Much of the material in this book comes from primary sources: diaries and letters gathered in various countries, some of which have only recently come to light. In addition to relationships with public figures and ecclesiastical issues, they reveal much of Ambrose de Lisle's own family life and the prevailing social conditions of his immediate neighbourhood. It becomes clear that the affection and support of his family of sixteen children, and particularly of his devoted wife, helped to make possible his unabated response to the calls of his faith.

FAITH AND FAMILY

AMBROSE PHILLIPPS DE LISLE
Posthumous portrait by Adrian Stokes, 1879

FAITH AND FAMILY

The Life and Circle
of
Ambrose Phillipps de Lisle

MARGARET PAWLEY

The Canterbury Press
Norwich

© Margaret Pawley 1993

First published 1993 by The Canterbury Press Norwich
(a publishing imprint of Hymns Ancient & Modern Limited,
a registered charity)
St Mary's Works, St Mary's Plain,
Norwich, Norfolk, NR3 3BH

British Library Cataloguing in Publication Data

A catalogue record for this book is available
from the British Library

ISBN 1–85311–073–6

*Typeset by Datix International Limited
Bungay, Suffolk and
Printed and bound in Great Britain by
St Edmundsbury Press Limited
Bury St Edmunds, Suffolk*

In memory of my parents
James and Lilian Herbertson

Ambrose Lisle March Phillipps changed his name to Phillipps de Lisle in 1862. In the interests of clarity, he will be referred to as Ambrose de Lisle throughout the whole of this work, but no alterations will be made to earlier MS references, where his name will appear in the original version.

Preface

THE gestation of this book has been a long one. By a set of fortunate circumstances I spent the years 1961–1965 largely in Rome, as a spectator of the proceedings of the Second Vatican Council. It was a matter of comment that several of its final Decrees seemed to reflect the mind, at an earlier date, of John Henry Newman. Of no area was this more true than that of the place and function of the laity in the Church. Some years later, while carrying out research for a book on Reunion movements, I came across in the Archives of Magdalen College, Oxford, letters written by Ambrose de Lisle to J. R. Bloxam in the 1840s. They caused me to make the connection between the dramatic changes I had seen take place in Rome and a situation and personal struggle that had existed for Ambrose more than a hundred years before, in which Newman also had been involved. Ambrose was part of the old order, but he did not accept its restrictions. His battle for lay participation in the affairs of the Church in his own day, against increasing clerical domination, can now be examined in a new light since the discovery that he was a precursor of things to come.

I offer a fresh evaluation of Ambrose de Lisle in these terms; in terms of the times and circumstances in which he lived, and the challenges he set himself. A two-volume biography, begun but not completed by E. S. Purcell, was published in 1900. Purcell's earlier book on Cardinal Manning received a worse press, because Manning was better known and his critics better informed. It may well be that after having been sharp about Manning, and having paid for it, Purcell decided to be unctuous about Ambrose. But the subsequent hagiography was equally unhelpful, and Ambrose's memory has not been well served.

Primary source material considerably beyond that contained in Purcell's book, has come forth. For the supply of this I am indebted to the help of a large number of archivists, both in England and abroad, whose collections are named in the Bibliography. The use of these letters and diaries has made possible the attempt to recapture attitudes towards daily living, and in particular towards religious matters, many of which are no longer current. Certain of Ambrose de Lisle's descendants have offered me help and encouragement beyond description. Mr Gerard de Lisle of Quenby Hall, present squire of the estates in Leicestershire which he has done so much to restore, has placed his considerable collection of manuscript material unreservedly at my disposal. To him and to Mrs de Lisle for her frequent hospitality, I owe much. Major and the Hon. Mrs Everard de Lisle of Stockerston Hall, Oakham, have given me access to their store of family memorabilia in a most generous way.

I wish to thank the Principal and governing body of St Hugh's College, Oxford, for the research award in the shape of the Yates senior scholarship in Divinity which they gave me towards the preparation of this book; also the Principal and Fellows of Lady Margaret Hall for part of the Susette Taylor Travelling Fellowship, to facilitate my work on archives in Rome. The British Academy made me a grant towards research expenses, for which I was most grateful. Among the friends who have offered help and advice I wish to thank in particular Mrs Rosemary Gilbert, the Revd Max Saint and Professor Ilsley Ingram; also the late Miss Eileen Ball for her skill in transcribing and translating early 19th century manuscript material in French. Mrs Deborah Webb and Mrs Meg Baxter-Shawe, who produced the typescript, have been patient and cheerful in their reception of my handwriting.

The events of Ambrose de Lisle's home and family life, as they are recorded, may appear perpetually, closely and curiously juxtaposed with his participation in the affairs of Church and State. This is how it was, and his choice. The paradoxes were endless.

Wye, Kent   MARGARET PAWLEY
1993

Contents

List of Illustrations

Introduction

A prophet, ecumenist, or meddler? The passage of time shows Ambrose de Lisle more properly in the first two roles. All too frequently his contemporaries thought of him purely in the third category. Though not strictly an original thinker, he was an inveterate collector of ideas, many of them visionary in the extreme in current terms. With interrupted initiative, zeal and resolution, he spent his life trying to put them into effect, undeterred by rebuff and disappointment. One of his attributes was his staying power, seen by many as wilfulness or obstinacy. His driving force was a search for the holy, and he felt it could be found most perfectly represented within one source, institution and system of doctrine, that of the Roman Catholic Church to which he had moved from the Anglican at the age of 16. Hence his anxiety that all men and women should embrace its beliefs and in some way unite with it. But his loyalty, though deep and lasting, was not uncritical and there were many instances, particularly towards the end of his life, when he found himself swimming against the tide.

Ambrose de Lisle founded a Cistercian Abbey and Roman Catholic missions, chapels and schools in the villages of Leicestershire and kept a constant watch over them; he promoted a crusade of prayer for the conversion of England which became widespread on the continent; he helped to import foreign missionaries. Through his determination to associate himself with the extension of Roman Catholicism in England, and to wave aside the growing body who objected to his so doing, he had a greater share in the developments which took place than most other lay persons. In a real sense the history of the changes within the Roman Catholic community, and reactions to those changes, in the 1850s and 1860s, was his personal history also, and can be seen through his eyes and experience.

With his feeling for the mediaeval, Ambrose played a part in the reintroduction of Gothic architecture, Gregorian chant and the Church ceremonial of earlier ages; he wrote a score of books and pamphlets. He was familiar with members of the Oxford Movement and his articles in *L'Univers* brought the attention of Frenchmen to it. His correspondence was prodigious and his house seldom empty of guests.

Almost alone among converts, he maintained a respect for the Church he had left and did not abandon his belief in the validity of its Orders. He designed various schemes for the reunion of Christendom with a variety of patterns, for he was essentially a pragmatist. He moved among a circle that was wide, yet distinctive. There were clear reasons, discernible 150 years later, why certain friends were close and others less so. The circle was by no means confined to those who shared his religious outlook. During a period when Roman Catholics tended to remain somewhat exclusive, Ambrose spent much of his time in the company of neighbours and friends who had a religious allegiance of another kind. The ties which bound together members of his particular social milieu in the county proved very strong. But closest of all were links with relations. Kinship was a powerful force and drew in quite distant cousins.

Conscientious recording of daily events showed the high proportion of family visits. Charles Montalembert, W. E. Gladstone, John Henry Newman, Nicholas Wiseman, Pugin the Architect, Henry Manning, the Wilberforces, Miss Nightingale and countless others, came and went, but it was Ambrose's father, his brother, his uncles, aunts and cousins who rode over day by day and were the more frequent visitors. It was part of a style and mode of life now gone for ever.

At times of acute social, political and religious disturbance, uncertainty and rapid change, members of a family tended to close ranks to help each other. With his privileged background, Ambrose had the added advantage of being able to call upon his relations to use their influence in high places to serve the causes to which he had dedicated his life. A source of particular strength was his wife, Laura Clifford; his dependence upon her, even in business matters was very great. She bore many children (sixteen were to come to full term) and she spent much time with them; she taught in schools, arranged the lives of priests, visited the poor, the sick and the dying; she copied her husband's letters, tried to help him with money matters (a hopeless endeavour) and to make peace with those he had displeased; entertained his friends.

Ambrose was never part of the glittering company that is axiomatic of parliamentary public life, although he was invited to stand for election and managed to influence what went on in the House of Commons. He became a Deputy Lieutenant, High Sheriff and Magistrate in his own county of Leicester-shire, and regarded this as his limit. There were probably two main reasons why this should have been so. One was that he was all his life very short of money (and left serious debts) because his plans always exceeded the means he possessed to execute them. His expectations from the substantial bequest made to him in the will of the 16th Earl of Shrewsbury came to nothing as the result of law suits initiated by the Italian members of the late Earl's family. With characteristic dogged-ness, through the 1850s and 60s, Ambrose pursued through the courts the chimera of financial independence; but in the end, only the lawyers became rich.

Secondly, it seems to have occurred to him that he was unsuited to public debate. 'I am of a very nervous temperament' he wrote[1] to Luigi Gentili in 1847 'and when I am excited I lose myself directly'.

A tendency for Ambrose to become irascible when thwarted in his plans was recorded by several of his relations and contemporaries. He would not have been the first man in public life to show traits such as these. But it is clear that by inclination he was happier trying to exert his influence in the designs that interested him, from a rural and domestic vantage point, than from the centre of a metropolitan political arena. In order to promote the causes inspired by and consequent upon his faith, he had need of the protection and support of his family.

Chapter 1

Youth

AMBROSE was born on the 17th March 1809 at Garendon, a mansion set in the 5,000 acre country estate near Loughborough of his paternal grandfather, Thomas March Phillipps; obviously a deliberate birth-place for an eventual heir; it was not yet his parents' home. Among his immediate surroundings there was comfort and plenty, but in the neighbouring countryside there was hardship and want. The war against Napoleon still had another six years to run. The supply of foreign corn had diminished just when the demand at home was greatest, for the population had been rising since 1760. There was a sharp rise in the cost of food, to some extent offset by a rise in agricultural wages, but the recent enclosures and consequent loss of grazing land and the reduction of cottage industries, particularly for women affected by the development of machines for spinning and weaving, contributed to a good deal of deprivation.

Ambrose's surname, by descent, should have been March; Phillipps had been added his grandfather, Thomas March, whose family had been members of the Levant Company, merchants trading with Turkey since the early 18th century; a wharf and a lane in Smyrna were named after them. Later they acquired land in Dorset and the Isle of Wight. Thomas March's grandmother, Mary Lisle, was the daughter of Sir Ambrose Phillipps, who, knighted in 1637 and King's serjeant, had bought Garendon and its park in 1683 from the Duke of Buckingham. It had formed part of the lands of a Cistercian Abbey dissolved by Henry VIII and given to Thomas, Earl of Rutland, from whom the Duke of Buckingham had acquired it. Sir Ambrose also bought the Grace Dieu estate, near its former convent, from the Beaumont family.

Sir Ambrose's grandson, another Ambrose Phillipps, though a Member of Parliament travelled widely in Italy where he developed a taste for the classical in architecture. He rebuilt the mansion in 1730, and in the grounds, as well as a vast triumphal gateway, a replica of Titus's arch in the Forum at Rome, constructed a round temple in the Greek style, an obelisk and portice approached by an avenue of cypresses;[2] the gardens were also laid out in a new design. This Ambrose did not marry; on his death in 1737 the inheritance went to his brother Samuel, who though he had married twice left no direct heir. He bequeathed the house and estate to Thomas March, grandson of his aunt, Mary Lisle; her ninth child, Jane, had married Thomas's father.

Ambrose the subject of this book, was Thomas's grandson. He was inordinately proud of the Lisle connection; it had been strengthened by Thomas's[3] own marriage to Susan Lisle, his cousin. The Lisles owned property in Hampshire and had been closely associated with the Isle of Wight. The family traced their descent from Fitzazor, a knight who came from Normandy with the Conqueror and had been rewarded by land on the island from which the name De Insula or Lisle derived. Their history during the middle ages filled Ambrose's imagination: there had been a Knight of the Garter and Lord High Admiral of England and a barony which had become extinct in the reign of Edward IV. Although the original 17th century Ambrose whose namesake he was, inspired him with a deep love for Wales, it was the Lisles with their chivalrous connotations, rather than the Welsh lawyer and Smyrna merchants, whose memories Ambrose chose to cherish and perpetuate. By middle life the profound influence of his inheritance was plain to see. An example was his change of name to de Lisle in 1862 when the estate came into his hands.

Ambrose's father Charles was the eldest son of Thomas March Phillipps and his wife Susan, who proceeded to have four further sons and five daughters. Although five of these uncles and aunts did not marry, the remainder provided him with 29 first cousins. Ambrose was baptised while still at Garendon by his uncle Edward Thomas March Phillipps, who held one of the family livings in the nearby village of Hathern from 1808 until his death in 1857. His biography[4] by his daughter Lucy gives some useful background to local conditions. On his arrival at Hathern, a village of some 1200 inhabitants, he found it 'almost a barbarous place'.

> The north side of the churchyard was the usual place for fights, and a recess between the north aisle and the vestry was used for fives and skittles ... At the first marriage Mr Phillipps solemnised, the crowd who followed the wedding party into the church began, according to their wont as the clerk told him, to amuse themselves, whilst the service was going on in the chancel, by pelting each other with prayer books and basses [hassocks] in the church; and one bass thrown by a bolder hand flew between the couple and fell within the rails. He stopped the service and ordered the church to be cleared: but the mob refused to go, till warned of the consequences and finding the service would not be completed till they obeyed, the church was gradually emptied and the doors were locked. The crowd clustered round the windows hooting and yelling defiance.[5]

Apart from the agricultural workers, as in much of the rest of Leicestershire most people laboured in the hosiery trade as stocking-frame workers. Frames were rented and the stockings completed at home. With the development of machines, demand for hand-made stockings fell sharply. Some men took part in the exodus from the country into the towns to work in the expanding factories. Others retaliated, determined to save their livelihood, by breaking up the new machines. Luddism was a secret society which was brought into being, with acts of fidelity undaunted by the execution or transportation of some of its members. When James Towle the Luddite was tried in Leicester on August 10th 1816, 'a great number of townspeople were sworn in as Special Constables'. He was executed on 20th November and six more Luddites on 30th March 1817.[6] Troops were called out to try to find offenders. The Rector of Hathern found the road no longer solitary at night: 'discontented, suffering men crept in twos and threes along its further hedge or in larger bands took possession of the footpaths and challenged all who passed with their watchword "Captain Ludd".' Edward, visiting his parishioners, was several times challenged but never stopped: he carried a lantern 'to satisfy the alarm of his family'.[7]

Another uncle, William, was also in holy orders and was much at home as he was very delicate and unmarried; he died of consumption in 1818, aged 28. The styles of the family show the occupations then open to men of their status. The most illustrious was Samuel, who was a lawyer and writer of legal text books: he became Permanent Undersecretary of State for the Home Department and a Privy Councillor. Henry was in the Royal Navy and Edward and William, as already mentioned, were clergymen. Charles March Phillipps, as well as managing the estates, was a Member of Parliament from 1818–20, 1831–32 and 1832–37. Charles, Samuel and Edward had distinguished careers at Cambridge and all won classical prizes; Samuel was the most brilliant academically; he and Edward were both Wranglers. It seems to have been the custom to call unmarried aunts by their Christian names, hence Aunt Harriet and Aunt Fanny, and married ones by the surnames of their husbands: Susan was Aunt Dawson married to Edward Dawson a nearby land-owner of Whatton; Sophia, Aunt Ryder, had 13 children as the wife of Henry Ryder, Bishop of Gloucester and then Lichfield and Coventry. Aunt Cowper, Catherine March Phillipps, was not on the scene long and died in 1830. In 1817 Charles March Phillipps inherited the Garendon and Grace Dieu estates on the death of Thomas, and his children moved into the house and grounds on a permanent basis. The unmarried uncles and aunts remained there also.

Accounts which survive of the early childhood of Ambrose reveal the contribution of his mother and her family to his personality.

Charles March Phillipps and Harriet Ducarel had been married in 1807 from Walford House near Monkton in Somerset, the home of her mother and brother. The bride was only seventeen years old and had been betrothed for a year. The couple had doubtless met at Launde Abbey,[8] a large house in Leicestershire with a particularly beautiful setting, where Harriet's sister Mary was married to its owner, John Finch Simpson. As in the case of several local landowners, he was a connection by marriage of the March Phillipps. Harriet Ducarel was of French descent on her father's side; her mother was Indian. Harriet's paternal great-grandfather, Jacques Coltee

Ducarel, though a Huguenot, was ennobled by Louis XIV, but later forfeited his property; on his death in 1718, his widow fled from France as a refugee. Her elder son, Andrew Coltee Ducarel, was in due course keeper of the Library at Lambeth Palace. The younger son, Adrian, became father of Gerald Gustavus Ducarel who, through the friendship of Clive, was offered an appointment in India; there in Burdwan he married Elizabeth (Bibi) Mirza. Harriet, the youngest of their six children, was born after the family's arrival in England.

At the age of sixteen in 1806 and 1807, before her marriage, Harriet wrote to Charles March Phillipps a spate of letters which would have done credit to one of the more spirited of Jane Austen's heroines, whose contemporary she was. The lack of eventfulness in her quiet life in Somerset did not stop the flow. She was clearly devoted to her older suitor, flattered by his attentions and determined on self-improvement. She undertook to apply herself particularly to her lessons with her governess. 'You dear darling man', 'You most conceited, charming, agreeable young man', 'My dearest, beloved Charles Phillipps', she wrote and assured him, '. . . I love you, I love you more than anybody in the world and most wretched should I be if I imagined you could for a moment doubt it. Believe me, since your departure you have never for an instant been out of my thoughts'. She wrote with a freedom and enthusiasm which would not later be characteristic of Victorian young women, but may have owed something to her gallic and eastern blood. Her affection did not prevent her from retaliating somewhat after criticisms on his part. He saw fit to suggest that she should not walk on the outer edges of her feet, nor smile unless with her back to the light on account of her teeth. Harriet acknowledged she had never seen a dentist and was unlikely to do so, though she believed there was one such in the suburbs of Taunton; she had been to a social occasion where she had been admired, and when, she inferred, there had been no talk of ugly teeth; nevertheless '. . . I think the want of candour between two persons who love must be fatal to their affection'. She urged him, on her part, of the dangers 'attending the impropriety of leaping over gates with a loaded gun and several other things that I could mention'. He had admitted to his quick temper, but she dismissed the warning briskly. Harriet considered him much less violent than her brother-in-law, an 'amiable and sensible man, but he requires a great deal of management, much more, I suspect, than you ever will'. Half way through 1807, she once more discussed her looks: 'I will tell you for your comfort, my teeth are grown so much whiter. I cannot help looking at them in every glass'.

After their marriage Charles and Harriet made their home in a series of rented country houses. It was to Gunby Hall, near Spilsby in Lincolnshire, that they returned from Garendon with Ambrose as an infant, and his earliest years were spent in that distinguished Georgian house with its large formal garden, described by Tennyson as 'a haunt of ancient peace'. One of the entries in Charles Phillipps' diary for 1810 was the payment of an account of a dentist in Spilsby. Later that year, in November, came a two-day journey to Garendon by way of Bourn, where they stayed the night, and beautiful Launde, house of Harriet's sister. Harriet gave birth to a daughter, Augusta, at the family home on 10th December during a particularly heavy fall of snow. She was churched at Hathern in the New Year, and the baby baptised. No move was made to return to Gunby in a hurry; Charles rode much in Leicestershire, went shooting and was out with the Quorn. During a visit to the West Country to see Harriet's relations, Charles, who was apt to lapse into French while recording his family's activities, wrote in his diary while at the sea 'Ambrose prend le bain premier fois'.

Soon after the arrival back in Lincolnshire late in July of 1811, French comments began to describe the onset of Harriet's ill health. In spite of it, a second son, Charles, was born in March 1812, but no journey was made to Garendon; the birth took place at Gunby. By the beginning of 1813, it was obvious that Harriet's sickness was mortal and she was unlikely to recover from the disease of tuberculosis which had taken a severe grip upon her and and was not confined to her lungs. A move was made to a house three miles from Bristol, no doubt on account of the more benign climate. Her husband's daily record of Harriet's suffering makes sad reading; it would seem that he shared the sleepless nights of incessant coughing, shortness of breath and loss of blood, her bodily pain, terrible headaches and sickness, when she would weep and long for release. There was little that could be done, in that age, to minimise her anguish. The effect of her condition on her children, her looks sadly altered, particularly on the four year old Ambrose, is not hard to imagine. Only occasionally was their mother well enough to drive out with them.

Members of the Phillipps and Ducarel families visited often, as did the clergy who prayed and sat with Harriet, read to her and brought the Sacrament. At last, in September 1813, Charles Phillipps wrote in his diary that the doctor had said 'que la fin s'approche'; 'my beloved darling is very ill'. On the twenty-fourth she died, after a short life of twentythree years. She was buried in Bristol Cathedral where her husband had constructed to her memory a monument surmounted by an urn in one of the side aisles. On a marble plaque a long poem records her charm, vitality and virtues.

Charles and his children left the Bristol neighbourhood immediately and within a week of Harriet's death he was living in another rented house in Brandon in Warwickshire on the outskirts of Coventry. It was near to his parents at Garendon and to his sister at Lutterworth Rectory. Here he remained, cultivating land, rearing some animals and taking part in country pursuits until 1817 when, on the death of his father, he came into his inheritance. His searing experiences clearly affected him, as they did his children. He made mention in his diary of the shortness of his temper on several occasions; he also suffered from frequent bouts of ill-health; his recorded attitude bordered on hypochondria. Charles never remarried, although there is evidence that he attempted to do so but his suit was not accepted. His relations with his children revealed affection and concern. Especially if they seemed ill they merited a notice in his diary; all three were clearly delicate; perhaps they realized unconsciously that it was a certain way of claiming his attention. In 1815 Ambrose was given a horse which cost £5; shortly after another came from his grandparents for him. Thereafter father and son would ride together often, which practice continued to the 1850s. Several months a year were spent at Garendon and in 1816 Charles Phillipps took his children to the sea at Barmouth for the summer. Ambrose expressed his pleasure at the scenery and his affection for Wales, homeland of the 17th century Ambrose Phillipps, and as a further sign of his awareness of his ancestry, in the future took his own family to the same neighbourhood on several occasions.

Shortly after the inheritance of the estate had fallen to Charles, there was another death in the family. William's health had been the cause of anxiety for many years. Aunt Dawson[9] wrote to Aunt Ryder about their brother which showed the family concern for each other:

> We dined at Garendon yesterday and rejoiced to see our dearest invalid better than he has been since the dreaded attack. They certainly mean to take him to town in the Spring and he needs us all to urge him to be careful. Yesterday was a wintry day, yet he went out in the carriage and what was worse, got out at Miss Combes' shop: we all shook our heads.

When he was well enough, William gave daily religious instruction to Ambrose and Aunt Fanny taught the children their other lessons. The death of William in March 1818 can be seen as a further shock to his nephew at the age of nine. It was decided that he should go away to school. A small private one twenty miles away at South Croxton kept by the Revd W. Wilkinson was chosen as the most suitable.

In the meantime, his father began to assume the role of Squire of his estate. He had been a magistrate for some years and was drawn into the maintenance of law and order in disturbed times. On 22 January 1817 he recorded that twenty-four Special Constables were sworn in at Shepshed; Charles personally swore in a further sixty-five from Hathern. On a more positive note he set about initiating repairs to his property for the farmhouses were in a dilapidated condition; he also took some measures to relieve distress. Fifty gallons of soup is noted as having been delivered to the parsonage together with £50 for the 'weekly indigent'. In December 1820 there is a diary entry 'Kill my second ox to be given to the poor'; the end papers show a list of linen for distribution in Shepshed: blankets, men's shirts, boys' shirts, women's shifts, gowns, gowns for girls; several hundred articles.

Charles Phillipps was an enthusiastic collector of pictures and other works of art with which to embellish the mansion newly in his ownership. He made visits to the Continent in search of selected pieces. A prominent interest lay in books, especially works of theology, history and biography, and not merely to possess them. He continued to read widely into old age, including classical texts in the original tongue. His eclectic library was extensive; it offered considerable opportunities to Ambrose who was by nature also a voracious reader.

The Parliamentary election of 1818 was an unusual affair. George Anthony Leigh Keck[10] of Stoughton Grange and Lord Robert Manners,[11] who were both Tories, stood for election for the County of Leicestershire; Thomas Babington of Rothley Temple who had represented the borough for fourteen years, was also adopted. Unexpectedly, Charles March Phillipps was nominated in the Whig interest, supported by the powerful Paget[12] family. At the last moment Keck resigned on grounds of ill-health. According to the *Leicester Journal*[13] 'As determined a contest as the County has ever witnessed' was expected. Voting began on Saturday 26th June. On Monday 28th

> Carriages of every description from the elegant barouche to the humble dung cart were put in requisition and came rattling in from all quarters to Leicester Castle.

During the weekend Babington decided to retire from the contest; the votes for the two seats then stood: Lord Robert Manners 391, Charles March Phillipps 307, Thomas Babington 257; more were to come but they did not affect the outcome. Lord Robert and Charles were returned, but the scene that should have been of triumph was one of uproar and violence. The *Leicester Journal*[14] reported:

> The populace appeared to be seized with a fit of revolutionary frenzy, and upon Lord Robert Manners appearing in the Chair, commenced a most brutal attack upon his person by a discharge of almost every species of missile accompanied with the most furious gestures and diabolical language. By the time Lord Robert reached the Committee Room he was battered, bleeding and coated with filth. It was one of the few ways open to the unenfranchised to express their view of Lord Robert's reactionary opinions.

Charles Phillipps fared better for he had made his attitudes plain at the hustings:

Man is no longer the same passive machine he once was:
ignorant, unlettered, uninformed. He has begun to think, reflect
and reason, and what is knowledge but power? Woe to those
who shut their ears to the popular voice.[15]

The *Leicester Journal* commented 'His election cry was
"Vox Populi vox Dei".' He still paid dearly for his success. In
the absence of a modern electoral system, secret ballot and
polling stations, candidates who wanted loyalty were obliged
to entertain their supporters among the local yeomanry for
days before the election in neighbouring hostelries. Charles
wrote in his diary on 21 July 1818 'My election expenses will
reach £8,000'. In 1842 Ambrose explained[16] to the Earl of
Shrewsbury his shortage of funds for the building of churches:
he believed that election expenses on three occasions cost his
father a total of £30,000. Charles Phillipps did not contest the
election of 1820 (nor in 1826) against Keck, now recovered in
health. The mood was, however, changing; both Keck and
Lord Robert Manners now expressed sympathy with the distress that affected the lives of manual workers. (When Parliamentary Reform was in the air in 1830 radicals again decided
to fight the County Seat and Charles Phillipps once more
entered the arena).

Ambrose, meanwhile, remained for two years at South Croxton. In 1820, at the age of eleven, he was moved to Maisemore
Court School, a few miles from Gloucester. Aunt Ryder's
husband had been Bishop of Gloucester since 1815: his confidence in the head-master, the Revd George Hodson, was such
that on the Bishop's translation to the see of Lichfield and
Coventry in 1824 he appointed him Archdeacon of Stafford
and caused the school to be removed to Edgbaston. Ambrose
went with it. His days at the school were crucial to the whole
of the rest of his life, for it was while he was there that he
decided to become a Roman Catholic.

As will later appear, the choice of school was not a happy
one, but it is clear how it came to be made. The influence of
personal recommendation in such matters was paramount.
Charles March Phillipps had been at Eton, his brothers at
Charterhouse. Public Schools at the turn of the century were
places of brutality and licence. William Wilberforce[17] in one of

the 600 letters to his third son Samuel[18] explained why it was
that such establishments were to be avoided[19]:

> When a youth who has been piously educated gives in to actual
> vice, there is no saying in what degree the Holy Spirit may be
> withdrawn. Pious parents do not like sending children to
> public schools for this reason.

Samuel Wilberforce at the age of twelve was sent to a
succession of tutors, all of them clergymen who took a number
of private pupils. In 1819 he joined the household of George
Hodson, then chaplain to a friend of the Wilberforces in
Sussex. Hodson had been a protegé of William's as a poor
undergraduate at Trinity College, Oxford. In 1810 he wrote to
his benefactor to say that he had been offered a fellowship at
Magdalen College and the second Chancellor's medal, and
would not need 'the remaining £20 which he had allowed me
to expect'. In due course George Hodson became even closer
to the Wilberforces by his marriage to a connection of the
family. On the tutor's move to the parish of Maisemore near
Gloucester in 1820 (no doubt on the recommendation of William's to his friend the Bishop), Samuel accompanied him and
it was there that he was joined by Ambrose, the Bishop's
nephew.

There were seven other pupils in the school: Albert Way,
son of Hodson's former patron in Sussex, Patrick Boyle[20] a
Scotsman, Henry Hoare,[21] boys called Colquhoun and Barker
and brothers by the name of Pringle. Sam Wilberforce left at
the end of 1821 for yet another tutor, this time the Revd F.
Spragge of Little Bounds, Ridborough. Albert Way followed
him there and Patrick Boyle departed also for an establishment
called 'Tucker's'. Descriptions of conditions at Maisemore
have survived through the letters of Henry Hoare to Sam at
Spragge's and Sam to Patrick Boyle. It does not appear as if
any of them were happy at 'Hod's'. In the Lent term of 1822
Henry Hoare wrote[22] to Sam from Maisemore:

> I should certainly have made a point of writing to you sooner
> was it not that Hod does not allow us to do anything when we
> are up in our rooms but private reading and fagging. I am glad
> to hear you are so happy at Spragge's. You may judge, however,
> that your description of yourself must be very tantalizing to us

at Maisemore. Hod has a little cold today and the brunt of it
has fallen on Ambrose's head for he has a small bruise on his
cheek from Hod's hand. I think I never once saw Hod put into
such a violent passion by such a trivial occurence [sic].

There were references to fines which Hod exacted of all
who came down to dinner after grace; of the answer 'Queen
Boadicea' given to Hod by one of the Pringles during a lesson
on Richard I, when asked who was the subject under discussion. Rabbits as pets had been given up 'for Hod says he is
convinced they were a source of great mischief to the boys'.

Charles Dawson, first cousin to Ambrose, had joined the
school, Hoare reported[23] to Sam; 'Not very religiously inclined,
I am sorry to say'. The other newcomer was John Bainbridge
Story,[24] son of a neighbour of the Phillipps;

He is of a Leicestershire *breed* and has been to school at East
Sheen, where as well as at home he has been *most shamefully*
neglected. When he first came he had not the slightest notion
where to find any place in the Bible.

Sam's letters to Patrick Boyle told of his relief that he had
left Maisemore. 'Did Hod make any row to your Dad? He did
rather to mine' he wrote. 'I quite agree ... as to the great
preference I should give to this place over Hod's'. Hodson had
changed his plans in taking Lord Castlestewart's son[25] 'Not
only as respects the age, but also the quality of his pupils as he
refused before to take any of the nobility and I know that he
has before refused some offers on this account'. He continued:

The noble lord's Irish is a great amusement to the boys ... To
be sure how very odd it does appear to me when I look back
on our mode of life there. Does it not to you? Hodson's mode
of boyishing us to such an extreme degree and treating us with
such uncommon strictness ... Do you look back upon them
with surprise? Hodson's was certainly a most excellent place
for making progress in classics, but his method of treating us
was I think extremely injudicious.

Later he wrote[26] from Oriel College, Oxford; Hoare had
written to say that Hod was always 'grumpy'; that 'After we
went it got infinitely worse and Hod insufferable'.

There was a certain amount of provocation for the Headmaster's uncertain behaviour: from the correspondence already quoted it would appear that Mrs Hodson's confinements were a source of anxiety, as also his children, who were extremely delicate. At one stage, two out of three were reported as close to death and unlikely to recover. Also he would seem to have been by education and temperament a classical scholar, and a teacher of young boys only by force of circumstance. The effect of the atmosphere at Maisemore upon the sensitive young Ambrose can be imagined. It provided a religious crisis for, as a contrast to the 'grumpy' Hod, there was an emigré priest who taught French, Abbé Giraud, who had come to England in exile during the revolution. His charming and benign character attracted the young Englishman who asked him questions and for the names of books to read.

From an early age Ambrose had been adventurous in his search for religious truth. He had previously put some inquiries about Catholicism to his Aunt Fanny at the much earlier age of seven or so: why in the Creed did the faithful say they believed in the Catholic Church, when it was considered full of error? She replied that it meant the assembly of all true Christians and that it did not refer to any particular Church. His next question had been whether it was *certain* that the Roman Catholics were wrong and in error. No, she answered, but before the next world it would be impossible for anyone to pronounce what was true and what was false. This vagueness he continued to find disturbing. On a half holiday from school Ambrose and some school fellows visited Abbé Giraud's chapel in Gloucester:

> the devout crucifix over the altar; the altar itself on which was engraved the figure of the Lamb of God, the vestments adorned with gold and embroidered flowers: all spoke to my heart. Everything showed such an appearance of holiness and of separation from all profane uses and associations, as was calculated to impress the mind with high and holy notions of God.[27]

He had already experienced a certain amount of religious tension at home: his uncles Edward and William had represented different theological schools of thought. It is not easy to determine their standpoints at this distance because a good

deal of bias is attached to the versions that have been handed
down. But what is clear is that William Phillipps was considered a high churchman, which at that time probably meant
that he took a more serious view of the Church as an institution
than Edward, who was regarded as a low churchman: personal
religion and the salvation of individual souls were of greater
importance to him. Both were contained within Anglican comprehensiveness; it being judged that the mystery of Christianity
could be expressed most fully within a number of emphases.
Vigorous expression of almost any sort was lacking in the
early 19th century. The fervour that had been engendered by
such as the Wesleys in the 18th century, in response to the low
moral standards and spiritual turpitude, had waned; churches
and cathedrals were in a bad state of repair, though there was
a good deal of individual private piety. The institutional aspect
of the Church of England was at a low ebb.

During Ambrose's schooldays at Maisemore, many Sundays
and some holidays were spent with Bishop Ryder and his aunt.
He saw practised another set of religious ideals, for they had
become Evangelicals, a term which had begun to have a
precise sense to denote churchmen who laid special stress on
personal conversion and holiness and on the death of Christ as
atonement for the sins of men.

A problem which had been laid upon him by words from his
Uncle Edward, had to be resolved. Edward March Phillipps
had begun as an Evangelical also; he came to the conclusion
that this standpoint was too narrow and static. He incurred
the criticism of the Evangelical clergy of his acquaintance who
regretted that he 'should waste his time in useless abstractions
and mystical distinctions; why should he teach more than
Christ Crucified?'.[28] He had written a treatise on the mission
and office of the Holy Spirit, preached on the priesthood of all
believers, and had given more emphasis to the Sacraments. He
increased the number of Communion services in a year in
Hathern Church from four to ten and as a result of his
teaching, though only about 10% of the inhabitants, two
thirds of church-goers were communicants. But in common
with Evangelicals he maintained his interest in the interpretation of prophecy contained in the Bible; in Christ's second
coming and in the last battle of Anti-Christ.[29] The latter he

identified, in common with some of his contemporaries, with the Pope of Rome whose Church he regarded with some vehemence as idolatrous. These latter ideas he communicated to his young nephew. Reinforced no doubt with similar teachings from the Palace at Gloucester, they began to prey on Ambrose's mind.

When Ambrose was about thirteen, his headmaster became alarmed on account of his obvious interest in the Church of Rome. Some books by learned Anglican authors were put into his hands, the object of which was to prove that the alleged corruptions of the Papacy were foretold in the prophecies of the Bible, particularly those concerning the predicted Anti-Christ who, as the 'man of sin', 'the false prophet', the 'little horn', was to contest the dominion of Jesus Christ over the nations, to persecute the Church and ruin mens' souls redeemed by Christ. Ambrose waded through the treatises: the conflict 'which now arose in my mind, filled me with sadness and dejection'. One day he felt sadder than ever as he walked alone by the banks of the Severn near Maisemore Bridge and he wished that someone would tell him who indeed was the great Anti-Christ. His eyes were looking into the sky, when a shaft of light came through what seemed like an opening in solid substance, while his ears heard the words 'Mahomet was Anti-Christ because he denied the Father and the Son and he denied them in those words of the Koran where he says "God neither begetteth nor is he begotten". I felt my soul filled with the most unspeakable consolation and peace'.[30] On his next visit home, he flew to the Koran. Many years later he wrote his own book on prophecy[31] largely as a result of this experience.

The nervous Hod next produced a history of the primitive church which helped temporarily to restore Ambrose's equilibrium. He was delighted with the piety of the early Christians and determined to read more patristic writers; he clearly did not care for compromises and was searching for certainties. Represented particularly imperfectly in the early 19th century was the Anglican spirituality which had been the fruit of the patristic scholarship of the 17th century and the group known as the Caroline divines.[32] Ambrose became much interested in the then neglected Anglican writers of that century with their view that catholicity rather than protestantism was the decisive feature of the English Church. From that vantage point he read Jeremy Taylor's *Holy Living and Holy Dying*[33] and Charles Wheatley's *Commentary on the Book of Common Prayer*.[34] The latter led him to suppose that the present age was neglecting the practices and teaching contained in that book. The matter of absolution in the Prayer Book office for the Visitation of the Sick harassed him particularly, for he had never heard it taught. He confronted Bishop Ryder with his anxiety, whose reply was that the doctrine was held. These excursions into 17th and early 18th century English writings were to prove of value in the dealings which Ambrose was later to pursue with the Tractarians; he was able to understand their origins when his contemporaries could not.

Abbé Giraud also lent him books and realised more wisely than Hod that the intellect is only part of a man. He produced *Mrs Herbert and the Villagers*[35] by the Countess de Bodenham, a cosy set of homilies in which Roman Catholic dogma and the duties of various stations of life were set out. Mrs Herbert 'a lady who usually resides in the city of York where she employs a considerable portion of her time and fortune in administering instructions to the ignorant and relief to the indigent around her' went each Sunday into the country. Her conversations with various village people, farmers, apprentices, servants, inhabitants of a workhouse, covered the obligations of the Sabbath, preparation for death, the meaning of the Sacraments, heaven, hell, judgment, eternity, prayer, and so on, in a simple and authoritative manner. They spoke to Ambrose's condition because clear, practical and uncompromising.

He began to dislike the attacks made upon Roman Catholics in writings and conversations, to feel that some accommodation must be possible between what were sister Churches,[36] and to look for resemblances.

In the spring of 1823 Ambrose, at the age of fourteen, travelling alone in a diligence, joined his father his sister Augusta and her governess, Mademoiselle Bertrand, in Paris. Six weeks of sightseeing followed, in which many visits were paid to churches. Ambrose enquired of Mlle Bertrand and others a great deal about the Catholic religion and the nature and meaning of its ceremonies, particularly of the Mass. The arrangement of the places of worship made a deep impression upon him for its solemnity and appearance of sanctity. The sight of so many emblems of Christianity, the praying people at all hours of the day, so he recorded later, all made him respond with feelings of devotion. On Whitsunday they attended the Ambassadors' chapel for the morning service. In the afternoon his father took Ambrose to Notre Dame for Vespers, where the Archbishop of Paris was officiating. At first, the sight of twelve priests in copes walking up and down during the *Magnificat*, amused the boy and Charles March Phillipps rebuked him saying that all Roman Catholic ceremonies had deep religious meaning. Presently the splendour of the ceremonial, the response of the people, and particularly the timeless solemnity of the chant, seized hold of him and it became an experience that was never forgotten. On the Feast of Corpus Christi they went to see the *Sainte Procession de L'Hostie*, but of the reception of this event no record survives.

Augusta had quite a different response to the French Church. Writing to her cousin Bessie[37] from Nice where she, her father, Aunt Cowper and Aunt Fanny had been staying before the Paris visit, she remarked that a great part of the population were priests. 'They are always walking about in their black robes: they have a most ridiculous degree of superstition'.

On his return to England, Ambrose made an attempt to find a place for his fondness for ceremonial in Shepshed Church (the second family living, three miles from Garendon). He persuaded the vicar to wear a cope and to put a cross on the altar from which it was removed by order of the Bishop of Peterborough on account of the complaints of some parishioners. Ambrose did not pursue the matter and back at school there was a lull before the storm. A report from Maisemore to his father at the beginning of January 1824, spelled out sound progress: Ambrose had applied himself very diligently to his books. There was a fondness for Latin and Greek and he composed very readily in prose but 'His style is at present too redundant'. (It was a fault he never eradicated and was much like his mother's). There was not much relish for mathematics, but since Ambrose was intended for Oxford, they would not be necessary. 'His temper occasionally shows itself, but very seldom' was also a lasting characteristic.

Relationships between the Phillipps' and Ryders were particularly close in these years which made even more painful, on
both sides, the withdrawal of Ambrose from the family's
religious conformity. On the Bishop's move to Lichfield, his
second son Charles, in the Royal Navy stationed at Malta,
commented[38] upon it to his mother:

> But now I must come to a subject that interests me particularly.
> The newspapers tell me dear Papa is translated to the see of
> Litchfield [sic] . . . I think on the whole the change will not be
> disagreeable to me, it will bring us *within hail* of that dear
> place Garendon which of all others I should like.

The house attracted them all for its beautiful surroundings and
for reasons of family attachment. Several of Ambrose's generation, children of Aunt Ryder, had, like himself, been born
there.

During the course of 1824 Ambrose was confirmed privately
by Bishop Ryder in Lichfield Cathedral, from the school at
Edgbaston. The white marble monument to Henry Ryder
which stands in the Cathedral shows his strong patrician
figure at prayer. The sense of authority it emanates, its lawn
sleeves, show him every inch a father in God; he was also the
parent of thirteen children. The Evangelical position which he
came to adopt, though it was to have strength by the middle of
the century, was not a popular one in the 1820s, with its
enthusiasm, its emphasis on personal salvation and literal
interpretation of the received text of the Bible. He was considered the first Evangelical to be raised to the Episcopate. Son of
a peer, grandson of a former Bishop of London, graduate of St
John's College, Cambridge, friend to William Wilberforce the
liberator of slaves, a persuasive preacher, though not in any
sense a scholar, it would seem he could not be overlooked. He
was at first vicar of Lutterworth, then Canon of Windsor, and
later Dean of Wells: he seemed to find it permissible to keep
the last named dignity in plurality with his parish. In his
dioceses he put as his priority the reclamation of the poor and
the provision of more churches and church sittings. After six
years at Gloucester, 20 new churches had been built and 10
were under construction. Bishop Ryder was said to be at his
best in confirmation addresses. He would certainly have encour-

aged Ambrose to make a personal commitment to Christ and
to be aware of his own unworthiness. This teaching was
received and lasted, but conversion, when it came, was not of
the sort that his uncle by marriage would have understood.

For his part, Ambrose was sensitive, lonely and short particularly of maternal affection; he could not forsake his sense of
personal illumination. In language that was ebullient and
elated, he afterwards described[39] his state of mind: his guardian
angel was prompting him; Mary the mother of Jesus was
interceding for him. He visited the Roman Catholic Church of
St Peter in Birmingham and spoke to the parish priest.[40] After
a long talk with his father on religious matters on Good Friday
of 1825 ('Un vif entretien des matières Ecclesiastiques avec
Ambrose le soir' wrote Charles in his diary), he made his
Communion with his family on Easter Sunday in Shepshed
Church. With the bare walls and austere appearance, (the only
visible aids to devotion the tombs of his Phillipps ancestors)
the liturgy, with no musical accompaniment, obviously did not
feed his soul. His experience in Notre Dame had remained a
vivid memory. He visited the Dominicans in Hinckley and
implored Dr John Ambrose Woods, OP., to admit him as a
Roman Catholic.[41] The priest gave him some small engravings
of religious subjects, but declined to take further responsibility.
Ambrose returned to school for the summer term.

A dream made him take the final step. He was being
reproached by the Lord for not having complied with the light
he had received. He wrote to Thomas Macdonnell and asked
to see him: he wished to be received into the Communion of
the Catholic Church. To the priest's surprise he was well
instructed by his own reading.

On May 4th Uncle Edward March Phillipps called at Garendon to see Ambrose's father. Archdeacon Hodson had reported
'An increased show of Catholic propensities' in Ambrose: his
views were beginning to affect other boys.[42] His family began
to close in on him. Painful letters home from headmaster and
pupil followed: Charles March Phillipps answered them and
showed all the correspondence to his brother. It was decided
to take Ambrose away from school in Edgbaston; this was
done on 6th June. Father and son spent some days walking,
riding and talking together. On going into Ambrose's room

the older man noticed a gold-looking cross tied to a ribbon; 'Price, he says, 2/6d,' he wrote in his diary. 'Upbraid him with the absurdity, and broke it into pieces, was loudly, alas, angry with him – it was unwise – it was unkind – it was unjust. He commended himself. Is this paternal prudence? Christian forbearance? Religious Tolerance? Alas. Oh my God, make me to subdue my temper, to govern my passion'. Charles March Phillipps was later to show himself as a remarkably tolerant father, whose bursts of hot temper were offset by a largely benign disposition: but his family loyalty and religious faith were strong and the circumstances acutely painful.

Like many parents before and since, he decided to ignore the crisis and hope that it would pass. Next Sunday he took his son to Hathern Church and it was arranged for a tutor who was in holy orders to come and prepare him academically for the university. The Revd W. Wilkinson who was selected, reported that Ambrose had faced him with a reference to Extreme Unction in the Book of Common Prayer and questioned why it had fallen into disuse.

At this point, news reached the family that Charles Ryder had been drowned in the Tiber where his ship was paying a ceremonial visit to Rome. (He had narrowly survived an earlier experience of this sort when he fell from a cutter in the Mediterranean). It was a bitter blow to parents, uncles and aunts and cousins, as he was a boy of promise and amiability and only nineteen years old.

Aunt Ryder was daily expecting her thirteenth confinement. Letters of concern went to the Palace at Lichfield from the family at Garendon. There was no inhibition to the expressions of grief in religious terms. The dead boy was Charles March Phillipps' godson and had been named after him. 'He is still yours, although as to this world a curtain has been dropped between you and him' he wrote to the Bishop:[43] he became sponsor to the child who was born a few days later.

Without the awareness of his family, Ambrose was conditionally re-baptised and received into the Roman Catholic Church. On 21st December 1825, he rode out from Garendon across the snow-covered park to a poor Irish paviour's cottage where, by arrangement, the priest was awaiting him. He made his

general confession and as he put it later 'Received for the first
time, the Bread of Life'. He was sixteen years of age.

It was an act of great courage. As eventual heir of the
beloved ancestral home, he had opposed his large and powerful
family in what he had done. From their point of view, he was
lost in a way that Charles Ryder could never be. From his, the
Church of England was no longer faithful to its original vision.
(John Henry Newman was to come to the same conclusion
twenty years later). He had gone into a world politically and
socially alien. He would have no civil rights[44] when he ceased
to be a minor. He knew no Roman Catholics apart from the
priest who had received him, who was an awkward man, and
in the future gave a good deal of trouble to successive Bishops
in Birmingham, and who did not share the authority and
prestige enjoyed by Ambrose's clerical uncles.

The English Roman Catholic community was undergoing
great changes. Its size had been calculated at 80,000 in 1770
and by 1830 it was considered to have doubled, though the
number of priests had remained static at about 400. Irish
immigrants were responsible for part, but far from all the
increase: middle class town congregations had grown considerably.[45] Ambrose had no experience whatever of any of these
people. The Roman Catholic gentry families, recusants from
penal times, he still had to meet. His loneliness must have been
very great.

On the religious plane, he took to the next phase of his life
certain qualities from the last: a recognition of the need for
personal holiness, and a sense of sin: also a deep interest in
prophecy. Almost as a paradox, he carried with him also an
awareness of his rank in society: this he was constantly to use
in the service of his new allegiance. He was slow to realize,
however, that having been of great importance, the powerful
layman in the English Roman Catholic body was to become an
anachronism and of far less consequence.

Charles March Phillipps wrote in his diary 'A heavy aggrava-
tion to my other sorrows' (His brother Samuel's wife,
Charemille, had died, leaving her four surviving children with-
out a mother). He set to putting Ambrose to the University.
During the early part of 1825 he had already written to Dr
Copplestone at Oriel, to ask for admission for his son; he

followed this up with a personal visit to Oxford but was told that the College was full: there were no vacancies. He turned to Cambridge; Ambrose was accepted at Trinity College to read Mathematics for the Autumn term of 1826. Meanwhile the private lessons at home continued.

His father accompanied him to Nevil's Court at Trinity on 16th October 1826. Ambrose was seventeen. The Master, Dr Proctor, invited them to dine, and the Revd Thomas Thorp[46] was engaged at £100 a year as a private tutor. Charles March Phillipps seems to have been concerned to keep close to his son in view of the differences that had come between them, for he went to Cambridge to fetch him home in December. He found Ambrose's room 'full of Catholic objects'. No doubt he had hoped that, in new surroundings, the attachment would fade. In fact it was to be reinforced, for Ambrose had found a friend, Kenelm Henry Digby.[47]

Chapter 2

Cambridge and Rome

FOR the next fifty years Ambrose was to gather round himself a number of men, and a few women, whose characters were out of the ordinary and somewhat larger than easily recognised as true to life by the criteria of the present day. The social climate encouraged the cultivation of friendships among the leisured; eccentricity was tolerated, even expected in persons of rank. Ambrose shared his hopes and aspirations with those he found congenial, and absorbed ideas and reactions in return. To see his friends can reveal something of the man he grew to be. Of no one was this more true than of Kenelm Digby, the first of the new relationships.

Digby was born probably about 1797 (the date is not certain), an Irishman whose forbears included Knights, a philosopher, Members of Parliament and a Bishop of Elphin. His father had been Dean of Clonfert and had married three times; Kenelm was born when his father was nearing 70. The Dean had been a good athlete; skated, swam, ran, jumped. He was a Hebrew scholar, loved nature and painting, and travelled a good deal in France and Italy. Kenelm inherited many of these traits. Moreover he had by his Trinity days acquired his father's (and mother's) money, for a brother had died also. There was no need for him to earn his living. He was tall and powerfully built, over six feet, with a swarthy complexion, dark hair and eyes and had considerable physical strength. He plunged into the Rhine opposite the Drachenfels on one occasion and was carried downstream for three miles by the fierce current before he just managed to reach the farther bank. In his eighties, and living in London with his only remaining daughter, he swam on many evenings in the Serpentine. Riding on the back of a lion in a travelling Zoo in Cambridge was another exploit.

By a narrow margin Digby scraped a degree in Mathematics in 1819 (it was obviously not his metier) but in 1820 he won a Norrisian Prize for an essay on the evidences of the Christian religion. A comment upon it pointed out that while not closely reasoned, the work showed a wide range of reading. The rest of his considerable literary output (about 40 volumes) was to show precisely these characteristics. With his academic attainments behind him, he began to travel in pursuit of his burning enthusiasm, which was the concept of chivalry and the culture of the middle ages. Fired originally by the poems of Sir Walter Scott, Digby went off in search of cathedrals, castles, abbeys, knights, tournaments, chronicles and legends. His best friend at Trinity as a student had been a fellow Irishman called George Darby[1] who lived at Markye in Sussex. Together they held tournaments with hop-poles as lances.

While in Normandy Digby drew up a table of the distinguishing features of the different epochs of architecture: the Norman, Early English, Decorated and Perpendicular. He made sketches of charm and creativity and added features which existed only within his imagination. With his known feeling for the middle ages, it cannot have been any great surprise when he became a Roman Catholic at the end of 1825, just at the time when Ambrose made his much more startling disclosure to his family. Digby's spiritual pilgrimage was clearly much influenced by the observances in Catholic churches in Europe: he saw there greater evidence of faith by which men lived than was generally the case in contemporary England. When he eventually decided to seek instruction from a priest, no one at first would take him seriously. A professor at the Sorbonne in Paris who did not wish to involve himself in controversy, advised Digby, who was nearly 30, to consult his family in England. In London he had two similar experiences until Charles Butler, a Roman Catholic lawyer who had been much concerned in bringing matters of faith into the open, introduced him to the Jesuit, Fr Edward Scott[2] through whom Digby's reception took place.

Trinity, which had allowed Digby to keep rooms in College since his undergraduate days, did not withdraw the privilege. It was thus that Ambrose found him there in the autumn of 1826. Digby had already one book to his credit, the first version of *The Broadstone of Honour* (named after the castle of Ehrenbreitstein) with the sub-title of 'Rules for the Gentlemen of England', and published in 1822. After his conversion to Roman Catholicism, he rewrote and expanded it into four volumes with the intention of demonstrating the close connection between the principles of chivalry and those of his new beliefs; re-publication brought with it a fresh sub-title 'The true sense and practice of Chivalry'.

The first of the new volumes, *Godefridus*, appeared in 1827 while Ambrose and Digby were at Trinity together. It is solid, defuse and intensely derivative: there are few paragraphs or structured arguments: Latin and Greek quotations are not translated[3]. Godfrey, a Crusading chief, does not make his appearance till p.322; characterisation and plot are sacrificed to the cause of extolling chivalry as 'that general spirit and state of mind which disposes men to heroic and generous actions and keeps them conversant with all that is beautiful and sublime in the intellectual and moral world'.

Digby's books were not widely reviewed and the extent to which they were appreciated in his lifetime is difficult to gauge. They reached Montalembert[4] who said he was edified by them, but their circulation cannot be assessed by the rate of re-printing, since all publication expenses were borne by the author; his works do not appear to have been given more recent attention[5]. However, they have a certain academic importance in throwing light on the personality and outlook of Digby, who emerges a good deal more interesting than his writings. One factor remains abundantly clear: Digby and his works exercised a powerful influence on the young Ambrose. Later some of their attitudes began to separate, especially their views towards Christian union and the methods by which it might be achieved; but in the 1830s their friendship was close. Digby was dominant and Ambrose somewhat undeveloped, so their opinions were similar.

Evidence for the day to day university life of Ambrose is scarce though certain details appear in Digby's books of verses. It is impossible not to be repelled by their banality, but they help to illustrate their subject. One of these, *Ouranogaia*[6] or Heaven on Earth, written many years later, described friendships at Cambridge. Digby introduced the names of various dons, Whewell, Peacock, Hare, Rose, Sedgwick and then those of his younger contemporaries among whom he included Ambrose:

> Phillipps, deep read in mediaeval books
> Had Heav'n around him. Heav'n in his looks

In the *Temple of Memory*[7], he referred to his young friend's bright and pure image and his white vellum-bound volumes in Italian, French and Spanish, clearly inspired by Digby himself:

> Little Latin volumes proved for him
> True cups Ambrosian that o'erflow their brim.

Other allusions were to the 'angel's smile that opened heav'n to earth'; and his 'fascination which made acquaintances 'humbly own the error of their nation'. That many of them did so is unlikely, but it reveals that Ambrose at Cambridge was obviously much engaged in attempting to bring about conversions to Roman Catholicism. A letter written from Trinity to Fr Scott[8] (to whom Digby had introduced him) concerned his hopes of bringing three Cambridge men to 'our Holy Religion'. He was anxious for the priest to make a visit to the University.

The names of Ambrose's friends, apart from Digby, are not well documented. In 1867 he told the Bishop of Clifton[9] that in his own college his acquaintance was largely with many 'who now hold some of the highest places in the realm'. Richard Monckton-Milnes[10], who made a reappearance in the 1840s was one of them; Edward Fitzgerald[11] later acclaimed for his English poetic version of the *Rubaiyat of Omar Khayyam*[12], was another; his brother John married Augusta, sister of Ambrose in 1832. Alfred Tennyson, afterwards Poet Laureate, was a Trinity contemporary, as was Arthur Hallam, but no trace of their close acquaintance survives. William Thackeray came the term after Ambrose had left.

Members of the University were expected to be at least nominal members of the Church of England, and appear in chapel; supplicants for all degrees had either to declare themselves members of the Established Church or to subscribe to the three articles of the Canons of 1604 and to take the Oath of Supremacy. This was a stumbling block for Ambrose and it is likely that he would have needed to cut short his career at

Cambridge, without taking a degree, had his illness not precipitated it.

During the summer vacation of 1827 he asked his father's leave (he was still a minor which had significance at the time) to attend Mass on Sundays at Leicester; the lack of reply he took as agreement. Later that summer his tutor, Thomas Thorp, came to stay at Garendon for a few days. His report was not encouraging to the recipient, for he told Charles March Phillipps that his son read nothing but 'Roman Catholic books and legends'.

From the pages of his father's diary it would seem that Ambrose did not present so amiable a front to his family, in his early twenties, as to his contemporaries at Cambridge. Both father and son were clearly hot-tempered and each was wrestling with problems: Ambrose was acutely aware of belonging to a different religious allegiance from that of his relations; Charles March Phillipps in the summer of 1827 was suffering from the pangs of unrequited love; so bitter that the pain of it is transmitted down the ages through the pages of his diary. The incident is not without significance in relation to his future attitude towards his son's forthcoming romance.

Charles had been a widower for fourteen years; he had discussed the question of second marriages with his brother's wife 'which she disapproves of if there are children'. A mysterious 'Miss Hall', clearly a friend of his daughter Augusta, was invited to stay at Garendon with her brother for over a month in July 1827. They both, with Charles, Augusta and Ambrose, rode a great deal in the park; Miss Hall on a grey pony. Soon Charles was listing her accomplishments and committing his feelings to paper. Miss Hall played the piano beautifully, including some compositions of her own; she danced the quadrille 'exceedingly well'. Charles wrote to her father 'announcing my affection for his daughter; request permission to address her'. At last: 'I have opportunity of speaking to Miss Hall privately; she gives me no ray of hope. Rashness had produced despair'. 'I am wretched' he confessed several times. Charles read aloud to the girls in an attempt to soften Mary Hall's heart: Pope's Epistles, Grey's Letters and Odes, *Childe Harold*. There were more conversations and 'delicious' walks in the park in the moonlight. 'The result as before', he wrote 'Age, age!'

At last it was time for Miss Hall to leave for home; Augusta accompanied her. 'My farewell with the darling creature most bitter . . . I was overwhelmed.' He wrote imploring help to his late wife's sister Mary Simpson, who came at once and he returned with her to Launde. 'She thought my case unfortunately hopeless'. Each day he exchanged letters with his beloved. As a result, after a brief interlude he set forth for Totteridge to stay with her parents. But failure attended his mission. 'I entertain faint, very frail hopes of Happiness here'. Another 'bitter farewell' took place and the relationship came to an end. Back at Garendon his health seemed to suffer for some weeks. A final humiliation was to follow: Ambrose returned from a visit to Launde with the news that a letter from Augusta had been read aloud to various members of the family which

> communicated the unfortunate result of my journey to Totteridge. It gives me excessive pain; the indiscretion of Augusta, so repeated, quite derange my health and temper.

Eventually he sent Miss Hall a pair of doves and took up his life again with a more than usual number of social and public engagements.

An additional anxiety for Charles was his mother's health; there had been several what seemed like final-partings here; she was living at Brislington, near Bristol, and suffering from dropsy. At home a prolonged drought affected the crops on the estate and much social disturbance and deprivation was apparent in the countryside. He was busy as a magistrate in attempts to keep law and order.

He and Ambrose came near to blows on more than one occasion:

> Ambrose is most violent . . . A personal scuffle on the stairs !!! Mrs Cowper [Ambrose's Aunt Catherine] condemns his conduct – she heard him use the words 'I will be revenged' thrice aloud on the stairs previous to the encounter.

It was a far cry from 'the Angel's smile' of Digby's poem and not an isolated incident. On 29 June 1827 Charles wrote

> Ambrose guilty of a dreadful *Ebullilene* as I talked of the Ceremonies of Holy Week at Rome

The nearest Catholic chapel to Cambridge was at the Seminary belonging to the London Vicariate, St Edmund's College, Old Hall, Ware. For the purpose of administration and oversight, the English Mission, for such was the Roman Catholic Church on this island deemed to be, was divided into four areas or Districts: London, Northern, Midland and Western. The Bishop responsible for each was a Vicar Apostolic and not a Bishop in Ordinary, and they held titular rather than territorial sees. In 1826 William Poynter[13] was coming to the end of a long period as Vicar Apostolic of the London District; Thomas Smith held the Northern one with Thomas Penswick as coadjutor; Thomas Walsh was single-handed in the Midland District, while in the West, Peter Collingridge was Vicar Apostolic and his co-adjutor Peter Augustine Baines.

Bishop Poynter wrote[14] to Ambrose in answer to his letter from Cambridge; he expressed pleasure at his conversion, his friendship with Kenelm Digby, and the prospect of their participating in the duties performed on Sundays at St Edmund's. It became a habit for the two men to ride the 26 miles from Cambridge for Mass, without breaking their fast. St Edmund's had occupied its present site only since 1793, when the college was refounded as a continuation in England of the Seminary which had carried on its work at Douai since 1568; it had been forced by the revolution to close. The site was a good one, on high ground surrounded by parkland; the long low building was large and dignified. It was a school for boys as well as a Seminary for the training of priests.

The chapel in the second decade of the 19th century was scarcely more than a large room with a gallery. It faced the front to the north (and right) of the house and acted as an extension to it; a similar building at the southern end was the refectory; the two together had cost little over £1,500. There were long windows which reached almost to the ground on the western side to correspond to those at Douai, to which the position of the stalls, benches and pulpit also bore a resemblance. The sanctuary was at the north end, where a vaulted ceiling (the roof of the building was flat) had at the centre the figure of a dove with outstretched wings, and the inscription *Laudate Dominum omnes gentes*. The high altar was of wood with an ornamental frontal and carved pillars; upon it was a

very large heavy tabernacle nearly 7 feet high, with a high
domed canopy over the ivory crucifix. On either side of it were
six tall candlesticks of gilt wood. At the back of the altar hung
a picture, usually taken to represent St Edmund, but in reality
a copy of a painting of St Andrew Corsini, the original of
which belonged to a palace in Rome.

Before the sanctuary was the choir with stalls and pulpit;
together they occupied half the available space. The floor of
the choir was 'covered with a carpet, of worse taste, it is said,
even than the sanctuary one, and moreover totally at variance
with it in colour.[15] The choice of the decoration in the chapel
was doubtless regulated by the need for economy. Much as the
attendance at Mass at St Edmund's must have meant to the
two Cambridge men; the lack of harmony and beauty and the
kind of antiquity that both admired so much in their surroundings, was surely a source of pain. So much so that the extreme
care which Ambrose was later to devote to the furnishings and
decoration in his chapel at Grace Dieu would seem to have its
origin in the experience of these earlier days.

Ambrose's health, precarious throughout his youth, continued to give him and his family cause for anxiety during the
Cambridge period. Worried letters passed between him and
Digby, for Digby was very ill in the winter of 1827–8; several
of their contemporaries died that year. Fr Benedict Caestryck[16],
parish priest at Leicester wrote[17] frequently urging caution. In
addition to his weak chest, Ambrose had a tendency for his
spirits to vacillate between depression and exaltation, and this
may have affected his resillience. He wrote[18] to Digby on the
first day of 1828.

> I am very wretched about something just now, it would not be
> worthwhile to tell you why, for to recount to one's friends
> one's miseries is always gloomy and therefore certainly not to
> enter into a letter.

A possible explanation for this anxiety may well have lain in
the debts Ambrose had contracted at Cambridge. Undergraduates were notoriously prone to overspend but in his case the
habit, unhappily, remained with him throughout his life. They
may well have been bills for books which were then bound in
white vellum (of which Digby had written), together with

supplementing the very poor fare supplied in Hall at Trinity, which were his undoing. Men who wanted to avoid the food merely went to Hall to be marked down for attendance, and dined in their rooms or in the town at their own expense.[19]

An attempt to denigrate Ambrose at a later date[20] seized upon some incidents during his undergraduate days and referred sarcastically to debts which had received some notice and described him as a

> ... silly young man of noble family, who at Cambridge gave promise of his capacity for nice distinctions, by not being able to distinguish as his boon companions between his tradesmen and his fellow students ...

Kenelm Digby considered the dons at Trinity to have over-reacted to the circumstances, when he wrote concerning the incident to a friend.[21] Once again it is Ambrose's father's diary which provides the clues. On 1 February 1827 he records telling his agent to pay Dr Peacock £305.5.9 on account of Ambrose's bills; a considerable sum in modern terms. On 1 May he heard from his son with a further bill from Dr Peacock of £149.1.9. In November he wrote

> Receive letter from Mr Thorp of Trinity College relative to pecuniary embarrassment of A.

Next day he wisely consigned the sum of £240 not to his son, but the tutor. Three days later, he sent his son a bill for Church Plate for the Catholic Church in Leicester.

It was during one of the Sunday visits to St Edmund's in April 1828 that Ambrose, already suffering from a severe cough ruptured a blood vessel and became seriously ill. His father was sent for,[22] as was a doctor from London. In accordance with custom, he was bled, 35oz, and it was recommended that winter be spent in Italy; not to start later than September. Ambrose's Cambridge days were over.

If Charles March Phillipps had reservations about the conversion of his son to Roman Catholicism, it might be supposed a strange decision to take him to the central stronghold of his new beliefs. Perhaps he felt that proximity to the papal seat of government might damp his enthusiasm: the administration of the papal states was regarded with particular horror in

England. Or perhaps again he recognised himself defeated and yielded to his own reasons which attracted him to Rome. It provided a society which he found congenial and works of art which were of interest to him as a collector: he had made several purchases on previous visits. His chief motive will have been to save his son from the fatal consequences of the illness which had already overtaken his wife and his brother, William. No price was too great.

The impact of the French revolution and the subsequent Napoleonic wars still retained their marks on the collection of Italian states in which Ambrose, his father, and his sister, Augusta, arrived in the autumn of 1828. Especially was this true of that part of Italy governed by the Papacy. At the outset, the over-running of the peninsular, the entry into Rome of the troops of Napoleon in 1808 and the forcible abduction of the Pope Pius VII to France in 1809, had aroused much feeling on his behalf. The States of the Church became part of the French Empire: the Pope was deprived of his patrimony. Pius behaved with dignity in exile, at first in Grenoble, then Savona and finally Fontainbleau, and by the time he returned to his capital in 1814 there was considerable sympathy for him in Europe. It was partly on this account, and partly because of the virtues and sagacity of his Secretary of State, Cardinal Consalvi, that the Papacy received such favourable treatment at the Congress of Vienna in 1815, where the map of Europe was redrawn. Consalvi visited England on his way to the meeting of the European powers at Vienna; he was received in his robes by the Prince Regent and a lasting friendship was established between the Cardinal and Castlereigh, the English foreign secretary. Later, letters and gifts were exchanged between the Prince, who had become George IV, and Pius VII and the leading English portrait painter, Sir Thomas Lawrence, was despatched to Rome to paint the Pope and his outstanding statesman. Consalvi's requests at Vienna were granted almost in full and the States of the Church returned intact into Papal hands.

Much has been written on whether this can be regarded as ultimately in the best interests of the Church. To have been able to relinquish the difficult undertaking of governing the papal territories in the 1820s and 30s would have enabled the Pope to devote his attention to his spiritual responsibilities. Certainly the later conflicts which were to surround the issue of the temporal power in the 1850s and 60s would have been avoided; as also the Pope's final humiliation with the removal of that power in 1870. But it is doubtful whether the role of the Pope as conceived at that juncture would have allowed for this development: he was an Italian territorial prince and his spiritual influence was tied up with his temporal sovereignty. There was uncertainty as to the position of the papacy within the Church from a doctrinal point of view. For example, during the 18th century, various bodies had gone on record in denying to the Pope authority beyond a primacy of honour: the theological faculty at Caen, the English Vicars Apostolic who, in pursuit of political rights for Roman Catholics said in 1788 'we acknowledge no infallibility'[23] and the Archbishop Electors of the Church in Germany in calling for an account of the papal position, had done just this. For some Roman Catholics ultimate sovereignty, in the matter of faith and morals, lay with a General Council. More dogmatic interpretations of the Pope's spiritual power, mainly from Italian and French sources, were on the way, but they had not yet received a universal hearing.

By the Congress of Vienna Italy was carved into eight portions: the Austrian 'Kingdom of Lombardy-Venetia' with an Archduke as viceroy; the Kingdom of Piedment-Sardinia with its accession of Genoa and the Genoese Peninsular ruled by the House of Savoy; the Kingdom of the two Sicilies (Sicily and Naples) under Spanish Bourbons; the grand-duchy of Tuscany and the duchies of Parma, Modena, Lucca; lastly the Papal states which stretched across the centre of Italy from the Po in the north-east, through the Marches of Ancona and Rimini, to Rome and the western coast.

The French regime having been swept aside, it should have been possible in theory for Pius VII and Consalvi to make a fresh start in the ordering of their territory. As Cardinal Chiaramonti, in 1797, the Pope had preached on the theme that the new ideas of the revolution were not irreconcilable with those of the Church, but they would only be effective if interpreted in a Christian way. Throughout Italy, however, the

forces of reaction prevailed. In general all French innovations
were suspect. Since these had included a measure of reform,
some return to obscurantist administration was inevitable.

Consalvi made attempts to disturb the clerical monopoly of
administrative posts by infiltrating some laymen into subordinate positions. His efforts did not meet with the approval of
all his brethren in the sacred college. He tried to reform the
finances of the Papal states, agriculture and transportation and
establish a textile industry. Nowhere had the industrial revolution touched Italian life: there were many small towns, some
of ancient origin, for Etruscan and Roman civilisation had
begun in them, but for the most part it was a land dominated
by agricultural values, which still remembered ancient gods,
where superstition and magic were live issues. The dispensation
of justice was less harsh and brutal than that in England with
its high rate of executions and transportations, but a good deal
more corrupt and arbitrary and filled with informers and
spies.

Ambrose, entering Rome in 1828, was hungry for visible
spiritual authority; for ceremony, form and drama in his
religious observance and for evidence of the entry of the
supernatural into the everyday world. He was to find it all.
The reign of the humble and gentle Pius VII, his character
manifested in the charming Lawrence portrait[24], had given way
to a different kind of regime. On Pius's death in 1823, Cardinal
Hannibal della Genga[25] was prevailed upon to accept election
as Pope, despite his poor health; he took the title Leo XII.

Pius VII and Consalvi had, in 1818, re-opened the English
College in Rome for the training of priests. Nicholas Wiseman[26]
who was later to play a considerable part in English public
life, as well as in that of Ambrose when both returned to
England, was one of the first students after the gap of a
generation. He left a frank appraisal[27] of the early 19th century
pontiffs from a close and favoured position. He wrote that on
the accession of Leo XII there were 'different sentiments prevalent in Rome' on the matter of Consalvi's principles of administration. The new Pope belonged to 'another school of politics';
was estranged from Consalvi whom he removed from the
Secretariat of State and replaced by Cardinal della Somaglia.
On 24th January 1824 Consalvi died and thereby passed from

the scene not only a servant of the Holy See respected by the great powers, but a system of government seen by Wiseman as 'just, liberal and enlightened'.

The new Pope, it would seem, decided to abandon moderate political and social policies and showed himself anxious to reverse recent changes. It is perhaps unfair to him that only the more ludicrous examples of attempts to raise moral standards have survived: he forbade the playing of games in the street, the waltz in carnival, encores in theatres, certain dress for ladies and tourists. He returned the Jews to the ghetto. A ban was placed on drinking in public places: drink might be bought in Osteria, but not consumed there. 'Nothing' said Wiseman's account, 'could exceed the unpopularity of this measure and it was abolished immediately on the Pope's death'. It has been said that he banned vaccination as a French fad, since he declared that smallpox was a judgment from God[28], but this is not so; it was declared no longer obligatory. His actions were not all negative: he reformed the universities; rebuilt St Paul's outside the walls on its original lines and just as large after the fire of 1824, reduced taxes and re-centralised government; but it is, in general, his strictness that is remembered.

Ambrose clearly regarded it as an asset. He wrote[29] to Digby from Naples:

> I have been much delighted with my stay in Rome how many profound and devout feelings are excited by a residence there ... it is impossible for me to be in a more edifying place ... the piety of the people is so great ... the numerous and vast colleges are so regulated and orderly ... it does one good to see the students walking about in their long gowns and one often sees a St Aloysius or a St Stanislaus amongst them.
>
> ... Everything is so piously regulated by the government of the Pope – even to the price of all merchandise and the just profit is fixed by a priest according in the rules of conscience. On every house in Rome are written up these words 'Almighty God sees us and Eternity'. No public houses are permitted and drunkeness is unknown, also very great means are taken to suppress vice of all sorts ...

He went on to describe the actions of princes and princesses who walked in poor habit to visit the sick and bury the dead:

one went continually to the hospitals to dress wounds. The contrast between these features of Rome and conditions in London clearly impressed itself upon the young man. The depravity, squalor, drunkenness, soot, of the English capital, the evils of the factory system, the dominance of the profit motive, the indifference of the well-to-do, were thrown into relief by the sight of a simpler and less brutal form of economic life.

Popular religion Ambrose found warm, exuberant and attractive; how different from the cool scriptural religious atmosphere in England with its lack of openness on spiritual problems. 'I was acquainted with very many priests and religious' he wrote to Digby[30] ... 'it was a great delight to converse ... what a consolation it was to our ancestors when there were convents in England in moments of despondency to have recourse to these monks and religious for advice to direct and soothe them'. He had been presented to Leo XII a fortnight before his death:

> He spoke to me with the greatest kindness and humility, asked me a great deal about my father and my family, whether they are kind to me and whether I had any hopes of them. He gave me blessing and a silver crucifix which begged me to keep for his sake and added 'Remember me in your prayers'.
> ... the ceremonies at his funeral were indeed awfully grand and worthy of the Church which the prophet likens to 'a city built on top of the mountains'.

One of the chief characteristics of Ambrose throughout his life was his search for the miraculous which he saw not so much in nature itself, as the work of the creator, but in the suspension of its laws in situations that were unexpected and seemed to defy rational explanation. Signs of miracles increased his faith. He referred to the 'many miraculous images of Jesus Christ and Our Blessed Lady before which the faithful go to pray. There is also a miraculous well two feet deep which St Peter made to baptise a gaoler in the Mammertine prison. There is no hole in it, which you may ascertain by groping about on all sides and yet if you carry away tanks of water, it never diminishes' A personal experience, told many years later[31] reinforced Ambrose's belief in what he saw as supernatural happenings.

On his way to Rome that autumn he had fallen ill of a fever which had claimed several victims. A doctor, so he related, had considered his condition dangerous: his father's servant wept at the prospect of his imminent death. As the fever was at its height, Ambrose had invoked the aid of the Blessed Virgin whose picture he carried with him, and soon after he had begun to improve '*mia salute fu notabilmente migliorato*'. A few days later the party were able to resume their journey to Rome and Ambrose received a premonition: that his life had been spared for the accomplishment of some good purpose.[32]

A feature of Ambrose's visits to Rome was that the extent to which his acquaintances influenced him, increased and accelerated. Many of the men and women he met there were considerably to affect the future course of his life and later to cross his path many times. Roman society was not a large group. Those Englishmen who possessed the entry to it, as did Charles March Phillipps as a former Member of Parliament and large landowner, were bound to meet each other. Chief among the family's acquaintances was Hugh Clifford[33], eldest son of a Roman Catholic peer and descendant of one of the five ministers of Charles II, whose surnames spelt the word CABAL. He had served as a volunteer in the Peninsular war and had attended Consalvi at Vienna. His young cousin, Laura Clifford, was to become Ambrose's wife; their first meeting later in England took place under his auspices.

The friendship of Ambrose with John, Lord Shrewsbury, formed in these Roman months was only slightly less significant. They were to spend the rest of their lives in close contact, developing the spread and influence of Roman Catholicism in England, and in particular in the building of churches and religious houses. Lord Shrewsbury's career reflected the contemporary scene as it concerned Roman Catholics. Deprived of opportunities in England during his youth by the penal codes, he had travelled to the countries round the Mediterranean and while in Spain during the Peninsular war, had been so sickened by the carnage that he had taken a small brig to return to England. He exchanged one kind of violence for another: the ship was captured by pirates and it was with difficulty and the loss of all his possessions that he reached home. On his succession to the earldom of Shrewsbury in 1827 he inherited large estates round Alton Towers in Staffordshire, but he, his wife and two daughters Mary and Gwendoline Talbot, continued to spend a large part of most years in Europe. Once he and Ambrose had embarked on their building programme, this exile was extended in order to save money and devote it to the cause they held so dear. The earlier continental journeys were devoted partly to the search by the Countess for Italian princes as husbands for her daughters. As a senior Roman Catholic layman in England, Lord Shrewsbury became albeit unwillingly a leader and spokesman of the community: many of his open (printed) letters on issues which concerned Roman Catholics, were addressed to Ambrose de Lisle.

There were two remarkable English clerics in the Roman scene of 1828–9; one was the aforementioned Nicholas Wiseman whom Ambrose did not begin to know well until his next visit, the other was Peter Augustine Baines.[34] He came into prominence by his criticism of converts in his Lenten Pastoral of 1840. (Ambrose was clearly identifiable.) Bishop Baines's earlier history has a good deal of bearing on the incident. Peter Baines was educated at the English Benedictine Abbey of Lampspring in Westphalia due to limited English alternatives. Suppression of religious houses in Europe followed the French revolution and he returned to England and re-joined his contemporaries at Ampleforth in Yorkshire, where a house had been found for them. He was professed as a monk, ordained priest, and in 1817 entrusted with the care of the Roman Catholic congregation at Bath. His strong personality, zeal and drive were recognised by his appointment as co-adjutor to the Vicar-Apostolic of the Western District in 1823: he was consecrated with the title of Bishop of Siga. Not content, as were some of his fellow bishops, that his faithful in England should remain part of a small and insignificant body existing quietly in backwaters, his plans for mission, education and development were always expansive and idiosyncratic. Soon his enthusiasm and efforts had wrecked his health and he left for the Continent to rest and revive. By the winter of 1826 he had arrived in Rome.

Nicholas Wiseman with whom, among many, Baines had a tremendous wrangle described the latter in his *Recollections*[35]; not without an element of spleen since they were written subsequent to the disagreement:

He came in a state of almost hopeless illness . . . in the hopes that a change of climate might do more than medicines or their administration . . . The mild climate, the interesting recreation, and perhaps more still the rest from the labour and the excitement in which he had lived, did their duty and a visible change for the better was observable by spring . . . By degrees the reputation he had acquired in England began to spread in Rome.

Wiseman's description, in which he failed throughout to conceal traces of envy, nevertheless showed Bishop Baines's capacity for influencing those he met and converting them to his point of view. When an English pulpit was opened in Rome the church became crowded whenever Bishop Baines was announced as preacher:

The flow of his words was easy and copious, his imagery was often very elegant, and his discourses were replete with thought and solid matter. But his great power was in his delivery, in voice, in tone, in look and gesture. His whole manner was full of pathos, sometimes more even than the matter justified; there was a peculiar tremulousness of voice which gave his word more than a double effect, notwithstanding a broadness of provincial accent and an occasional dramatic pronunciation of certain words. In spite of such defects, he was considered, by all that heard him, one of the most eloquent and earnest preachers they had ever attended.

Shortly before his death in February 1829, Leo XII appointed Bishop Baines a domestic chaplain at the Vatican. The news began to circulate that it was the Pope's intention to make him a cardinal which was contrary to the Bishop's own plan to return to England and work there for the extension of Catholicism. The Pope died before any decision was made, and since the Vicar Apostolic of the Western District, Bishop Collingridge, also expired two weeks later, Bishop Baines hastened back to England to take up the administration of the Vicariate. He and Ambrose did not appear to meet or communicate again for six or seven years, but from then onwards, despite an equal total dedication to the same causes, there were sharp differences of opinion as to their method of achievement.

A frequent companion of Ambrose during the first visit to

Rome, and one who has left a clear picture of him, was the
extraordinary Mary Arundell, 43 years old, and wife of a
Roman Catholic peer. Her eccentricities and excesses would
probably never have been tolerated had it not been for her
exalted ancestry. Born Mary Anne Grenville Nugent Temple
in 1787, only daughter of the 3rd Earl Temple and 1st Marquis
of Buckingham, she was witty, fascinating, obstinate, fond of
society and had a fierce temper. Her childhood was spent in
Dublin where her father was twice Viceroy of Ireland. At the
age of 23 she became a Roman Catholic, largely it would seem
owing to the influence of her mother who was a secret Catholic; forbidden to practice her religion for many years by her
husband. Their home at Stowe was filled with Mary Anne's
suitors who included, it was said, the Comte d'Artois later
King Charles X of France. The offer was declined for her by
her father and she married James Everard Arundell of Wardour, later 10th baron and perhaps not the exciting companion
for which she might have wished.

Financial pressure drove them from England in 1828, when
the upkeep of Wardour Castle proved beyond their means and
they ventured on a continental tour. Lady Arundell clearly
enjoyed Roman society and she soon formed a deep attachment
to Ambrose whom she treated as a son: she had no children.
She admired his appreciation of all things Roman, his devotion
and seriousness, in contrast to the frivolous behaviour of many
young English bloods; and his youthful and pleasant appearance.
Ambrose returned the affection and remained attached to her
for the rest of her tempestuous life. Lady Arundell's letters[36] to
her sister-in-law Mrs Doughty, give a graphic impression of
the young protegé:

> Then I have a Platonic and *haute devotion* friendship with one
> of the other sex, as we say in shriving with whom I pass whole
> mornings in various churches and who is always ready for a
> *funzione* – the most delightful young man that has existed since
> the days of St Stanislaus Koska[37], the son of March Phillipps,
> once member for Leicestershire – who became a Catholic,
> withstanding persecution of family, father, uncle, Bp Ryder
> and all the University of Cambridge. His father, a very gentle-
> manlike, well-informed, pleasant man, and a nice little sister,
> are here with this young saint, who has reconciled all his

family now by his excellent conduct and does nothing but pray for their conversion. At breakfast the carriage comes to the door. Now says Evd[38], I shall not see you till dinner: of course you'll be till then in churches with *that boy*. Such masses at the Gesu! after which we adjourn to the outer sacristy and there such conferences with Padre Glover[39] who is by the bye one of the dearest, most agreeable and delightful of men, and best of confessors. He will be one of the thousand things I shall deeply regret in leaving Rome.

His pleasure in his surroundings did not compel Ambrose to accept with equal enthusiasm all the examples of art and architecture around him. The classical style reintroduced and adapted by the Renaissance and continued in the Baroque tradition disgusted him. His love for all things mediaeval, fostered and developed in him by association with Kenelm Digby, was made stronger by exposure to what Ambrose derisively called pagan art. It was the same with music: much of what he heard in religious settings he considered 'uneccclesias-tical'. These opinions may have been a youthful arrogance, but he held the same views for the rest of his life and many were the controversies that they engendered. They were only partly intellectual and derived more from association with an age which he held to have provided men with sound religion, stability, beauty and honour.

Eighteen years later Ambrose compiled and had published a manual of plain chant for use by his own chapel choir[40]. In the preface he referred to his experiences in Rome in the year 1828 and showed how seminal they had been and how much of his later development he owed to them. Late in October he had ridden out into the compagna and back through the Porta San Paolo.

> ... my friend pointed out the distant turrets of the venerable basilica of St Paul, three miles from Rome on the Ostian way ... and my heart beat as he told me how it was destroyed by fire and was now being restored once more with greater magnifi-cance than ever, and I thought it might be an emblem of a Catholick resurrection in England, and I fancied my country once more taking its special charge, and serving it anew with devotion and faith renewed ... suddenly my friend drew in his bridle and halting bid me dismount, that we might visit the

ancient basilica of Santa Sabina, one of the martyred virgins of the primitive Roman Church . . . we entered the sacred building. Never shall I forget that sublime moment: the monks to whom it belongs were just chanting the concluding antiphons of the complinehour. Oh! what sweetness, what majesty, what inexpressible devotion, what sorrow for sin, what peaceful humble hope of forgiveness were concentrated in that divine chant, the sonorous voices of the older monks, the high clear melodious notes of the youthful novices, blending with the sweet deep tones of the organ, and echoing the constant psalmody of eighteen centuries amid these venerable aisles, consecrated as they were from the times of Constantine, brought before me all the solemn grandeur of the primitive Church, that manly and heroic period of Martyrs and Saints. I knelt down with a mixed feeling of heavenly awe and delight, and blessing God, that He had of His infinite mercy made me a member of His Holy Catholick Church, I thanked Him that He had brought me to hear at the threshold of the Apostles that 'New Canticle of the Lamb' the divine chant of St Gregory: I besought Him to confirm my faith, which I felt strengthened by this living image of the Church of the fourth century, this Church which is the same yesterday, today and for ever. I conceived a love for the old chants of the Church, that has since deepened, becoming more and more intense, as I have studied them more, and learnt to perceive their various and hidden treasures: and though we must go to some of the old monastick churches of Rome to hear them in all their grandeur and perfection, still in the furthest west we may echo their divine sound, and though they die out faintly on our lips, our heart at least will never cease to beat in unison with them, and loving them intensely, we shall not only have a Catholick, but an English motive for praising the memory of England's blessed Apostle, St Gregory the Great![41]

The Conclave for the election of the new Pope, following the death of Leo XII opened on 23 February 1829 and lasted until March 31, by which time Ambrose had left for Naples. If he wrote an account of that part of the proceedings which reached public ears, it has not survived. Antonio Rosmini[42] one of the most original minds in Italy in the 19th century, and later a frequent and important correspondent of Ambrose, was in Rome; he wrote to his bishop[43] (of Trent) who was avid for news:

The Conclave is this time being held at the Quirinal. The Cardinals left the church of San Silvestrò in procession on foot and the *Veni Creator* was sung among an immense concourse of people ... three more Cardinals went in yesterday [making 40 in all]. Our Cardinals are there, that is the Hungarian and the one from Milan but not the Archduke Rudolph and the French Cardinals. I do not think the Spanish and Portugese will come, partly because they are too old and partly because they are too busy. In the first scrutinies it is stated as a fact that Cardinal Pacca[44] had 20 votes: he only needed 5 more for two thirds[45]. M. de Chateaubriand [the French Ambassador] said he wanted Cardinal Pacca excluded, but this appears to have been a private bomb-shell for he had not yet received his credentials from the Court to the Sacred College. Nothing is known of the scrutinies that followed, but it seems that Pacca is out of the running. This Cardinal has the reputation of great piety, of being a good theologian and a good administrator; but he is supposed to be too gentle and easy to influence. He gained a great reputation during the persecution of Pius VII. As Pacca's supporters have not succeeded it is thought that the Conclave will be somewhat prolonged ... Cardinal del Gregorio in conversation said he thought that if he were supported, he would be excluded by Spain ...

On 3rd March Cardinal Albani, accredited representative of Austria, charged with the veto held by the Emperor, entered the Conclave, and the lengthening of the proceedings was assured. Eventually Cardinal Francesco Saverio Castiglioni[46] was elected and took the title Pius VIII. He was a specialist in Canon law and a favourite of the moderates. It appears he tried to improve conditions economically and socially in the papal territories and promoted a policy that was milder in general than the extreme conservatism of his predecessor. He was dogged by poor health which prevented him from officiating at the liturgy. Wiseman did not give Pius VIII a very good mark in his *Recollections*, and wrote of his bowed figure and invisible features; 'the functions of the Church were beyond his strength'.[47] Rosmini told his bishop[48] 'all think we have a learned and holy Pontiff, but in the midst of this satisfaction is the fear that the reign will not last long: he is 68 years old and not strong'.

Ambrose had travelled south on his way home and has left

another illuminating account[49] of a ride, this time at dawn, to
the monastery of the Camaldolese hermits situated at Phlegrean
Fields, overlooking the bay of Naples. In lyrical terms he
described the landscape which had been immortalised by Virgil
in the sixth book of the Aeneid, and become even more
transported by the life and aspect of the monks. Their rule
led them to spend their days in separate little detached hermit-
ages, each enclosed by a small garden with a chapel. The
monks in their long white habits and beards, some of them
very old (a proof that the great austerities of their rule were
not otherwise than conducive to health and longevity) never
tasted flesh, meat or even fish, but lived on bread, fruit and
herbs. They hardly ever spoke, nor even met together except in
their church when they sang together. There were to be two
consquences of this visit: the first was the birth of interest in
contemplative monasticism which had its culmination in the
founding by Ambrose of the Trappist Abbey of Mount St
Bernard on land adjacent to his own, in Leicestershire in 1836:
the second was his discovery at the Convent dei Camaldoli of
a book on the Maxims and Examples of the Saints which he
later translated and published in England.

Turning north, he visited Bavaria and the Tyrol where he
again admired the open religious nature of the people. Later he
described[50] the Austrians to Kenelm Digby as 'a sublime and
such a noble and chivalrous race; heroism and Christian piety
are indeed united in the characters of these mountaineers and
combined with such a patriachal simplicity . . .' Many people
went daily to Mass, 'No one can form an idea of the height of
perfection to which Catholick religion can raise [sic]', Children
knelt before crucifixes wrapt in meditation and upon the
graves of their friends. Ambrose had been much struck with a
'real Christian fountain' in which water gushed from the side
of a wooden statue of the Saviour. The shocked effect that
such a construction would have had upon the religious sensibili-
ties of Church people in England is not difficult to imagine. In
relation to Bavaria, Ambrose described a different situation.
The late Elector had been a sacrilegious innovator and had
laid his Kingdom open to the bad effects of the free circulation
of the principles of the French revolution: Jews had been
admitted to equality with Christians and the press had been

allowed to publish as it willed. The present King of Bavaria, however, according to Lord Shrewsbury, was a most chivalrous monarch with 'genuine ancient ideas', who had done something to restrain liberty of conscience. The young Ambrose thought this wise.

On his return to his father's home in Leicestershire, Ambrose was sad and lonely. Although deeply patriotic with one side of his nature, spiritually and psychologically he was at one with the religious ethos of Southern Europe. He had been much fêted in Italy, enjoyed its heady atmosphere and the society of clerics and lay people. Now he was isolated from much that made him happiest, in what now seemed a largely alien environment. For the only time in his life and in contrast to his later enthusiasm and application, he became listless. 'I have sought in vain to collect my thoughts. I can never sufficiently thank you for the excellent advice you were so kind as to give me with that regarding sadness. I wish indeed I could always bear in mind what you say . . .' he wrote to Digby.[51] He looked forward to his coming of age in March 1830 when he would be more of a master of his own movements and might be able to join his friend on the Continent.

In the meantime, he read much; the Life of St Aloysius Gonzaga, the contemplations of Padre Venturelli and other works in Italian and a book in French concerning the *Révélations*[52] of Soeur de la Nativité, a nun in France, which was reinforcing all that Ambrose had already absorbed from other sources that the time of Anti-Christ was very near. 'Never was there such profligacy, such infidelity, such open profaneness. It is impossible for things to go on: there must be something coming.' A sign in the sky in the shape of a crucifix had been seen against the moon on the 15 September; it had been reported in *The Times*. Popular opinion had held it to be a natural phenomenon, but 'I have talked about it to several Catholicks and they all think it is a wonderful and miraculous sign and certainly Our Lord said in the latter times there should be signs in the sun and moon'.

Ambrose's moods could swing very sharply from one extreme to another: in the same letter in which he exposed his gloom to the Jesuit, Fr Edward Scott[53], he changed key and began to register the extreme optimism which was to become an enduring characteristic. Catholicity was making a wonderful progress: new missions and churches were being opened and everywhere converts were pouring into the ark of Salvation. He worked on a translation of the *Maxims of the Saints* he had found at Naples which was, he thought, the most charming book he had ever read. The plan of the work was to present a virtue for each month and for every day a maxim inculcating the practice of it by holy people 'and then beautiful instances from the lives of the saints illustrative of it, so that it is full of the most beautiful and sublime stories that you can possibly conceive'. He intended to publish the finished work as he felt it would be useful, but not before he had submitted it to some learned priest for approval.[54] He thereby assured the Jesuit that he recognised his lay status.

Some writings he was later to send to his grandmother[55] received a kindly but rather less than complimentary reception; the attitudes of his family became plain to see. She thanked him for the beautiful engraving which he had sent from Rome:

> The subject is most interesting. I also thank you, my dear Ambrose, for the translation which you have made from the Italian. I will only remark that I am sure you are doing well not to print any for publication, but *only* your *family* friends.

She ended with some pious sentiments, as if to show that her grandson had not the monopoly of a personal understanding of the Christian religion.

Now deprived of close contact with Roman Catholics, Ambrose wrote frequently and fulsomely to Fr Glover at the Gesu in Rome. And it is in a letter in this series that can be found probably the most accurate account of the greatest triumph of Ambrose's early life, and one with which his name is widely remembered: the conversion of George Spencer to the Roman obedience in January 1830. The event was a watershed. Before it Ambrose was an untried boy; after it his confidence grew, his name emerged as a force to be reckoned with. He became increasingly certain he had some part to play in the destiny of the country to which he was devoted and the Church whose faith he believed so fervently. The next years were spent testing what could be the nature of that role and his exact status: should he be priest or layman in the English Mission which was his dearest cause.

Chapter 3

The English Mission

(i) Plans

George Spencer who was to become one of Ambrose's closest friends, was born in December 1799 at the Admiralty in London of illustrious parents. His father was George John, after 1835 2nd Earl Spencer; as Lord Althorp, First Lord of the Admiralty 1794–1800, and who in 1831 and 1832, managed in Committee the revolutionary Reform Bills. His mother was daughter of the 1st Earl Lucan. George was the youngest of the seven children. During childhood at their country seat at Althorp, his mother decided in 1810, when George was 11, that he was to take Holy Orders and fill one of their country livings. His brother Frederick, always called Fritz, was told that he was to be a soldier and it is clear that the nature of the careers were thought equivalent. Their sister Sarah, later Lady Lyttelton and in her widowhood governess to Queen Victoria's elder children, has left a set of correspondence in which she describes George in his youth[1]. 'He could scarcely keep grave the whole day after he had heard that he was to be a clergyman'.

After Eton and a private tutor (Charles James Blomfield, later Bishop of Chester and then London), George Spencer went to Trinity College, Cambridge in 1819. He made many friends, though he did not approve of the frequent drunkeness, and rode a great deal. His mother rebuked him at the end of his second term for spending too much time shooting and at hunt balls and said he must return to his studies. Lady Lyttelton thought him at this time 'as near perfection . . . as it is possible to reach as to mind and disposition'. His preparation for ordination was meagre in the extreme. In March 1819, having

attended 25 divinity lessons at Cambridge he received a certificate which allowed him to proceed without further training.
He passed out as Bachelor of Arts that June in the first class;
as the son of a peer, he completed the requirements in two
years. On 26 June he received the honorary degree of MA at
the hands of the Chancellor.

Some months followed on the grand tour of Europe with his
parents. In September 1822 the Bishop of Peterborough suggested that George should be ordained at Christmas. He asked
the Diocesan examiner what books to read and how to prepare,
and received the following reply[2]:

It is impossible that I could even entertain any idea of
subjecting a

> gentleman with whose talents and good qualities I am so well
> acquainted as I am with yours, to any examination, except one
> as a matter of form, for which a verse in the Greek testament
> and an Article of the Church of England returned into Latin,
> will be amply sufficient.

George Spencer was examined by the Dean of Peterborough
on 19 December and made Deacon by the Bishop on the 22nd.
On Sunday 29 he preached his first sermon as curate of the
family living of Brington; the Rector being absent on the
continent on account of debt (a frequent state of affairs), the
conduct of the parish devolved upon Spencer's inexperienced
shoulders.

For the next six years he remained at Brington, for most of
them promoted to Rector. His care of the poorer elements of
his flock was exemplary, but his theological opinions were not
so steadfast, and swung frequently and violently between various schools of thought. During 1828 he was close to resigning
his living. It seems clear that not only was he at that period
uninstructed and had no assurance of a call to the ministry,
but he lacked effective help and oversight from a superior. His
sister put the matter clearly[3] on his conversion:

> My other dear and poor brother! What shall I say of him. I
> mean George, who is become a Catholic – we fear a Catholic
> priest. His motives have been pure and such has been his state
> of uncertainty and doubt and unfixedness upon all but practical
> piety in religious matters for years, that we have no reason to
> be surprised at this last fatal change.

During the course of 1828 and 1829, Spencer met two or three
Roman Catholics, prominent among whom was Father Foley,
missioner at Northampton. In his house Ambrose and Spencer
met for the first time and spoke for five hours; an intention to
resume the discussion at Garendon followed and Spencer
wrote[4] to accept and explained his position. From the letter
and his later account of his conversion[5] it seemed that he had
experienced two major problems during his life as an Anglican
cleric: the first concerned the scriptural basis upon which, he
had been taught, all doctrine was founded. It had struck him
that the Athanasian creed could not be said to be based
entirely on Scripture. He had spoken to an Anglican divine on
this subject who had told him that the Spirit of God spoke
through the voice of the Church as well as in the written word.
Up to that point he had been unaware of the existence of
unwritten tradition: he could imagine no way for the discovery
of the truth but perservering study of the Scriptures; they were
the only divine rule of faith with which he was acquainted. He
was forced to 'a new observation that the system of religion
which Christ taught the Apostles and which they delivered to
the Church, was something distinct from the Scriptures'. Secondly, he disliked discord and hoped that the time was not far
off 'when God would inspire all Christians with a spirit of
peace . . . To the procuring of such a happy termination to the
miserable schisms which had rent the Church, I determined to
devote my life'.

During the few January days of 1830 when Ambrose invited
Spencer to join him at Garendon, there was a large party of
guests which included several clerics. One was Henry Ryder,
Bishop of Lichfield and Coventry, husband of Aunt Ryder.
Uncle Edward March Phillipps, Rector of Hathern, was another; also Henry David Erskine[6] then Vicar of nearby Swith-
land, a recent widower and close friend of Ambrose's father.
Spencer and Ambrose spent many hours daily in conversation.
Spencer had been struck with the ardent zeal of his young
friend at their previous meeting. Ambrose's answers to the
questions he now posed about the principal tenets and practices
of Catholics he found satisfying beyond his expectations. 'I
was prepared to accept with joy the direction of the Catholic
Church' he wrote later 'when once I should be convinced that

she still preserved unchanged the very form of faith taught by the Apostles'. This conviction Ambrose sought to provide.[7]

The day before Spencer was due to return to Althorp, his young host accompanied him to Leicester to speak to Fr Caestryck, the missioner there. Spencer's basic anxieties centred upon the role of tradition in the Church and the authority by which it was maintained. The priest explained that the way to come to a knowledge of true religion was not to contend, as men were disposed to do, about each individual part, but to submit to the authority of Christ and of those to whom he had committed his flock; of the unbroken chain of Roman pontiffs who through the ages had exercised authority. The rest of Spencer's opposition was overcome. He decided not to return to his parish, but on the following morning to make his submission.

Ambrose did not know how to express his joy; for two nights, he told Fr Glover[8], he could hardly sleep at all. Spencer had acknowledged himself convinced by his 'poor words under God'. And this was not all: he had received a letter from a very dear friend[9] in the north of Ireland announcing his conversion also. He had only just come of age and was now able to throw off the mask and profess his faith openly. 'We were schoolfellows and when but boys we never used to converse on any other subject but about the Catholick religion . . . Good news for the Catholick cause'. In his elation Ambrose saw these events solely in their personal aspect. Conversions among the prominent were not, however, regarded as a private matter. Both these were to create a considerable public stir.

Much of what was said and written was inaccurate. In the case of Spencer, it was suggested, for example, that a consultation or specially arranged dialogue had taken place at Garendon with the Anglican clergy on one side and Ambrose defending the infallible position of the Roman Catholic Church on the other. After the furore that followed Spencer's departure from the Church of England amidst full press coverage, attempts were made to put the record straight. Edward March Phillipps in his letter to the *Leicester Chronicle*[10] said that his brother in law, the Bishop, was at Garendon not for controversy, but in order to see a dying sister living in the neighbourhood.[11]

Edward Phillipps protested that he had been in Mr Spencer's company for about three hours and a half during his stay and conversed with him possibly for 20 minutes. Spencer had told him of his trials and perplexities and Edward Phillipps had advised him not to be in a hurry. Ambrose was also forced to address a letter to the same editor.[12] His objects were first to correct various false statements perpetrated by the *Wexford Evening Post* concerning the Bishop of Lichfield, and to prevent further attacks on George Spencer; and secondly to redeem some mistakes made by his Uncle in the paper's previous edition. The Bishop had not come to Leicestershire for the express purpose of holding a discussion, that was true; but although he declined to discuss the points of faith with his nephew requested by a letter from Mr Spencer, the prelate had changed his mind and did hold a discussion one morning in the presence of Mr Erskine; 'Mr Spencer was not a little shaken in his faith by what appeared to be the weakness of the Bishop's arguments'.

Another legend which grew up (and has been continued whenever Spencer is mentioned) concerned his stipend at Brington. 'There goes £3,000 a year' he is reputed to have said as he resigned his living. The exact annual value of the Brington parish in 1830 is difficult to establish. It was included in a list[13] of 1831 which contained livings not exceeding £150 per annum, but only the value in the King's Book (Henry VIII) was shown, as £40, and the current value was not reckoned. Those parishes where sums had been re-calculated mainly had annual values between £100 & £150. The 1855 Clergy List and Whellan's Directory of 1849 record the benefice of Great Brington as worth £485 annually,[14] which since the average gross and net incomes for all benefices[15] at that period in England and Wales were £303 and £285 respectively, would seem to present a more realistic figure. If the sum mentioned by Spencer was accurately recorded in the first place, it could hardly have represented his stipend, but probably largely an allowance made to him by his father. This continued after his conversion. Spencer wrote[16] to Ambrose to say that he had passed through an interview with his father. 'His kindness was very great, joined with great depth of feeling . . . My father has made me quite comfortable for money, and in the most prudent way'. Spencer's sacrifice in

becoming a Roman Catholic in 1830 was very considerable but
to construe it in the way in which it has often been construed
is to over-simplify a complex set of inter-related religious,
social and political factors. To reduce it to (false) economic
terms is to do Spencer an injustice.

From Fr Caestryck's house in Leicester, Spencer reported to
Ambrose on 2 February:[17] he was to visit Bishop Walsh (Vicar
Apostolic of the Midland District) in Wolverhampton and it
had been suggested the two might accompany one another.
'God Almighty be with you', he wrote, 'And help us together
to keep up a good profession'; so it proved to be. The
friendship, forged under such dramatic circumstances, was
life-long and Ambrose gained his staunchest ally. Spencer was
a big man, in stature as in his expansiveness: he had a large
head with heavy lidded eyes and the rounded jaw which is still
a characteristic of the male members of this family. He was
good natured and kind and incapable of succinct writing: his
generosity spread to a liberality with words as well as with his
substance. He has left a large number of long letters, many of
them written to Ambrose, which give in immense detail accounts of his experiences.

Spencer's immediate act was to offer himself to the Roman
Catholic priesthood, and with typical exuberance felt drawn to
return to his old parish of Brington in a new guise. Bishop
Walsh, who was probably the most sagacious of the Vicars
Apostolic, decided that it was important to improve on the
parlous state of Spencer's knowledge of theology and not to
send him to Oscott, his own seminary, but out of the country
immediately to the English College in Rome. This action was
to have profound consequences both for Spencer, the English
Mission and for Ambrose.

After conveying to Fr Glover the momentous news of the
conversion of his friend, Ambrose discussed his own future.
He was torn in two directions: he realized the shortage of
priests hampered the progress of Catholicism in England. Fr
Caestryck was instructing several converts in Leicester. This
could be extended if there were more like him. On the other
hand, as heir to important estates he could in time exert
influence as a layman, as the Roman Catholic gentry had done
in the past. He seemed to think he might combine the two.

'The present situation seems to point out I ought to marry tho'
always with that intention of separating to become a Priest.
Then sometimes I have doubts and think perhaps I should be a
priest at once. Will you soon write me a long letter all about
this and recommend the matter to God.[18]

The familiar pattern of alternating elation and sadness followed: elation when a Roman Catholic procession on Easter
Day through the streets of Leicester with a banner, designed
and provided by himself, had been admired and not a word
uttered against it; as word came from Spencer, happy and
edified with Rome; unhappy when Spencer's conversion produced such an uproar in the press. 'It has really worried me to
death'[19]; 'Indeed I am in a very desponding mood about
everything just at the moment[20]'; 'How miserable I am not to
see you, the only person who cares about me[21]', he told Digby.
His relationship with his father was obviously at low ebb due
to the notoriety following the Spencer affair. Ambrose described[22] his efforts to placate Charles March Phillipps; 'I do
all I can to please him with a view to his conversion. I walk,
shoot, ride with him, so that I may gain some influence over
him'.

On 17 March 1830 Ambrose came of age; his health was
moderately good, though the doctors still put some prohibi-
tions on his movements: he was not well enough to go to St
Edmund's for Holy Week. Spencer's letters from Italy no
doubt increased his own anxiety about the future. In the late
summer, with his new found freedom, he made up his mind to
return to Rome and seek an answer to the matter of his vocation.

His journey took him by way of Loreto, to that most
Southern European of all shrines, the house of the Holy
Family purported to have been carried by angels to Trieste
from Nazareth in 1291, and on to Loreto in 1294. There he
wrote[23] to Fr Glover in terms that were uncharacteristic of
English piety, and revealed both his happy acceptance of
Italian forms of devotion, and the turmoil within his own soul.
It had meant so much to him to receive the Body of the Lord
within the walls of the very place that Jesus had lived in as a
child. 'Oh if you knew how much I have suffered internally
from the Devil since I last saw you. Oh I have suffered a cruel

torture and constant pain near a year and in consequence my health has been much weakened, tho' I am now much better. I have suffered very much both bodily and spiritually and would to God I had suffered it with a greater conformity to the divine will'.

Of Spencer, Ambrose was to see a great deal in Rome. His regime at the English College was not that of an ordinary student 'since I am a *convictor*, that is paying my own way'[24]. He kept company principally with the Rector, Nicholas Wiseman, and Vice-Rector, George Errington, who taught him at the College rather than his going to public lectures. It was in this way that Ambrose's long and crucial relationship with Wiseman had its beginning.

Nicholas Wiseman was born in Seville in 1802. Debarred from the professions as a Roman Catholic, his grandfather became a merchant in Waterford and then having trade with Spain, emigrated there in the 18th century. His mother travelled back to Ireland as a widow, and at the age of eight the young Nicholas was sent to St Cuthbert's College, Ushaw, in County Durham for his education. Though he cannot have recalled in later life many memories of his infancy in Spain, he was to develop markedly latin traits, with his charm, exuberance, sense of occasion and love for ceremonial and flamboyant, princely personality. Ushaw was a robust school with a straight-forward spirit, where no use was made of the system of informing in respect of misdemeanours. This was a feature of Italian seminary training, a cultural difference, which caused offence when brought to bear on English religious institutions. But as in Ambrose's case, it may well have been the lack of feminine presence that most affected Wiseman. He found the atmosphere cold and uncongenial: doubtless he missed his mother; he was still shy and introspective and his ebullience and good intellect did not emerge at this stage. When in 1818, at the age of 16, he was chosen to be one of the six Ushaw students to join the newly opened English College in Rome, it was the beginning of his spiritual and intellectual awakening.

Wiseman's inclinations led him towards the study of Oriental languages: he specialised in Syriac and Arabic. There being no English preaching then in Rome, the Pope asked Dr Gradwell[25] for such to be provided, Wiseman began to make a

reputation as a powerful communicator. It led to his appointment as Vice-Rector of the College in 1827 and when in 1828
Dr Gradwell was appointed Co-adjutor of the Vicar Apostolic
of the London District, and left for England, Wiseman was
chosen to fill his place at the age of 26.

He had become a well-known and respected figure in Rome;
he was thrilled by the ceremonies of the papal court and the
liturgical functions in the churches. His limitations came in the
administrative field where he was markedly bored by day to
day management of affairs. Later he was to show himself
unable to keep track of vital pieces of paper, which had dire
consequences[26]. As Rector of the English College, Wiseman
was representative in Rome of the Vicars Apostolic in England.
Though intellectually somewhat limited, most of them had
good sense and experience of native, though not Roman,
conditions. Wiseman had little in common with them. There
were problems in this area, and more ahead when he left
Rome to serve on the English Mission.

For the help he later gave Ambrose during his attempts to
come to an understanding with the Oxford men, Wiseman was
much criticized. Despite his good academic record (better than
any of his fellow bishops in England) his practical sagacity
could be called in question. It was not always easy to tell
whether his clumsier actions were a device covering an underlying design, or whether in fact the simpler interpretation was
the correct one, and Wiseman had misjudged the issue. He was
for all his outward pomp, a simple man who his life long
needed sympathy and companionship. Ambrose was one of the
few who consistently gave it to him.

Spencer's arrival at the English College was a turning point
in Wiseman's life. The latter recognised his new student was
'destined to do wonders in England' and Spencer for his part,
began to persuade the Rector that he should set aside the study
of ancient languages for the greater importance of the souls of
the British nation. Aided by Ambrose and a series of English
visitors, Wiseman eventually became convinced that his ministry also did not lie in Rome, but in England.

Meanwhile Ambrose consulted Fr Glover at the Gesu as to
his vocation. The Jesuit counselled that he should remain a
layman: the over-riding consideration, according to Ambrose's

view of it[27], was the benefit that he could bring to the cause of
Catholicism in England from so favoured and prominent a
household. Ambrose resolved to show his willingness to fulfil
this role. Within a few weeks he had met two priests whose
interest in England he began to encourage. Their eventual
ministry on the English Mission, due very largely to his devis-
ing, was to help to change the appearance of English Catholicism.

With a view to avoiding a language problem, Ambrose
made his way to the Irish College in Rome, in search of
missionaries. On the feast of St Stanislaus Koska[28] (with whom
he was sometimes compared) Ambrose was introduced by the
Rector[29] to a remarkable Italian, Aloysius, (or Luigi) Gentili
who had just been ordained and was living at the College. He
had committed himself to a new religious association, the
Institute of Charity, or Rosminians, as they more frequently
came to be called, and was studying divinity and philosophy in
Rome before leaving for Domodossola to join the noviciate.
He wrote[30] to his superior at very great length to describe the
request Ambrose had put before him. A young English gentleman, convert to the Catholic faith, had come to Rome to
consult about a state of life. Being advised to choose the
matrimonial one and therein to promote the spiritual welfare
of his neighbours, he wished to accomplish this holy design.
He wanted to find a priest to establish a parish in Lester [sic] a
town roughly in the middle of England, where Catholics were
multiplying every day. Gentili asked Rosmini whether he was
in favour of according to this request of Sigr Fillips [sic]. At
one time he had really wanted to go to England and shed his
blood there, but the possibility would expose him to continual
warfare, not only with heresy, but with its effects which were
corruption of the heart and low degrading vice.

This proposition of Ambrose has been variously interpreted
in recent accounts of it: some have suggested that he asked for
a chaplain for his estate; that his marriage had been arranged
and he was already in possession of his inheritance. This was
not so. He was barely 21 years old and was still living under
his father's roof, upon whose estates no Roman Catholic
mission could at that time be established. In so far as work in
the town of Leicester was concerned, Ambrose needed to

consult Bishop Walsh, Vicar Apostolic of the Midland District: this was precisely what he did on his return to England. In Roman circles, ignorance of the English scene credited the earnest young man with a good deal more power and wealth than he, in fact, possessed; he was often referred to as 'il nobili'.

Antonio Rosmini replied[31] to Gentili's anguished appeal immediately in terms that were characteristic of him. His letters almost invariably contained an air of wisdom, directness and shrewd practicality. He declared that the interests of English Catholics were close to his heart: there was little in his power that he would not do to promote their welfare, so he would like to comply with this request. If Gentili felt inclined to undertake this mission, he should undertake a year's noviciate in Northern Italy and prepare himself for the work by learning and practising the rules of the Order. Then Rosmini would be ready to give him two companions with whom to establish a house wherever the young Englishman pleased. The second year of noviciate could be continued while labouring in the ministry; this arrangement Gentili could communicate to Ambrose.

In Gentili, Rosmini had an aspirant of rare gifts and unusual qualities, but his training and progress were never going to be straight forward. His route to the present offering of himself to the Rosminians had been tortuous: there had been many changes of direction, but to every intended goal he had given the same intense dedication and zeal that were to mark him for the rest of his life. Gentili began as a lawyer and the study of jurisprudence at the Roman University called the Sapienza. He carried off prizes and became a doctor of both canon and civil law. In his spare time he studied and wrote poetry. To amuse his younger brothers and sisters he designed a puppet theatre and costumes, for he was clever also with his hands. Some legal work for Cardinal Consalvi gave an indication that Gentili might become a judge, but the Cardinal's death put a stop to this, and the disappointment induced the young man to leave the law altogether.

The next cause was the study of foreign languages. By intensive application to the exclusion of all else, even conversation with his own family, Gentili mastered French, English and

Spanish in twelve months. He began to mix with foreigners in Rome, to study music and give Italian lessons. In order to increase his prestige he persuaded the Duke of Sforza Cesarini, who had the patronage, to create him a Knight of the Golden Spur. His appearance was described as striking: he was tall with shining black hair, a pale complexion and sharp blue eyes; his voice was deep and pleasant. He had amassed a good deal of money from his teaching which he invested in some land on Monte Mario, near the Vatican. He began to cultivate a vineyard and drive his own plough. Unused to hard physical work and pushing himself with customary zeal beyond his strength, Gentili was forced to abandon his newest enterprise. He returned to the study of art.

It was at this point that he met and became deeply attached to Anna de Mendoza y Rios. Her mother was English; her father had been a Spanish admiral on whose death Bishop Baines had become her guardian. With Anna's consent, Gentili asked the Bishop if they might marry. His refusal and the swift removal of the young woman to England wounded Gentili and caused another reversal in his plans. He decided to become a priest. His piety had been constant throughout his varied career and it struck him that he was being led in this direction by the unsatisfactory outcome of his other enterprises. He applied to the Jesuits, but his health seemed then to prejudice his chances of enduring the long noviciate.

In November 1828 he met Antonio Rosmini who had just drawn up the *Constitutions* of his new Institute of Charity and was in Rome recovering from an attack of smallpox. Rosmini agreed, after several consultations, to allow the young enthusiast to try his vocation after a period of study and ordination to the priesthood. Despite his strange path to the present decision, Rosmini was impressed by the new recruit. The fact that he spoke English was recorded (Rosmini had a high opinion of the English nation) and a future extension of the work of the Institute of Charity in England became a possibility.

But Gentili's vacillation was not over. Although he managed to extricate himself from invitations to New York from Bishop Duboy and the English Western District from Bishop Baines by explaining his commitment to the Rosminians, he found conscientious reasons for delaying his journey to Domodossola

and the noviciate. Eventually his zeal triumphed: he decided to
walk the 400 miles, which Rosmini was quick to forbid. The
erratic swing of competing enthusiasms marked much of the
remainder of his exceptional ministry and caused many clashes,
particularly when he eventually became chaplain to Ambrose
in England in 1840. But in the meantime a move in that
direction was in abeyance. First, Ambrose had not tied up the
Leicestershire end of the scheme with his Bishop. Secondly he
had met another remarkable Italian who was against it.

Dominic Barberi[32] whom Ambrose met through Spencer,
was a Passionist. Often the three men would walk together on
the Coelian hill, overlooking the Coliseum where the Passionists had their Roman house. The Italian founder of the Order,
Paul Francis Danei (St Paul of the Cross 1694–1775) had a
particular devotion for England and a special inspiration had
come to him to pray for her conversion. Dominic as a young
man had also received a mystical experience that he would
minister to the English. At the time it seemed most unlikely.
He was born in rural surroundings near Viterbo, the youngest
of six children. His father died when he was 3; his mother
when he was 8. He joined the household of an uncle who had
a farm, but no family, with the possibility of inheriting it. He
never went to school. His deep piety inclined him to become a
Passionist but the lack of education at first seemed to inhibit
him and suggest that he should be a lay brother. Dominic set
about teaching himself to read and learn some latin and was
able to re-enter as a clerical postulant. Although his writing
remained very unformed for the rest of his life, his good innate
intelligence helped him through his theological studies.

His appearance was uncouth and ungainly; his voice unmusi-
cal and weak. His lack of early formal education affected his
capacity for expressing his thoughts eloquently, as his
concentration on study had damaged his eyesight. Yet the
impact of his personality with its humility, dedication and
sincerity, was considerable. At the time that Ambrose met him
he had been teaching theology to Passionist students in Rome
since 1824. His great preoccupation became the conversion of
England and, though he did not speak the language, he longed
to make a Passionist foundation in that country. Ambrose
responded with enthusiasm and worked to this end intermit-

tently for twelve years, despite the disapproval of friends such as Lord Shrewsbury who thought[33] Italian missionaries quite unsuitable for England.

Neither Dominic Barberi nor Spencer were relaxed about the Rosminians. Their founder was an intellectual: his thought was ahead of his time and therefore threatening. As well as being a priest, Rosmini was a philosopher who was accused of attacking Scholasticism, whereas his concern was to reconcile it with modern thinking. His political thought embraced the concepts of liberty and social justice; his theories of education the rescue of teaching from being mechanical and from failure to understand pupils. He stood for liturgical involvement and Catholic action among the laity. Rosmini was to endure a rough passage: his *Five Wounds of the Church*, written about this time was not published till 1848. A series of constructive reforms reflecting the ills of the Church, it was placed on the Index through pressure from his adversaries. The struggle endured for many years until his orthodoxy was established. The approval of the Holy See of the *Constitutions* of the Institute of Charity hung fire till 1838.

It was partly this lack of official sanction which so much worried Dominic Barberi who had been raised in circumstances of conventional piety in the Italian countryside, and within a more conservative Order. He told Ambrose he was anxious and sent him his *Lamentations of England or the Prayer of the Prophet Jeremiah applied to the same*, prayers for the return of the Kingdom to the bosom of the Catholic Church. Ambrose replied[34] (in Italian):

> ... Here is the first step towards the conversion of our country. ... At this moment the Catholic Faith is increasing every day in England and I believe that within 50 or 80 years this dear but unhappy land will be wholly Catholic.

On his return to Garendon he translated the *Lamentations* into English and at the end of the following year they were published in Leicester.[35]

Ambrose was to witness another set of papal obsequies before he left Rome, for after a short reign of 20 months, Pope Pius VIII died on Nov 30th 1830. The *Catholic Magazine*[36] in its first issues dealt with him rather insensitively when it wrote of 'this uninterrupted career of mental fatigue and bodily infirmity . . .' A disturbed and disturbing inheritance waited for his successor. Revolution had broken out during the past months in France, Belgium and Poland and an inflammable situation existed in the papal territories. The conclave called to choose a new Pope lasted over 50 days. At one time Cardinal Giustiniani seemed likely to be elected: he had many English connections. His grandmother had been a Clifford; his great-grandfather a Weld, while his brother by right and his niece by naturalisation, inherited the Newburgh peerage. But the Spanish veto excluded him on account of his complicity in the appointment of bishoprics to Mexico. In fact the Pope elected had taken a more prominent part in this process.

On 2 February 1831 Cardinal Mauro Cappellari[37] received the required majority. He was a Camaldolese monk; Abbot of San Gregorio on the Coelian hill for 20 years. He became a cardinal in 1825 and Prefect of Propaganda. He took the title Gregory XVI. As an extreme conservative, his election was thought opportune at a time of crisis. In 1799 at another period of decline and ferment, he had written a treatise entitled *Il Trionfo della Santa Sede*[38] (at the time an unlikely possibility) which provided a blue print for the extension and development of papal power. He had been a near neighbour and well acquainted with Dominic Barberi; also with Nicholas Wiseman (Cappellari had corrected his proofs). These facts were to be important in relation to later English affairs.

Two days after Gregory's election the revolt which had been simmering in Modena, broke out in Bologna and spread quickly to Umbria, Romagna and the Marches. An assembly of representatives from the risen districts was held at Bologna; the abolition of the temporal power of the Pope was decreed and it named itself the 'Assembly of the Free Provinces of Italy'. The newly elected Pope appealed to Austria for military help: the rebellion was soon extinguished. (In May 1831 the European powers presented a memorandum to the Pope which asked for enforcement of the 1816 constitution, reforms such as representative assemblies on municipal and provincial levels, the creation of an auditor's office and admission of laymen to official positions. Gregory's theories of papal authority found these suggestions difficult to assimilate.)

Ambrose witnessed the solemn entrance of the Pope into St
Peter's on February 3, accompanied by Pasquale Aucher, a
priest of the Armenian Mechitarist monastery[39] on the Island
of San Lazzaro in the Lagoon in Venice. The priest's diary of
the Roman visit has been preserved there with an English
translation from the Armenian original. It describes the 'young
English neophyte and an angel in behaviour' who was dressed
in 'the princely uniform of his family' (presumably a frock
coat). They were given 'praiseworthy seats' because Ambrose
was English and in the evening the young man took the priest
to the house of Duke Torlonia to a gathering of more than a
thousand 'illustrious personages' both ecclesiastical and lay, of
whom six were cardinals. 'After the public conversations and
games, the Duke honoured them with syrups and pies'.

The coronation of Gregory XVI took place on February 6th.
The two friends went again to St Peter's where with much
ceremony the Pope received first the episcopal order and then
celebrated his first papal mass. Later the papal tiara was
placed upon his head by Cardinal Albani on the balcony of St
Peter's and he gave the papal benediction with plenary indulgence to the huge crowd. Ambrose and Pasquale Aucher
lunched with Cardinal Zurla[40] and in the evening saw the
'incomparable lighting of St Peter's facade [torches] and of the
castle of St Angelo followed by skilful fireworks'. Three days
later Ambrose was received by the Pope and kissed his foot as
a mark of obeisance. Ambrose answered questions about his
conversion; Gregory patted his face and blessed the religious
objects in his possession. In a subsequent conversation with
Cardinal Caizrug the conversion story had to be repeated and
the Cardinal said he wished to see Ambrose often. The ten
days of festivities were rounded off by a visit to the Englishman, Cardinal Weld, by which time the city was in a state of
agitation. Carnival was prohibited and soldiers were posted at
various points; rifle shots were heard and the population 'shut
the doors of their houses and shops'.

It was a heady time for Ambrose, but none of these occasions
was the most memorable of his Roman visit. During the early
months of 1831 he had an experience which moved him so
intensely that the impact never left him, and he remained
always faithful to its vivid message. He had heard of the

sanctity and miracles of a certain holy man, Marco Carricchia, who lived in the Convent of St Mary Magdalene belonging to the Brethren of St Camillus of Lellis. Marco had chosen a hermit's life and supported himself by painting sacred pictures. The newly-elected Pope was in the habit of seeking his advice and asking for his prayers, and had a copy of one of his pictures of the Madonna. Ambrose described[41] many times in the future his meeting with the hermit:

> As soon as I entered the room, Marco almost ran across it and embracing me, he said with tears running down his cheeks, 'O how I rejoice to see you – for 15 years how have I prayed every day to God that He would convert England and Russia ... now I was praying this morning as usual, and suddenly I saw an angel, who told me he was your guardian angel and that he would bring you to me today, and as I prayed to the Mother of God concerning this, she assured me that she had chosen you for this work of the conversion of England, for which I daily prayed. And therefore I rejoice to see you, and I tell you that God has chosen you for this work.' When I heard this I was much astonished ...

Ambrose then expressed the doubt whether he should remain a layman if chosen for high a destiny, and whether he ought not to become a priest. Marco said not

> 'For you shall marry and God has prepared for you a holy wife and you shall have a great family of children, and they shall be holy' then I said 'How then am I to labour for this great work?' He said 'God will show and He will put it into your hand' I said 'But how will the conversion of England come?' He said 'There will be a great movement of the learned men of that Kingdom and this shall be the sign of near accomplishment of the event. God has chosen you to work with them, and to confound human pride; and know this for certain, that you shall not see Death till you have seen All England united to the Catholic Faith'. He then said, sighing 'Here in Italy we are losing the Faith, but our loss will be your gain'. He said also many other things, but I could not quite understand them all, as he spoke fast and his Italian was rather provincial.

Ambrose was stunned by these words. He hurried to the Gesu to consult Fr Glover who said that the Jesuits would commit these issues to prayer, and counselled that he should return to

Marco Carricchia after three days to see if the message was repeated. This Ambrose did, and at the second meeting he was astonished to receive an accurate account of the near fatal illness in Florence in 1828 and his miraculous recovery. He became assured of the authenticity of the revelation that had been granted to him.

Before leaving Rome for Northern Italy he became affiliated to the Passionist Order by a document which still exists. On May 25 he had a crucial meeting with Antonio Rosmini in Milan at the house of his friend and patron Count Giacomo Mellerio. It was the only time they were to come face to face, though the empathy on both sides was real and lasting. Rosmini wrote[42] of the encounter:

> How much the dear spirit of Phillipps appealed to me. We were able to establish in the few hours that we were together a sacred friendship which I hope will never cease. He opened his heart to me: he showed his plans, to please the Lord.

To the still doubtful Spencer, the meeting was described[43] in the following terms:

> When I was at Milan I heard that Rosmini was then staying at the palace of the Count Mellerio. I called on him and began a friendship that I trust will never cease. He is no ordinary being, I can assure you – depend upon it. God has raised him up for some grand purpose in the universal Church ... At the same time I would be very far from advising anyone to take a decided step in reference to Rosmini's society until it has received the formal approbation of the Pope. At the same time that is no reason why one should not have one's eye upon it now: you in case it should be the will of God that you should serve him on it, and I as a member of the Third Order.

Ambrose completed his journey home by way of Venice and the Mechitarist monastery on the island of San Lazzaro. The past six months had provided much encouragement and the clearer indication he craved as to what was expected of him. His state of life pointed towards marriage, although Spencer continued to unsettle him on this score. Acquaintance with the members of two religious orders held promise and he intended keeping his options open. His correspondence with the Rosminians and Passionists was to bear fruit with the arrival in

England, in due course, of the Italian missionaries. But although their eventual achievements were due partly to him, he was to be victim as well as perpetrator. Within the changes they introduced, the power and influence of the English laity were considerably diminished.

(ii) Achievements

On his arrival in England Ambrose travelled north by way of Canterbury. He described[1] his thoughts in that place to Spencer still in Rome. It was clearly distressing that Anglicans should possess 'the sublime Cathedral' while those who, like him, held the true Faith worshipped in mean chapels and drawing rooms. A resolve to build something worthy in the future was, no doubt, in his mind. The influence of Digby in what he wrote was obvious, both in style and content:

> Oh England if but once I could see the holy Catholick faith of Jesus Christ flourish again throughout thee, I could die contented! ... Tears fell from my eyes with many a sigh when I thus mused on the desolation of our renowned sanctuary ... How sweet was it for me to kneel down ... and there recite the office of Our Lady. I conjured our Lord to return once more to take up His merciful abode in that solemn temple in the sacrament of His love. I besought our dearest Mama, our Lady, and our Queen once more to come back to her English subjects and children, I implored the mercy of our most glorious apostle S Austin, of S Anselm, S Edmund and S Thomas and all these innumerable Saints whom God had once honoured in that Church, and I felt an answer to my prayer. I felt that the day would come when I should myself behold the blessed consummation to which alone I look forward and for which I will never cease to sigh and pray. I think in about 50 years England will be Catholick again ... that something will very probably take place in England in favour of Catholicity before the end of the year '32, I believe and hope, but I cannot anticipate the '*total* reconversion of the country in *so short* a period ... Oh that there was not such a deadly apathy on the part of the English Catholicks generally ...

Ambrose concluded with the intelligence that his father had

been returned once more as Member of Parliament for the County of Leicester. 'His election was most satisfactory to us all, as he was earnestly solicited by all the gentlemen of the County to come forwards. There was hardly anyone who did not press the matter. I rejoice in it, as I trust it will indirectly advance Catholick interests . . .'

Spencer had written a very lengthy and somewhat unsettling letter, for he had discovered that the Religious state was considered more perfect than the secular:

> You must have observed plainly by my conversion sometime back that I had not come to a correct understanding of the religious orders, and vows of the Church. I could not see what Catholics in general seem to look upon as undoubted, that *vows* of poverty and obedience and chastity were meritorious in the sight of God and decidedly advantageous to the man who makes them with due dispositions. I have long been convinced that the *practice* of these counsels was an excellent thing. But I thought it was better to retain one's liberty and so go on making continual sacrifice (or rather repeated sacrifices) of one's self from time to time . . . I now see more clearly the Catholic view of the thing.[2]

It is hardly surprising that Spencer should have been ignorant on the possibility of gaining merit, an issue upon which views had become polarized between Roman Catholics and Anglicans, and no reconciliation of them had been attempted or set forth. On the death of his sister, Samuel Wilberforce had written to Patrick Boyle expressing the belief held by the English Church:

> When last I left Maizemore my dear departed sister was thought rapidly recovering – but I was coming to watch over her death bed: she died a little before 1 in the morning of 30 Dec, relying solely on the Saviour's merits and in joyful hope of a glorious resurrection through him alone.[3]

According to this view, justification (to be pronounced righteous and therefore to be saved) was held to depend upon the disposition of faith alone (*sola fides*) and was brought to the sinner by the merits of the sacrifice of Christ. To 19th century Roman Catholics the possibility of being able personally to acquire merit in the sight of God, under certain circumstances, was a very real one: it was to be the mainspring of many of Ambrose's activities, and illustrated by an incident which concerned his wife. Travelling on a boat in the Highlands in 1874, she was struck in the eye by a rope thrown by a sailor to the shore. Her first thought was to offer her eyesight to God, for she thought that it was gone. 'What else could I have done', she explained later, 'I was not going to lose the merit of the accident'[4].

Spencer had mentioned, he wrote, this matter of vows to Fr Glover who said that he saw no sign of his vocation to the Religious state. Spencer had already written to Bishop Walsh of the Midland District at the time of receiving the sub-diaconate, explaining his feelings, and the Bishop had replied that experience convinced him how much better fitted secular clergy were for the work in England. Spencer might practise poverty of spirit if he wished to an eminent degree, and every other virtue, as a secular priest. Spencer's introspection at this point grew tedious: he went on to argue that he felt Bishop Walsh's expression almost a tacit acknowledgement that a state of Religious vows was in itself better, and that it was only on account of the condition of England that made him consider that Spencer should be a secular. He thought of placing the whole problem before the Pope, but had been dissuaded by Nicholas Wiseman.

Unbeknown to Spencer, Bishop Walsh had already written[5] to the Rector of the English College:

> . . . Inter nos I hope you will kindly and prudently watch over him that he may not in his enthusiastic feelings and earnest drive to become more and more perfect be induced to embrace a religious life. I think he will be most useful on the Mission and that in this country there can not be a more holy and charitable employment than to be engaged on the mission in labouring to promote the salvation of souls. For that purpose with all my respect for the religious orders, I had rather have secular clergymen. Will any efforts be made, do you think, to engage him to enter with the Society of Jesus?

Two serious issues for the Bishop were raised here: the first was that the work of the English Mission was limited through lack of priests. 'We need more churches, chapels, priests and money';[6] 'Had we in England the means of supporting priests, we should be able to extend much more widely the influence of our holy religion'[7]. George Spencer was a recruit not to be lost. Secondly, the relationship between the Vicars Apostolic and the Religious Orders (Regulars) was a critical one (and became more so) since the Bishops had no control over the latter in their own Districts: juridiction over the members of the Order of Benedictines, Jesuits, and so on, was exercised by their own superiors.

If Ambrose was under the impression that it would be an easy matter to persuade Bishop Walsh to invite the Rosminians into his area, he was wrong. In Aug 1831[8] he addressed the first of a series of letters to Rosmini at Domodossola representing the Bishop as enthusiastic over a plan to found a House in his District, after the society had received the Pope's approval. Bishop Walsh may have been interested in very general terms, but as the correspondence developed, so did the problems. Ambrose reported that he was about to visit Lord Shrewsbury and it is obvious that he was intending to ask him to support the mission. By November the visit of three weeks duration to Alton Towers had taken place; but his host had not made any promises of financial help for the Rosminians. Although Ambrose did not say so, Lord Shrewsbury was not in favour of foreign missionaries in England and later made this quite clear in writing. What did emerge from the visit was the young man's growing attachment for the peer's elder daughter, Mary Talbot[9]. Ambrose seems to have confided in Fr Caestryck, the Dominican missioner in Leicester who replied[10],

> Yes, my dearest friend, commit yourself to the holy and fatherly providence of Almighty God, trust in him alone and in the all-powerful protection of the Blessed Mother of God, may the young lady never become a victim, in punishment of the ambitious views of the mother, but I fear much that this may happen to be the case. How little Xtian this is in the Mother. And if Lord S suspected your desire, he might bring her over, and if he would not he ought to conclude at least by saying it shall be so. But after all, my friend, we do not, we cannot know the designs of God upon the young person, nor upon yourself.

Mary Arundell had formed the opinion in Rome that Lady

Shrewsbury had aspirations for her daughter. 'She is good and good-natured ... she likes diamonds and going out and great dinners and driving with her four horses on the Pincio, instead of enjoying the beauties of Rome', the former had written to her sister-in-law[11]. 'Her great aim is intimacy with the great and to please and court them her occupation ...' Mary Talbot became formally engaged in 1834 to Prince Frederick of Saxe-Altenburg, cousin to the King of Bavaria, but for a reason which it has not been possible to discover, the marriage did not take place. In 1839 she married Prince Filipo Doria Pamphili and spent the remainder of her life in Rome.

Ambrose, disappointed on two counts, pressed on with his main objective. By the spring of 1832 he said he felt that Loughboro (sic), rather than Leicester, might be a better place for a Rosminian foundation. It was a smaller town, but it had good potential. A new mission was flourishing; it was near his father's estates. But after all his bravado in Rome, Ambrose was forced to be realistic about finance. It was impossible for him to promise support himself; he was still totally dependent upon his father[12]. Bishop Walsh gave permission for Benjamin Hulme, missioner at Loughborough, to go on a begging tour for money to build a larger chapel and house for priests there, but as he wrote to Ambrose, who passed the words on to the Superior of the Rosminians[13], it was something which required 'Molto prudente considerazione'. The Bishop clearly did not intend to risk the arrival of missionaries in his District who would not be subject to his jurisdiction. He had written, he said, to the English Cardinal Weld in Rome asking for more information as to the Constitution of the Institute of Charity. This move in fact shelved the whole issue.

Nicholas Wiseman's comment on Cardinal Weld in his *Recollections*[14] would appear to have been accurate when he wrote that the latter had found it difficult to master a new language on going to Rome or 'perfectly learn ways of transacting high ecclesiastical business'. Born in 1773, he was a member of the English Roman Catholic gentry family who owned Lulworth Castle and were considerable landowners in Dorset. On the death of his wife in 1815, he became a priest in Paris and in August 1826 was consecrated bishop in London; the Vicar Apostolic of Upper Canada had made him his co-adjutor.

He remained another three years in England preparing for his journey, when the health of his only child Lucy (who had married the son of the 7th Lord Clifford) gave him anxiety and he travelled with her to Rome. There he was made a Cardinal in 1830. Ambrose showed his obvious alarm at the inevitable delay by writing to Domodossola to make sure that the Cardinal was correctly briefed on the suitability of the Rosminians for England. Rosmini, via a correspondent in Rome, sent[15] the Cardinal a full explanation of the Constitution of the Society which included safeguards for the rights of bishops.

The correspondence endured for much of 1831 and the whole of 1832. Ambrose's immensely long letters translated badly. His confidences expressed in early 19th century Italian do not reproduce well in 20th century English. From his spiritual exile he poured out his pious longings; perhaps he felt that hyperbole was expected of him to demonstrate the measure of his fervour, as he wrote in fulsome terms of his commitment to the conversion of England, his devotion to Mary, the Mother of God, and to Rosmini himself. There was plenty of background agony too; the unsettled state of England, for example: 'We are in a sea of misery . . . blow after blow'. Every kind of disorder existed, he claimed, in all the great cities, connected with the Reform Bill crisis. There was also a serious outbreak of cholera. Some felt that the age was coming of which St John had spoken in the Apocalypse, the thousand years when the Church would triumph: the writer was one such. Rosmini replied in calm, reasonable, constructive terms, answering each point put to him. Ambrose was particularly incensed to hear of Dominic Barberi's grave doubts and hints of heresy concerning the Rosminian Society. Rosmini replied[16]

> How deeply indebted I am to you, my dear Phillipps, for your sincerity and frankness with which you treat me . . . Do not be surprised, however, if I appear unconcerned about the suspicions which are being circulated by P D [Padre Dominic] They are horrible certainly, but I believe he is acting from a good motive, and is under a misapprehension with regard to the Institute of Charity and myself. I feel sure that as soon as he knows the true state of the case this good priest will retract all that he has said and written against us. In any case I can hardly take these suspicions seriously.

An offer to Bishop Walsh for the existing mission at Leicester to be transferred to the secular clergy was made by the Dominicans in the autumn of 1832. It could not be accepted since there was a debt of £500. Ambrose tried hard, but unsuccessfully, to persuade Rosmini to assume this responsibility. There was no word from Cardinal Weld and therefore stalemate, and a lull in letters between Leicester and Domodossola.

Meanwhile Dominic Barberi had been appointed to the Passionist house at Lucca and letters passed between him and Ambrose on the possibility of a Passionist foundation in Leicestershire. Barberi longed to take part in the English Mission: 'I rejoice in the hope of being one day able to reach it: Dear England, Beloved Nation! When shall I behold thee restored to the loving bosom of our holy Mother the Church'[17]. 'How much I have at heart the return of that island to the Catholic Faith. If with my death I could procure such a grace, how willingly would I die. Well, I hope against hope'[18] Ambrose continued to support these expectations. 'I trust the air of Lucca has done you good and will put you in a condition to be able one day to come to England and establish here your holy Congregation of the Passion of Jesus Christ'[19].

Spencer also exchanged letters with Dominic Barberi. Spencer had begun to spit blood in the spring of 1832 and was sent to the sea at Fiumicino. Fr Dominic invited him to Lucca to recuperate, but Bishop Walsh demanded his immediate return to England upon his ordination. As it happened, they did meet, since the boat on which Spencer was to sail was temporarily detained for 10 days at Leghorn. It was to be a crucial meeting; his affection for the Passionist Congregation was further cemented thereby.

At the General Chapter of the Passionists held in Rome on 18 April 1833, Dominic Barberi made an appeal for a foundation in England; letters from Ambrose and Spencer demonstrated their support. But it was not the Chapter's policy to create new Houses without a request from a local bishop: the matter was postponed for six years.

In spite of the disappointing progress of his plans and the unsettled state of the country, the lot of Ambrose had improved. His personal life had taken a more favourable turn; he

reported[20] an better relationship with his father. The intercession of Mary had been very powerful. One day his father had
been talking to friends of current affairs and the crisis in
England. Ambrose had made an interpolation which showed
an ignorance of the customs of Parliament. Charles March
Phillipps had been impatient with his son and said that it was
a pity that he spent his time reading the lives of saints and
remained extremely ignorant about the laws of England. Ambrose in his humiliation turned towards Mary in spirit, became
quieter in his own soul and his father began to speak to him
with gentleness: times of happiness between them had been
spent. Later he wrote[21] that his father had increased his allowance, and that his sister, Augusta, was to be married to John
Fitzgerald, an Irishman; many of his relations were Catholics,
though he was not. Their conversion, that of his father and
George Spencer's family, was a constant preoccupation. Several
missions were being established locally and many individuals
were under instruction. If only holy priests could arrive from
Italy, great things would come; English gentlemen would rather
speak to a foreign priest. They had a horror of talking to an
English one.[22] Lord Clifford had been to stay at Garendon:
this intelligence heralded the most auspicious news[23] of all.
Ambrose had married, on 25 July, Laura Clifford, the peer's
young cousin:

> I went with my father to London where I saw my friend Lord
> Clifford . . . He is a truly Catholick man and most devoted to
> the Saintly Faith as his illustrious family have always been . . .
> Lord Clifford introduced me to his beautiful and devout cousin
> Laura Clifford. And what will be your response, dearest Father
> Rosmini when I tell you that Laura and I are now married. I
> cannot thank loving providence enough for giving me such a
> loving and devoted wife, a woman so well learnt, and blessed
> with every virtue of mind and heart, such is my Laura. All my
> relations and the Clifford family are most happy about this
> marriage, which has given joy to all the Catholics of England.

Laura was 21 and an orphan. Her father, Thomas[24], was the
4th son of the 4th Lord Clifford. Denied a career in England
by his religion, he had gone to Mecklenburgh Schwerin and
become Chamberlain to the reigning Duke. There he met

Obermarschal Count von Lutzow[25] and his wife the former
Bernadine von Kurzrock[26], and married Henrietta[27], the youngest daughter of their nine children. Their nationality is difficult
to determine before the map of Europe was tidily divided into
unified national boundaries. It can best be described as Holy
Roman Empire, from whence the title derived from 1643: they
were part German, part Italian, part Austrian and lived sometime in France. Laura was born in Mecklenburgh Schwerin on
26 October 1811, the eldest of three daughters. Her father died
in Liège in 1817; her mother in Aix-la-Chapelle in 1822. Lord
Clifford had become her guardian.

Ambrose had given Rosmini a less than accurate picture of
the events leading up to the wedding and the reception of it,
which were nothing like as straight-forward as Ambrose had
described. What is certain is that it was a whirl-wind romance;
both he and Laura fell violently in love in a matter of days.
They were able, on account of the strength of their feelings, to
convince their families that their marriage should take place at
an early date. From the letters they exchanged during the next
forty years, and outside observation, their level of affection
remained constant.

Ambrose told his father of his attachment on Monday 10
June 1833. Charles followed his practice of committing private
family items to his diary in French.

> Mon fils avait commencé me dire l'histoire de sa passion, de
> ses vues, de ses espérances.

They were interrupted by the arrival of Charles' brother
Samuel. The conversation continued the following day, 11
June.

> Ambrose m'announce son projet. Je lui dit je n'approve pas à
> cet heure, mais je ne denounce pas. Vous serez pauvre et la
> pauveté sera votre lot.

He ended 'On l'accepte sans doute'. Had he but known it,
Ambrose was not in a mood to accept any opposition. On 14
June he wrote from London to Laura, who had gone on a visit
with her sister Mary Lucy to New Hall, near Chelmsford, the
Convent School of the Canonesses of the Holy Sepulchre
where she had earlier been a pupil. It was clear that whatever

the opinions of others, their minds were made up. Ambrose had been to Communion in honour of the Sacred Heart of Jesus.

> I recommended myself to your Angel Guardian begging him to unite his prayers with those of my angel that both you and I may be blessed and protected by God and that I may have the grace to make you a most affectionate husband. My Sweet Laura, I look upon you as the most precious present I have received from the blessed Virgin and I only hope that I shall always prove myself worthy of you.

He assured

> ... my dearest love that you have made a great impression on all my relations and that they have all concerned a great admiration for you, especially my father and sister and I do hope that my father will consent to our living at Garendon with him.

Ambrose pointed out this would be a considerable point of vantage

> ... and it would enable us to do a great deal amongst the tenantry and dependants and also amongst the neighbours throughout the County.

Their conversion, as that of his father, was obviously uppermost in his mind. 'But, of course, this is a point which can only be determined upon sometime after our marriage'.

Charles March Phillipps had only, in fact, met Laura once, two days earlier, on 12 June at a musical evening party given in London by his Dawson relations. His comments were not particularly flattering

> Ni riche, ni belle, ni jolie, une figure Saxone, une taille assez bonne; elle paraît aimable, bien née.

During the course of the next few days, he agreed to the match, in that he met Lord Clifford's man of business and together they drew up a marriage settlement which would give Ambrose an increased allowance for a wife and children. Very likely the wretchedness that Charles had endured in his failure to secure the hand of Miss Hall, helped him not to inflict similar pain on his son. Laura's family were not strangers; he had known the present Lord Clifford's father in Rome. He bowed to the inevitable.

Meanwhile Laura had replied to Ambrose's letter with enthusiasm equal to his own,

> A thousand thanks for your dear affectionate letter, which I shall always keep as one of my most precious treasures and every moment I feel more thankful to Providence for having blessed me in so far a superior a manner to what I deserve by having permitted that you should have taken a fancy to me. I hope and pray I shall never give you reason to regret our choice of each other: I am sure I shall never regret it and my visit here convinces me more than ever how very necessary you are to my happiness ... the thought of you never leaves me a single moment ... I think of you the first thing in the morning and the last thing at night. I am longing for Monday ... my dearest Ambrose you cannot be more anxious than I am that there should be no delay to our marrying as soon as possible ... I am so happy there is only one day more before we shall again meet, and I trust we ere long be united, never again to part.

Her future father-in-law paid several visits to Laura at her guardian's home. On one occasion he found her and her sister 'renewing their knowledge of their native tongue, German, being born in Mecklenburg Schwerin, with a master'. Events seemed to be taking a smoother turn, until in mid July, Charles discovered Ambrose's intentions as to his living arrangements.

> I learn that Ambrose imagines he is to live at Garendon, quite impossible ... at night j'ai un trop vif entretien avec lui sur ce sujet.

Ambrose wrote Laura a downcast letter. They were not to be allowed to be at Garendon. How will they live on such a small income; they would need to go abroad.
Next day his father wrote

> Ambrose takes leave of me, returns to Town; proposed building at Grace Dieu a small house for himself and Laura, Preposterous idea.

As usual Charles March Phillipps' spleen was short-lived. He left for London during the last week of July for Ambrose's wedding and took with him a collar of pearls he had bought in Venice, for which he ordered a topaz clasp from Wilkinson's of Piccadilly, and gave it to Laura. He bought a travelling carriage to take the newly married couple on their honeymoon. On 25 July he accompanied some of his relatives, Samuel and his daughter Emily, and Mrs Dawson, but none from Leicestershire, to the 'Catholic Chapel' (St James's, Spanish Place). The celebrant was Bishop Bramston, Vicar Apostolic of the London District. Immediately after, the exchange of vows had to be repeated in an Anglican Church, since weddings in Roman Catholic churches were not then lawful in England. At St Mary's Church, Bryanston Square, Charles March Phillipps gave the vicar a fee of £3 and the clerk £1. The guests took leave of Ambrose and Laura, who left in their new carriage for Lyndhurst in the New Forest and thereafter to Weymouth; Charles and the others repaired to a 'dejeunée à la forchette at Countess Constantia Clifford[28] a very handsome one, prepared by Gunters'

By his marriage Ambrose acquired relations on the maternal side who were to increase his cosmopolitan outlook and enrich his visits to the continent. Through the Cliffords he became connected to many of the 'old' Catholic families of England, the Blounts, Arundells, Constable-Maxwells, Langdales, Fitzalan-Howards, Welds. But his marriage was to bring him more than influential relations. It was to change him more than any other single event, except his conversion. Laura's whole-hearted devotion and single-minded care for his needs were what he had obviously craved for all his life, at any rate since the death of his mother. From that stability much was to spring. His health improved, his lassitude vanished and was replaced by a burning energy. Laura was on many counts a remarkable woman. Whereas the death of his mother had left Ambrose introspective and melancholy, her early sufferings in the loss of both parents before she was 11, made her resilient, resolute and imperturbable.

Mary Arundell was delighted[29] at the match and thought Ambrose's choice 'much more worthy than any I know among ye present race of Catholic spinsters, for if you recollect I always after mentioning a name instantly found some personal objection except in one case, and when Laura C's name came

on the tapis, my utmost powers of criticism were taxed in vain
. . .' During a stay at Ugbrooke[30] she had seen nothing in 'Miss
L C but what I *liked, admired* and *approved*, and everything I
have ever heard has tended to raise my opinion of her: but this
I have said 100 times'.

That his father changed his mind on the issue of building a
house for Ambrose and Laura at Grace Dieu, may partly be
attributed to his favourable impression of his new daughter-in-
law. He was also encouraged to be generous by the safe arrival
in September 1833 of a son to his daughter Augusta who had
been married the previous year, to whom he was very close.
When, after delay a boy was born, he wrote,

> Grant O God that I may daily be sensible of this and all thy
> other mercies. Give me grace to be thankful.

The child was small and very feeble, but survived.

The anticipation of an heir for Ambrose in the Spring no
doubt prompted a resolution as to where he and Laura should
live permanently; they had been staying at Garendon and
making long visits to relations. On his marriage Ambrose had
received an allowance from his father of £1,200 a year; to this
was now added possession of the manor of Grace Dieu and
promise of a new mansion on the site of the old, which had
fallen into disrepair. Much of the cost seems to have been
borne by Charles, although some of Laura's dowry was added
to the sum which was needed to complete the house and
chapel. Frequent alterations to the plans of the architect,
William Railton, prevented the completion of the house until
1835. By this time the first of sixteen children had been born at
Garendon on 11 May 1834. He was christened Ambrose
Charles and known in the family as Amo. or A C.

To her sister-in-law, Lady Arundell described[31] the attitude
of her young friend to his forth-coming parenthood

> I find a letter from my son Ambrose almost hourly expecting
> his wife's lying in, and talking so obstetric and so paternal. I
> fancy it is my little Stanislaus Koska and glad as I am that his
> race should be continued, I almost regret that my little saint is
> no longer in his niche but talks like any other man.

A fulsome letter of congratulation came from Bishop Baines[32] on the birth of the first born 'and destined, but I hope very distant heir'.

In the early 1830s it was the Western District that contained much of the energy in the English Mission due to the enterprise and zeal of the Vicar Apostolic. (The centre of gravity was to move to the Midland District after 1840. Key figures left the West to be drawn to the middle of England; Ambrose was one of those responsible for this shift in direction). One of the problems that afflicted Bishop Baines, as it did the other bishops, was the shortage of priests in relation to the increase in the number of the faithful. The Benedictine monastery of Downside was within the Western District, but over its school and monks who had almost no conventual life, but were scattered in missions all over England, he had no control. Bishop Baines conceived a bold plan: to constitute the District as a Benedictine one, with Downside as its seminary. He was himself a member of the Order: he and after him his successor, he decided, would be Superior of the community and all the priests ordained there could be called to work locally under his jurisdiction. His struggles with the Benedictine Chapter lasted several years, produced repercussions that were far-reaching and went beyond the local issue. Kenelm Digby wrote[33] to Ambrose from Downside, where he had been spending Christmas 1832 that he hoped the troubles caused by the Bishop would soon be at an end. 'I could only infer from the monks' conversation generally that they were in no fear of being disturbed. Truly it would be a curious thing if they were to be. Prior Park seems a Princely place, but it would be horrible if Downside were sacrificed to it'. First Bishop Bramston and then Nicholas Wiseman from Rome, were called in to arbitrate.

The scope of Wiseman's activities was extended during the year which followed. Visitors to Rome gravitated to the English College: the nature of several of them were to affect Wiseman's ministry and outlook in the future. Hughes Félicité Robert de Lamennais[34], Charles de Montalembert[35] and Jean-Baptiste Lacordaire[36] were three such. It was a formative experience for Wiseman to be thereby exposed to evidence of Catholic revival in France. The results of this experience have their place in chapter 4, since Ambrose also became acquainted with two of these Frenchmen: he and Montalembert met and corresponded for the rest of their lives: visits and letters were exchanged with Lacordaire.

Wiseman in 1832 was unable to unravel the Benedictine confusion, but he did on his visit to England see Spencer who had returned in July, and was assigned for three months to a mission in Walsall. He and Wiseman went to stay with Spencer's father (Lord Spencer) at Althorp: Spencer wrote[37] to Ambrose:

> My father wrote to desire that I would go with Dr Wiseman to Althorp which I did on Friday the 2nd ... at Northampton where I went for Sunday morning and my reception was delightful among my old parishioners ... what a grand point was this and a Catholic Priest and D D Rector of a College received with distinction at a Protestant Nobleman's! ... Oh, come Ambrogio & help us here.

A new church was being built at West Bromwich towards which Spencer had contributed £2,000; his ministry was exercised there until 1839.

The failure with the Downside plan drove Bishop Baines in the direction of another grand expedient in his efforts to have his own school and seminary. For £20,000 he bought the mansion of Prior Park with 180 acres of ground, over-looking the city of Bath, and built two extra wings. It became, as it was intended to be, the most splendid building allotted to education in Roman Catholic hands in England. In order to find teaching staff and boys for the school, he made a visit to the Benedictine monastery of Ampleforth where he hoped to detach some of the members of the foundation by reason of the fact that the validity of their vows had been called into question. Eventually, the Prior, Sub-Prior and Procurator were secularized and transferred to the obedience of Bishop Baines; three novices and between 20 and 30 boys out of 60 came also. Such was the force of his personality that a procession of hired wagons with furniture and belongings and a large herd of cattle, for which a sum of £720 was paid in compensation, was driven all the way from Yorkshire to Bath.

Three other problems of jurisdiction where he had found himself not a free agent, assailed the Bishop almost simultaneously: the first was an altercation with the Benedictine nuns at Cannington in his District on the the subject of the appointment of a chaplain. The Prioress claimed an ancient right to choose whom she willed. An immense correspondence[38] in the files of the Propaganda Fide in Rome (which Vatican department dealt with the affairs of England, as a missionary area) shows the gravity accorded to the matter by the sisters in their struggle for independence in relation to the Bishop; the Pope withdrew the community from him and took it under his own direct jurisdiction, appointing Cardinal Weld his vicar. Secondly, there was a dispute as to the ownership of a church in Trenchard Street, Bristol, which had been built by an ex-Jesuit. When the restoration of the Order was formerly recognised in England, the Jesuits wished to recover the church; Bishop Baines disallowed the claim and the appeal went to Rome. Thirdly a Pastoral issued by him in 1834 suggesting that devotions to the Sacred Heart were not suited to the English religious scene, was reported[39] to the Pope by Mary Arundell's husband.

Bishop Baines made his way to Rome in February of 1834. Mary Arundell, who had returned to Rome and acted as Ambrose's Roman correspondent, wrote[40] that she hoped the Bishop would 'profit by the *severe* lessons he there received from the Papal lips'. There were two important consequences of the visit. He invited Nicholas Wiseman to Prior Park which he intended to turn into a Catholic University, and it is probable that it was then that he indicated to the latter that he should become his co-adjutor in the Western District. The second event was his visit to Rosmini at Domodossola in September, when he repeated his invitation to the Institute of Charity. The two other claims on the Rosminians in England had come to nought: Ambrose was forced to abandon his first attempt to import the Order into Leicestershire; Sir Henry Trelawney who had asked for a missioner based on his chapel in Cornwall, had died. Bishop Baines's offer was accepted.

Luigi Gentili had completed his noviciate under conditions of great austerity: he ate little, no meat nor fish, drank no wine and practised many bodily mortifications after the manner of the times. His aim was the total destruction of any self-love. He had taught other novices because he was better educated

than they, had carried out much pastoral work in the neighbourhood of Monte Calvario where the noviciate was situated, and
was in demand as a director of spiritual exercises in seminaries
and convents; this was work at which he excelled. Gentili was
dedicated and full of zeal for the English Mission, but as he
was to show on his arrival, his was a volatile, impetuous
nature; he was gripped constantly by a powerful and vivid
imagination and beset by a series of violent alarms as to
situations in which he might find himself trapped. He had
made up his mind about the horrors he would experience if he
went to England. As early as December 1831 he wrote to
Rosmini:

> For my part, I consider the English Mission the most difficult
> in Europe, for there error and vice are greater than in any
> other.

In 1833 his anxieties took another turn and he feared the
reaction of the English secular clergy if he and his brethren
were to join them:

> I know all about England, not only the Protestants, but also
> the Catholics ... you take my word for it, our settling in
> England will be more opposed by the Catholic clergy than by
> the Protestants.

The English clergy he thought tainted by Gallicanism[41]; were
often vain and proud. He knew some Regulars who had to live
in private houses as chaplains without their brethren; he
thought this very dangerous as they soon lost all their spirit
and turned out worse than secular priests; this was not hearsay,
he maintained, it was 'What I myself have seen and heard and
what all good men of that unhappy nation complain of'.
Rosmini answered with his customary good sense 'If God is
with you, what have you to fear? It is also a mistake to build
up a prejudice and hostility against anyone beforehand ...[42]'
Gentili's devotion persuaded him to set aside his fear; he
answered[43] Rosmini's call as to his willingness to go to England
with an affirmative, referring to that country as the former
dowry of Mary and Island of Saints. He would go as her
advocate and champion to reclaim 'my Mother and Queen's
rich domain from satanic usurpation'. It was decided that

Gentili and two other members of the society, both French priests, Emile Belisy and Antoine Rey should go to Prior Park. They would teach French and Italian, philosophy and theology: they would receive no salary, but they would have a house, and their travelling expenses would be paid. On 25 April 1835 Rosmini gave Gentili his instructions:

> You are constituted Superior over your companions who are, however, to be your counsellors. In the college, never assume a critical or magisterial tone, but remain submissively and dissimulate indulgently those customs which to you may not appear appropriate, and seek to gain the hearts of all, only by modesty and prudence – awaiting the hour of the Lord.

It would have been well for Gentili if he had been more able to heed these warnings.

The three men left Northern Italy for Rome to receive a personal blessing from the Pope before they sailed for England. Gregory XVI was very cordial. They made a pilgrimage round the 7 Roman Basilicas and renewed their vows in Santa Maria Maggiore. On May 22 they embarked on a steamer at Civita Vecchia. It was to sail immediately but the Pope was in the town; he unexpectedly came on board, gave the party another blessing and they kissed his feet. The enterprise was obviously considered one of extraordinary difficulty and danger. Needless to say, Mary Arundell had heard that Gentili was in Rome and sent[44] Ambrose her views:

> I hear that he is preparing with others of his Order to set out for England to establish themselves, at Bp Baines's *request*, in a house near Prior Park, and under his *sanction* and *protection*. I do not know what surprised me most, Bp B the *mortal enemy* of all religious orders, the persecutor of regulars, requesting that such an establishment be made, or that after the opinion I heard expressed of him by Padre Rosmini, not a year ago that he should consent to it! I only hope that Rosmini will reserve all authority over his Padri & *not* allow the Bp to have any.

A month later, she wrote[45] again; Fr Glover S J had expressed himself freely on the Rosminian move to the Western District:

> Says he is no prophet, but that he gives them but three months at most to remain at Prior Park, *probably one month*. I think so too, and so I saw, did P. Gentili. It is impossible that people

holding such different opinions as the Rosminians and Bp B. should go on together.

The Rosminians left the boat at Genoa and travelled overland across France: they arrived in London on 15 June. Gentili's first impressions were not favourable:

> We seemed to be entering the very city of Pluto: black houses, black ships, dirty sailors – all was covered with filth.

Everything seemed to him unpleasant: the colour of the Thames, its smell, the noise on land, the confusion of horses, carriages, persons in crowds: 'in short the devil is here seen enthroned, exercising his tyrannical sway over wretched mortals'. His opinions were not to change a great deal. A courtesy visit was made to Bishop Bramston, Vicar Apostolic of the London District, who surprised his abstemious guests with his generous helpings from a joint of meat. Differences in culture, customs, attitudes were very great. Stormy incidents lay ahead. Ironically enough, the British government, (together with other European powers[46]) was pouring criticism upon the Pope for maladministration in the Papal states, and illustrious British visitors bewailed the lack of law and order on their journeys through Italy and the inconvenience of brigandage.

It was August before the three Rosminians began to live at Prior Park. Gentili was no happier about conditions in England: clearly the weather, particularly the overcast skies and lack of sun, affected him. Although he could hardly attribute these to the Reformation, he saw this event as responsible for most of the evils that surrounded him in religious, political and social scenes. He was prone to sweeping, unanalytical condemnation, but it would seem that it was individualism, and its fruits, private judgment and initiative (which had led to industrialisation), that was most under censure. He wrote to a friend[47]:

> The scandals, the softness, the immorality ... In this country though it has fallen so low, our religion has a great harvest, but is without labourers ... all is melancholy, a heavy atmosphere hangs over a monotonous countryside, the poverty is frightening. People shout at you that they are free, but they are slaves to a nobility that wallows in opulence.

Rosmini exhorted[48] him to overlook difficulties and sent advice that was very hard to follow:

> I recommend you three to become gradually English in everything that is not sinful, for there you will practise the device of St Paul . . . It is not good to oppose anything that is not sinful: every nation has its customs and each country thinks its own to be good. You must adopt those of the country you are in and you must approve of them with the eyes of charity. To be too attached to Italian, French or Roman customs is a great defect in servants of God, whose real country is heaven.

A letter from Ambrose[49] to Gentili congratulated the country on its happiness at having received such a friend, such a shepherd. He felt a great epoch had begun, issued a warm invitation to Grace Dieu and, somewhat rashly, asked to know Gentili's impressions of England and the 'magnificent college worthy of the zeal and piety of Bishop Baines'. He spoke of the progress made in his own neighbourhood. Since his move to make his home at Grace Dieu in February 1835, Ambrose had achieved a great deal, chief among which was to found a monastery.

His first meeting with a Trappist was during the early part of 1833 while he was engaged, but yet not married, to Laura. They attended St Mary Moorfields together, chaperoned by Laura's cousin, Constantia. Fr Norbert Woolfrey was the deacon at High Mass. He was commissioned to raise funds in England for a new Irish monastery of Mount Melleray. The Cistercians, as Ambrose was later to emphasize on many occasions, had flourished in the pre-Reformation England of the 12th and 13th centuries and had built many abbeys of exceptional beauty in remote places such as Rievaulx and Fountains. The Order had originated in Citeaux in 1098 when a stricter and more primitive form of Benedictine rule was established. After a period of decline, there was a new burst of life in the 17th century and a number of congregations emerged from the renewal, the most famous of which, La Trappe, was to give the name Trappists to the Reformed Cistercians of the Strict Observance. Their emphasis was upon liturgical worship, contemplative prayer and manual work, chiefly agriculture; their diet was sparse and they lived in silence.

In 1791 La Trappe was attacked by the forces of the French Revolution. A small group of monks after having escaped to Switzerland, arrived in England with the intention of going to Canada. They eventually made their home at Lulworth in Dorset in 1794, under the patronage of the Weld family. In 1802 a House of Trappist nuns was set up at Stapehill nearby, on land given by Lord Arundell. The Prioress was Madame de Chabannes[50], an intrepid French nun who had led her community first to Russia for safety and then back to the West. The Lulworth community attracted some new vocations, survived for 23 years and grew to over 60 in number, when problems arose under the penal code affecting Roman Catholics on the matter of accepting English novices. In 1817 all 64 monks moved to Melleraie in Britanny, which monastery had survived the Revolution.

In 1831 another anti-clerical movement broke out in France and revolutionary guards marched upon the Abbey of Melleraie with its 175 monks; of these 25 were men of education and choir monks; the remainder were lay brothers. Many were of English and Irish origin and caused suspicion and jealousy locally by using English Farming methods. They were forcibly expelled, manhandled four to a monk, one to each arm and leg, when they refused to leave. Fifteen of them decided to stay in Nantes to wait for better days, when they might return to Melleraie; 64 sailed for Cork, 4 Choir Religious and the rest lay brothers, in the frigate Hebe. Four monks died, but the remainder eventually set up a new monastery of Mount Melleray in County Waterford near Cappoquin.

Once established in his new home at Grace Dieu, Ambrose wrote[51] to Norbert Woolfrey, who with his brother Odilo was based at Stapehill, the latter as chaplain to the nuns:

> Do you mean that you have any prospect at present of being able to found a Cistercian monastery? Should this be the case, both I and Mrs Phillipps would be much pleased if you could be induced to carry your foundation into execution in this neighbourhood.

He asked the monk to pay a visit for Holy Week and stay over Easter (April 19th), when Bishop Walsh was expected. Dom Antoine, Abbot of Melleraie, in answer to letters from the

Bishop and from Ambrose, replied that as he had no jurisdiction in England; the Vicar Apostolic of the Midland District could do as he thought fit in regard to a foundation in his area.

> Lui en laisse, s'il veut s'en charger, le soin et la responsabilité ... J'ai laissé tout sur les bras de l'évêque[52].

Spencer, hearing of the proposal, urged[53] Ambrose not to let Bishop Walsh slow him down:

> The Bishop told me of your proceedings about the Trappists. As might be expected, he was anxious to make out all about them and seemed to fear some inconveniences. He is remarkable for not closing with schemes quickly. This is a Catholic disposition in a prelate: for what can be slower than Rome in her decisions! ... my little experience makes me very earnest in recommending to you to express with all your energy your eager desires to carry forward the operations which you have so zealously set on foot ... not only with regard to the monastery but also evangelising the neighbourhood.

Ambrose did not need the warning, for he had lost no time. By May 7th he was able to write to the Bishop that he had purchased 230 acres of land at £12 per acre from Thomas Gisburne, MP for Derbyshire, with the funds the former had lent him. The exact amount borrowed in the first instance is not very clear (since further sums were later added to the debt, and some spent on other projects) but was probably about £4,000. Ambrose was, as usual, sanguine on local reaction to the arrival of Roman Catholic monks. His father had taken an interest, he wrote[54], and 'all the Liberal Protestants were delighted ... and all this neighbourhood bids fair shortly to embrace the Catholick Faith'.

The land given by Ambrose to the monks was for the most part wild and uncultivated, and formed part of what had been once Charnwood forest, then moorland covered with fern, gorse, heath and beds of loose stones, with several projections of sharp, deeply cleft granite which was characteristic of the area. Among the 40 odd acres of cultivated land was an enclosed area known as Tin Meadow, on which stood the near derelict Tin Meadow House, 12 feet by 20, with two rooms below and two above. On 18 Sept 1835 Bishop Walsh wrote[55] to Madame de Chabannes from Grace Dieu. For the glory of God and the salvation of many souls, she must very much wish for a Trappist monastery to be established in his neighbourhood, and be willing to do what lay in her power to assist the holy work. Consequently, he had concluded that she would cheerfully and on the altar of Divine love, make a sacrifice of her chaplain, Odilo Woolfrey; and since he was a very necessary person to aid the promotion of the monastery, he had desired him not to return to Stapehill.

Odilo Woolfrey took charge of the new community as prior: he was the only priest. The six monks he chose to join him were lay brothers from Mount Melleray in Ireland: Xavier Johnson (brother of a choir monk Benedict who had led the party from France) was born in Oxford in 1801 and entered Melleraie in 1818: Luke Levermore, born in London in 1797, formerly a gardener to the Benedictines at Dunkirk, had entered the same year: Placid Boardman, born in Lancashire 1803 went to Melleraie in 1824, as did Simeon Commins, an Irishman born in 1796 who had previously also worked as a gardener, in his case to the nuns at the Presentation Convent in Manchester; Augustine Higgs was born in Worcestershire in 1788 and went to Melleraie in 1828. The sixth name is uncertain, probably Cyprian Slattery who entered Melleraie in 1823 and was a short time only in Leicestershire. Vincent Ryan, the Abbot of Mount Melleray in Ireland, gave his assent to the new foundation which was to be called Mount St Bernard, and placed under the patronage, as in the case of all Cistercian houses, of the Blessed Virgin. On 29 September 1835 the title deeds of the property in Charnwood forest were signed. Augustine Higgs took possession of the Tin Meadow Cottage on behalf of his brethren: the founding of the Abbey is now calculated from that day.

Ambrose kept Bishop Walsh aware of developments in the construction of a more solid building. The community had decided, he wrote,[56] to put up a temporary monastery and chapel before attempting 'a great one'. The monks had endured a hard winter in their poor dwelling with snow falling through the roof into the dormitory, and it was important to make provision for the next 7–9 years for about 30 monks, the estimated growth. So that there should be no complaint of wastage from the neighbourhood, Ambrose and Laura had given timber and slates and sand and £45 in money: stone could be dug from the ground. Although Ambrose himself favoured a modest start, it is clear he had a vision of a permanent monastery of splendid aspect and proportions to echo the Cistercian glories of a past age.

He pressed[57] Bishop Walsh on his forthcoming visit to Rome in April 1837, to ask that the prior of Mount St Bernard be raised to the status of a mitred Abbot. 'Now, my dear Lord, I entreat you for the love of God not to neglect this, upon which depends the very existence of Mount St Bernard'.[58]

The existence of a Cistercian abbey at Garendon in the middle ages from 1123, would seem to have been one of the reasons that prompted Ambrose to choose to establish a monastery of this particular order. He saw it as an act of reparation for the dissolution of the earlier foundation and purchase into lay hands by his ancestors. He believed in the power of prayer, which was an integral part of the Cistercian life: his love for the liturgical offices of the Church, particularly when sung to old Gregorian chants, continued to increase since he was first introduced to them in Rome in the early 1830s. Digby's current literary output would certainly have reinforced Ambrose's attitude towards monasticism.

Digby had been living abroad in France, Switzerland and Italy almost continuously since he and Ambrose were parted at Cambridge. Their correspondence, on both sides, was of a self revelatory kind. Digby, as his friend had been, was (despite his physical strength) prone to fits of melancholy and inertia, and found the world a troubled place. 'Come remember you have always been my comforter . . . I am a good for nothing fellow . . . It can't be helped, there is no use in complaining' Digby wrote.[59] 'We are like buckets in a well, up and down alternately'.[60] In Nov 1832 he complained of Ambrose's treatment of him 'I have no one to correspond with but yourself . . . You have never known what it is to be as I have been since the death of my mother'. Later[61] he described Christmas with the Downside monks:

O what a contrast to the world is the interior of such a House! What peace and order and leisure. I was not surprised at their cheerful faces. They may well feel that they are happy, but they deserve to be so,

He spoke of the celebration of the Mass:

They keep choir so that the sound of their chant is still in my ears and though the community is small, there are still voices enough to produce a most solemn effect.

He concluded that he was about to go back to London 'to resume my wretched course of useless and pernicious solitude' and there would be nothing agreeable to write about for some time. A few months later came more pain 'I only write[62] to put you in mind that there still lives such a one as myself, just that I may have the sweet consolation of receiving a few lines from you, to inferior me' [sic].

During the years 1831 to 1842 Digby wrote eleven long volumes of his *Mores Catholici* or Ages of Faith. It would appear that he escaped from contemporary unhappy realities to what he saw as pleasanter times. He explained in his Book I:

My thoughts were carried backwards to ages which the muse of history had taught me long to love; for it was in the obscure and lowly middle time of saintly annals that multitudes of these bright spirits took their flight from a dark world to the Heavens. The middle ages, then I said, were the ages of the highest grace to men, ages of faith, ages when all Europe was Catholic, when vast temples were seen to rise in every place of human concourse to give glory to God.

His thesis was that the beatitudes that were propounded in the Sermon on the Mount were upheld by the Church in the middle ages and permeated every part of life; that more recent history had seen a decline in these values.

Ambrose read each volume as it appeared and was captivated by the theme, the long sonorous sentences, passages of description, the catalogues of deeds of chivalry and evocative allusions to past heroes. In November 1834 he expressed his appreciation of Volume V:[63]

In reading it I seem to be listening to one whose voice fills one with the most enchanting delight and calm contentment . . . How you discover to everyone the sublime views of the Church! . . . Your vision of the saintly crowd of all degrees whose pursuit is the thirst after justice is quite enrapturing . . . But how sad it is to turn from such a scene to contemplate the melancholy change that has taken place all over Europe.

Later[64] he pursued his appreciation further:

I have done nothing but read and meditate upon your Golden Book ever since I last wrote. I cannot describe the impressions it produced on me . . . I can express myself so poorly in praise of a book to study which would delight the Angels. You tell me sometimes that I look at the bright side of things, well now, you shall never tell me again that I am too hopeful . . . the age that could produce such a work is one preeminently calculated to inspire hope . . . To praise your book, my dear Digby would require an angel's tongue . . . the disquisition on the ecclesiastical Chant and Musick is sublime.

Book V[65] to which Ambrose referred, described the ancient liturgies, the beauty of the offices and ceremonies of the mediaeval Church, vigils, incense, lights, the use of the latin tongue, symbolism, processions and the importance of music in its various styles, especially the chants. The substance was heady and affected author and reader; it filled Ambrose with a longing to introduce these observances to his neighbourhood.

Ambrose did not stop with the foundation of Mount St Bernard. He also cajoled[66] Bishop Walsh into lending him more money for extensions to the Chapel at Grace Dieu Manor. He and Laura had opened a 'Catholick school' to which nearly 200 children had come during the first week. '. . . besides which we have a great many applications from other villages round Grace Dieu besides Whitwick requesting admission for their children'. It was of importance that these children should attend a chapel on Sundays. It was clearly too small to contain the present congregation. 'Last Sunday not only the chapel but even the long corridor was compleatly [sic] crowded with people' A week later he wrote again thanking Bishop Walsh for the loan of £600 from the Mission Fund. Brother Xavier would see to the work and Mr Railton would again be

the architect. By September Ambrose was sending his gratitude[67] for an additional £500 which he had been forced to
borrow:

> It was a great relief to myself and Laura that you agreed to our
> request because otherwise we should have been placed in such
> difficulties that I think it would have been impossible for us to
> have remained in England ... Even as it is, unless my Father
> enlarges our income, we must I think give up our horses, for I
> do not think we can afford to keep them ... the difficulty is
> for us to ask my Father ... because, of course, he has no idea
> but that we have our present income clear or very nearly so.

As Spencer had recognised, Ambrose intended to embark on
two major enterprises, the foundation of the Trappist monastery and the conversion of the neighbourhood. He was under
the mistaken impression that the first would help the second.
His original draft Founder's deed[68] gave the following stipula-
tion:

> 'that the Monastery shall supply the Grace Dieu Mission with
> a daily Mass and all other Ecclesiastical duties for ever, unless
> the Possessor of Grace Dieu and Garendon in conjunction with
> the Bishop of the Diocese shall otherwise appoint'.

The discovery that these duties were not permitted under
Cistercian rule must have come as a blow. Fr Odilo, the only
priest at the monastery until 1838, agreed to serve the Grace
Dieu mission as a temporary measure, and the one at Whitwick
which Ambrose set up in 1837, but it was clear that other
priests must be found. Ambrose began to renew his enquiries
of the Rosminians and Passionists. The prior of the monastery
was joined by a second choir monk, Bernard Palmer[69] in 1836,
but he was not ordained until 1838. Shortly after his arrival, in
a letter to Madame de Chabannes at Stapehill, he gave[70] a
graphic picture of the life of the emergent community:

> Things gos on here as well as can be expected for a new
> foundation. Our dormitory is finished and the Refectory and
> we have just begun our Chapel it is to be covered in in two
> months it is to be built by contract. Monny is the chief thing
> that is wanting here every thing is going out and very little
> comeing in for Fr Norbert has left off begging for us ... so I
> leave you to judge of our present circumstances, but I hope our

good Lord will come to our assistance if we serve him faithfully. Mr Phillipps has bought the land for us, and helps us all he can but as his Father allow's him but a very small income he cannot do much. If we can rub on untill next harvest we shall not have our wheat to by as we have sowen about 8 acres of wheat. Our land is very good when ones tilled but it is expensive to tille it on account of the quantity of very large stones. [sic]

Fr Vincent from Mount Melleray had been to see them and left a copy of the exercises adopted there, but he did not oblige the monks at Mount St Bernard to follow them; for example the taking of mixt (a kind of breakfast meal) 'at half after leven ... none of us take it at present, we dine at the usual time of half after two', so that their lives involved a high degree of fasting.

> I have to go to 3 different parishes [he continued] Now you know it is quite contrary to our state, but there are two or three observations to be made first, it is only on those conditions that our land is givin to us, and that our Bishop protects us. Secondly there is no Priest in the neighbourhood ... our holy Fr St Benedict went out of his monastery to preach to the peopel. And St Anthony went out of his seel to encourage the faithful in the time of persecution, therefore to refuse the poor peopel instructions that desier it, and ask, it would be cruel to refuse them, and contrary to Christian Charity ... we have many converts, two of them died a few days ago after havin receiving the Sacraments in the best dispositions ... [sic]

On three successive days in the autumn of 1837 there were moments of joy for Ambrose for on the 10th, 11th and 12th of October the chapels of Grace Dieu, Mount St Bernard and Whitwick were consecrated with ceremonial of great splendour. Local papers in Leicestershire and Staffordshire described the scenes, the banners, the 'highly creditable singing'. Bishop Walsh had vested in the Tin Meadow hut for the occasion at Mount St Bernard. At the head of the procession was the cross bearer followed by six other acolytes in surplices holding candles, followed by six more acolytes, walking two and two: then a banner of yellow satin damask, embroidered in silver and bearing the name of Jesus in the centre, carried by Ambrose in the uniform of a deputy lieutenant of the county. Four ecclesiastics in cassocks and surplices walked in front of Sir Charles Wolseley Bart, recently converted by Ambrose, and wearing court dress, who bore the banner of the Blessed Vigin Mary. Thirty clergy preceded the Revd Edward Huddleston as archdeacon, and Bishop Walsh in full pontificals with mitre and crozier, his train borne by an acolyte. On the summit of the hill, the Prior of the monastery with sixteen monks, was waiting: the processions joined up. Singing the Litany they filed into the monastic church. Spencer preached the sermon.

The consecration of Grace Dieu chapel was solemn, thorough and lengthy. The procession walked round the exterior and interior of the building sprinkling the walls with holy water and chanting the Litany and three psalms: high Mass followed. Upon the altar stood massive gilded candlesticks and a profusion of artificial flowers which gave it 'a most beautiful and striking appearance'. It was not a sight in the English tradition, but perhaps one to cheer the hearts of those who led lives of drabness and poverty. At Whitwick on the third day of celebrations, a burial ground was consecrated also: the Bishop blessed 'a large handsome cross 24 feet high' in the centre of the graveyard.

During the summer of 1838, the feared need for economies pressed upon the de Lisle family: Ambrose and Laura now had three children, Everard[71] and Philomena[72] usually known as Mena had joined Amo. Laura had miscarried a fourth child in the spring. It was possible to live cheaply and anonymously in lodgings in France without the style of life dictated by convention in England. For three months they lived at Dieppe. Spencer, whose health had broken down once more, accompanied them. He and Ambrose who had been giving thought to how it would be possible to encourage prayers for the conversion of England, found themselves launching a crusade. Spencer began with a lecture in Dieppe and through Laura's cousin Lord Clifford who was staying in Paris, found himself introduced to the Archbishop, Monsignor de Queslin. The latter suggested that in two days' time Spencer should address a gathering of 70–80 French clergy at St Sulpice on this theme: he further proposed that prayers for the conversion of England be said in French churches every Thursday. Letters of introduction to heads of Religious Houses followed. The Crusade had begun in such a rapid and open way that news of it soon reached the English newspapers.

The Times of 3 Nov 1838 reported that George Spencer 'brother to the present earl' and Ambrose 'have been in Paris where they have been busily occupied there in establishing an association of prayers for the conversion of this country to the Roman faith. They have had several interviews with the Archbishop of Paris on this subject, who has ordered all the clergy to say special prayers for this object. A number of the religious communities in France have already begun to follow the same practice'.

The Crusade spread to Holland, Switzerland, Germany, Ireland and Italy, encouraged by the two architects of the scheme. Spencer found himself having to explain their actions to the cautious English Vicars Apostolic. His interest in the Crusade caused Monsignor Forbin-Janson[73], Bishop of Nancy, to introduce himself to Ambrose and Laura at Digby's Paris home. The Bishop took them to his house at Mont Valerien where the first public mass in the campaign for the conversion of England was said before a large concourse which included the Papal Nuncio. The friendship with the Bishop of Nancy was to develop and endure: several of his enthusiasms were to be transported to Leicestershire.

Meanwhile at Prior Park the expected situation had arisen. At first Gentili had been well received by Bishop Baines. He had been given a great deal of responsibility and had thrown himself whole-heartedly into his teaching work: so much so that the parents of his pupils had begun to complain. Shocked at the secular environment and lack of what he considered the essentials of Catholic devotion, Gentili had ignored Rosmini's advice and introduced many customs hitherto unknown in England, but popular in Italy. The two priests who had accompanied him found him very severe as a Superior as he demanded of them the high standards he set himself: tale-telling letters reached Rosmini.

Correspondence flowed between Gentili and Ambrose as soon as the Rosminian came to England. In July 1836 Gentili paid a visit to Grace Dieu and to the Shrewsburys at Alton Towers. Ambrose consulted him over various personal problems and was fulsome in his thanks for the advice given. He offered advice also which doubtless greatly surprised the recipient with his Italian background. A certain amount of anticlericalism was endemic in the latin world, but it was accompanied by formal deference in relationships with the priestly caste.

One of Gentili's austerities was a reluctance to shave: Ambrose wrote[74]

> Before I say anything further in reference to more spiritual matters, I must proceed frankly to say a few words in reference to certain points on which I am anxious to do what will perhaps appear very presumptuous on the part of a layman towards a Priest and a Religious, and that is to give a word of advice . . . If you wish to do good in this country you must conform to those customs, which however different from those of Italy, are innocent and indifferent in themselves. Hence I do not approve or admire that spirit which would urge a man to abstain from shaving his beard in England, because it is esteemed a mark of effeminacy in Italy to do so every day, or because certain Saints in different ages and countries allowed their beards to grow. In England it is the custom for men of the rank of Gentlemen to shave every day. Hence when a man in that rank of Life (and Priests are esteemed Gentlemen whether by birth or by courtesy) neglects this custom he is looked upon as a man of slovenly or dirty habits & as being guilty of disrespect to the society in which he moves.

Ambrose went on to prove the point by referring to Jesuit practice in England: the fathers conformed to local custom.

> There are several other *little* matters of the same kind in which it strikes me that your opinions are somewhat too severe.

He was probably referring to Gentili's negative attitudes towards regular washing, which had caused some misgivings: anything that conspired towards self-love and against poverty he thought suspect.

> I am not singular in thinking so, for Lord and Lady Shrewsbury made the same remark to me a few days ago, and I can see that their thinking so makes them esteem your judgement less than they otherwise would do; and that therefore your means of usefulness might be diminished.

In 1837 Rosmini sent reinforcements to Prior Park, including

Giovanni-Battista Pagani[75], his future successor as Superior. He came just in time, for relations between Bishop Baines and Gentili deteriorated so much by the summer of 1838 that the Bishop took most of the Italian's duties away: he despatched him first to Stapehill to make a visitation to the nuns and then to Spettisbury near Blandford to the Augustinians. Rosmini believing an absent Superior to be no help to his brothers, demoted Gentili and replaced him by the new-comer Pagani. Then seizing on an opportunity to recall him to Italy, did so in the summer of 1839. Six months later Rosmini re-opened negotiations once more with Ambrose who had rashly said he would provide the Institute with a noviciate house in Leicestershire. His ideas were, as usual, more extensive than his means. Rosmini wrote[76] of Gentili.

> He is all yours, and he seems to me to be growing all the time in holiness and learning. If things go well with his health as at present, I shall send him next spring.

Ambrose had expressed a wish to have Gentili in his own house which the Superior doubted was according to their rules of poverty, but he agreed to let him come without conditions. Whether Rosmini realized it or not, Ambrose was quite unable to finance a separate building for the missionary. 'Here at last is dear Gentili' was the message that Rosmini despatched[77] on 5 May 1840 'May he be a new Augustine for England . . . Look after his health for his is not strong'. Luigi Gentili arrived at Grace Dieu on 12 June.

Ambrose's negotiations with the Passionists were also bearing fruit. Through the good offices of the new English Cardinal[78] in Rome, (Cardinal Weld having died in 1837), a memorial was drawn up to the Passionist General Chapter meeting in April 1839 for an English foundation. In it was stated that Ambrose, a Catholic landowner, was willing to make the offering of a house in the County of Leicestershire which might contain six or seven Religious. A devout lady was said to be willing to give £50 sterling each year and other resources might come from alms of the faithful.

Dominic Barberi, saddened once again to be elected Provincial, this time in the South of Italy, was suddenly summoned to form a House at Ere in Belgium in the summer of 1840. That autumn, encouraged by Spencer and empowered by his Superiors, he set foot in England for the first time on a visit of reconnaissance. December found him as a guest at Grace Dieu. He described the visit to the Passionist General[79]: Gentili was in the house also; he had made many converts in the neighbourhood; his host had read him an article he had written in defence of Gregorian chant and Latin psalmody. Ambrose's happiness at that moment was surely very great.

Chapter 4

'Negotiation with the Oxford Divines'

(i) Prelude

Of all the participants with Ambrose in his dealings with the writers of the *Tracts for the Times*, later called the Tractarians, in the years 1840–1, none was more enigmatic in his approach and motives than Nicholas Wiseman. One reason why it is so difficult to shed light on him 145 years later is that, as in the case of Ambrose himself, attempts have so often been made to shelter him from accusations of lack of orthodoxy and to protect his posthumous reputation. It is not easy to separate factual evidence from the glosses. For example, as late as the 1920s when at the time of the Malines conversations[1] Vincent McNabb, OP wrote an article entitled *Cardinal Wiseman and Cardinal Mercier on Reunion*,[2] permission to publish was refused. It was said that McNabb might have misunderstood Wiseman. It would not have been difficult.

Wiseman was better qualified than many other contemporary Roman Catholic prelates to take part in conversations where the subject matter stretched beyond previously accepted boundaries. He had a good intellect, had received an academic education and could think conceptually. He had shown himself to be particularly interested in the ideas on Catholic renewal that were emerging in France and Germany in the 1830s. Above all, he had valuable experience in international communication when he was Rector of the English College in Rome; no longer shy nor socially inhibited, he was pleasant, friendly and liked to be liked. Wiseman increased his acquaintance and his influence by keeping in touch with former visitors. Ambrose and Spencer were prominent among these.

The visit of Montalembert, Lacordaire and Lamennais in the autumn of 1831 was to stretch over a long period during which they and Wiseman became closely acquainted. Lamennais had changed his political opinions several times. By that year he had begun a newspaper *L'Avenir* which set out to show that a free church could exist in a free state. He and the two friends who shared his enthusiasm had gone to Rome to ask for the approval of their ideals by the Holy See. After a formal audience with Gregory XVI, they sent a memoir for examination. It was not to be the only document for scrutiny: several French bishops sent a request for the principles proposed in the memoir to be dismissed; the French and Austrian governments did likewise.

While the three Frenchmen were enduring their wait for an answer, they were joined by two friends; the life of one of them later impinged on that of Ambrose. Alexis-François Rio[3] was a young Breton writer, fervent Catholic and art historian; his predilection for specifically Christian art was to endear him particularly to Ambrose. Rio also become a close friend of William Gladstone[4] whose first visit to Rome was during this period. In search of Spencer, Gladstone made his way to the English College on 14 April 1832[5] and saw in Wiseman 'an agreeable and I believe able man; went over the college'. Ten days later[6] he met Spencer:

> ... We had a conversation, long and friendly: bearing much of course upon our differences in religion. Much of it touched upon himself, yet there was not the smallest appearance of egoism ... He rested his defence of Roman Catholicism not on any single, but rather on a constructive argument, founded partly on miracles and partly on historical testimony – for which he did not seem to have gone deep. He appeared very *ignorant*, considering the circumstances, of the true character of the Church of England on the question of private judgment; spoke generally with clearness and good sense and whether in their communion or ours, he is doubtless a single-minded and devoted servant of God.

The papal answer to the French group came in August 1832 in the shape of the Encyclical *Mirari Vos*. Within its terms came an implicit censure of *L'Avenir*. The suggestion of collaboration between Catholics and all who wanted to work for liberty 'was most disturbing to the Pope'. The consequence to Lamennais is beyond the scope of this book. Sufficient is it to say that by 1834 he had abandoned priestly functions and published *Paroles d'un Croyant* which denounced political tyranny; it was placed on the Index. Eventually Lamennais broke with the Church and his former associates with him. But his influence remained. He brought to the notice of his contemporaries several important issues: the involvement of the laity in the Church; the need for better clerical training; reconciling the Church with democracies; longings for social justice. Among Catholics who were influenced by his views were Antonio Rosmini[7] and to a lesser extent Nicholas Wiseman. Lamennais' ideas also interested some contemporary German thinkers whom Wiseman was to visit in Munich on his way to England in 1835, chief among whom was J. J. Ignaz von Döllinger[8] soon to become a correspondent of Ambrose also. Going through Paris Wiseman renewed his acquaintance with Lacordaire and Montalembert who, with Rio, had likewise made a recent journey to Munich and spoken with Döllinger and his colleagues. This circle was becoming increasingly closely knit. (Ambrose was to make the pilgrimage to Munich in 1844). Among those responsible for the condemnation of the views of Lamennais in Rome was the Passionist, Dominic Barberi[9]: the formation of the pro and anti-liberal Catholic camps was taking place.

The base of Wiseman's knowledge and experience continued to broaden. Before leaving Rome in 1835 he delivered a course of lectures in Cardinal Weld's rooms on the connexion between science and revealed religion which increased his reputation. His object in the English visit of that year was mainly to see Bishop Baines, for it had been suggested that Wiseman might become his co-adjutor and head of a possible Catholic university in England. It was also clearly important for the English Vicars Apostolic as a whole to be in touch with their representative in Rome.

The meeting between Bishop Baines and Nicholas Wiseman at Prior Park in August 1835 was not a pleasant one and Wiseman left with the possibilities under discussion perma-

nently ruled out. The offer of appointment was merely tenta-
tive, in the first instance only for a year, and not renewable if
unsuccessful. Moreover Wiseman's suggestions for an educational programme at Prior Park were ill received and produced
a rebuff such 'as I have never had before, and never since'[10].
There were happier incidents elsewhere in England generally.
On Sunday afternoons in Advent, Wiseman delivered sermons
in English in the old Sardinian Chapel in Lincoln's Inn Fields
in London on what Roman Catholics actually believed. Such
success greeted the experiment that he gave a further series of
popular lectures in the following Lent at Moorfields when a
large number of non-Roman Catholics attended. He agreed to
prepare the substance of the talks for publication. Gladstone
met Wiseman for the second time on 28 July at breakfast with
Monckton Milnes and wrote in his diary 'A long *sederunt*'. He
had recently read the lectures on the *Principal Doctrines and
Practice of the Catholic Church* between 12 and 20 July and
noted 'remarkably able'.

Another important action of Wiseman's during this summer
was to establish the *Dublin Review*, a periodical of intellectual
and literary standing designed to appeal to a wider readership
than Catholics alone; Wiseman became the first editor. There
were losses and gains in this visit: Wiseman's reputation with
the Vicars Apostolic in general and Bishop Baines in particular
deteriorated. This was partly on account of his frequent critical
attitudes and lack of understanding of local conditions seen
from the Roman view point. His partiality for the deployment
of members of Religious Orders was a further cause for
division. Wiseman's reputation among the English laity was,
however, enhanced by the tour of the great Catholic houses
and families, and by the ability of his lectures and writings.
These attitudes in regard to Wiseman were to endure and
harden. He returned to Rome in Sept 1836.

Gladstone made a second visit there in 1838: on 4 Dec he
renewed his acquaintance with Wiseman. He bore a letter of
introduction from Rio, with whom he was by now on intimate
terms, which said that Gladstone wished to know more of 'the
practice of the Roman Catholic Church with its moral and
spiritual results on its members', Wiseman proved himself very
obliging and the two men had long talks. The Missal was

explained to Gladstone so that he might understand services more perfectly and arrangements were made for him to attend various ceremonies. Gladstone wrote in his diary[11] 'I am confirmed in the idea that the mass implies and carries less of active mental participation than the English Liturgy'.

On 12 Dec Gladstone took Henry Manning[12] who was also staying in Rome, on a visit to the English College. The object was to borrow that edition of the *Tracts for the Times* which dealt with the Roman Breviary. It was Tract 75, written by John Henry Newman[13]. Wiseman remarked that 'with some inaccuracies, it is on the whole a good account'[14]. He was clearly greatly interested in the Tracts; as was Gladstone; they spoke at length about them and their writers. Ever since the visit from Oxford of J. H. Newman and his friend R. Hurrell Froude[15] to Wiseman in March 1833, as he wrote[16] later, he

> . . . watched with intense interest and love that Movement of which I then caught the first glimpse. My studies changed their course, the bent of my mind was altered, in the strong desire to co-operate with the new mercies of providence.

In a letter[17] to his sister on 27 April 1839 Wiseman acknowledged that he was anxious to leave Rome. 'England is in the most interesting condition and calls for all the exertions of those that wish her well'. An appointment for him in England was part of a larger problem. That the English Vicars Apostolic should become diocesan bishops within an established hierarchy had been mooted for a decade. Opinion in Rome by the end of the 1830s was in the main that they had not exhibited sufficient initiative nor regard for the Holy See to be trusted with increased status. Letters in the Archives of the English College in Rome show how hard Bishop Walsh was pressing for Wiseman to become his co-adjutor in the Midland District. On 26 December 1838[18] he wrote to the Rector: he had applied to the Pope, the Propaganda Fide, Lord Shrewsbury, Prince Doria and Lord Clifford in this interest. By 1 December 1839[19] he revealed that a scheme to divide the Districts was being worked out. Bishop Baines had a plan of which he did not approve since it would involve 'unmercifully cutting up the Midland District' By 24 January 1840[20] Bishop Walsh felt that the situation was becoming urgent. He was conscious that it was in his District that most of the activity in the English Roman Catholic community was taking place among which was church building by Lord Shrewsbury and missions by Ambrose. Now possibilities of contact with the Tractarian movement in Oxford were opening up:

> You my dear Dr Wiseman are the proper person to meet the Oxford divines and I feel satisfied that were H H and Propaganda fully aware of what is going on in Oxford and of the real state of religion in this country, they would rather press you than otherwise to come amongst us.

In the summer of 1840 came developments. The Vicars Apostolic did not change their status; no hierarchy was established, but the existing four Vicariates created in 1688 were increased to eight. The London and Western Vicariates retained their titles though their boundaries were redrawn and a new District for Wales was carved out of the latter. Bishop Walsh became Vicar Apostolic of a smaller Central District, having lost part of his area to a new Eastern one. The Northern Vicariate was divided into three parts: the two new jurisdictions were to be known as Lancashire and Yorkshire Districts. Nicholas Wiseman was appointed co-adjutor to Bishop Walsh and President of the Seminary at Oscott. On 8 June he was consecrated Bishop of the titular See of Melipotamus. He left Rome for England the following September.

Though solving some administrative problems in the English Mission the scheme created new ones. In order to accede to the wish of Bishop Walsh for the assistance of Wiseman and his presence at Oscott, some way had to be found to remove the sitting occupant of the post of President. Monsignor Henry Weedall, a studious, pious man but delicate, had been appointed in 1826, having been at the college, student and teacher, since 1804. It had become his whole life. His health had always given concern for he was prone to 'a mischievous affection of the nerves of the head'. His eyes were very weak and at times in his life he could not bear the light, nor could he read for more than a few minutes. In 1830 he went abroad for two years to try to recover and returned the better for the change, and threw himself whole heartedly into plans for a new Oscott building 2 miles from the original. Bishop Walsh wrote[21] to Wiseman in Rome:

> Dr Weedall, ... improves in health and is become quite an efficient man. He surpasses my expectations. I do not allow him to preach or to apply his mind to deep study. His situation in the College enables him to take horse exercise which is of great service to him.

The expedient employed to create the necessary vacancy at Oscott in 1840 was to appoint Henry Weedall Vicar Apostolic of the Northern District. He was, as Bishop Walsh described[22] to Monsignor Acton (not yet until 1842 a Cardinal) in Rome, 'overwhelmed with grief'. The poor man himself wrote some pitiful letters to Acton pointing out that he did not 'possess one requisite on the score of theological attainment' for the vicariate. 'I can assure you that the very shadow of a mitre has made my head sorely to ache' he wrote to a friend[23]. Bishop Walsh threw his weight against the appointment: the situation had worsened, he wrote[24], in that there had been an unpleasant intimation from the clergy of the Northern District that they wished to avoid Henry Weedall as their Bishop.

A rumour reached Bishop Walsh, 'the astonishing and heart-breaking intelligence' that it was Wiseman who was now to go to the Northern District, while Weedall was to remain at Oscott and be co-adjutor. The Bishop protested[25] in the strongest terms:

> I should consider myself bound in conscience to use every means in my power to oppose it which was consistent with the most perfect obedience to the Holy See ... For the good of my poor dear District, may Heaven grant my fears are un-grounded.

He had earlier solicited the help of Acton to obtain Wiseman's services, which would seem to explode the theory (often expressed) that Walsh did not want him in England.

Eventually the storm blew over: Weedall went to Rome to appeal to the Pope to be relieved of the burden. After some difficulties and due to the help and kindness of Bishop Baines who had been called there, the appointment was rescinded. Weedall retired into obscurity for a while, until he reappeared at the new Cathedral in Birmingham. He returned to Oscott, again as President, in 1853, for six years more, in spite of the fact that although 'entrusted with teaching he did not possess the art of conveying every kind of knowledge . . . and failed to adapt himself to the capacities of children in Catechetical instruction.' He was apparently more successful with older pupils. Ambrose, seven of whose sons were educated at Oscott, had an acquaintance with him on this account. Francis Mostyn[26] became Vicar Apostolic of the Northern District in Weedall's place. Seriously ill with tuberculosis for most of his episcopate, he was assisted after 1843 by William Riddell[27] as co-adjutor. Bishop Mostyn died in August 1847 aged 47; three months later Bishop Riddell died also aged 40, of 'Irish fever' contracted while working among the poor in Newcastle.

This episode, minor in itself except to the unfortunate Henry Weedall, is of importance in demonstrating three facts: first, the authorities in Rome were out of touch with the English scene; second, the English Roman Catholic community were particularly short of leaders. When Nicholas Wiseman wrote to Ambrose in the context of his conversations with the Oxford men and said 'Let us have an influx of new blood'[28], it is now clearer why he said so. It may well be that this need dominated his relationship with the Tractarians, and explains it. Third, the education of Catholic students and boys would seem to have provided problems; certainly many come to the surface in the 1860s. Ambrose, with his family of 16, was in a position of experience when he became involved in this issue.

The arrangements made for Wiseman's arrival at Oscott on 9 September 1840 reflected a significant side to his character. His view of the importance of his position and forthcoming role were shown in the full ceremonial of the Roman Pontifical for the entry of a new Bishop to his diocese (although he was only a co-adjutor). From accounts in the Catholic press it would appear that vested (at the lodge) in the Odescalchi cape presented to the college by Lord Shrewsbury and a jewelled mitre, Wiseman was conducted in solemn procession with many robed clergy up the drive lined with schoolboys while the choir sang *Ecce Sacerdos Magnus*. They were prophetic words. Once inside the chapel the *Te Deum* was sung. A link and contrast with the style in which the 'old' Catholics had conducted themselves in England was provided by the 80 year old Dr Kirk, trained at the English College in Rome in the Jesuit days (before the suppression of the Order) 67 years before, who rode from his mission in Lichfield on a horse.

Bishop Walsh had transferred Spencer to Oscott a year before, partly it would seem for Spencer's good and partly for the good of the college. He named him spiritual director to the young men preparing for the priesthood: he 'needs a sensible guide to regulate his movements and sober down his enthusiastic spirit'[29] The scene was set for Oscott to become the power house for the (now) Central District, to which men from Oxford were to gravitate.

One member of the staff who was to play an important role as a go-between, has not yet been mentioned: Augustus Welby Northmore Pugin was probably the most gifted and certainly the most unusual of Ambrose's close friends, and one whose cultural pedigree is the easiest to trace. He was clearly an inheritor of the European Romantics of the late 18th century. Ambrose himself shared some of their characteristics: their search for eternal truths; their emphasis on the pre-eminence of vision, the culture of past ages and its elitist nature. But he had absorbed these tendencies at second-hand and somewhat accidentally, it would seem, as an Englishman from a conventional, establishment background and was not an original thinker. Ambrose's originality lay rather in the daring of his approach and methods. (Digby's claim to be considered a Romantic was stronger, with the same attachment to the past but a more cosmopolitan cultural inheritance. On the other hand his creativity, though life-long, was rather derivative and he relied, in his writings at any rate, more on the books of others than on imagination). Pugin was the most idiosyncratic of men, and it is his very excesses that place him most firmly in the Romantic tradition.

He was a creative genius, with burning enthusiasm, imaginative power, and dedication of such high degree that he overworked himself to the point of madness. Emotionally susceptible, he was married three times and two unsuccessful love affairs caused him much grief. His father, Augustus Charles Pugin who was of Swiss extraction, had taken refuge in England at the time of the Revolution. He became an apprentice to John Nash and his son was born in London. By the age of 15 so precocious was Pugin the younger that he was helping his father with his architectural drawings and in fact completed the latter's commission for gothic furniture for Windsor Castle.

His attraction towards the gothic dominated his life and although he was to deny that his conversion to Roman Catholicism was consequent upon it, the connection was undoubted.

One of the younger Pugin's characteristics was the breadth
of his talent: having begun as a furniture designer, he then
turned to scenery and stage sets; next to architecture and a
range of decorations: wallpaper, stone and wood carving,
ceramics and so on. Some of his finest work was executed in
metal. He concentrated on developments in styles prevalent in
mediaeval times. In 1834 he became a Roman Catholic. Having
married at 19 in 1832, and having soon been bereaved, he
married again in 1833. In 1836 he published his book *Contrasts*
which illustrated vividly the drift of his thinking. 'Everything
grand, edifying and noble in art is the result of feelings
produced by the Catholic religion on the human mind'[30] he
wrote in a later explanatory volume.

From this premise Pugin deduced that art in England since
the Reformation had become degraded. Unable to find a
publisher, he had the book printed at his own expense. During
the course of the following year he was forced to retract many
of the ideas contained in it; for example he was to find that
gothic architecture, the ancient liturgies, chants and vestments
were more in favour among some Anglicans than among his
19th century Roman Catholic contemporaries. Moreover Rome
itself contained much of the detested 'pagan' (classical) architecture. In common with Ambrose, he allowed his artistic prejudices to gain the upper hand over his judgment. Pugin's profound intolerance towards those whose opinions differed from
his own was his most serious fault, and it was to lead Ambrose
into controversy in company with him.

The two men met through Lord Shrewsbury (who had
asked Pugin to stay at Alton Towers, initially to advise on
some furniture) about the year 1834. The formation of a
lasting friendship would seem to have been inevitable: there
was so much common ground. Pugin was to become more
than a friend: he was architect and adviser on many projects
for buildings, decoration and expansion; colleague and confi-
dant in the Catholic revival movement and schemes for Christian reunion. By 1840 he was stretched almost beyond endur-
ance, designing cathedrals and churches, mansions, chapels,

convents all over England. His programme was relentless; he would travel all night, appear at Grace Dieu at 6. a.m, inspect the work in hand and be off again an hour later. The pattern was general. Amidst the other calls upon his time he became in 1837 a member of the teaching staff at the seminary at Oscott, under the title of Professor of Ecclesiastical Architecture and Antiquities. With Wiseman and Spencer he formed a triumvirate for the reception of any of the Tractarians from Oxford who could be persuaded to come to the college.

It was not to educate a few boys that this Oscott was erected, Wiseman wrote[31]

> But to be the rallying point of a yet silent, but vast movement towards the Catholic Church, which has commenced and must prosper.

Much to the disappointment of Wiseman, at first no visitors from Oxford seemed to wish to come. It was Pugin, then Spencer, and then Ambrose (the most successful) who were to make the moves. Although the four men were committed to the same cause, the restoration of England to what they termed 'Catholic Unity', they saw it with varied emphases. These were to be reflected in the conduct of their relationships with the Oxford men, for they were based on different interpretations of the term 'Catholic'.

For Wiseman, the overwhelming criterion was not only communion with the see of Rome, but acceptance of methods, outlook and practices that were specifically *Roman*. He considered the type of Roman Catholicism that had developed in England to be a travesty of the faith and devotions as practised in Rome; priests and lay people were too independent and lacking in respect for the authority of the Holy See. But he appreciated that the standard of leadership was a reflection of lack of education and background; this the Oxford men could provide. It would be worth granting a few concessions to gain their adherence.

Spencer was sufficiently influenced by his period of fairly recent training in Rome to be similarly motivated, but his own English education had been so sparse and inadequate that he was unable to grasp the issues at stake. Pugin warmed to those who embraced customs and forms he saw as derived from

pre-Reformation times, the love of plain chant and the wearing
of gothic vestments; he recoiled from those who derided them.

Ambrose was firm in his loyalty to the see of Rome but at
the same time intensely patriotic towards his native land. He
was sufficiently informed by his reading to appreciate that the
pre-Reformation Church in Europe, and more particularly in
England, had not been monochrome in its rites, practices and
forms, but had contained considerable local variety within a
universal framework. To allow this once more would create
unity in diversity. As will be seen in Chapter 8 he had chosen
an unpropitious time to promote this outlook, when the trend
at the centre was to secure the adoption of the specifically
Roman rite internationally.

It would be unfair to Ambrose to suggest as has often been
inferred, that his view of what was 'Catholic' concentrated on
forms only, and that it was common interest in those of earlier
times that drew him to the Tractarians. Ambrose's definition
of 'catholicity' was related to an attitude towards the doctrine
of the Church which the Tractarians held and to which
Newman referred when he later declared that it was Oxford
that had made him Catholic.[32] Ambrose was more impressed
by the presence of what he saw as Catholic revival in these
terms than were Wiseman or Spencer; he conceived it as a sign
of grace wherever it might be located. It was a point of view
unique at the time, but upon which modern ecumenical dialogue has been fruitfully based.

Ambrose felt himself to be in some way destined to bring
about reconciliation between Christians. What form the reconciliation was to take he never quite knew; sometimes individual
conversion seemed indicated; corporate reunion of groups he
thought appropriate in other instances. The emergence of signs
of 'catholicity' among such groups gave him hope, in fact he
saw it as assurance that unity must be the outcome. It had
been promised to him by prophecy. Entry into the jurisdiction
of the Holy See was axiomatic, for only there could full
reconciliation take place at the source for him, of all true
union.

In January 1840 Spencer made a visit to Oxford with the
object of trying to gain John Henry Newman's support for his
Crusade of Prayer. Newman had been disturbed by an article

written by Wiseman in the *Dublin Review*[33] in which he compared the position of the Donatists, a schismatic body in the African Church of the 4th and 5th centuries, with that of Anglicans in their relation to the see of Rome. Partly on this account and partly because of his antipathy towards the political activities of Daniel O'Connell,[34] Newman's welcome to Spencer was not warm. Spencer had been in correspondence with William Palmer,[35] fellow of Magdalen College, with whom he had a very one-sided encounter. His adversary's knowledge of the Fathers and ecclesiastical history in general was greatly in excess of his own. He wrote to Ambrose[36] describing the episode:

> The result was very different from what I expected ... I shall not go there again, please God without special direction ... I had sailed right down into the enemy's fleet, my little ship had been terribly battered and mauled. But I had made good my retreat, with colours at the mast head ... The others of the same class whom I met, to whom young Mr Palmer of Magdalen introduced me, and amounted to 8, hardly hit me at all to hurt, all the glory was with him ... I can hardly ... give you an idea ... of the sort of course by which I was brought during the first day's fight, to the most astonishing point, not only of having my battery regularly silenced, but of being in a complete maze in my own head.

He had passed the next two days with Palmer, he explained:

> ... I cannot look on him in any light but as one who is to be a brother to me and you and perhaps now only kept from us by prejudice on his part and faults on ours which make our cause not appear in a true light. Both you and others speak of the necessity of learning to make one fit to meet the people and therefore it is concluded that a visit to them by one such as I, who have no learning could not be expedient ... Again I say I am not going again ...

Bishop Walsh gave his account[37] to Wiseman (who was still in Rome) and showed a great deal of sagacity and grasp of reality

> Mr Logan[38] has made known to you good Mr Spencer's failure at Oxford. He is so humble that all will no doubt contribute to his greater sanctification and to his becoming more strong in

faith. At the same time, it would be most dangerous to raise him at present to the Episcopal responsibility [this possibility had already been suggested twice and must surely have reinforced Wiseman's worst fears regarding lack of leaders in the English Church] for if when more left to himself he should again indulge his enthusiastical schemes, again commit himself with the acute learned Oxford divines and fall, the scandal and injury to our holy religion would be the more to be lamented. He is quite willing to follow the plan which we all here think the best for him, that of being more fully employed in spiritual[?] in the College, in zealously exerting himself under prudent advice, to promote piety and the religion of the heart and of improving himself in the knowledge of Ecclesiastical history, particularly that of his own country, in which he is very deficient, and which gave a triumph to the Oxford divines over him. I am inducing him to curtail his extensive foreign correspondence which is calculated to elevate him too much, and to turn his mind from what is more solid and more to the purpose.

Pugin's relations with the Tractarians were created initially by demands for his professional advice on the restoration of churches and their decoration. He made several visits to Oxford during the course of 1840 and began a correspondence among others with John Rouse Bloxam[39] a considerable liturgical scholar and fellow of Magdalen College. Pugin's letters to Ambrose reveal the identity of views he had established:

We nearly *stand alone* if we except the Oxford men, for among them I find full sympathy of feeling. But the real truth is the churches I build do little or no good for want of men who know how to use them ... the present state of things is quite lamentable, and were it not for the Oxford men I should quite despair.[40]

Later he wrote[41]

Rely on it these Oxford men are doing more to Catholicize England and to work the great internal change of mind than all our joint body. I consider them quite as raised up by God in the present emergency, for we seem sinking into utter degradation ... I had a most delightful letter 2 days ago from Mr Bloxam of Magdalen, breathing a most Catholic and reviving spirit. They are really the only sort of letters I read with

Mount St Bernard's Abbey, Charnwood Forest, from an early 19th century engraving
(Architect: A. W. N. Pugin)

JOHN ROUSE BLOXAM, Fellow of
Magdalen College, Oxford; Chalk
drawing for his painting on Magdalen
Tower by William Holman Hunt.

WILLIAM ULLATHORNE, Bishop of Birmingham.

LAURA 1811–1896
(at the time of her marriage)

AMBROSE CHARLES
1834–1883

EVERARD V.C. 1835–1857

MENA 1836–1903

ALICE 1840–1926

WINIFREDA 1841–1909

MARY 1843–1860

BERTHA 1844–1913

(There is no extant likeness of REGINALD 1839–1845)

pleasure, for any communication from other quarters is full of amazing information. You will be grieved to hear that all the altar fittings that were made for Birmingham have been condemned by Dr Wiseman because they are all in strict conformity with antient solemn practices.

The violence of Pugin's reactions were to become a source of embarrassment to Ambrose, but his contacts in Oxford were useful. During the course of 1840, Ambrose was to make his own.

His growth in maturity is apparent in the letters that followed. By the autumn of 1840 his and Laura's family had grown to five children: Reginald, whose life-span was to be short, was born in 1839 and Alice one year later; hers was long and full of tragedy. Beautiful and talented, she was from the start a much favoured child; as 'darling Alice' Laura referred to her in her diary. All the omens were good. Grandpapa[42] had caused a box of 'magnificent' baby-clothes from a grand shop in Cheltenham to be delivered at Grace Dieu to await her birth. It was the first and last time he was to do so. 'Cost £50' Laura recorded, obviously astonished, on 20 August. Mr Eddowes was as usual too late for the birth on 3 September (two maids were with Laura) but Ambrose nevertheless gave the doctor £8, a very large sum by the standards of the day.

Ambrose's own achievements had included two more books, both translations, since the *Lamentations* of 1831. J.C.L.S. de Sismondi[43] a Swiss national of Italian descent had published in 1809–18 a history in many volumes on the Italian republics of the middle ages: it was critical of the role of the papacy. Alessandro Manzoni[44] whose works included *I Promessi Sposi* which Ambrose greatly admired, wrote a *Vindication of Catholic morality* to offset the view portrayed by Sismondi, and this Ambrose translated from the Italian and published in 1836 in order that the English reading public should see the papacy in a more favourable light. In 1839 he translated Charles de Montalembert's *Histoire de Ste Elizabeth de Hungrie* from the French and established a close friendship with the author (who became godfather to Reginald). Their lengthy correspondence endured until the death of the Frenchman in 1870. Ambrose who did nothing without principle, clearly intended the book as an inducement to the nobility to emulate the example of the thirteenth century saint who gave up children, position and riches for the cloister and a life of austerity, self-giving and care of the poor.

Ambrose's approach to the Tractarians, as with his other efforts at reconciliation, was pragmatic and mainly conducted from his Leicestershire base. He had no overall strategy, though he had been long prepared by reading the *Tracts* as they appeared[45] and some of the works quoted by their authors. As a result of some newly established European connexions, he began in the early months of 1840 to write letters describing the movement which 'est connu en Angleterre *sous le nom des "principes de L'Université d'Oxford"*' to the French journal *L'Univers*, through the good offices of Jules Gondon[46] the editor of English religious affairs. These letters he was to continue to write during the rest of 1840 and 1841. They are important on two counts: first they reveal Ambrose's opinion of the Tractarians: secondly as Louis Allen has pointed out,[47] they were the chief medium by which the French public was introduced to the Oxford movement and led to the first biography in any language of J. H. Newman.

In his letter of 12 March 1840[48] Ambrose said he believed this to be a movement which sooner or later would lead to the return of the entire Anglican Church to unity with the Catholic. The principles for which it stood were not new to Anglicans; they had always existed among a fairly numerous section of this Church. He went on to show an acquaintance with 17th century ecclesiastical history:

> Donc vous voyez que nous avons des raisons historiques pour nous féliciter de voir ces principes, qui touchent de si près à ceux de l'Église catholique elle-même, professés aujourd hui si hautement par un si grand nombre de membres et du clergé et des laiques de l'Église d'Angleterre.

He described these principles: the ancient form of the liturgy had been retained and the three-fold hierarchy of bishops, priests and deacons; the first four ecumenical Councils were recognised and nothing was professed to be taught which did not conform to the consent of the Fathers of the primitive

Church. Ambrose felt the English Church could be regarded as schismatical, like the Greek, rather than heretical as the Protestants of Europe. Points of agreement existed: the system contained many Catholic precepts; there were upright souls, sincere and pious, touched by the grace of God, but also many contradictions. He asked for prayers from the 'elder sons of the Catholic Church' for England.

On 24th August 1840 Ambrose and Laura left Grace Dieu in the 'poney' carriage for Glenn where they were to stay until the 26th with an Anglican clergy family called Apthorpe. They were late in starting at 11.30 am, and as they drove near to Mount St Bernard, they passed a carriage containing John Rouse Bloxam and one of his five brothers (incumbent of a Leicestershire parish) to whom he was on a visit. Both Ambrose and Bloxam descended and the latter presented a letter of introduction which he was intending to deliver from Dr Rock, Chaplain to Lord Shrewsbury, whose acquaintance Bloxam had made as a fellow liturgiologist. Their intention was to visit the monastery. A brief conversation followed and both carriages went their way. In January 1841 Ambrose decided that this chance encounter had been engineered by Providence; he must seize the opportunity thus offered. On the feast of the Conversion of St Paul he wrote Bloxam at Magdalen College a very long letter[49] It was the forerunner of many, in both directions, and drew in others among Tractarian contemporaries of Bloxam. Ambrose's contacts with the Oxford men had begun.

(ii) Finale

The hesitation which Ambrose showed (he met Bloxam in August 1840, but did not write to him until the following January) once more illustrates the nature of that innate pragmatism which he would have considered inspirational in origin. There were factors required to make the moment of initiative propitious. Ambrose was particularly concerned during that autumn whether it should be Passionist or Rosminian missions which were to be permanently established on the estate. But it is doubtful whether the extent of his involvement precluded other commitments: it was his custom to operate on a broad

front. As ever, his writings, theological discussions and missionary plans were woven into a social and family life which
continued to be full and varied.

Alice was born a few days after the visit to Glenn and the
crucial meeting with Bloxam. This was followed by a visit to
Grace Dieu by the Shrewsburys and Pugin (who left at 6.30
am). Later Ambrose and Laura made a return visit of ten days
to Alton Towers; the infant Alice accompanied her parents
and became very ill. A return home on her account was
prevented by a doctor who said it would not be safe: he found
her suffering from 'spasmodic affection occasioned by wind';
he ordered two grams of 'soda' and two drops of sal volatile in
a tea spoonful of dill water; her back and stomach were to be
rubbed with oil and brandy and as a last resort she was to be
put into a warm bath. The remedies, or nature, effected a
rapid improvement. On their arrival back at Grace Dieu Ambrose and Laura found 'all our darling children quite well'; but
not for long, for in November Amo was thrown from his
donkey and broke his collar bone.

M. Jules Gondon of the Paris *L'Univers* made a significant
visit during the following month.

Both Bishop Walsh and Bishop Wiseman had been guests at
Alton; also Pugin who made the customary early departure.
Developments at Oxford were certainly discussed. Lord Shrewsbury was not in sympathy with the Tractarians whom he thought
not to be trusted: they professed Catholic beliefs, but would not
leave the Anglican Church for the Catholic. No doubt he made
these views as clear in his conversation with Ambrose as he did
in his letters (some of which have survived). It may partly have
been this that acted as a temporary brake on Ambrose, but not
for long; he was on several occasions to show himself capable
of defying his chief benefactor. Spencer's unhappy experience
at Oxford may also have caused momentary hesitation.

By the beginning of 1841 Ambrose had clearly reached a
decisive phase in his thinking about the writers of the Tracts.
Since 1839 he had come to the conclusion that he could no
longer continue to oppose the validity of Anglican orders. In
that year he wrote[1] to the Prior of the Dominican Convent of
the Holy Cross at Leicester: he cited various historical prec-
edents and arguments deduced from them:

. . . I think it impossible for me to argue any further against the Anglican Orders . . . As far as my own feelings and wishes are concerned I have always wished that the Anglican Orders might be admitted, as I am certain it would be a great point gained towards the reunion of the High Church party with the Catholick Church, and I am inclined to think that if a certain number of the leading English Catholicks were agreed to this, the Holy See would be very glad to open a negotiation with the Oxford Divines on the basis of this admission . . .

To the embarrassment of his biographers, Ambrose clearly maintained his opinion on the validity issue; in 1862, for example, he included[2] in a form of prayer 'for the reconciliation of the Anglican Church with the Church Catholick' the phrase:

Behold O Lord the Tears of thy antient and noble spouse the holy Anglican Church, for holy she is in her hierarchy, and in her sacraments . . .

An article in the January number of the *British Critic*[3] became the final catalyst. Two letters of the period illustrate Ambrose's state of mind: the first was to Lord Shrewsbury[4]

The new number of the *British Critic*, which has just come out for this month of January, I particularly recommend; it is beautiful, full of Catholick feeling and sighing for the restoration of Catholick Unity for our distracted and divided England; . . . the Catholick movement at Oxford I certainly regard as the brightest symptom of England's reconversion . . .

The second was to Laura's cousin and former guardian, Lord Clifford[5]:

I do not know whether you keep yourself *au courant* of the Anglo-Catholick movement at Oxford, let me urge upon you to get this January's number of the *British Critick*, you will find ten times more genuine Catholicism in that, than in all the numbers of the *Dublin Review, Tablet, Cath Magazine* yet published put together, and without that coarseness that vulgarity that frothiness, that base political truckling, that littleness of Nationality as contradistinguished from genuine patriotism, which I must say marks and disfigures everyone of our so-called English Catholick publications. Fortunately it does not matter that such stuff is written by our little *Penmen*, for the great Anglican Families trouble themselves mightily little about such insignificant writers.

A selection of the letters that passed between Bloxam and Ambrose in 1841–1842 form part of a volume published by R.D. Middleton[6] in 1947. It draws upon documents which are still contained in the archives of Magdalen College. But the communication between the two men needs orchestrating, as it were, with correspondence between Ambrose and other Tractarians in order to provide a more complete view of the episode. Most notable, for their interest and importance in regard to future events, were the letters which Ambrose exchanged with J. H. Newman. Those with William George Ward[7], Frederick William Faber[8] and John Dobrée Dalgairns[9] have an additional significance since these Oxford figures also were to leave the Anglican communion and their futures were, to some extent, tied up with Ambrose's own.

The letter of 25 January 1841 which Ambrose addressed to Bloxam at Magdalen College was the first of over forty within the next ten months. They were, for the most part, long, discursive, enthusiastic and concessionary, in contrast to the letters of Bloxam which were brief, cautious and donnish. Ambrose's starting point was the *British Critic*. It becomes increasingly clear that it was two recent articles in that periodical which precipitated his action: their subjects could not have been closer to his heart, for one concerned Anti-Christ (written by Newman) and the other by Frederick Oakeley[10] on Plain Chant. Ambrose had passed the first, he said, to several learned continental theologians who in pronouncing it worthy of Bossuet[11], did not object to 'the castigation bestowed on the English and Irish Roman Catholic body'. The article on Plain Chant was 'most satisfactory and truly Catholick, indeed much more Catholick than one written three or four years ago . . . on the same subject in the *Dublin Review*'. What had struck him quite as much as the Catholicism of that article, was its deep and devotional spirit.

Ambrose proceeded to explain how he laboured on every occasion to 'soften down the asperities which exist on our side, and which I candidly acknowledge display too often in Catholick writers amongst us a spirit quite unworthy of Xtian

Charity'. He continued:

> I am convinced that what I have urged in this point of view in several quarters has had its effect, and though unpalatable to many, it will serve in some measure at least to restrain them. Nor will I ever lose an opportunity of thus opposing to the utmost of my power that bitter spirit against the Anglican Church which too many among us entertain.

With these words Ambrose outlined the attitude he was to carry with him to his grave. It was a courageous and at the time idiosyncratic stand, denigrated by many as failure to cast off former Anglican traits, but represented by himself as the pursuit of Christian charity and a comprehension of the meaning of catholicism[12]. After some passages of a historical kind, he concluded by saying that it was no new thing for Catholics of *various rites* to live together in the same country, each being governed even by *Bishops in ordinary*[13] He himself had joined the Roman rite 17 years before, though for several years before he had regarded himself as a Catholic, while still following the modern Anglican rite. It should be possible, in the interests of unity, for Anglicans to lay aside the Book of Common Prayer, the Roman Catholics, the Roman rite, and let 'the antient rites of Sarum and York' resume their place. As was often to be the case, he had chosen an ill-timed moment for this statement; authorities in Rome were pressing for a uniform Roman liturgy and the Pope had declared variety 'deplorable'.[14]

The wretched state of the poor in England with their 'miserable clouded countenances' was a reproach to the nation, he claimed. It was the Church which should rescue and restore them.

After suggestions of some reasonableness, Ambrose departed from what could, by any stretch of the imagination, be considered acceptable in Rome: it might be possible he thought for Anglican Bishops and priests to retain their wives as the price to be paid for union; and certain relaxations of ancient canons could perhaps be permitted in future. The Holy See might sanction 'the suppression of the direct invocation of saints in the publick liturgy'; the use of pictures and images might be regulated, so as to be considered proper by Anglicans.

My earnest hope and prayer is that *negotiations* for this re-

union, as rather for the solemn declaration of an union . . .
should commence as soon as possible, there is surely no reason
now against negotiation anymore than in Archbishop Wake's
time or in that of Archbishop Laud, and this is unquestionable
that at the present day the probabilities of success are much
greater that they were then . . .

Twice Ambrose referred to the *Catholicks* of Oxford; he
declared that 'on all the fundamental points of Xtianity, there
is no difference between the real Anglican and Members of the
French, Spanish, Italian, German or American Churches'; he
was disposed to admit the genuineness of Bloxam's priesthood.
With the presentation of two books (his translation of Montalembert's *Life of St Elizabeth of Hungary*, one on John Shrewsbury's holy daughter Gwendoline) and the expressed wish that
visits might be exchanged, Ambrose brought his letter (which
was more like a tract) to an end.

Bloxam replied briefly[15]: the main thrust of his answer was
that with permission he was circulating Ambrose's letter to
some friends. One of these was Oakeley, enthusiastic to follow
up the suggestions made; he asked that the circulation of
Ambrose's letters be increased; Ward to be included. The
former should be asked to Oxford, but it was important to be
guided by Newman, who was not encouraging and wrote
Bloxam a note[16] which could be sent to Ambrose 'from an
anonymous friend who had seen his letter'. Newman mentioned the doctrine of transubstantiation as set out by the
Roman Church as a difficulty: 'whether it be a large or a small
difficulty is not the question, but whether I can subscribe that
to be true for which I can see no reason'.

Ambrose's next excursion into print was a letter to the
Tablet, a Roman Catholic publication which had been inaugu-
rated in May 1840 under the editorship of Frederick Lucas, a
former Quaker who was converted in 1838. His early moderation was of short duration and by the beginning of 1841 his use
of unrestrained language and abuse of those whose opinions
differed from his own (such as the Catholic aristocracy and the
Oxford men) became causes of offence. Ambrose wrote[17] to
accuse the *Tablet* of discourtesy: the 'Puseyites' as the Tractarians were apt to be called as a term of mockery, had been
referred to as 'a new sect'.[18] He did not hesitate to declare:

The reunion of the Churches would not be a difficult matter at the present day and at the present favourable juncture. Take the Church of England as her canons and her liturgy testify her to be, and I declare that the chasm which separates her from the Catholic Church is but small.

Although Ambrose received some sporadic encouragement, the entry aroused protest in the main which persisted for some months. A correspondent[19] from the Isle of Wight whose views found frequent exposure in *The Tablet* took particular exception:

The writings of Mr Phillipps are not only injurious, but as he is a layman, highly censurable.

But a prominent Anglican had taken note; he knew of, but had not yet met the writer[20]: W. E. Gladstone wrote in his diary on 18 February[21] 'Read A. Phillipps' beautiful letter in *The Tablet*'.

While he was waiting for response from Oxford, Ambrose wrote several more letters to *L'Univers*. He set himself the role of interpreting the mind of the Tractarians to the French intelligentsia. It can well be compared with the interpretative part played later by Pusey addressed to Anglicans, in regard to Roman Catholic belief and practice. Ambrose was anxious that the catholicity of the Anglican Church should not be measured by the current utterances of the Evangelical or liberal wings, but by her historical precepts, orders, canons, hierarchy, liturgy and so on. Likewise Pusey was to maintain that the orthodoxy of Rome should not be regarded as invalidated by the superstitious practices, with their connotations of magic, developed over the years by peasant populations in southern Europe.

In the first letter[22] Ambrose illustrated the place of the Anglican Church within the Catholic whole in relation to the reasons which prompted him to leave 17 years before: in practice at least the body of members had become separated from Catholic Unity. He used the word practice, he said, because he knew that in theory a great many of the most learned and most pious members of the Anglican Church had never been separated from it. Catholic principles had, he believed, never been entirely given up, although in practice perverted, trampled underfoot by the great majority of members, but the theologians called Puseyites whom he held to be the true representatives of the Anglican Church, continued their chain of tradition. The Oxford Anglicans, in trying to rekindle these embers which had been nearly extinguished, instead of being the object of jeers by the advocates of Catholicism, should on the contrary, receive in their efforts, kindness and encouragement. Ambrose asked the rhetorical question why should he become involved in this vexatious affair. It was because of his wish to see every English Catholic similarly involved: because hope for the return of England to Catholic Unity lay in the scene before them. He repeated his *Tablet* statement that the distance which separated the two Churches was small: he identified the similarities.

The second letter[23] made many of the same points at the same great length. Ambrose gave some historical data from the 17th century and concentrated on the sacraments where he did not see 'any difference between true Anglicans and Catholics'. He expanded the contrast between theory and practice, already touched upon. He ended with some words of 'your sublime Bossuet' which he felt to be an apt interpolation:

> Such an intelligent nation ... will not remain ... in this establishment. The respect that it retains for the Fathers and its continuous and careful researches will bring it back to the doctrine of the early centuries.

He was more right than he knew.

Before a full reply came to his original proposals, Ambrose wrote Bloxam a second very long letter.[24] It would not be advisable, he thought, for Anglican clergy to make any advance to Roman Catholick authority, certainly not in England: 'I put them wholly out of the question; it would be most injurious ... to negotiate with them'. A rough scheme of the terms on which reunion might be effected should be drawn up at Oxford, circulated privately among the clergy and once a majority were in favour, to come to an understanding with parliament: then a double mission from Church and state could go to the Pope with their plans. It was for the Church of England to formulate the nature of the terms. Ambrose insisted that he knew from authority that concessions could be made. He inferred that he had gathered such from 'learned theologians' whom he did not specify. Luigi Gentili was no doubt one who had shared discussions on the Tracts: another may have been Fr Pagani, the Rosminian English Provincial. Ambrose showed some correspondence with the Tractarians to Dominic Barberi, but no concessions would have been forthcoming from this quarter. Newman's comment on transubstantiation drew forth Ambrose's response that the term be excluded in any scheme of reunion: the Greeks had never used the word, but expressed belief in the mystery: he thought Anglicans held a similar view. Copies of *The Tablet* and *L'Univers* articles and a communication[25] from the monks of Mount St Bernard (sixteen men; three priests and thirteen lay brothers) addressed to 'the Reverend Clergy of the ancient Anglican Church residing at Oxford and elsewhere', completed the package. 'Let hostilities cease', they wrote 'Let there be sweet reconciliation, a perfect union . . . May the God of Love . . . be pleased in his tender mercy to remove all obstacles; and inspire the authorities of the Catholic Church to grant you every *possible* concession that you may reasonably desire'.

Bloxam's reply[26] enclosed a copy of the latest of the Tracts which had reached the number 90; written by J. H. Newman under the title '*Remarks on Certain Passages in the Thirty Nine Articles*',[27] it was to become the most celebrated of all. Bloxam invited Ambrose to Oxford after Easter; it is not his letter, but that from Newman[28], from which he sent some extracts, which is of the greater interest:

> I feel most strongly and cannot conceal it, viz that, while Rome is what she is, union is impossible – that we too must change I do not deny.
> Rome must change first of all her spirit. I must see more sanctity in her than I do at present . . . I do verily think that, with all our sins, there is more sanctity in the Church of England and Ireland, than in the Roman Catholic bodies in the same countries.

Newman expressed himself as particularly offended by political intrigue: 'Never can I think such ways the footsteps of Christ.' Barefoot preachers in manufacturing towns, pelted and trampled upon might convert England. (They were prophetic words, for Newman was to make his own submission to one such). In the meantime he found many portions of formularies interpreted 'in a sense which seems to us very uncatholic'.

Ambrose reacted[29] patiently: he had stopped the circulation of Wiseman's tracts against high-church claims in his neighbourhood; he felt the Oxford men should encourage the same attitude towards Roman Catholics. Newman wrote[30] to Bloxam again at length a few days later, which letter was passed to Ambrose. The latter's correspondence breathed a beautiful spirit, he thought, but he could not agree that 'the time is arrived for the holy endeavour to effect the reunion of the Churches'. To anyone with a proposal of negotiations for reconciliation he would recommend they address the bishop, not himself. He used harsher words than heretofore in relation to the Roman Catholic Church: hollow, insincere, political, ambitious, unscrupulous. 'Where was written work', he asked 'which evidenced any heart, any depth of spiritual experience, or fullness of faith and love?'.

Bloxam felt the contents would cause pain, which they did: he also had to tell Ambrose first, that Newman did not see fit to meet him during his Oxford visit; secondly, that contained in a subsequent note was a message 'as from a friend': 'If Mr P. [Phillipps] wishes to *extinguish* the Catholick movement among us, he cannot take a better way than by introducing foreign divines to Oxford'.

Ambrose faced[31] the criticisms and sought at length to provide evidence to offset them: he rejoiced at the prospect of meeting in Oxford; official negotiations were far from his thoughts; he would certainly come alone, without 'foreign divines'.

By mid-March Bloxam had become increasingly cautious:[32] everything that had passed between them must be kept secret. 'There is a heavy storm brooding over us'; considerable excitement was raging in the university. Newman's intentions over Tract 90 on the 39 Articles had been misunderstood. A Preface which E. B. Pusey (who was a close collaborator) wrote to the 1865 edition[33] of Tract 90, tried to make clear what they had been:

> We had all been educated in a traditional system which had practically imported into the Articles a good many principles

which were not contained in them nor suggested by them, yet which were habitually identified with them. The writers of the *Tracts for the Times* as they became more acquainted with Antiquity and the Fathers, gradually and independently of one another laid these aside . . . we proposed no system to ourselves, but laid aside, piece by piece, the system of ultra Protestant interpretation which had encrusted round the Articles . . . the expositions to which we were accustomed, and which were, to our minds, the genuine expositions of the articles, had never before been brought into one focus, as they were in Tract 90. What was to us perfectly natural was, to some others who had not examined the Articles from the same point of view as ourselves, unnatural . . . We had examined the Articles in order to see whether or no they contradicted other truths; they who did not believe these other truths, had no occasion to examine them in this aspect, and consequently had not so examined them . . . We had an interest . . . to vindicate our Church from unsoundness as to any Catholic truth.

On 8 March four senior tutors in the University addressed the Editor of the Tracts and charged No 90 of a highly dangerous tendency in suggesting that certain very important errors of the Church of Rome were not condemned by Articles of the Church of England. The Hebdomadal Board (Heads of Houses) took up the challenge and without giving Newman the chance to explain his tract, resolved[34] that it had evaded rather than explained the Articles. Next day appeared Newman's explanation in the form of an *Open Letter to Dr Jelf*[35]. He contended that he considered the 39 Articles to condemn the authoritative teaching of the Church of Rome on the subjects which the four tutors had suggested he did not. 'I only say that whereas they were written before the decrees of Trent they were not directed against those decrees'.

Ambrose was on the whole encouraged by what he saw as Newman's firmness and courage in opposing the view that the 39 Articles were irreconcilable with the teaching that Newman saw as Catholic, on the authority of earlier Anglican divines. He decided to answer those points in Newman's *Letter to Dr Jelf* with which he disagreed, by a publication of his own. Bloxam, still alarmed by the climate of controversy and by the fear that his letters were being opened, wrote[36] to postpone temporarily the visit to Oxford. But the process that he had set in motion continued its momentum. Faber[37] wrote at length commenting upon Ambrose's 'interesting and important letters'. Bloxam could pass on that 'there is at least one clergyman of our Church who cordially enters into his wishes and desires to give in his prayers for the restoration of unity throughout the whole Catholic body'. Faber felt that Ambrose seriously miscalculated the feeling of the Anglican Church as it affected the point of union with Rome. He had 'no scruple in saying ... that the actual condition of the Roman Communion, as brought before our eyes in this country ... is likely to continue a most serious evil ... to the speedy accomplishment of our mutual wishes'.

W. G. Ward[38] wrote also, delighted with Ambrose's letters and appreciative of his 'generous and Christian wishes for our Church ... would that the time for that union were as near as Mr Phillipps in his earnest wish for it considers it to be'. J Brande Morris[39] sent a poem which expressed longing for unity, for transmission to Ambrose.[40]

Dalgairns and Ward chose this disturbed moment to write a long letter for publication in *L'Univers*[41]. It was anonymous and bore only the signature 'A young student at the University of Oxford' and the date Passion Sunday [March 28th] 1841. Ward wrote the substance and Dalgairns, as a Guernseyman bi-lingual, translated it into French. The editorial preamble reflected on the movement towards the return to unity which the great powers of grace seemed to inspire in the Anglican Church at that moment. The letter itself expressed a longing for union; it gave a lengthy resumé of Tract 90 and mentioned Newman by name. It was sent to Ambrose for onward despatch to *L'Univers*; he took it first to the monastery to show it to the monks: a course he later had reason to regret.

Reactions began to reach him from Roman Catholic quarters to whom he had shown correspondence with Oxford. Nicholas Wiseman wrote[42] to say his object was to temper the minds of Catholics 'to the feelings with which he thought they ought to view the actual state of controversy'. (Clearly both he and Ambrose were aware of the grip held by bigotry and prejudice on all sides.) Wiseman said he had not read Newman's *Letter to Dr Jelf*, but when he had he would see if he could be of service by writing on it. 'God knows that I would give my life if it would hasten the reunion of this country, or a part of it, with the Apostolic See and the Church Catholic'.

Five days later came the much fuller letter already referred to[43] in which Wiseman expressed the need for new blood in the English Catholic community and the advantages that the Tractarians could bring. '. . . If the Oxford divines entered the Church, we must be ready to fall into the shade and take up our position in the background'. Bishop Walsh had said that since this movement had occurred in his District 'We should both be guilty of a serious neglect of duty were we to omit anything in our power to smooth the way towards a reconciliation. In fact it would be the happiest event in our lives to be in any way instrumental in bringing it about'. He intended to write to Newman.

Ambrose communicated[44] his joy at Wiseman's response: 'He is decidedly one of the first men in Europe'. He also spoke of the revival of 'true Catholick' literature on the continent, no less than 'true Catholick and Christian' art, which he saw as indications of the return of a healthier state of mind. Bloxam refused an invitation to Grace Dieu for Easter, enclosed a copy of Newman's *Letter to the Bishop of Oxford*[45], and commented favourably on an encouraging note which Digby had sent Ambrose. Bloxam, who liked Digby's *Mores*, had lent a copy of it to the President of Magdalen.

Ambrose's pamphlet[46] which replied to Newman's *Letter to Dr Jelf* reached him on April 2nd; a remarkable feat of typography by modern standards; the manuscript was completed on 25 March. He and Pugin took it immediately to the monastery and a copy was despatched to Newman. It was the first piece of work other than translations that Ambrose had written. He expressed his admiration for Newman's stand and said that he was not aware of anything which could appear objectionable to Catholic minds in Tract 90: but there were some protests he must make on the *Letter to Dr Jelf*: Newman has contrasted the Council of Trent with the authoritative teaching of the Church of Rome: it was not a distinction nor a definition Ambrose could allow. He also took offence against the phrase 'the Roman system preaches the Blessed Virgin Mary, the saints and purgatory, instead of the Holy Trinity, heaven and hell'. The reflections on infallibility, pardons and St

Bonaventura's Psalter and honour due to the saints, all received notice.

It drew from Newman the first letter addressed to Ambrose personally, and was followed closely by another[47]. Newman had found the pamphlet 'to be like everything you undertake, full of earnestness and charity'; it was inferred that this was in contrast to the outlook of Wiseman. He did not see any prospect of unity 'within our time and I despair of it being effected without great sacrifices on all hands. Were the Roman Church in Ireland different from what it is, one immense stumbling block would be removed'. The Bishop of Oxford had asked him to stop the Tracts; to have resisted him would have been to place himself in an utterly wrong position from which he could never have recovered. At the end came a warning: 'I can earnestly desire a union between my Church and yours; I cannot listen to the thought of your being joined by individuals among us'.

In Ambrose's reply[48] he expressed surprise that any spirit save that of charity should have emanated from Wiseman: 'If as yet circumstances are destined for a little while longer to keep us separated . . . there is at least no reason why we should add expressions which serve to make still more bitter a division, which already to noble and generous minds is almost too bitter to be endured'. These sentiments were a constant refrain throughout Ambrose's long years of attempts at reconciliation. He pleaded on Wiseman's behalf that the latter had not had the opportunities which he himself had experienced of knowing the mind and heart of so many both of the clergy and laity of the Anglican Church. It was a particular feature of Ambrose's life (which can be seen in detail in chapter 6) and one that singled him out among his contemporaries. He felt that Newman's *Letter to the Bishop of Oxford*, like all writings from this pen bore a stamp of learning and power of argument that would do honour to a Father of the Church, though it struck him as 'less Catholick in its tone' than others.

Bishop Wiseman sent Ambrose an important letter on Good Friday:[49] he had been the victim of condemnations and insults as the result of the position he had adopted towards the Tractarians. But believing that a fire had been kindled, not by them, but by God, he felt that the state of things in England ought to be made known to the Pope. He was conscious that 'erroneous and prejudiced views of matters were circulating' [much of it in the pages of *The Tablet*]; it was his intention to write a full report for Cardinal Mai (secretary of the Propaganda Fide) with a request that he show it to none but the Pope. He would do nothing until Ambrose gave the word.

> Let me know that the Viceregent of Xt approves of my cause and understands my motives, and I shall not care for all the world nor allow difference of opinion to check my exertions.

Ambrose sent[50] Newman a copy of this letter with a lengthy accompaniment. He had been to Oscott to consult Wiseman on some interesting matters:

> We feel, my dear Sir, that God has raised you up as a glorious instrument in his hand, not only for the reconciliation of the English Church with the Church Catholic, but likewise for the purpose of working out a renovation and a reform in the whole of Christendom … *you will find henceforth* in our Church powerful assistance towards carrying out the great end we all have in view. Bishop Wiseman authorizes me to say that he for one intends to devote himself to the object of facilitating matters, not only with the Holy See, but with the Catholick Bishops generally … Abuses in the practise [sic] of the Catholick system so far from constituting a legitimate bar to reunion, form perhaps a powerful argument in favour of it. If you wish to see them reformed, let the Anglican Church unite herself to us, and we shall soon be strong enough to reform them.

The meeting with Mark Carricchia in Rome twelve years earlier was again recounted, as evidence of Ambrose's commitment to the cause of reunion. 'I believed the word of that most holy man and every day of my life confirms my belief in his simple but wonderful words'.

Anxious to keep Lord Shrewsbury in touch with events, Ambrose wrote[51] to him in Rome to tell him in particular of the 'young student of Oxford's' letter in *L'Univers*. He gave an enthusiastic picture of Wiseman's intentions and the fact that 'Mr Newman has lately received the adhesion of *several hundreds* of the clergy: this is publickly known and therefore I can state it'. He was glad the peer was returning to England the following year, '. . . If things go on as I expect, you will be wanted then' Ambrose made it clear that corporate reunion was the ideal to which he was dedicated.

> Meanwhile I beseech you to give us all the assistance you can. Urge at Rome the necessity of extreme prudence and forbearance, to do everything to *encourage*, nothing to *damp*: not to call upon those men to quit their own communion in order to join ours, but to proceed on courageously with their holy and glorious intention of *reconciling* their Church to ours . . . a false step would spoil all.

The news that Bloxam's friend Bernard Smith[52] had visited Oscott and that there were so many urgent topics to discuss, prompted Ambrose to visit Oxford immediately without consultation. He booked in at the Angel Inn on 30 April; fortunately Bloxam was in residence at Magdalen. In a letter to Laura, her husband described his delight at all he was shown: the beautiful, glorious and solemn buildings by moonlight; breakfast with Bloxam in Magdalen College; three parish churches 'fitted up in a very Catholick way'. He dined in hall where the Fellows were polite and kind. Mr Newman was unfortunately in London. The Roman breviary had been translated into English with everything precisely as in the Latin. 'Nothing can be more determined than they are to reunite their Church to the Catholick'. The chanting in Magdalen Chapel was very beautiful: matins and vespers were sung each day; a latin hymn was to be sung on the tower at five a.m. the following morning. Dr Rock, chaplain to Lord Shrewsbury, who was on a visit to Bloxam had dissuaded Ambrose from attending, but he followed his own inclinations and was present at Evensong the following day. 'My holy confessor here thought very differently from Dr Rock of my being present at the Divine Office . . . But he is a foreign priest and that makes all the difference' he wrote[53] on his return. Ambrose sat up half the night with W. G. Ward discussing the possibilities of reunion, but as Ward's biographer[54] put it, while concerned with the subject, he was against any sudden action at the time, beyond the reform of abuses in each Church. Ambrose also met John Brande Morris.

That members of the Church of England might be encouraged to change their allegiance consequent upon consultations on reunion, worried Bloxam. He asked[55] Ambrose what was his position in relation to the Anglican clergy of his neighbourhood: he received several long replies and the assurance that there was no state of hostility. Ambrose felt he was on terms of a most friendly nature, particularly with the clergy of the parishes on his father's estate. A large number of the inhabitants were dissenters belonging to several sects:

> In all that we do we put prominently before the people that we look forward to the holy reunion of the Anglican Church with the Church Catholick, and we hope that the day is not distant, when that antient Church will again possess all the privileges of an undoubted Catholic Church. Hence we are preparing good and sound members for your Church, as soon as she shall be in a sound and healthy state so as to receive us back into her fold.

Meanwhile local clergy were being encouraged to return to their 'antient practices'.

Wiseman, pleased with the report of the Oxford visit, told[56] Ambrose that he would send a second letter to the Pope through Cardinal Mai. It might be necessary to make a visit to Rome if he were destined to become a channel of communication with the Oxford men; papal instructions as to recommending mildness, prayers, calling on bishops for reform would be necessary.

From an unexpected source came a response to the Ward/Dalgairns letter from 'a young student of Oxford' in *L'Univers*. Dominic Barberi[57] from Ere in Belgium wrote at length in Latin a communication addressed to 'the Professors [sic] of the University of Oxford on the occasion of seeing an Epistle from one of their body in a Journal called *L'Univers*'. It was forwarded to Bloxam by Spencer. The fervent, emotional style expressed ideas that were received rather than conceived and showed the restricted nature of his background. Of Tract 90 and its authors he was sharply critical. But a correspondence opened up with Dalgairns which was to have remarkable and lasting consequences.

Wiseman in his efforts to be more conciliatory received a blow which he took very hard. He had written to Newman, he

explained[58] to Ambrose, and the response was 'a most distressing letter . . . which has thrown me on my back and painfully
dispirited me'. He kept back a communication he had written
to Rome. Newman had expressed his regret that Wiseman had
attempted to vindicate the invocations of the Blessed Virgin in
the Church in his discussions with William Palmer. Ambrose
told[59] Bloxam that the Bishop was greatly dismayed, grieved
and annoyed. He allowed himself a certain degree of spleen of
his own over the difficulties he faced. 'My battling for your
Church . . . I find dreadfully uphill work owing to the terrible
state of division in which I find your clergy . . . nevertheless in
spite of discouragement, I shall go on'.

Bloxam was puzzled as to what there could have been in
Newman's letter so to upset Wiseman.[60] He did not think it
advisable for Ambrose to mix Anglicans in his societies for
prayer; 'Our Bishops would strongly object to it . . .' Ambrose
tried to explain[61] the unhappy impressions received by Wiseman's mind. He had feared that Newman was drawing back
from the position he had held in Tract 90. Ambrose had done his
best to counteract this view while the Bishop had been a guest
at Grace Dieu; Wiseman had replied that he hoped his host
was right. Ambrose asked why Bloxam persisted in referring
to his *Communion*; why not speak of his *rite*. In the Catholick
Church there never had been any difference of *Communion*;
but from Apostolic times there had been difference of rites,
and in that sense a diversity of churches, but no other.

Wiseman recovered sufficiently by July to contemplate talks
with some of the Tractarians on a forthcoming visit to Oxford.
He had received a visit at Oscott from F. T. Wackerbarth an
Anglican cleric from Lichfield: 'Very little will, I think', he
wrote[62] to Ambrose 'fix him amongst us, and give us the
primitiae of the Oxford Movement. He is particularly anxious
to visit Mount St Bernard and if you could give him hospitality
for a day or two, I think you would do an immense amount of
good'. In spite of having received a severe letter from Newman[63]
who was clearly seeing all the correspondence, Ambrose agreed
to try and fix an Oxford meeting between Wiseman and the
Tractarians.

Whilst admiring Ambrose's zeal and charity, Newman had
written that he did not welcome a movement being started on

behalf of a union between the Churches. 'I cannot be party to any agitation; but mean to remain quiet in my own place and do all I can to make others take the same course . . .' He felt it a painful duty to keep aloof from all Roman Catholics. Ambrose sent a long and patient reply,[64] merely remonstrating mildly at the use of the word agitation. Bloxam wrote Newman a worried note[65] on receipt of the news of Wackerbarth's presence at Oscott: Bernard Smith had attended, as the only Anglican, the ceremonies in connection with the opening of St Chad's Cathedral at Birmingham and the ceremonial had a great effect upon him; 'still he makes no mention of any sudden resolution of leaving us'. A discussion of Ambrose's letter followed. Bloxam did not see fit to receive Wiseman on his Oxford visit, but Newman agreed to do so and the two men, with Dalgairns, met in Newman's rooms at Oriel for the first time since the spring of 1833 in the English College in Rome.

Ambrose, Laura, Amo and Ebby (Everard) left for Barmouth in the poney carriage on 6 July: the doctor had to be called before their departure, as Reginald had an accident, but it was not serious. (The three younger children made a separate journey with their nurses in the chariot and arrived in Wales on the 10th). The first night was spent at the George Inn at Lichfield where Ambrose took tea with Wackerbarth who had visited Grace Dieu a fortnight earlier. In the morning they breakfasted with him in his lodging in the Cathedral close, went to the Cathedral at 10 a.m. and remained for the service. A further call was made on Wackerbarth on the return journey on August 21.

Spencer joined the de Lisle family in Wales and despite the ceaseless activity of bathing, boating, visits to Snowdon, Carnarvon, Festiniog, Beddgelert, Bala, Dolgelly, Ruthin, Denbigh and Holywell, the output of writing was undiminished. Spencer wrote a long letter to *L'Univers*[66] in which he added his witness to what Ambrose had already written on the Tractarians. The nearer they drew to Catholic ideas, he said, the more they seemed determined to rectify their position not by leaving the boat as though despairing of it, but by bringing it with them to the port of unity. They insisted that it was a misunderstanding on the part of Catholics to imagine that the succession

of Anglican orders had been broken. Ambrose found time to
write two further letters to the French journal,[67] in the second
he added a long paper on the intercession of Mary the mother
of Jesus.

The long awaited visit of Bloxam to Grace Dieu took place
on the 23 to the 26 August: Wackerbarth came also. Gentili
and Pagani, the Rosminian Provincial, were present, as was
Moses Furlong[68] who preached at Benediction on the first
evening. Wackerbarth attended in choir in Anglican surplice
and hood, but not Bloxam. After High Mass in honour of St
Bartholomew on the 24 August, all went to spend the day at
the monastery. On the following day they went to Garendon
and walked in the grounds; a visit to Oscott completed the
stay. Bloxam then drove to his brother at Twy Cross. Wackerbarth returned a few days later and was joined by the son of
an Anglican cleric from Edinburgh by the name of Greensides
who was a convert to Roman Catholicism on his way to Rome
to train as a priest. They spent the night at the monastery. All
their names, as that of 'Blocksom' [sic] found their way into a
report in *L'Univers* on 12 October, to Ambrose's intense indignation.

Newman, with an explanation that he had received several
of Ambrose's letters from Bloxam, now wrote[69] to Ambrose at
some length. He expressed his concern at the exaggeration on
Ambrose's part, particularly on the attitude towards Mary:

> And now I fear I am going to pain you by telling that you
> make approaches in doctrine on our part towards you closer
> than they really are. I cannot help repeating what I have many
> times said in print that your services and devotions to St Mary
> in matter of fact do most deeply pain me. I am only stating it
> as a fact.

Ambrose's reply has not survived.

Bloxam's thanks[70] for his visit were warm and appreciative:
he was particularly grateful for Wiseman's 'laborious attentions'. He had great hope 'in spite of certain unpleasant
charges, that prospects were really brightening'. Newman was
reading over Spencer's letters and would send some remarks
on them. Bloxam had prepared him for what Wiseman was
about to send out. The next day Bloxam continued: Oakeley

and Ward, who had been to Oscott, had been delighted with the truly Catholic ethos there. He was anxious for Pugin's health which had been reported as poor: 'we must all persuade him to take care of himself, for his life is most valuable'. A first mention was made of Bloxam's friend Richard Waldo Sibthorp[71] a former demy (scholar) of Magdalen, as anxious for an opportunity to pay Ambrose a visit. It was his action that brought the Ambrose /Bloxam correspondence to an end.

Bishop Wiseman published his *Letter on Catholic Unity addressed to the Earl of Shrewsbury*, at Ambrose's insistence, on St Matthew's day. It was a relatively conservative document dwelling on the evils of disunion, but there was an emphasis on realities and a sense of urgency. The Church of Christ seen exclusively as that whose jurisdiction stemmed from Rome, had a paramount duty

> to heal schism and not to be deferred by past failures, nor by present difficulties, to begin at once and to persevere energetically in such measures as *directly* tend to the work of religious reunion: not to say that the time is not yet come, but to hasten it forward.

Mischief had to be ended; obstacles removed, so that people could be brought back to kinder, juster, truer views between Catholics and Anglicans. Phrases used in popular devotion should be explained; deficiencies lamented, so that prejudice might be overcome. The friendship between the state and the Established Church had cooled: worldly ties no longer meant so much.

Bloxam, writing[72] to Ambrose, said it was impossible to help liking the contents and that he was annoyed at current rash judgments passed on prayer and practices in the Roman Church. He thought the Letter would do good eventually. At Grace Dieu there was a spate of visitors: Abbé Bouqueau from Malines arrived on the 17 Sept and was despatched to Oxford to see Bloxam at the beginning of October: Bernard Smith came on the 22 Sept and Bishops Wiseman and Errington[73] on the 25th. On the 26 Ambrose sent for Mr Eddowes on account of Laura's 'fullness of blood to the head' and she was bled 10 oz; as she was awaiting the birth of her next child (Winifreda) in December, it was in modern terms an unwise procedure.

The following day Wackerbarth came once more, also W. G. Ward who was greatly impressed by the liturgy in the chapel and the life of the monks at Mount St Bernard and spoke of his host's thoughtful kindness during 'the happiest week he had ever spent'.[74] He went on to Oscott.

During the next weeks Ambrose was much taken up with writing in French to *L'Univers* who had published material with which he disagreed. First a quotation from an article in another French periodical, the *Journal des Debats* required to be answered. He thought it gave a quite erroneous view of the Anglican Church. He sprang to what he saw as its defence.[75] In *L'Univers* of 12 October he was furious to find 'copious extracts from a most injudicious and absurd letter written by one of the monks of Mount St Bernard, in which the writer had mentioned *names* … I always dreaded Wackerbarth's indiscretion, but not that the inconceivable folly of this monk has published such indiscretions to the world, I fear much mischief may result,' Ambrose wrote[76] with heat to Bloxam. He intended to write to the Editor; fortunately every name had been mis-spelt. His anger at the threatened miscarriage of his plans made him high-handed: he had written to Bishop Wiseman to ask him to forbid any of the monks for the future ever to write in the newspapers; he did not know which of them was responsible. In kinder vein he said how delighted he would be to receive Sibthorp at Grace Dieu.

At the end of October Ambrose and W. G. Ward[77] exchanged long letters on the reunion issue; they were to come closer together as Bloxam withdrew; Ward was anxious to press onward; Bloxam felt that it 'may be a duty for many years to remain as we are'. Newman's attitude, according to Ward's conjecture, was that 'We ought hardly to look forward beyond the present time'. Sibthorp appeared in Oxford and told Bloxam he wanted to consult Bishop Wiseman about a member of his congregation. Newman, who did not know Sibthorp well, but thought him psychologically delicate, tried to prevent the visit to Oscott. It took place, and Sibthorp there became a Roman Catholic.

Bloxam wrote the last letter in the series to Ambrose on 31 October.[78] It had appeared to him, he said, that the latter had expectations that certain members of the Church of England might leave it: this had now occurred; it was not as he saw the reunion process. 'I have never yet felt the slightest conviction that it is my own *individual* duty to leave the Church of England; and my repugnance to the notion is so great that I must decline any discussion of it ... Things are upon the whole working for good, and will continue to do so: if we look to God's will that we may know it ...' Bloxam later added an explanatory post script[79] to his collection of letters:

'... the secession of Sibthorp and the ardent eagerness of Dr Wiseman and Mr Phillipps to receive deserters from our camp, whilst these negotiations were being carried on, at once dispelled the notion of a Re-union of the Churches which vanished like a dream; and I no longer took any part in the correspondence with Mr Ambrose Phillipps ...'

Wackerbarth came to Grace Dieu on 20 Nov and on the 26th told Ambrose that he had decided to become a Roman Catholic. On the 1 December Bishop Wiseman arrived with Sibthorp; he received and conditionally baptised Wackerbarth who on the following day, with Sibthorp, was confirmed. On the 6th Laura stayed in bed all day and Mr Eddowes sent for Mrs Squires, the midwife, and remained till she came. All the children began to have colds except Amo. There was another false alarm on the 17th; the doctor came and soon left. Next day Sibthorp received minor orders. On the 20th Laura went to Mass but not feeling well she came out at the Communion: Winifreda, third daughter and sixth child, was born at 12.30; (Mr Eddowes arrived half an hour later); Bishop Wiseman agreed to be her godfather.

A few scattered letters passed between Ambrose and Bloxam in 1842 and the former made a second visit to Oxford in the company of Luigi Gentili in November of that year. But the spirit had gone out of the relationship because of the misunderstandings that had occurred on both sides.

Ambrose interpreted the emphasis placed by the Tractarians upon the Catholic base of their religion and the re-introduction of forms from the 17th and earlier centuries, as a sign of a desire (even if at the time unconscious) to be placed under the jurisdiction of the See of Rome as it then was. For example

Bloxam's translation of the latin Breviary, of which Ambrose bought some copies secretly, ('no one would know whence it came') appeared to him to lead in this direction. Because his own spiritual pilgrimage had caused him to place himself under the Roman obedience, he thought this must be the direction in which the Oxford men were bound. Although some Tractarians did change their allegiance, it was not in the minds of any that they should do so in 1841. Those who later went acted independently; as a movement they stayed in the Church of England, their object to influence it from within. As late as 6 October 1841, when the correspondence was about to draw to a close, Ambrose showed how far his enthusiastic longings had led him off course. He wrote[80] to Montalembert and said of the Tractarians,

> Their great object is to reunite the Anglican Church and the Catholick Church: but I think it very probable that a large body of these zealous men will join the Catholic Church at once, before the reunion takes place; so ardent are their longings for Catholick Communion.

That Ambrose should have experienced confusion in grasping the Anglican position is understandable. He did not recognise that comprehensiveness was included within the concept of catholicity; nor that to members of the Church of England 'antient formulas' (to which they gave assent) were those which belonged to the original deposit of the faith and the Fathers of the primitive Church, not to mediaeval or Tridentine times. Almost alone on the Roman Catholic side, Ambrose accepted the Tractarian view of the Anglican Church as part of the Church catholic; it would seem inconsistent of him therefore to act as if he felt they would be prepared to leave it. His tendency to create catogories of 'true' Anglicans and 'true' Catholics (the criterion of authenticity being agreement with his own point of view) was highly subjective.

Wiseman clearly thought in terms of absorption, though it would seem that his realisation of the potential value of the Oxford men made him consider the possibility of some concessions. An opinion outside ecclesiastical circles comes from the diary of C. C. F. Greville[81] who wrote of a dinner with him in August 1841:

... He came in full episcopal costume, purple stockings, tunic and gold chain. He talked religion, catholicism, protestantism and puseyism, almost the whole time ... He talked much of Pusey and Newman, and Hurrell Froude, whom Wiseman had known at Rome ... and gave us to understand not only that their opinions are very nearly the same, but that the great body of that persuasion, Pusey himself included, are very nearly ripe and ready for reunion with Rome, and he assured us that neither the Pope's supremacy nor Transubstantiation would be obstacles in their way.

Bloxam's conception of reunion was unformulated and he was very largely feeling his way throughout the correspondence; but it did not involve absorption, or submission by Anglicans. When it became obvious that such was involved, he withdrew at once. As so often, it was Newman who put the Tractarian case most clearly. In the letter to Ambrose last mentioned he wrote[82]

'I am sure, that, while you suffer, we suffer too from the separation; *but we cannot remove the obstacles*; it is with you to do so ... I have nowhere said that I can accept the decrees of Trent throughout, nor implied it. The doctrine of Transubstantiation is a great difficulty with me, as being, as I think, not primitive ... thus, you see it is not merely on grounds of expedience that we do not join you. There are positive difficulties in the way of it. And, even if there were not, we shall have no divine warrant for doing so, while we think that the Church of England is a branch of the true Church, and that intercommunion with the rest of Christendom is necessary, not for the life of a particular Church, but for its health only. I have never disguised that there are actual circumstances in the Church of Rome, which pain me much; of the removal of these I see no chance, while we join you one by one; but if our Church were prepared for a union, she might make her terms; she might gain the cup; she might protest against the extreme honour paid to St Mary; she might make some explanation of the doctrine of Transubstantiation. I am not prepared to say that a reform in other branches of the Roman Church would be necessary for our uniting with them, however desirable in itself, so that we were allowed to make a reform in our own country. We do not look towards Rome as believing that its communion is infallible, but that union is a duty.

The endeavour to make contact with the Oxford men was not a complete failure and waste of time; the record stands. Ambrose's overall attempts to overcome bitterness and prejudice, to reconcile disparities, cannot be set aside nor despised; it would seem that current factors beyond his control not his methods conspired to make them fruitless. More recent times have shown[83] how close it is possible to draw in such a process.

Chapter 5

Young England

(i) The Ideals

Attention has been drawn to the fact that Ambrose shunned
the political scene. If by this is meant membership of the
House of Commons, this was so. But his determination to
make the whole of English life aware of the claims of his
Creed, meant that he was bound to operate in several areas at
once. This he did without hesitation. While 'negotiating with
the Oxford Divines', therefore, he was simultaneously active
trying to bring his influence to bear in political and social
spheres.

Despite his Whig background, Ambrose's attitude towards
Liberalism was ambivalent. One reason for this was that early
19th century liberal principles were themselves capable of
varied interpretation. No one has stated this more clearly than
J. H. Newman at the end of his *Apologia Pro Vita Sua*[1] 'Liberty
of thought is in itself a good; but it gives an opening to false
liberty'. It could lead, he contended, to denial of the truths of
Revelation in the name of liberal rationalism. Newman's withdrawal from the Church of England was the result of his
seeing just such a tendency within it.

The overall liberal and tolerant views of Ambrose's father
served his son's own religious standpoint well; just as the
Whig party of the 1830s proved a greater friend than the
Tories to Roman Catholics in England as a whole. It was a
state of affairs Ambrose was constantly to bewail, for it
involved association with radicals and free-thinkers. On the
continent of Europe no such anti-dogmatism was implied by
the term Liberal. Ambrose's two friends Montalembert and
Lacordaire openly declared their membership of the Liberal

Catholic camp and meant nothing more by it than reserving the right to a certain independence of mind. As the Roman Catholic Church in England grew increasingly reactionary and governed from the centre at Rome, both Newman and Ambrose began to adopt increasingly liberal attitudes, in the continental, rather than the English anti-dogmatic sense.

In the meantime, Ambrose allied himself with the Conservatives in politics and in 1843 he became associated with a group of Tories who were to be called Young England; what drew them together is once more revealing of him. The history of Young England has yet to be written and traces have to be collected piecemeal. There is much scattered in the pages of *Hansard*. Its particular flavour can be seen in the highly idealistic and romanticised writings, mainly verses (as opposed to poetry, which certainly they are not) of some of its members. Most clearly it reveals itself in the novel *Coningsby* which Benjamin Disraeli[2] published in 1844. Here the characters in the book are based on the personalities within Young England. Ambrose de Lisle emerges clearly as Eustace Lyle, a young Roman Catholic of strong philanthropic and romantic leanings. Although obviously allowances must be made for Disraeli's discretion to make of the characters what he needed for the over-riding demands of the novel, the personality of Eustace Lyle is sufficiently compelling for it to be worth scrutiny for what it may tell of his contemporaries' view of Ambrose.

On 2 June 1841 the Whig government led by Lord Melbourne fell[3]. The *laissez faire* liberal policies of successive Whig adminstrations (apart from a short Tory break in 1834) had produced some significant legislation. The 1832 Reform Act, which had increased the middle class vote, and the 1834 Poor Law Amendment Act, were the most notable. The latter had sought to reduce the running costs of providing relief for the poor and alter its parochial basis. A central authority was set up under commissioners: Edwin Chadwick[4] was its secretary: parishes were grouped into unions in which areas workhouses were built: local boards of Guardians were elected to supervise paid officials. Allowances in the form of out-door relief were stopped for the able-bodied. Separate workhouses were intended for diferent classifications of paupers: old, young, sick, mentally-ill; but these did not materialise. Hideous conditions were the result; too comfortable a refuge was held to demoralise. Married couples were split up; young children never saw their parents and did not go out to school until after 1842. Public opinion was critical of the terms of the act; many letters to the newspapers were devoted to it, as also to conditions endured in factories.

Whether or not the Corn Laws should be repealed was another crucial issue, revived in 1836. This form of Protection for home agriculture had operated since the last third of the 18th century. After the end of the Napoleonic war the price of home-produced corn showed its dependence on the English weather. The harvests of the early 1840s were good, so bread which had been expensive in 1839–41 was unusually cheap in 1843. The Free Traders pressed that total freedom of entry be given to foreign corn to the advantage of developing commerce. The members of Young England were to split on the issue, for some could not reconcile themselves to the consequences that must follow to British agriculture. Perhaps the most dangerous of all the legacies left to the new parliament was the Peoples' Charter, a petition which had been presented in 1838 with its six points. Adopted by what came to be called the Chartist movement, it was followed by riots, particularly severe in Leicestershire, and a second petition to the House of Commons in 1842.

A Tory government was returned in July 1841 with a majority of 90 and Sir Robert Peel[5] as Prime Minister. Several gifted and enterprising mainly younger men became Members of Parliament. They began to act as an association and gained the appellation Young England. Lord John Manners[6], then 22 years of age, became (with W. E. Gladstone[7]) one of the Members for Newark; the size of the electorate now appears remarkable. He received 630 votes and Gladstone 633: the unsuccessful third runner had 394. George Smythe,[8] of the same age, had already won Canterbury at a by-election in February and was returned again. Other members of the group were Alexander Baillie-Cochrane,[9] 4th son of a Scottish admiral; Henry James Baillie[10] a young relation of Smythe's; Peter Borthwick[11] who conducted *the Morning Post*; Augustus Stafford O'Brien,[12] a high spirited and amusing Trinity contemporary of Ambrose and large Irish land-owner; William Bousfield

Ferrand[13] son of an industrialist who never lost his Yorkshire intonation, shared the outlook of his colleagues, though not their aristocratic background; Richard Monckton-Milnes moved fitfully in and out of the clique; Benjamin Disraeli, who had formerly held a seat for Maidstone, now represented Shrewbury.

By 1841 Disraeli had established himself, after a poor start, and was piqued not to be given office. Under his leadership this group of young men began to exercise an influence in the House of Commons, particularly on the issues that have already been described, together with that recurrent bugbear of English government, the maintenance of peace in Ireland. There was never any certainty on Disraeli's motives; those of his young companions were a generally idealistic concern for the extreme suffering conditions of a large proportion of the population in Great Britain. The country had become the workshop of the world at the expense of adequate feeding, housing and education for the majority of inhabitants. Disraeli did not take the sole initiative in drawing the members of Young England together. This they largely achieved themselves and some of the origins of the group's existence were of longstanding, based on common ancestry and education; some were tenuous, almost accidental; some dependent upon a similar attitude towards redress of grievances. Its amorphous nature gave Young England a certain initial degree of strength in that its movements were not restricted by manifesto. The lack of an accepted programme, however, led to eventual weakness, but not before it had added some interesting pages to parliamentary history.

One of the bases of Young England had been laid at Eton, where John Manners and George Smythe had been schoolboys in the 1830s. While Manners was able and good natured, George Augustus Frederick Percy Sydney Smythe's 'brilliant gifts and dazzling wit' did not conceal his also dissipated character which showed itself early, and he was nearly expelled twice during his five year stay. *Fraser's Magazine* for March 1847[14] took a sombre view of the contrast between Lord John and

> the majority of our young nobles ... who would seem to have but a low opinion of public virtue ... A scoffing sneering

GWENDOLINE 1845–1914

BERNARD 1846–1856

OSMUND 1847–1869

FRANK 1851–1883

EDWIN 1852–1920

RUDOLPH 1853–1885

MARGARET 1855–1895

GERARD 1860–1924

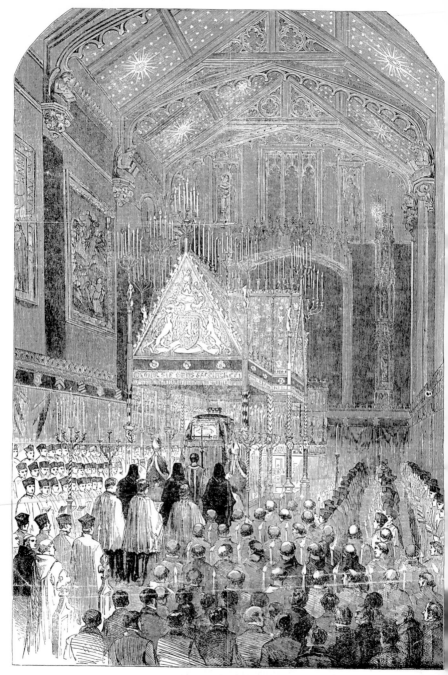

Funeral of John 16th Earl of Shrewsbury, 14 December 1852, Alton Towers.

spirit, an adopted levity of manner, and apparently a low estimate of the other sex, detract from their value as citizens.

This was a remarkably accurate description of George Smythe who in 1836 was admitted to St John's College, Cambridge. In the same year John Manners entered Trinity.

They took an active part in undergraduate politics and formed a small ultra-Tory group in the Union. Their views owed something to the particularly romantic brand of toryism of Robert Southey[15] (whom they considered the real founder of Young England) and something to Ambrose's friend Digby and his *Broadstone of Honour*. They criticised Liberal capitalism and the predominance of the bourgeoisie whom they held responsible for the sad condition of the labouring classes. Their solution lay in a romantic revival of the ethos of an earlier age, when the prestige of the aristocracy was imagined to rate high, and with it benefits for the poor. These views were poured into verse. It was the triumph of feeling over intellect, and of lack of a most elementary knowledge of the economics of the middle ages. A past golden age was created in which a powerful and benevolent nobility and almsgiving Church protected a dependent peasantry, acted in its interest and gained its affection. John Manners went first into print with his *England's Trust*[16] and other poems, which he dedicated to George Smythe:

> Each knows his place, King, peasant, peer or priest
> The greatest owned connection with the least,
> From rank to rank the generous feeling ran,
> And linked society as man to man.
> Gone are those days, and gone the ties that then
> Bound peers and gentry to their fellow men.
> Now in their place, beyond the modern state,
> Doomed from the very cradle to the grave
> To tread his lonely path of care and toil.
> Bound in sad truth and bowed down to the soil.
> He dies and leaves his sons their heritage –
> Work for their prime, the workhouse for their age.
> . . .
> Oh would some noble dare again to raise
> The feudal banner of forgotten days.

It was precisely the same view of history as held by Ambrose; its message was the one he had put forward in his *Life of St Elizabeth of Hungary* and he adopted the principles with which he had credited her, as his own. The almsgiving he and Laura practiced among the poor in Leicestershire were inspired by his interpretation of past virtues. He identified his wife with the Saint in an affectionate letter which he wrote to her on 29 May 1836

> I think you are just like her in her charitable feelings for the poor and your ardent love for your husband.

Nothing comes more clearly out of the character created by Disraeli as Eustace Lyle than his assumption of a beneficient, but none the less feudal, role towards his neighbours.

George Smythe wrote in the same vein. A sonnet in their Cambridge days described John Manners and extolled similar virtues.

> Thou shoulds't have lived, dear friend, in those old days
> When deeds of high and Chivalrous enterprise
> Were gendered by the sympathy of eyes
> That smiled on Valour – or by roundelays
> Sung by the palmer minstrel to their praise.
> Then, surely some Provencal tale of old
> That spoke of Zion and Crusade, had told
> Thy knightly name, and thousand gentle ways.

More poems of a similar kind were to follow and, dedicated to his friend as the 'Philip Sydney of our generation' were published under the title *Historical Fancies*[17]. Their subjects ranged from the crusades and the aristocracy of France, to the events of the reign of Charles I and the later Stuarts. Smythe observed in a note that he had made no distinction in his ballad between the Churches of Rome and England, since he thought that the limits which separated them were not broad, nor the obstacles to union very strong.

Despite their differences, Manners and Smythe formed a close bond. The former's innate virtue and generosity enabled him to tolerate the waywardness of his friend, but it would seem that despite Smythe's Roman Catholic sympathies, Manners did not risk an introduction to Ambrose after they had become friends in 1843. Ambrose was not to meet Smythe until 1847 and then through other auspices. Noting in her diary the guests they had met at a London dinner party on June 15th, Laura wrote 'George Smythe-Coningsby' for it was in the title role of the novel that Disraeli cast him.

In the summer vacation of 1838 Manners and a group of undergraduates from Cambridge were staying in a cottage above Windermere in the Lake District. Frederick Faber, then still Fellow of University College, Oxford, had taken a similar reading party to Ambleside where he officiated in the church. His eloquent and stirring preaching transported Manners and his friends as they sat at his feet, Sunday by Sunday, listening to 'the music of his voice'. He inspired the young men to adopt more thoroughly the Tractarian ideas being developed at Oxford: they had already been prepared to receive them through the influence of a Cambridge source, Hugh James Rose of Trinity; the 'solid Rose' of Digby's *Ouranogai*,[18] known to Ambrose ten years earlier. The friendship begun between Manners and Faber was to endure until Faber's reception into the Roman Catholic Church in 1845. Inevitably, Faber wrote a poem on his new friend.[19] Such of their correspondence that has survived is enough to show the close identity of their interests. 'I had a deal of talk with Faber' Manners wrote on 29th August 1838.[20] 'His idea is that Church and State must first of all be separated. The internal struggle would soon be over, though it would be fierce and keen'. Manners was prompted to spend the Epiphany season of 1838 in Oxford, where he fell under the spell of John Henry Newman.

A close associate of Smythe and Manners in their Cambridge days was Alexander Baillie-Cochrane, 'Kok' to his friends. Sir Charles Buckhurst in *Coningsby* was based upon his character. He was two years older than the others and President of the Union in the Lent term of 1837. In his reminiscences[21] Kok, then Lord Lamington, appeared to be anxious to make it clear that he began as an outsider and joined Young England later which, as can be seen, does not entirely correspond with the facts. Perhaps some jealousy and the ultimate weaknesses of Young England, made him loath to go down in history as one of the founders of it. He stressed that it had its origins in early friendships and good fellowship derived from a public school background; 'the air was full of Byronism'. Love of order, he said, and love of kindness were the first principles of Young England: radicals proposed to counsel the sufferings of the masses by votes and speeches; the philosophic school gave them tracts and essays; Young England set out to lighten their servitude and to put the 'merrie' back into England. (It was supposed that the epithet had once been apposite).

Causes that interested the young men included the romantic claims of absolutism and legitimist rulers (Manners visited Don Carlos claimant to the throne of Spain, in France in 1839) and the Cambridge Camden Society. Its belief that the gothic was the only Christian form of architecture was one of the most firmly held assumptions also of Ambrose and it was most surely one that endeared this group to him. Alexander James Beresford Hope,[22] one of the leaders of the Camden Society, was a Trinity friend of Manners. Elected for Maidstone in 1841, aged 21, although of Tractarian sympathies, an admirer of the mediaeval and writer of their kind of verse, he was kept from closer association with Young England by a desire to act independently, by a dislike of Smythe and Disraeli, and a quarrel with his brother Henry[23] mainly about money.[24] On two occasions Laura marked in her diary with approbation Beresford Hope's exploitation of the gothic; once on his re-establishment of St Augustine's Abbey, Canterbury, as a theological college, and secondly on the occasion of their visit to the church of All Saints, Margaret Street, which was built through his efforts. Later they were to become acquainted.

Disraeli first met Manners at a dinner party in London in February 1841, when the latter wrote in his diary 'D'Israeli talked well, but a little too well'.[25] Ambrose and Laura met the Disraelis in similar circumstances, but not until 16 June, 1847.

Disraeli had known Smythe in childhood, through acquaintance with his father. In the summer of 1842 Smythe and Manners were in Geneva together and they spoke of their combined political future. Smythe went on to Paris in the autumn where he found Baillie-Cochrane and Disraeli, with whom he dined one evening in October. Smythe's letter to the latter of October 20[26] was the first written evidence of the formation of the group that was to be Young England. 'I have fulfilled your instructions and written to John Manners and to H. Baillie', he wrote:

> The first I have told that we are to sit together and vote as the majority shall decide, and that any overture involving office ought to be communicated to the esoteric council of ourselves. To the Celt [Baillie-Cochrane] I have been more guarded and reserved, having only proposed that we should sit together in the hope that association might engender party ... It cost me three hours' walking over the Place Vendome after your dinner to reconcile him anew to our plan. He was all abroad – angry, jealous because you had talked to me more than to him. He said you did not appreciate him, that you had known me longer, but that him you did not understand ...

Disraeli set his own value on his ginger group. It would provide a section of conservative members 'full of youth and energy and constant in their seats', to keep an eye on Peel. Very sharply from the pages of *Coningsby* arises the notion that Disraeli was concerned to use his idealistic young men, with their romantic and nostalgic views, to give principles to policies of expediency. Disraeli could be a gad-fly or thorn in the flesh of the Prime Minister under the cloak of high-flown ideology. With the elaboration of these principles Ambrose de Lisle/Eustace Lyle was to be much concerned.

By the spring of 1843 Young England was given many opportunities to start: topics under review were frequently germane to the interests and inclinations of its members. The more prominent sat behind the Treasury benches and made their presence felt. And it was during this session that Ambrose began his acquaintance with some of them. He continued to act, as throughout his life, according to his customary plan: he exerted his influence from the now well-known background and drew people towards him. Spencer wrote from Oscott: Manners had been there and had expressed the wish to meet Ambrose and to see Pugin's work in the neighbourhood. The visit was arranged and Spencer replied[27] to Manners:

> I am mistaken if you do not find in each other a great deal to create warm and pleasing sympathy; and certainly in these days of dissension and coldness, we ought to seize all occasions by which a little of the pure fire of Christian friendship may be kindled.

It was the beginning of a close association which lasted until Ambrose's death, and welcomed with enthusiasm. 'We are expecting a visit from Lord John Manners shortly' he wrote[28] to Lord Shrewsbury as part of an on-going communique on his activities in the Midland District,

> but it is a secret, so do not speak about it. The more so as very likely the Duke of Rutland will take fright and advise him to put it off after all. You heard of his going to Oscott, of course, Spencer and Bishop Wiseman were pleased with his conversations etc. It was a silly thing of the Duke of Rutland putting himself at the head of the Loughboro' Protestant Association. I should think he regrets it now; at any rate it is not the line his son is taking. For my part I don't care about it, for it advances rather than hinders the progress of our Faith in the neighbourhood. Thank God we have now more than 1,000 converts in our own villages; and every day they are becoming more and more organised.

The first month of 1843 saw life at Grace Dieu at its most integrated and characteristic: events of a domestic, religious and educational sort, as always, closely followed on each other. On January 18 William Ullathorne[29] then a missioner at Coventry, arrived to take part in the blessing of the Calvary. During his travels in France and in the villages of Bavaria as a young man, the many crucifixes on the wayside had affected Ambrose deeply. The lack of images to convey the popular mind in England towards piety, concerned him and he saw his opportunity on his own estate. An outcrop of rocks over a hundred feet high about a mile from Grace Dieu, surmounted a natural amphitheatre of grass. Upon the highest rock Ambrose placed a wooden Calvary. In the future, visitors were invariably led to this place and on holydays processions with increasingly elaborate ritual over the years, would wind their way to this site of great natural beauty in the manner of mediaeval pilgrimages.

Early on that brilliant, mild, sunny January morning ceremonies followed one another with customary thoroughness: Ullathorne said Mass at 7 and this was followed by High Mass chanted in Grace Dieu Chapel according to the Gregorian mode, at which Fr Caestryck was the celebrant and everyone made their Communions. All but Laura went to Holy Cross at

Whitwick for High Mass at 10, after which Ullathorne preached on the occasion of the reopening of the Chapel after alterations. At 3 Gentili came from Shepshed to bless the Calvary and preach there. Writing in 1850, although he got the date wrong, Ullathorne recalled[30] the occasion in some detail and a description of the event also appeared in the Catholic Magazine.[31]

A multitude was gathered round, which included the congregations of the four Roman Catholic Chapels of the neighbourhood, mixed with strangers. They chanted the *Our Father* and *Hail Mary* in a 'Roman' chant and sang several hymns that Gentili had taught them. The last rays of the sun bathed the scene in a rich red light as he opened the Scriptures and declaimed his text. 'As the serpent was exalted in the desert, so shall the Son of Man be lifted up'. Finally, his sermon over, with the help of four priests, he pronounced the blessing on the Calvary. 'It was one of his happiest days' wrote Ullathorne, 'to see this public memorial of faith displayed thus openly in the very centre of England and for the first time in modern ages, in the midst of the scenes of his own labours, seemed . . . to open a new era in his missionary life'. No such spectacle had been seen in England for centuries. Vespers were sung at Grace Dieu at 4 when Ullathorne preached again: the Service of Benediction completed the day's ritual.

de Lisle experience continued to swing rapidly from the intense to the familial. Laura recorded on January 3rd that Everard, then aged 8, had burnt his lip with the poker: an experiment rather than accident, no doubt, on the part of the future VC. The first Vespers of the Epiphany were sung in the Chapel at 7.30 p.m. on the 5th. After it was over, Laura felt unwell and went up to her room: her fourth daughter and seventh child was born at half past ten. No one was with her but Mrs Squires, and Mr Eddowes was late as usual: he arrived two hours after the event. On the following day, High Mass for the feast was sung in the morning and at 3 Fr Caestryck baptised the child and she received the name of Mary. Monsignor Forbin-Janson, Bishop of Nancy and Mrs Stourton were godparents[32].

The hard frost which began earlier in the month had continued and on 14th January came the hardest fall of snow that could be remembered (winters remained intensely cold for the whole of the 1840s). Manners arrived for his visit on the 18th. Three accounts of the events of the next three days survive: in Manners' own journal: in Laura's diary entries which, since she did not leave her room, and she did not meet her guest, were clearly related by her husband; and most explicit of all in its graphic detail, the description of Eustace Lyle's surroundings in Disraeli's *Coningsby*. Though possibly embellished, it reflected the impact made by the personality, ideas and lifestyle of Ambrose. Manners' own account held him a mixture of Faber and Gladstone, who did not disguise his ambitions and hopes. Fr Gaestryck, the old chaplain made his appearance and Gentili came to dinner the first evening.

The following day, host and guest walked after breakfast to the wood and after luncheon they rode to the monastery. 'Nothing but monastic institutions can Christianize Manchester' Manners is reported to have said after his visit to that city. It may be that the afternoon at Mount St Bernard had something to contribute here. There was much to draw Ambrose towards him: he was a man of handsome looks and considerable personal charm: Lady Diana Cooper[33] found him still so during her childhood in the 1880s. Though not an intellectual, he had ability and integrity of the highest degree: above all, as a recommendation to Ambrose, he had private as well as public virtue. Dr William Whewell, Fellow, later Master of Trinity, told[34] a friend that he had rather be Lord John Manners than any other young man who had passed through the University.

Like his host, Manners had suffered the early loss of his mother which doubtless increased his sensitivity. Born to luxury, he had a keen appreciation of the sufferings of the poor. He and Ambrose shared a similar view of the remedies: a return to the customs and institutions of a past feudal age and the reorganisation and re-invigoration of the Church. Moreover Manners had written a pamphlet on the position of English Roman Catholics[35].

Ambrose obviously lost no time in extolling the benefits of a united Christendom. He assured his guest (according to Manners' account) that the Pope eagerly desired a union of Catholics and Anglicans and would grant the latter terms: the present Anglican clergy would retain their wives and livings, appointing curates to administer the Sacrament; the English liturgy would be continued with some alterations in the Communion Service; Chapters would choose bishops, subject to the approval of the Queen and Pope. The Creed of St Pius, that is his additions to the Nicene Creed, would be given up; all but celibacy and 'that I think we shall never grant'. If these concessions appear strange, they were similar to those put forward by Ambrose in his letters to Bloxam, and confirms their accurate recording. Notes of a sympathetic kind were made on the Chapel at Grace Dieu and 'the far seen calvary set on a hill, at which pious pilgrims pay homage'.

The weather changed on January 20th: the snow had gone and on a bright, mild morning the two began their ride by way of the Church of St Winifred at Shepshed, built by Ambrose in 1842, to the mansion and parks of his father at Garendon and Longcliffe. There can be no doubt that Eustace Lyle's character and neighbourhood had their origins on that shining winter day. Ambrose was equally impressed: his views conveyed in a letter to Montalembert[36] are of interest on account of his priorities:

> We have also had a most interesting and agreeable visit from Lord John Manners, the Duke of Rutland's second son. He is one of the most fervent of the Oxford school, though he was educated as I was, at Cambridge. He is a very young man, but in Parliament, and likely to distinguish himself as a speaker – he is a person of most elegant accomplishment and full of devout Catholick feeling . . . he sympathizes with all our ideas on Xtian art, architecture, etc. He gave me very interesting information respecting the progress of these ideas amongst the leading families of the County, so that we may truly consider, as I have always said, the conversion of England as a certain event, though the precise Epoch of it be still uncertain. Lord John Manners published about two years ago a little volume of poems, which do him great credit, full of Catholick sentiment, *disfigured* here and there with some relicke of *Anglican* notions: however since he wrote them he has made great *progress* in that respect.

Two days after the departure of his new friend, Ambrose walked with his sons, Ambrose Charles and Everard, to the

Grace Dieu school at Turry Log, a small hamlet two miles from his home and the same distance from Whitwick. They found 63 pupils. Boys and girls, they heard, were to be separated (although all were very young). This was probably at the instigation of Gentili who had strong views in this direction brought from Italy. Laura came downstairs for dinner for the first time since her confinement on the 26 January: she had suffered from fainting fits and a great deal of pain in her breasts. The month closed with the news, alas not infrequent, that cousin Mary Dawson 'had spit blood'. She died of consumption on 21 March aged 35, leaving five children; the sixth had predeceased her.

Manners clearly communicated an account of his visit in some detail to Disraeli, and prompted Faber to make a similar call of his own in March. Ambrose was delighted: besides the personal pleasure of extending his circle of acquaintances by entertaining the like-minded, he saw in these encounters the success of the methods he had chosen to further the object he had set himself: to make England what he recognised as Catholic. 'It will always be a real kindness to ourselves to send any of your friends here' he wrote[37] to Manners 'who may like to see a Cistercian Abbey once more in the heart of England, so the more you send the better, and I shall be truly grateful, besides which this sort of intercourse between members of the two Churches may do some good, and hasten on what we both long for'.

Although Young England was essentially an association of men in Parliament who brought their outlook and principles to bear on current issues, Faber, outside the political scene, occupied a position similar to that of Ambrose: they were, in the modern sense, a type of consultant. There were others like them who added their particular kind of support. One such was Henry Thomas Hope, brother of Alexander, who had lost his seat[38] when the borough of East Looe, which had been bought by his family (formerly rich bankers in Amsterdam), became disenfranchised under the Reform Act of 1832. As the owner of the Deepdene, a mansion in Surrey which combined the beauties of the country with proximity to the House of Commons, he was of particular use to the members of Young England in providing a headquarters of the party and a retreat in which Disraeli could devote himself to his writing. John Walter, contemporary and friend of Manners and Smythe at Eton, was another fringe member of the group. Heir to the owner of *The Times* newspaper, his influence was valuable in securing its interest.

Faber, who had just become vicar of Elton, a small parish in Huntingdon, appeared to stay with Ambrose and Laura at Grace Dieu on 23 March 1843. Laura and the five eldest children had 'hooping cough' which was so serious that Mr Eddowes called a specialist from Nottingham who did not allow her to go out or eat meat for another fortnight. The guest's programme took much the same form as that of Manners. There was a considerable degree of common interest to bind Faber and Ambrose together, but both had volatile temperaments which during the course of their future acquaintance caused at least one serious disagreement. Ambrose remained faithful to the gothic style: Faber, as a Roman Catholic after 1845, began to espouse the Baroque and did not yield much importance to what Ambrose called Roodskreens. In April 1848 matters were to come to a head[39] and there was some shouting. John Henry Newman became the reconciler.

Faber clearly also suffered through early deprivation of parental affection. No appraisal of his character is fair to him which does not take sufficient account of this fact, for it rendered him psychologically vulnerable in later life. He explained[40] to Manners 'In rapid succession my mother (while I was at school) and then my father died. I was not only broken by these horrible blows . . . I was so stunned that for one whole year my intellect was struck dead'. To John Brande Morris, an Oxford contemporary, he elaborated[41] 'People who have not been deprived of home and all home thoughts as I have in early boyhood, who are not sick with pent-up domestic wishes, and have not had "the vents of mortal feeling closed with cold earth from the grave" having expended part of their nature, are ill-fitted to judge the trials of men left in early orphanhood, with hot feelings glowing in them unexpended skill'. He became captivated by the personality of Smythe, though he never had any illusions about his many faults, and realising the harm that the relationship could cause him, bravely broke it off.

Since his last meeting with Ambrose in Oxford, Faber had travelled to Rome and felt the pull of Roman Catholicism. Twice he had drawn close to going to the English College to make his submission. As a young man his imagination had been caught by the mediaeval age, particularly by what he conceived to be its religious and chivalrous ethos: gothic architecture still, at this moment, appealed to him, so all boded well for a successful visit. Faber walked to the monastery and Calvary and 'was most pleased with both'. Next morning he accompanied the family to the chapel at Grace Dieu for High Mass for the feast of St Joseph; his departure was remarkable in that he left by train from Loughborough; the date was only 1843.

Ambrose was delighted by the visit; 'We were quite enchanted with your friend Mr Faber' he wrote to Manners. 'He is a glorious man and I formed quite a friendship with him which I hope will never end but in heaven: what talent he has: what elegance of mind and what true Catholick Devotion!' He ended by imploring Manners to persuade Lord Adare, son of an Irish peer, to come to Grace Dieu. Ambrose perceived that his influence was beginning to spread, and it excited him. Lord Adare did not come until April 1845 when he was accompanied by his brother-in-law, William Monsell, but the visit had profound consequences: both men eventually became Roman Catholics. (William Monsell was later Postmaster General and created Lord Emly, thereby increasing the number of Roman Catholic peers in the House of Lords). The Baillie Cochranes came that year also.

As the members of Young England under the leadership of Disraeli attacked Peel and his administration, Ambrose in a series of letters[42] supplied facts, feelings and support. One of Manners' solutions to the extreme poverty of the labouring classes was to suggest that poor families be provided with allotments, so that they might grow their own food, and he spoke on this cause on numerous occasions in the House of Commons. Ambrose thanked him for mentioning[43] the efforts of the Cistercians at Mount St Bernard in their cultivation of waste land which he had seen on his visit to their neighbourhood. Ambrose gave him statistics for future debates. In 6 or 7 years, 250 acres had been brought under cultivation where was formerly wild heath; now it supported a community of 25 people. Besides this, the monks had supplied in the last two winters almost entirely as many as 90 families from surrounding villages. When the community expanded there would be greater production and the land could support 45–50 monks.

Ambrose dismissed Joseph Hume's sneering refutation of Manners' claims, and went on to describe the waste lands which he had given to the poor of Whitwick and Thringstone, about 30 acres, for gardens. They paid ten shillings an acre for ten years; Manners might have noticed the plots on his way to the calvary rocks. It had all been highly satisfactory: rents had been paid, the waste land cultivated and many of the people had told their landlord that during the insurrectionary movement and the *turnout*, that they did not know what would have become of them but for their potato gardens. Ambrose offered that Brother Francis Murphy of Mount St Bernard should go to London and explain his oversight of the Abbey's lands. 'I have told the Prior to tell him to take his Monastick Habit along with him . . . some of your friends might be interested to see it'; Ambrose seldom failed to make use of opportunities. Excellent results would follow if only the government would take up 'the monastick system' as a means of directing the cultivation of waste ground. He explained that a system of this sort had been begun in France, under the inspiration of Viscomte Alban de Villeneuve for relieving the poor, and drew attention to articles in *Université Catholique* on the experiment: a report of the scheme had been made in the *Catholic Magazine* by Mr Anstey[44], entitled 'a crusade of the 19th Century'.

Manners in the meantime, had published another pamphlet[45] on a subject dear to his heart, the return of public holidays on holy days when factories would be closed and workers have leisure. Ambrose was instantly enthusiastic: 'I think it difficult to over estimate the importance of all such steps as these . . . they give to Catholick minds in both our Churches occasion to act together and to proclaim their sympathy . . . in your beautiful pamphlet . . . you have admirably shown how much of temporal happiness and comfort would result to the poor from carrying out the beneficent provisions of the Church'. Others were less complimentary. In response to Manners' call[46] for 'healthy recreations and manly outdoor sports' to improve minds and promote happiness, his fellow MP's scoffed. *The British Critic*[47] remarked that within two or three days the pamphlet's arguments were fully and freely criticised by almost every London journal. Would he ask his father to reduce the rent of his tenants on the understanding that they should not deduct holy days from labourers' wages?

Ambrose had another holy day of his own to describe to Manners. May 3rd was the feast of the Invention of the Cross; a further vast concourse had made its way to the calvary. Lady Mary Arundell wrote[48] an account of the ceremonies. Her comparisons between the peasantry of Catholic countries and those in the same category in England, merry no longer, but toil-worn and lacking in recreation would appear somewhat senten-tious and begged a few questions, but the numbers present suggested that there were many (about 800) in the neighbour-hood who were drawn to the occasion. Vehicles of various sorts, horses and riders, were mingled with foot passengers. The ritual was much as before, except that according to the account of eye-witnesses, Whitaker, missioner of Whitwick, clad in a richly embroidered cope, bore in his hands a reliquary containing a particle of the true cross, given to Ambrose by Prince Doria.

At the end of the ceremony Ambrose and Laura, with their guests, ascended the summit to kiss the relic. 'Our service far exceeded my expectations' the former wrote to Manners. 'It was really a most striking fact to witness the enthusiasm of the people collected round the Calvary . . . it was *wonderful* to see how they all pressed forwards at the end of the service' to follow Ambrose and Laura's example. And when the priest pronounced the blessing with the relic, every individual threw himself on his knees; hats were raised in a seemly fashion and many were in tears. Lady Mary could not restrain herself from the comment that it was a far cry from the drunken beer shop festivals customarily known to the peasantry of England. But it would not have been easy so to persuade the members of the House of Commons.

(ii) The outcome

The attempt to create legislation on allotments had been the brain child and private member's bill of W. Bousfield Ferrand who shared Manners' and Ambrose's faith in this expedient, but they did not succeed in getting it through the House of Commons. In 1841 and 1842, Ferrand had made his reputation on supporting every endeavour to legislate on industrial conditions, hours, child labour, and so on; he spoke often on the poor law. 'It was the foulest conspiracy' ever entered into against the rights, liberties and privileges of the poor.[1] He produced the startling statistic that the annual deaths in England and Wales from preventable typhus were double the allied losses at Waterloo.[2] Manners, speaking in the same debate,[3] thought the administration of funds for the maintenance of the poor should be in the hands of the Church; it was Ambrose's view entirely. Ferrand also spoke in the protectionist interest against the repeal of the Corn Laws. In his opinion the state had a duty to protect home agriculture from foreign competition and the working classes from exploitation. He and Manners became close friends, though Ferrand did not accept the religious outlook of the Tractarians. Ferrand and Ambrose met at Beauvoir Castle.

Ambrose writing to Manners, drew attention to letters he had written in *The Tablet*[4] on the Factory Bill then before the House (at the instigation of Sir James Graham, the Home Secretary). Ambrose criticised that part of the provisions which concerned the education of young factory workers who were Catholics, and true to form as part of a lengthy case, added for good measure some remarks about the Oxford men. The reaction of the Editor of *The Tablet* and others was instantaneous. A letter from a correspondent under the pseudonym Sacerdos[5] was typical, when it observed 'Permit me, through your columns, to beg of Mr A. Phillipps to keep himself strictly to lay subjects. Whenever he goes into theology, he always gets out of his depth'. Ambrose was unrepentant: 'From the very unfair way that he [the Editor] deals with my letters, I can see that he is stung by them . . . I am determined never to let an occasion pass by without entering my protest against the odious manner in which some of our body attack the Church of England . . .' It must be added that Sir James Graham withdrew the Education clauses of the Factory Bill, but mainly on account of the petition of Bishop Wiseman and other Vicars Apostolic and the antagonism to it by Dissenters; the era of the powerful Roman Catholic layman was being taken over by the clerical ascendancy.

A bill concerning the provision of arms to quell rebellion in Ireland drew a speech from Smythe:[6] 'Some of our suburban pulpits are still disgraced by exhibitions which would be revolting if not ridiculous'; and one from Manners[7] in which he was rash enough to suggest that the Roman Catholic Church was not the original Church of the Irish people. He received a swift rejoinder: Ambrose was delighted with the report of an admirable speech, but it contained certain errors.

At this point Ambrose and his family proceeded in various stages to Rhyl in Wales for the summer. The expedition shows the nature of contemporary cross-country travel; the close relationship which both father and mother had with their children; and the maintenance of interest in political and religious affairs though on holiday. In fact, letters from Denbighshire were even longer and more diffuse than usual. The debates on Ireland, Manners' speech on the advisability of sending a British Minister to Rome as diplomatic envoy, the censure of Dr Pusey, and the reunion of the Churches, were all touched upon. Ambrose had visited St Winifred's holy well, he wrote, where he would have been happy to see Faber who no doubt would have written an appropriate poem. The renovation of the fabrick [sic] of the monument was so vile that Ambrose told Manners that the Camden Society should rescue it from vandalism.

Ambrose, Laura and the two elder boys, Ambrose Charles aged 9 and Everard 8, left Grace Dieu on July 11, and made their way across England to Chester. They travelled in their own carriage, drawn by a mare and accompanied by John, the groom. No arrangements whatsoever were made in advance, not even as to the final destination where a party of 11 were to remain for nearly two months. It would seem that they had not made up their minds where to stay. On the first day they covered 42 miles, which was rather more than usual, but they took on an extra horse at Uttoxeter: the average daily mileage was around 32. At Aston Hall they stopped to see Fr Dominic Barberi and the Passionists, and spent the night in Stone.

The following night was spent at Taporley (very good inn) where Laura felt very unwell and took a blue pill. She was by now carrying another child (Bertha, who was born in February 1844). New Brighton, a seaside resort at the top of the Wirral peninsular, was reached by the evening of the 13th. It was very full indeed and only one house was empty at £10.10sh a week and the owner insisted it could only be rented for a month, so after a fruitless search next day, they decided not to remain. The other five children with their nurses were due at Chester on the 14th in their own conveyance, but as they did not come, the parents made an expedition to Holywell and slept at Northorp (very bad inn). The younger children appeared the next day and together the family made its way via St Asaph where they saw the cathedral, to Abergele. Since it turned out to be one mile from the sea, Ambrose and Laura went the 8 miles to Rhyl in a hired gig, and booked Moorland Cottage there for £4 per week.

It became their base although with customary energy expeditions took place as far afield as Bangor, Carnarvon, Conway and Llanberis, where the mare developed inflammation of the lungs. Another horse was hired (the mare recovered quickly). Visits were made to castles, mansions and gardens, although occupied. It would seem that random calls to see the property of the Welsh gentry were quite in order. In fact, Laura recorded, with some indignation, the unusual fact that they were refused admission at Kinmel Park. Letters re-addressed from Grace Dieu began to arrive by 19 July, so contact was re-established with the affairs of the world outside their own.

Regular attendance at Mass was a difficulty; Roman Catholic chapels were scarce in Wales. Sir Pyers Mostyn, a relative of the Vicar Apostolic of the Northern District, had a 'handsome private chapel' in his house at Talacre, and with a horse put before the mare, it was feasible to make the journey on Sundays. Low mass was said with English prayers and, Laura recorded, a sermon read from a book. An invitation to remain to luncheon was often made by Sir Pyers and his three unmarried sisters.

The younger de Lisles spent their days largely on the sands where they were invariably joined by their parents, unless away on an expedition. Laura did not bathe, but Ambrose did so on numerous occasions, with every child except Mary. When the carriage was taken down to the shore for a drive it

became stuck fast: 'We were obliged to send for another horse
to clear us out'. Jones, Lord Westminster's harper, came to
play twice for two hours. They all went out in a boat. Pony
and donkey races, a sack race and splendid fireworks, took
place at other times. On 5 September there was the most
beautiful moon as they 'walked on the shore for the last time.
Alas!' Laura clearly enjoyed the family holidays far from the
demands of life in Leicestershire. The drive home went by way
of Oscott and Birmingham, where they met Fr Mathew the
celebrated Temperance Missioner in full cry touring the town
in a carriage, administering the Pledge. They reached Grace
Dieu on 11 September.

Of the activities of Young England that autumn, one of the
most important for its consequences, was the visit to Manchester of Manners and Smythe. It was a step into the real world.
The latter was intoxicated by the mystique of 'Commerce', its
wealth and energy, and the skill of manufacturers. Manners,
on the other hand, was appalled by the humiliation and
suffering endured by the work-force. It was October, and
many had no food, fires nor blankets. During that month,
most significant of all, Disraeli finished his novel *Coningsby*
which he had been writing at the Deepdene.

Disraeli had been invited by Henry Hope to stay at his
mansion in Surrey whenever he needed its peaceful surroundings. It was an exotic and apt setting, with its woodland
glades, its house in the Italianate style with galleries and
balconies adorned with busts, its two chained bear cubs in the
garden, in which to write a book of the imagination. For
despite the living basis of many of its characters, there was an
overwhelming unreality about *Coningsby*. It did not so much
tell a story as illustrate a point of view. When the book was
published a cartoon appeared which showed Disraeli blowing
a trumpet; on its banner the word *Coningsby*. After some
indecision, Disraeli had chosen fiction as his medium which 'in
the temper of the times offered the best chance of influencing
opinion'.

So *Coningsby or the New Generation* was, though a political
novel, by intention a Tract: its plot was minimal but its
messages many. First it sought to show the party within a
party as youthful and therefore possessing the attributes and

virtues of youth: vision, enthusiasm, energy, dedication. 'It is a holy thing to see a state saved by its youth' is put into the mouth of Coningsby/Smythe. Secondly, though essentially aristocratic (the *Coningsby* scenes were in the main staged in mansions, as Young England enjoyed the Deepdene and John Walter's[8] Bearwood), the group had a deep concern for the poor. Both in the book and out of it, came the formation of principles to govern their case. Thirdly, political power, Disraeli felt, should be vested in those most responsible and 'associated with great public duties';[9] by implication the privileged, and not the manufacturing classes.

Henry Coningsby, the ostensible hero of the piece, is a boy of 14 when the novel opens: his mother has died when he was 9: he is the grandson of a marquess. At Eton he meets and befriends Lord Henry Sydney 'sweet tempered and intelligent' and Sir Charles Buckhurst, representing Lord John Manners and 'Kok'; also Oswald Millbank, the son of a rich manufacturer (based on the character of John Walter) whose life he saves from drowning. A close companionship develops and Coningsby/Smythe spends holidays with Henry Sydney/John Manners at Beaumanoir/Belvoir.

As they grow to maturity, the friends react to the big questions of the day and the views of their peer group, and by their expressed opinions fulfil Disraeli's purposes. A particular house-party at Beaumanoir sees the principal characters at their most loquacious. They enjoy the company of their host, the Duke, father of Henry, and his daughter, and Lord Vere, son of a Whig peer (based upon Lord Edward Howard,[10] future son-in-law of Ambrose and husband of Winifreda). They are joined by Eustace Lyle, a young Roman Catholic, who has just inherited a large estate and they discuss, among other current events, the new Poor Law and out-door relief. 'Henry thinks' says his sister 'that the people are to be fed by dancing round a maypole'. The Duke relates that his daughter brings him terrible accounts of the sufferings of the poor, and asks Lyle/de Lisle what he does about it.

'"I have revived the monastic custom at St Geneviève"[11] said the young man, blushing. "There is an almsgiving twice a week"' An expedition is arranged for the following day to ride to the Eustace/Ambrose estates to see for themselves. '"What

sort of fellow is Eustace Lyle" says Coningsby "I rather like
his look"' and Lord Henry replies '"He is a great ally of mine
and I think you will like him very much ... he does an
amazing deal of good"'.

The description of Lyle's splendid house 'in the finest style
of Christian architecture' and 'verdant' park is clearly intended
to reflect the benign influence of its owner. He comes to meet
the party on a small, fawn-coloured pony; the company has
been prepared by the Duke for much beauty 'but the reality
exceeds his report; ... It was like suddenly visiting another
country, living among other manners and breathing another
air'. All are admiring St Geneviève/Garendon and its chapel,
when a bell sounds: it is almsgiving day and the poor arrive.
Eustace agrees with Lord Henry and Coningsby that ceremony
(which they have been discussing) is not, as too commonly
supposed, an idle form. 'I wish the people constantly and
visibly to comprehend that property is their protector and
their friend', he says. In sympathetic vein, Disraeli enables
Eustace/Ambrose to make an apologia at some length for his
Roman Catholic views, and ancestry.

Little of the remainder of the novel is of present concern.
Sufficient is it to say that the members of Young England
continue to explain at length their stand on the meaning of
Conservative principles. His friends acknowledge their indebt-
edness to Eustace Lyle for his influence upon them. Their
pleasure is great when he announces his engagement to one of
the daughters of the Duke. Christmas is spent at St Geneviève
according to the mediaeval pattern. 'Their host had entrusted
to Lord Henry the restoration of many old observances'.
Mummers are revived and, somewhat ironically, the hobby-
horse. Beef, ale and bread are given away: a red cloak for each
woman; a coat and broadcloth for every man. 'An indefinite,
yet sharp sympathy with the peasantry of the realm as a
characteristic sensibility' was one of the attitudes Disraeli
wanted his public to recognise. He could not have made it
plainer.

Despite its heavily overlaid didactic intent, or was it perhaps
because of it, *Coningsby* was an instant and considerable
success. The novel was widely read and commented upon, and
pronounced fascinating and original. The first edition of 1,000

copies was sold in a fortnight and was followed by two other editions within three months. It reached the continent of Europe where it had a wide circulation, and it is said that 50,000 copies were ordered in the United States. Ambrose commented favourably to Manners:

> I have read *Coningsby* and we are all charmed with it and especially with Lord Henry Sydney, and no one can mistake the person represented by so accurate a portrait. We were much amused with Eustace Lyle, and I did not feel disposed to quarrel with his sentiments, or at least with most of them, not but that here and there I might find a word I would not quite venture to use . . .

Another child, the eighth, was born to the de Lisles at 6.30 a.m. on February 9th, 1844; her birth was even less expected than that of Mary. Not only was the doctor absent, but the midwife also. On the 7 February Laura had walked to the school; on the 9th 'I woke up about 2 a.m. and not being well, I sent off for Mrs Squires who arrived about ½ past six. ½ an hour after Baby was born. No one with me but Hadley [the nursery maid] who managed extremely well'. The doctor arrived about 10 and 'decided I was not to nurse'. At 6 p.m. Gentili baptised the child and she was given the name of Bertha; Spencer and Henrietta, Laura's sister, were godparents. From a book of family ailments left by Laura it would seem that she had suffered a good deal from inflammation of the breasts as a result of frequent child-bearing. Alice, the de Lisle's second daughter, told her grand-child[12] that Laura had nursed fifteen of her children; all in fact but Bertha.

Laura was up after six days and on the 15 February recorded that she had eaten meat for the first time since her confinement, but as artificial feeding was still undeveloped, the child was sickening. On the 20th Mr Eddowes came to see her twice, and gave hope of her recovery with the help of a wet nurse. Mrs Goddard of Whitwick came for 10 shillings a week, but only stayed three days as 'she did not wish to remain' and Mary Spencer came instead, through thick snow. Bertha after being fed every half an hour all night, recovered quickly, and within three days, in spite of the outstandingly cold weather, was said to be out of danger.

During the early part of 1844 Ferrand and Manners spoke in favour of Lord Ashley's (unsuccessful) attempts to convert the Home Secretary's 12 Hours Factory bill to a 10 Hour measure. Members of Young England, apart from Smythe, backed him. 'Kok' in his reminiscences said that it was the suggested repeal of the Corn Laws in 1846 which was the first occasion of difference of opinion within the group. Clearly his memory was at fault, for Smythe had earlier begun to take an independent line. He, however, accompanied Manners and Disraeli in October to Manchester once more, and all made notable speeches at the Athenaeum at a meeting for young operatives, although he did not go with the other two on the next leg of the journey. The others, in the company of Ferrand, went to Bingley.

Here, on the 11 October they took part in a memorable occasion. Ferrand's aunt had given 15 acres of land at Cottingley as allotment gardens for the poor. They were opened with ceremony appropriate to the character of Young England. A cricket match was included in the celebrations; it was a scene which would have thrilled the feudal heart of Ambrose and one that he was to repeat many times when he inherited Garendon Park from his father. The description that survives[13] records Manners' underarm bowling, as he took part in his 'manly sports with the peasantry'.

Ambrose addressed several letters to him in 1845 in regard to issues before Parliament. The most important of these[14] was in respect of Catholic Education in Ireland and Peel's current bill. He agreed with the stand that Manners was himself taking:

> I can but echo the sentiment you so wisely express about it . . . It would seem almost hopeless to induce legislatures to legislate on sound principles in these days in any Country, Catholick or Protestant: we are all in a state of transition, and transition states are always more or less a state of confusion. It would seem then that the hope for each country lay rather in the efforts of individuals at such times, efforts to mould the chaos into some form, sooner or later, rather than to abandon it altogether.

How fervently was Ambrose to take this attitude personally to heart. He professed himself in favour of the secular Irish colleges as an expedient, if positive evil were not taught. 'I have no doubt that some of our Bishops will be violent against the measure, but I dare not say these are my types of true Catholick bishops'. He was grateful, he wrote, for the acquaintance of Lord Adare and his brother-in-law, William Monsell, whose visit, arranged by Manners, had finally taken place. 'Two more delightful or interesting men I have not yet seen . . . It is a consoling thought that there are so many young men now united together in the generous determination to work for those grand principles which can alone restore England to its proper condition or preserve it from that dreadful ruin which evidently menaces it on all sides.' The visitors were going on to Alton to see the interesting objects in Lord Shrewsbury's neighbourhood and to Oscott.

Ambrose was keenly awaiting the publication of *Sybil*, Disraeli's second political novel, enthusiastically described by Manners. 'It is a glorious thing that a man of D'Israeli's fine mind and brilliant talents [they had still not met] begins to take a Catholick view of things' wrote Ambrose. He ended with an appreciation of a book of his sermons which Faber had sent him ('what great good he must be doing in the parish'), and a review of the religious and educational picture in France.

From subsequent correspondence, it would appear that Manners found useful the views expressed by Ambrose on Irish education. During the spring of 1845, the whole issue came to a climax from which Young England never recovered. Peel decided to treble the grant to the college at Maynooth for the training of the Irish clergy. Manners spoke in favour in a very long speech[15] '. . . Nor when I come to consult the standards of our Church and the works of her holiest and most learned divines, can I find anything which would lead me to think I am acting disloyally towards her in sanctioning this grant. The English Church acknowledges the validity of Roman Catholic orders, acknowledges that Church as an authorized administrator of the Sacraments, and as a true, though not altogether blameless portion of the Church universal . . . as a loyal son of that English Church I do not consider myself bound to withold my support from this proposition'.

Smythe defended the increased Maynooth grant for necessary training of the Irish clergy: 'Priests for the people should be of the people'. Disraeli opposed it, for reasons that were never very clear, since he had hitherto shown himself sympathetic to the Roman Catholic cause; but to offend Peel was more necessary to him than to continue to support Young England. This need became even more evident in the following year when Peel decided that the time had come to repeal the Corn Laws. Manners supported Disraeli in opposing the measure, but Smythe followed Peel (and was accompanied by 'Kok'). But it was not the removal of a colleague of such exceptional ability, and the certain knowledge that Disraeli would now vote independently and just how it pleased him that was the main cause of the end of Young England. It had ceased to serve the purpose intended for it by Disraeli.

It only remains first to look briefly at the activity of a politician who was on the fringe of the party (though never entirely committed), for he had some links with Ambrose; and secondly to assess the whole movement.

Richard Monckton-Milnes, who was elected MP for Pontefract in 1837, had been a contemporary of Ambrose at Trinity. He spent some months in Rome and developed a certain interest, though a rather objective one, in Roman Catholicism. There was some correspondence between them, and Milnes sent Ambrose a copy of his *One Tract More*[16] which he had written, impressed by Pusey and Newman and furious at the attitude of the Church of England towards them, as a protest against injustice. Milnes came to stay at Grace Dieu in September 1845. He made the usual itinerary of those sights which established the extent to which Ambrose's ideals had been carried into practice; few men could show so much. They rode, with A. F. Rio who was a mutual friend, to the Monastery and so on. Milnes was on Laura's 'beautiful white arab, "Sultan", given to me by Ed. Dawson' He lamed her completely and she had to be returned to the donor. There is no evidence of a further visit. *Fraser's Magazine* (which did not like Milnes) thought his appearance slovenly and his speeches, despite his originality and obvious intellect also showed lack of care; nevertheless it granted that those on the subject of Roman Catholics 'have always been remarkably liberal and bold[17]'. Ambrose's influence may have acted here.

Although a close friend of Augustus Stafford O'Brien, Milnes had an intense dislike of Smythe and was sensitive to disparagement by Disraeli, who ridiculed him and caused offence by failing to include him among the characters of *Coningsby*. Despite the fact that Milnes frequently voted with Young England, he was never committed to the group as a whole, and gave further evidence that it was more than mere identity of views that had formed it.

Milnes' character was strangely paradoxical: even his nickname 'the cool of the evening' was such. He was kind to poets in financial straits and his feeling for the underprivileged in factories and mines probably accounted for his proposal to Florence Nightingale, oppressed as he was by the luxury and aimlessness of his life. She rejected him in favour of another mission. Largely no doubt on account of early insensitive treatment by his father, who taunted him with a bitter taste in humour, there was a coarseness in Milnes' nature which would have prevented a closer association with Ambrose and Laura. Although a reformer in the matter of capital punishment, his interest in punishment *per se* became somewhat of an obsession: he waited for hours for a public hanging in July 1840 and had a collection of sadistic literature in his library at Fryston, said to have been well known. Swinburne wrote to Rossetti July 1869[18] 'There is every edition of every work of our dear and honoured Marquis [de Sade].' Milnes was a living example of the undercurrent beneath Victorian society where all was not necessarily as it seemed.

Young England did not break up as a political combination when members ceased to be united; they had seldom been that; only some few broad principles of a social kind were shared. It was perhaps salutary that there were members of the legislature who seemed to have concern for the poor, though here again, their solidarity was in doubt. 'Could I only satisfy myself that D'Israeli believed all he said, I should be more happy' was Manners[19] uncertainty, Smythe joked about their Diz-Union. But if its members could not be relied upon to act together, at least they could be relied upon to act. It was because, apart from Manners, they were basically idiosyncratic, elitist and often awkward characters, that they were so useful. Disraeli harnessed their nuisance value.

Smythe's erratic behaviour was proverbial; Greville wrote in his diary[20] on 11 August 1843 'Disraeli and Smythe, who are the principal characters together with John Manners, of the little squad called Young England, were abusive and impertinent'. Ferrand was called to order by the Speaker in a speech[21] on the Poor Law Commission when the latter said that he was quite sure 'that the hon. member when he had a little more experience of the House would see that the language he had used was unbecoming to the dignity of debate'. The Speaker was mistaken; such caution was not part of Ferrand's nature.

Though limited in voting power, this trouble-making should not be minimized. In 1844 it formed part of a threat that the Government would be brought down. Queen Victoria[22] wrote to her uncle, King of the Belgians, on June 18, when the danger had passed, of the narrow escape caused by 'the recklessness of a handful of foolish ½ Puseyites, ½ Young England People'.

By 1845 Disraeli was beginning to find methods other than the use of Young England in his campaign against Peel. The latter's decision to change sides on the repeal of the Corn Laws played into Disraeli's hands: here was ammunition indeed. (Ambrose had already expressed his arguments on the Corn Laws issue in answer to questions sent to him by Lord Shrewsbury[23]; he was against repeal and his views had their place in Shrewbury's published *Third Letter to A. L. Phillipps Esq: On the Present Posture of Affairs*[24]). Greville wrote in his diary for 21 May 1846[25] 'Last week the debate in the House of Commons came to a close at last, wound up by a speech of Disraeli, very clever, in which he hacked and mangled Peel with the most unsparing severity, and positively tortured his victim ... they hunt him like a fox'. Young England was needed no longer. No one recognised Disraeli's tactics more clearly than the Home Secretary, Sir James Graham, when he wrote[26]:

> 'With respect to Young England, the puppets are moved by Disraeli, who is the ablest man among them: I consider him unprincipled and disappointing ... they will return to the crib after prancing, capering and snorting, but a crack or 2 of the whip well applied may hasten and ensure their return, Disraeli alone is mischievous and with him I have no desire to keep terms ...'

Of the 'puppets', Manners remained in Parliament for 39 years (during which he achieved Cabinet rank in 1852) and retired in 1880 on succeeding his brother as Duke of Rutland with a G.C.B. and pension of £1,200 a year. He continued to correspond with and meet Ambrose and turned his attention to the establishment of Anglican Sisterhoods with the latter's encouragement. O'Brien died before he was 50; 'Kok' became a peer in 1880; Smythe's innate but sporadic brilliance won him a brief period as Secretary of State for Foreign Affairs, but the darker side of his nature kept asserting itself; he fought the last duel to take place in England in 1852 and it cost him his parliamentary seat at the following election. He succeeded his father as 7th Lord Strangford 2 years before his death in 1857 when, leaving no legitimate heirs, and worn out by extravagancies of various kinds, brandy and consumption, he expired, taking bets on his life, aged 41. Benjamin Disraeli became Prime Minister in 1868. By that time Ambrose, though a lifelong Conservative, was about to begin what was to be a long and intense acquaintance and correspondence with William Gladstone, whose administration was to succeed Disraeli's within ten months, in the Liberal interest.

Chapter 6

Leicestershire Squire

'I think Grace Dieu may boast of more romantick charms than most places in England'[1] was a characteristic comment upon the locus of Ambrose's domestic happiness and springboard for his many activities. The manor house, Elizabethan in style, which was built for Ambrose on his marriage (with money settled upon him by his own and Laura's families) had a setting of great beauty. The immediate vicinity was the wildest and most unusual in the entire Phillipps' estate. All that happened there has left to the area a residual attraction and interest; the remarkable natural features still continue to enchant and amaze.

Grace Dieu manor lay in a hollow flanked by cedar-bordered lawns from which rose steep banks covered with many different species of trees. Beyond, spectacular crags and jagged rocks of granite towered among the gulleys and hills created by the undulating nature of the terrain: they bordered the road towards the Monastery 2 miles to the east, and that to the village of Whitwick the same distance to the south. High Cademan, High Sharpley, Great Gun Hill, Ratchet Hill, Pedler Tor, were the names of nearby prominences. To the north lay the ruins of the 13th century priory of Grace Dieu, founded in 1240 by Roesia de Verdon for 14 nuns and a prioress of the Order of St Augustine. Suppressed in 1536, the priory came into the possession of the Beaumont family who in Ambrose's time still lived at Coleorton, 3 miles off. The villages of Thringstone, Osgathorpe and Belton were a distance of one, two and three miles respectively. In all of them Laura visited regularly on foot and Ambrose's missionaries laboured at conversions.

Ambrose and Laura's partnership had been tested by the

early 1840s and had become stable and close. Their common
religious dedication, the creation and nurture of their many
children had brought them to a state of intense interdepend-
ence. They chose seldom to be parted. Abbé Vandrival from
Boulogne who made a long stay at Grace Dieu in 1847,
remarked in his diary[2] on the disinclination of Ambrose to
leave his wife even for a short visit to Derby and Alton in the
priest's company, and his constant acknowledgement of the
fact that he missed her. Mary Arundell commented upon the
couples evident enjoyment of each other.[3]

> You really are the beau ideal of a happy couple ... My best
> love to Laura. I will not tell you all the Fathers and I thought
> or said of her, for you are too fond of her already; and well
> you may be. You have indeed gained a prize ...

and described them as 'one of the happiest marriages I ever
saw': she wrote to her sister[4] on their appearance and their
activities after Ambrose and Laura had made a visit:

> They were so positive that everything would go wrong if they
> did not get back for *Tenebrae* in their own chapel ... that off
> they all set in an unpromising day and I fear from the heavy
> snow that fell soon afterwards must have had a terrible journey.
> I think he looks ill but he says he was never better, and he
> looks as well as Laura, happiness itself. She is altered, grown
> thin, but he says she is beautiful and *reckoned a beauty* in
> Leicestershire, so it is quite as well. We had most delightful
> spiritual days and they were indeed a refreshment to my poor
> harassed spirit. It is amazing what the good little couple do.
> They have just built a church two miles off their house and a
> school beside the church which adjoins their house. I imagined
> this to be a small domestic chapel, and found it to be 97 feet
> long ... La Trappe is most flourishing, and they left me full of
> pious envy ...

The precise form that their devotional practices should take
and the detail behind the chapel decorations were no doubt
due to the initiative of Ambrose. His was the inspiration
behind the gothic arches, the mediaeval-style vestments, the
Gregorian chant. But they were grafted in her case upon the
solid basis of religious duty that had been laid by Laura's years
at the convent of New Hall. His predilections became hers;

also his prejudices: 'dreadful figured musick' she would write in her diary. But if she echoed his sentiments and executed his instructions, she was a great deal more than an imitator or automaton. Besides Laura's management of the household at Grace Dieu with its servants and the large number of children, there is a good deal of evidence of initiative on her part in unobtrusive ways both outside and inside her home.

Laura's piety was very deep: she went frequently to confession (once a fortnight in the 1840s) and attended a great number of religious services; often two or perhaps three masses on one day, together with Vespers and Benediction. Her religion did not appear to be a constraint, rather a further fulfilment in an already fulfilled life. She did not have a developed intellect and there is no record of books read, though one of a book translated; but she had an analytical mind and was quick to see the issues in a situation, and a nice sense of irony which was more acute than that of her husband. She seemed to enjoy teaching in the schools of their neighbourhood, also the production of plays, outings, picnics. She grasped the hardness of the system whereby the payment of school grant was dependent on the results achieved by schoolmasters and mistresses on the occasions when she was forced to tell some of them that they must go. She bathed until October one year in Boulogne where the seawater is notoriously cold, and appeared to have been particularly happy on seaside holidays.

As a negotiator she was frequent in smoothing out relationships between others; often when her volatile husband was concerned. On 23 January 1840 she wrote in her diary that she had gone to her father-in-law's room before dinner 'to make up between him and Ambrose'. It was a role she was to play on subsequent occasions. Ambrose affection for her was coupled with a recognition that without her he was lost: hers was the greater psychological maturity. On the death of Reginald he was beside himself because Laura was so full of grief on the eve of her next confinement that Ambrose felt he might lose her also: he wrote to Gentili[5]:

> Do at least beg of Our Lord to protect my wife and to preserve her to me. Oh, if you could see my wretchedness you would pray for very pity.

On Laura's serious illness in 1848 he was again brought very low: 'I am stretched on the rack still, my angelic wife is still not out of danger and so picture to yourself my misery'.

Both were small and slight. Spencer in letters to friends often referred to 'Little Phillipps'. On finding a weighing machine on Loughborough station in 1844, Ambrose, then aged 35, discovered he weighed 9 stone and 5 lbs; Laura two years younger and having already borne eight children, was two pounds more. There are references to his pleasing delicate features. F. J. Baigent, an antiquarian, wrote of his visit to Grace Dieu in 1856:

> Mr P is a short and small-made person, but quite a good size head ... a deal of quietude and mildness in his eyes, mouth delicately marked, a deal of fineness of feeling, with a trifle melancholy look.

Photographs which survive corroborate the melancholy: the slightly hooded eyes are sad and the small, sharply defined mouth has no trace of a smile. Such a disposition would have been regarded as levity, and like many of his generation he was essentially serious: he treated his many projects with seriousness and himself most seriously of all. His greatest blemish would appear to have been a difficulty in accepting slights and small insults without rancour. Real opposition he met with extraordinary courage and determination: he would exuberantly return again and again with fresh plans.

Ambrose was sensitive to inferences that his wife and children might not be receiving sufficient care. Lord Clifford, formerly Laura's guardian, insinuated after seeing the family in 1838 that too great a portion of income was being devoted to missionary activity and going to Passionists and Rosminians; that Laura and the children were not looking well as a result. Ambrose denied this hotly[6]. He said that he did not intend to involve himself in any further pecuniary embarrassments, whether for the sake of establishing Passionists, Rosminians or any other object whatever. He clearly meant this at the time, but his zeal and enthusiasm later got the better of him and took over once more.

> If I were a more perfect Christian than I am I should also thank you for the humiliation and mortification I received from your

communicating to me as the groundwork of your advice your erroneous impressions about dear Laura and the children.

They had indeed been ill; they had been to France; and the French air had not agreed with them; (the words 'fretful' and 'delicate' had been used) but they were, he reported, all now looking the picture of health.

Laura on her marriage was regarded as lively and full of spirit. A miniature shows a smiling face with blue eyes and fair ringlets. There are few photographs of later date because she did not like the process; from one in early middle-life she had undoubtedly begun to look thin and wan; her hair had darkened and was taken straight back into a somewhat severe coil. But it would be wrong to draw from this image any deduction except that she took no interest in her appearance: her daughters have left such a record. She was self-effacing and disliked show: there is hardly an entry in the 56-year diary sequence about clothes or shopping. Most of the comments are about others; frequently, her husband and children, guests who came and visits made. Laura's feelings were recorded seldom: there are relatively few expressions of emotion. A curious exception occurred on her birthday, 26 October, in 1842, and perhaps thinking it might be misinterpreted by Ambrose's biographer when she lent E. S. Purcell her diaries in 1896, she struck out the words with dark ink, but they are just visible:

> I this day complete my 31st year. How many more shall I have to live? God only knows and may He grant me grace to employ them well.

They were typical of her; acceptance was her outstanding attribute and she was exceptionally acquiescent to sources of authority: the words of clergy, her husband and doctors were commands to be obeyed. She would write to Ambrose to ask permission to stay one more night in London; she came downstairs after her confinements when her doctor 'had given me leave'. The redoubtable Mary Arundell, who missed nothing, told Ambrose[7]

> I evidently saw when at GD that you have your own way, *not sometimes*, but *always*, and specially admired among Laura's *many* other excellent qualities, her *very* prompt obedience to a VERY wilful man.

On foot, on horse-back, by carriage or train, the members
of the de Lisle family were constantly on the move within their
tract of country. The demands of local government, estate
managing, family loyalty, church-going, works of charity,
social obligation and friendship were the ostensible causes of
this perpetual motion. But it is clear that physical exertion for
its own sake and at all cost had to be engaged upon. Rides or
long walks set off from Grace Dieu daily if there was no other
programme, in snow, heat or driving rain. Inactivity was
unacceptable and since domestic drudgery was the province of
others, some form of exercise had to be devised.

This had one overwhelming consequence: parents and children saw a great deal of each other. Day after day, unless
otherwise occupied, Ambrose and Laura, or often he alone,
would set off with a cavalcade or crocodile, Amo, Everard,
Mena, Alice, Winifreda, Mary, and when the older children
went away to school, with the younger ones.

Throughout the long series of her diaries, Laura never
mentioned punishing her children, nor once dwelt on a misde-
meanor, and this in a censorious age. She seemed to be amused
rather than aggravated by their behaviour and (particularly
after the death of Reginald) acutely anxious for their health.
Although overindulgence would not have been in their nature,
both Ambrose and Laura emerge as caring, interested, proud
parents. 'Some of the girls are very beautiful, though it is
hardly right for *me* to say so', Ambrose wrote to Montalembert. For Laura a prize-giving at Oscott was the 'proudest
moment of my life'.

Privileged in contrast to the deprivation endured by children
of the surrounding villages, the young de Lisles lived secure
but reasonably austere lives: religious observances were de-
manding; their conditions were spartan: water froze in their
bedroom jugs; money was short. Yet together with their clear
responsibilities towards the poor, it was required that they
become part of their own social scene in the county. With
great difficulty, arrangements were made for them to ride,
hunt, shoot and when they became old enough attend balls
and eventually take part in a London season. It was a constant
nightmare of contrivance, since so much money was being
directed elsewhere.

The individual characteristics of the children emerge from the pages of letters and diaries of their parents: Amo, born in 1834, the most headstrong, became a fanatical sportsman and rider to hounds; Everard a year younger and killed in the Indian Mutiny was clearly his parents' favourite among the boys with his particularly affectionate nature. Mena born in 1836 was always dependable and mature. Reginald who much resembled Everard in looks, died when he was five in 1845. Alice born in 1840, often referred to by her father as 'Chickie', was the favourite among the girls. Her parents considered her a great beauty, but there were compliments too[8] on

> ... her excellent qualities particularly of her real sincerity, simplicity of her manners and exquisite *tact* and judgement. So I can truly say that she has attracted my admiration and respect for her to a high degree.

Winifreda, born a year after Alice, enjoyed hunting and the social scene; 'danced every dance' was a frequent comment of her mother. Mary, two years younger, a favourite also, resembled once again in looks and temperament the much mourned Everard; Bertha, born in 1844, was early very devout; Gwendoline her junior by fifteen months, was born a few days after the death of Reginald. Her health was always rather precarious, having begun with measles at nine days old. Photographs would seem to show her as more beautiful than any of the other girls, but no mention is ever made of her looks; nor were the same efforts made to launch her in society as some of the others. Bernard was born in Dieppe in 1846 where all the family had gone to save money; he lived to be nine when he died from a fall on the ice. Osmund called 'Ossy', was a year younger; his qualities of kindness did not go unrecorded.

It was in the year following his birth that Laura had her serious illness in 1848 and there was a suspension of childbearing for three years. On her recovery she bore five more children in the next nine years; Gerard, her sixteenth, a few months before her 49th birthday. Although none of her children (with the possible exception of Amo who was sometimes rather erratic) seem to have presented any serious problems to their parents, the first eleven were rather more straightforward than those born after 1851. More effort could be devoted to them when household and parents were geared to the needs of young children. By middle age Ambrose and Laura had less time to give and other claims had increased, but in spite of them, their close fond relationship managed to continue.

Frequency of association with the Phillipps' could hardly have been greater. During the 1840s Ambrose and his family spent days, weeks, sometimes months at a time living under his father's roof at Garendon; this was largely because there were periods when they could no longer afford to maintain their own household at Grace Dieu at full strength. But even when they were in their own establishments, visits between the two houses were frequent.

Mr Phil, C.M.P, or Grandpapa, as he was referred to by his son's family, was a considerable local figure. The election of 1832 was the last in which he was called to represent the Northern portion of the county in parliament in the Whig interest. According to an obituary notice[9] 'It was at one time expected that Mr March Phillipps' service to his party would have raised such an extensive landowner to the Upper House and we well remember, on the creation of a large batch of peers, our own disappointment at not finding "Lord Garendon" amongst them'. The revival of the ancient barony of Lisle, in abeyance since the time of Edward IV was judged a possibility. (Ambrose, in company with several of his contemporaries, notably the Herries, Camoys and Mowbray and Segrave families, thought to initiate this process in his own favour in order to increase the number of Roman Catholic peers; whereas they were successful, he was not).

Charles March Phillipps gave up his London house when he ceased to be an M.P. and devoted himself to the duties of deputy Lieutenant, county Magistrate and landlord in Leicestershire. He accepted the responsibilities seriously. The 1840s in particular were times of social and political unrest, with riots a constant threat and frequent occurrence. On 10 June 1842, for example, a request came at 10 p.m. that Charles March Phillipps should sign a requisition for a regiment of soldiers; on several other occasions he was required to swear in special constables. Recent research has shown that Chartist strength was greater than the leaders of this popular movement realized.

Had they not been intimidated by the reactions of magistrates proclaming law and order, and resistance which was largely traditional and moral and had little force behind it, they might have carried the day.

His father introduced Ambrose to a world in which he would later have to take his place. In the evenings at Garendon he would read aloud the accounts from the newspapers of the trials of those Chartist leaders who had been caught trying to overthrow privilege and property. Ambrose had his own tenants on the land acquired at the time of his marriage. Rent days took place twice a year, in January and June. In January 1840 tenants appeared with a total of £120.3.7; £20.3.6 was owing by those who could not pay. In June the sum was £127.5.8, with a deficit still. Substantial tenants were sometimes provided with lunch with Ambrose and his agent in the dining-room at Grace Dieu. It was not considered appropriate for Laura and the children to be present, so they had their meal elsewhere.

A feature of Charles March Phillipps' tenure of Garendon Park was his enthusiasm for beautifying his surroundings. He gave his attention to the large formal gardens, shrubbery and green houses of exotic plants; also to forest rides of exceptionally fine turf leading to plantations of new trees; long avenues were created towards Nanpantan and Longcliffe where father and son would ride together. Ambrose's acres included some plantations also: marking trees to be felled was many an afternoon's occupation; the wood sales (£167 at the beginning of 1840) were a welcome augmentation of income. The gift of a pike or strawberries out of season from the glass-houses would accompany the older man when he rode to Grace Dieu on a call. Sometimes Laura would record her father-in-law's particular good humour, which implies that it was not invariable; but it would seem that he was a genial host. H. D. Erskine, while Dean of Ripon, wrote[10] to his daughter from Garendon in October 1857:

> Phillipps is as well as ever, very lively more fat than formerly with rosy cheeks, and walks and rides and talks all day.

Numerous members of the family were there including 'the

Ambroses'; Charles' deceased wife's sister, Mrs Bevan (formerly Jane Ducarel), 'a capable musician', had played the piano.

Erskine continued:[11]

> I preached yesterday at Hathern . . . Phillipps who had warned me against undue length of sermon saying he would have liked much more . . . I enjoy this visit much . . . I never knew Phillipps better company . . . I am recommending the removal of shrubs, but Phillipps is obdurate – however I got some large bows [sic] out of a tree before the dining room window which he admits to be a vast improvement for light.

His father seemed to bear with tolerance that Ambrose's religious convictions were at variance to his own; at least such was the interpretation: 'My father is in excellent dispositions in regard to the Catholic religion' and 'He went with us to the monastery; he is very fond of the good Cistercians'; 'He is much pleased about my going to Oxford and he feels very anxious for the reunion of the Churches'. He would ask the chaplains from Grace Dieu to be his guests; Anglican clerics were often at Garendon, as were prominent laymen of the neighbourhood. Thus Ambrose met them also and received invitations, though the social life of the de Lisles was restricted during the 1840s and the youth of the first eleven children, and it was not until the next two decades that they began to entertain and be entertained on a wider scale.

Augusta March Phillipps, sister to Ambrose, had married in 1832 John Fitzgerald[12], brother of the poet Edward, a contemporary of Ambrose at Trinity; she had borne two sons, and a daughter who did not live long, and was by 1835 very seriously ill. Edward wrote to a friend[13]:

> My brother John's wife, always delicate, has had an attack this year which she can never get over; and while we are all living in this house [Boulge Hall Woodbridge] . . . she lives in separate rooms, can hardly speak to us, or see us . . . and bears upon her cheek the marks of death. She has shown great Christian dignity all through her sickness [tuberculosis]: was the only cheerful person when they supposed she could not live, and is now very composed and happy.

Two years later he wrote again:[14]

My brother John's wife is, I fear, declining very fast . . . they
say her mind is in a very beautiful state of peacefulness. She
may rally in the summer, but the odds are much against her.
We shall lose a perfect lady, in the complete sense of the word,
when she dies.

Augusta died on 30 July 1837 aged 27. A few days previously
Uncle Edward March Phillipps, Rector of Hathern, had written
a very long letter.[15] 'Rely confidently on the things in which
you have been instructed; so will an entrance be ministered to
you abundantly into the everlasting Kingdom of Our Lord and
Saviour . . . Farewell, till we meet again in another world'.
Ambrose, on the other hand, was in an agony of doubt. He
had prayed and longed for his sister to become a Roman
Catholic, but she had not. Where was she now? Brother
Joseph of the monastery (who had a reputation for visions) to
whom he had gone in his distress, had said that she was
among the number of the redeemed and was in purgatory. He
pleaded with Gentili to tell him this was true and not an illu-
sion.[16]

The de Lisles' Roman Catholicism did not isolate them in
the neighbourhood: Grace Dieu was no ghetto. Many neighbours were also members of the family and kept Ambrose in
touch with county and national affairs. His brother Charles
Lisle Phillipps survived until 1875, three years before Ambrose's
own death. The two were close and saw each other frequently,
which was significant since Charles was admitted to Holy
Orders in the Church of England in 1844; largely it was
recorded as the result of the example and influence of Aunt
Fanny.

After a private education on account of his ill health, Charles
went to Magdalene College Cambridge where he graduated
Junior Optime in 1835. In September 1844 he was made
deacon by Dr George Davys, Bishop of Peterborough and after
a short curacy of 2½ years at Rothley, Leics, went to the
benefice of Queniborough. At the age of 39, in 1850, he
married Elizabeth Dixon who was 21 years his junior. Particularly after his preferment to the family living of Shepshed in
1856, the exchange of visits with the de Lisles was on a regular
basis: Ambrose would walk and ride often with Charles; the

former remarked approvingly in 1841 that his brother had 'joined the Anglo/Catholics of Oxford' and in company, it was said 'of a great number of young men all over England.'

Charles' obituary in 1875, described a genial disposition and warm pastoral heart; that he had given up shooting since he was 'scrupulously careful to avoid forms of pleasure not compatible with the growth of the higher Christian life'. Laura appeared kindly disposed towards 'Mrs Charles' who was only a little older than several of her nieces and nephews; the only mildly adverse report lay in her inclination to prolong visits to invalids and make them tired; she had no children of her own.

The Rectory family from Hathern were much in evidence in the 1840s: Uncle Edward Phillipps, his wife, and their surviving son Wilfred, and daughters Elizabeth (Bessie) who married her father's curate, Edward Smythies, in 1845, Rose, Lucy and Emma who remained single. Lucy, born in 1820, was an early blue-stocking, who not only wrote the life of her father, but some excursions into social science[17] and addresses to teachers on 'evidences of divine revelations.' Although strongly derivative and depending largely on quotations from the printed works of others, her books show a breadth of reading that was remarkable and an undeveloped potential that needed a liberal education to give it life.

Uncle Samuel Phillipps had the greatest intellectual gifts of the family. After an exceptional career at Cambridge, he was called to the Bar in 1806; he wrote a treatise on the law of evidence and *A selection of State Trials*. His tenure at the Home Office as Permanent Under Secretary of State spanned the years 1827–48; he later became a member of the Privy Council. As a widower, he went often to stay with his relations, especially at Garendon; his sons Spencer, Alfred (who went into the Bengal Civil Service) and surviving daughters Florence and Adelaide, were well-known to their de Lisle cousins; Aunt Dawson's family of four sons from the near-by estate of Whatton, likewise. The eldest, Edward, was a Member of Parliament.

Aunt Ryder and the Bishop's surviving children provided twelve more cousins: Annie Ryder married Sir George Grey who became Home Secretary twice between 1846 and 1866 and held other Cabinet posts; a situation of which Ambrose

made good use: Henry and George Dudley Ryder were clerics;
of George, and his sister Sophia, more will be heard since they
became Roman Catholics (causing thereby a great stir); Ambrose made it possible for them to live on the Grace Dieu
estate.

Ambrose's assurance to Bloxam in 1841 that he was on
friendly terms with local Anglican clergy can be easily substanti-
ated: for one thing he was closely related to several of them.
With others he chose to be friends on account of similarity of
tastes and natural sympathies. Ambrose and Laura deliberately
sought out the company of J. Bridges Otley, vicar of Thorpe
Acre, near Loughborough and his family; there were to be
many others. Closest of all was Henry David Erskine, originally
friend to the older generation of the family, Rector of Swith-
land before he went to the north. To him Ambrose wrote
more relaxed and expansive letters (some of which contained
mild jokes) than to any other correspondent. The extent to
which Erskine was able to keep a balance between Ambrose's
sound ideas and his more illusionary ones, and thereby sustain
a lasting friendship, becomes apparent in some of the younger
man's letters:

> I know you think us all visionaries, nevertheless our work
> proceeds and will proceed in spite of obloquy and ridicule –
> not that I mean you are inclined to heap either the one or the
> other upon us or it[18]

and again

> Dr Gentili would beg me to add his kind remembrances, if
> he knew I was writing – but he is out of doors, what you
> would call *making mischief.*[19]

'Pray do not disappoint your truly loving friends' were the
terms in which an invitation was given; they were pressingly
welcoming:

> Laura is returned to her usual post downstairs and ready to
> welcome any of my friends and hers. How much we shall have
> to talk over. I will not say discuss for happily each day opens
> men's eyes to see that they have *more* in common and *less* to
> divide, than they imagined before, not to say that each day
> furnishes new proofs that the Mother Church of Christendom

is not that compound of idolatry and absurdity, which certain isolated judgments under very chilling and blinding influences heretofore represented her.[20]

There was not a general acceptance of this view. The founding of the monastery and Roman Catholic missions provoked come sharp local reaction. The columns of the local newspapers provide evidence of protest meetings and preaching courses: 'to expose and refute some of the tenets of the Church of Rome'; 'the Church of Rome, persecuting and Erroneous,' and so on. Prominent among those who were fierce in their denunciation of the developments was Francis Merewether[21] vicar of Coleorton since 1810 and Whitwick in addition since 1819. Well educated and member of a distinguished family (his brother was Serjeant-at-law and Recorder of Reading) he was presented to his living by George Beaumont, 7th baronet, founder of the National Gallery and friend to Southey, Coleridge, Lawrence, Constable, Joshua Reynolds, Walter Scott and William Wordsworth, some of whom came to stay at Coleorton Hall. (Wordsworth continued to be a friend and young John Wordsworth, his son, became curate of the parish). It was a rich pasture, in spite of a high proportion of the population being Dissenters; the presence of so many dissenting chapels caused the vicar some dismay.

Although he has been described as an Evangelical, Francis Merewether was in fact an early sympathizer of the Tractarians and as he explained in his *Letter to Dr Pusey*[22] (and others) on 'certain contemplated theological publications at Oxford', he was an upholder of the traditions of primitive Christianity; the distribution of the works of the Fathers and Christian writings of earlier ages; the promoter of private devotional exercises, observances of feast and fast days and the right use of the Sacraments. He disliked 'popery', he wrote, because Christian antiquity he considered silent on the errors made points of view by the Roman Church; untenable interpretations of Scripture had been presented. Idolatry and superstition were further criticisms. Through his tendency too readily to leap into print, Merewether became divisive. (It was a trait not confined to matters Roman Catholic. Dorothy Wordsworth wrote to her nephew[23]

Mrs Merewether has always a thousand cares and apprehensions whenever a Tract or pamphlet is meditated).

In 1835 had come '*Popery, a new Religion*' which title describes the contents. He compared some of the tenets of 19th century Roman Catholicism: transubstantiation, Mariolatry, the invocation of saints, the doctrine of purgatory, with Apostolical Christianity. He noted that he wished to reserve for another occasion comments regarding the Mass, Indulgences, private confession to a priest as obligatory, and the position of the Pope.

Fears in regard to the spread of Roman Catholicism in England had several bases: one was a deep seated anxiety which stemmed from the 16th and 17th centuries, that Roman Catholics were planning to overthrow the realm, since they owed their prime allegiance to a foreign sovereign. While no one could have presented a more loyal attitude to the British crown than Ambrose and his patriotism was never held in question, his introduction of foreign (particularly Italian) missionaries to his estate did give credibility to the notion that the influence from Rome itself was increasing. An emphasis on greater centralisation (and therefore less local authority) was taking place and there was developing in England an attitude known as Ultramontane which welcomed such a trend; Wiseman was the chief protagonist. When it had become a considerable force, Ambrose was one of those much affected.

The standpoints of Ambrose were often liable to disparagement; criticism followed his response to happenings that could be regarded as unusual and not capable of an obvious and immediate rational explanation. Since the period of the Enlightenment of the 18th century and the impact of Newtonian physics, there had come a change of attitude in many minds towards the subject of miracles. The creation of the world with its fixed laws was still generally regarded, in England at any rate, as the work of the one true God; in a sense nature was the huge miracle. The gap between the natural and the supernatural widened. Since revelation of the divine took place within the visible universe, the realm of the supernatural in so far as it touched *matter* (the direct intervention of God within the hearts of men was different) was a far more shadowy area and one that became harder not only to define, but to understand.

This did not diminish, in fact tended to increase 19th century preoccupation with the supernatural in its broadest sense. By the 1850s attempts to speak with the departed, table turning and so on, reached many households; the de Lisles were one of them (see p 283). For Ambrose the divine initiative in the design of the universe and its laws was corroborated by the Creator's constant suspension of them in favour of those who had been specially chosen. One might even go so far as to say that a natural explanation of an event was to him suspect; a miraculous (in his terms) far more likely. It was part of the spectrum of the holy, the other; manifestation in this world from the one beyond human sight and understanding, the reality of which was so vivid to him. But when claims were made that miracles and visions vouchsafed to members of Ambrose's family and circle were divine revelations and acts in response to the prayers of the saints, provocation was the result. To those Leicestershire Anglican clergy who had been reared on the doctrine of salvation by faith, here were grave stumbling blocks to smooth relationships. This was equally true of the reactions of certain members of the Roman Catholic hierarchy in England, as will soon be apparent.

A test case came with the so-called Grace Dieu miracle. At Vespers on the second Sunday in Advent in 1835 in the chapel of Grace Dieu Manor, Anne Fullard, a young married women of Whitwick was seized by an epileptic attack of great severity. She was carried into the house where her struggles and aspect caused much alarm, until a certain metal object was placed on the sufferer's breast: all the violent symptoms ceased. It was a medal, struck in Paris in 1832 at the instigation of Catherine Labouré[24], bearing an inscription of the Blessed Mother of Jesus and said to have miraculous powers. Laura had bought several of them for occasions such as this.

During the following February, Francis Merewether issued a broadsheet[25] to his parishioners denouncing 'the subtle attempt' that had been made to 'palm on you with very insufficient evidence, the notions of supernatural, or at any rate superhuman aid in the services of the Romish Church'. A counterattack came in the shape of a much longer pamphlet[26] by Fr

Odilo Woolfrey of the monastery who had been present at the incident. He introduced a set of incendiary ideas:

> ... The well-proved existence of this divine power in the bosom of the Catholic Church, is at once its glory and principal ornament, and the irresistible proof of its divine veracity ... this it is that torments those 'who wish evils unto her'. They know well that miracles can be wrought only by the members of the true Church.

Francis Merewether responded with a crude satire[27] and there were other publications and comments in the newspapers until the episode died down. But the vicar had not tired; he wrote another pamphlet in the shape of *A Pastoral Address to the inhabitants of Whitwick on the Opening of a Monastery within the limits of that parish*[28] (upon the creation of a new building). He said that although the monastic state had advantages in the middle ages, it did not have relevance in the 19th century. Since the monks relieved the wants daily of innumerable poor people (some of whom even made their home there) the remarks would seem to have been insensitive at least.

A year later, three of the lay brothers announced they were receiving what were referred to as 'extraordinary supernatural communications made by an interior voice'; the three were Simeon Commins, and Luke Levermore, both professed and original members of the Community, and Brother Joseph, a novice whose surname has not survived. The principal subject of the communications at that stage was a change in the state of the lay brothers to a greater approximation to that established by St Benedict. The Abbot of the Trappists in Ireland had hitherto opposed this; so had Fr Bernard one of the oldest and most respected choir monks; the Prior, W. O. Woolfrey, seemed inclined to think the communications were from God.

In April 1837 Ambrose wrote to Bishop Walsh who was about to set off for Rome, asking him whether he thought it advisable to lay before the Pope the project recommended by the visions: that choir Religious and lay brothers be united in one class[29]. There is no record that Bishop Walsh mentioned the matter. The visions continued and in the late autumn came prophecies which affected Ambrose very closely; their content was not recorded in the letters of the time, only that they were very remarkable. Their nature becomes clearer at a later date in correspondence between the Provincial of the Rosminians in England and the Founder in Stresa, as the result of a conversation with Ambrose in January 1841. To follow the course of these unusual happenings is of some importance because it is only by this means that it is possible to come to a fuller understanding of Ambrose and of the opinions of others in respect of him.

Brother Joseph's belief was that his voices demanded that there should be a test to decide whether the visions and prophecies had a divine origin by asking for a miracle. Ambrose and Spencer were deeply involved, so much is clear from Spencer's letters to his friend[30]. Brothers Simeon and Joseph left their strict enclosure to go to Manchester with Spencer, there to meet Bishop Briggs. Meanwhile Lady Radcliffe Eyre with her parish priest were making their way north by road. Lady Radcliffe Eyre had shingles on her face and was praying for a cure. Bishop Briggs forbade the test and everyone returned home. Spencer wrote to Ambrose[31]:

> My own advice is . . . that we should be perfectly obedient and thankful for the stoppage and esteem it a great deliverance, there will be more honour done to Almighty God and for consolation for us in the practice of humility than in working the most splendous miracles.

On Dec 11th he wrote again of the wonderful matters in which they had been together engaged and in which 'we cannot but sympathise with one another'. He continued:

> I have come myself to the conclusion to allow nothing of the past to have any place in my mind. I cannot see just how to explain all that has been seen and heard on the supposition of its being an illusion or the fruit of imagination, but certainly the enemy is deeply clever in deceiving and if he could not manage to make falsehood appear truth to us, he could not be wiser than we are. Our Lord tells us that false spirits will deceive . . . Thank God, in obedience to Bishop Briggs to whom I found myself referred to by Dr Walsh, I gave up the wish to try this thing . . . the whole thing looks to me more and more like a great dream. I tell you my thoughts because I wish you and your amiable wife to unite with me in this determination. You have been led indeed to expect things for yourselves

and those belonging to you and it is hard to resort again to the poor prospects of a common life with all its trials and inconveniences, yet it is not in this life as we must remember that our hopes are to rest. You have come, as it were by the will of God . . . to be filled with these exceeding glorious prospects for the present life. Now he calls upon you to renounce them for obedience sake . . . assuredly one point of humility and patience is better than all that has been held out to us lately . . . Most thankfully then, let us now come down from our dangerous heights and devote ourselves to the pursuit of perfection.

These words showed the degree of maturity which Spencer had attained; they also revealed the readiness on the part of Ambrose once more to place high hopes on the outcome of prophecies which concerned his family.

A few months later the Abbot of Mount Melleray in Ireland, in whose jurisdiction Mount St Bernard lay, wrote to expel Brother Joseph from the Order; according to Ambrose to the grief of Bishop and Prior who thought this unjust. Since the Brother's prophecies had included 'the speedy reconversion of England', Ambrose was deeply hopeful that they should be true. But as he wrote to Lord Clifford[32] 'For some good reason God is very sparing now in the communication of the high spiritual gifts to the members of His Church'. Perhaps there is some connection here with a letter[33] sent by Ambrose (and signed by all the monks) to Cardinal Acton in Rome asking for Mount St Bernard to cease to be ruled by the Irish Cistercian house and placed under the jurisdiction of the General Chapter of the Order in France[34].

Laura writing to Fr Joseph Hirst, Principal of Ratcliffe College, many years later[35], admitted that she had not cared for Brother Joseph but that 'my dear husband' had been impressed by him and believed in his visions. Since the experiences in Rome in 1831, those who might be in touch with the source of all truth drew Ambrose like a magnet. He continued to consult Brother Simeon when he had to make decisions in the future, and even after some of the monk's prophecies did not become realities, Ambrose's faith and trust in the gifts were not destroyed.

The visit of Ambrose and Laura to the so called 'miraculous virgins of the Tyrol' offers a further illustration of the attraction for them of manifestations beyond the purely natural. Lord Shrewsbury had published a Letter[36] addressed to Ambrose which described the Estatica of Caldaro (Maria Mörl) and the Addolorata of Capriana, Maria Domenica Lazzari; there was a later supplement which told of three successive visits to another Estatica in Monte San Savino, Domenica Barbagli. This encouraged Ambrose to gain permission to see these holy women also. 'We visited with wonder and edification the Estatica Maria Mörl' he wrote[37] to his mentor.

Apart from members of the family, clergy and enquirers from Oxford, there were Leicestershire neighbours and friends too at Grace Dieu in the decade after 1839, though not as many as were to come in later years. Lady Sitwell, as she continued to call herself despite her second marriage, probably had the greatest influence upon them and one of whom the de Lisle family saw most. She was born Caroline Stovin of Whitgift Hall in Yorkshire and according to the Sitwell histories was a 'celebrated Blue-stocking' and friend of poets. She married Sitwell Sitwell as his second wife in 1798 when she was 19; their only child died in infancy. Her husband's surname at birth had been Hurt; his father, Francis Hurt had inherited Renishaw from a maternal uncle, William Sitwell, and in common with many Victorians had altered his name on the change of his fortunes. An iron works and a large sum of money came his way also from a cousin. By the time Sitwell Sitwell was grown up the family's trade connections had been severed; instead they had extensive estates and a large income. In 1808 Sitwell Sitwell had entertained the Prince Regent at Renishaw; when he died in 1811 he was a baronet. His son George, and two daughters of his first marriage were left to be brought up by Caroline, the 'handsome step-mother whose ideas ran upon education and progress'.

In 1821 Caroline Lady Sitwell married, as his second wife, John Smith-Wright, a Nottinghamshire banker and acquaintance of Gladstone; he had three daughters. They came to live at Rempstone Hall, a distance of three miles from Grace Dieu. In company with other widows of her day who remarried[38], she continued in her old style thereby avoiding a drop in rank; a matter of importance as would appear. She also continued to draw £3,000 a year from the Renishaw estates for the 49 years by which she survived her first husband. Kind and generous and much given to charitable works, she built and maintained three schools, aided two others, she ran clubs to encourage savings, managed her own farm; so there were interests in common with the Grace Dieu family. After Laura's illness in 1848 Lady Sitwell drove Ambrose and Laura with Mena and Alice to Matlock, a spa in Derbyshire, in her carriage for a few days to stay at an inn at her expense.

Step-son George married Susan Tait (sister of the future Archbishop of Canterbury); they were one set of forbears of Edith, Osbert and Sacheverell. Under Lady Sitwell's hospitable roof Ambrose and Laura extended their range of acquaintances; the Bishop of London (Blomfield) was one; the Nightingale family[39], was another; the party, including Florence, was escorted to the Monastery. The visit was repeated to Grace Dieu.

Charles Montalembert made his first visit to Leicestershire during the summer of 1839 and there followed a friendship with Ambrose which, although maintained very largely by correspondence on both sides, was extensive and expansive, and not only lasted until death, but survived some differences of opinion. They had much in common: a love of chivalry (Montalembert said in the French House of Peers 'We are the sons of the Crusaders, and we will not fall back before the sons of Voltaire') and of monasticism; the Frenchman's *magnum opus The Monks of the West* was still unfinished when he died in 1870. Both valued their independence in relation to the clergy, and their freedom to express their views.

Montalembert's letters to his wife gave details of the English visit. After seeing Alexis-François Rio who introduced him to William Gladstone in London, he made his way to Leicestershire. Ambrose showed him his father's house, Garendon Park, his own home, and related the story of his life and what he was attempting to achieve in the neighbourhood. Montalembert was deeply impressed[40]. He had assisted at the 'abjuration and baptism of six protestants' in a touching ceremony with beautiful chants excellently executed: the young seigneur dressed in a mantle of gold walked in procession with his servants; two young sons, five and four years old clad as choir boys, preceded their father: their sweet voices brought tears to the eyes of the French visitor.

Together Ambrose and Montalembert visited the ruins of some of the former Cistercian abbeys of England: Kirkstall, Rievaulx and Fountains, at the last of which they had made a joint vow, consecrating their services to the Church. It was a friendship that provided each with introductions that might not otherwise have come his way: for Montalembert the sight of some prominent Englishmen travelling through Europe, and for Ambrose meetings with continental writers and thinkers, Rio, Lacordaire, Dom Gueranger, the liturgical scholar, to name a few. Their voluminous correspondence gave them an opportunity of airing their views to a sympathetic ear, and posterity the chance to know what these had been.

The most fruitful friendship continued to be with Lord Shrewsbury. Within it the strength of the persuasive powers of the younger man are revealed for he cajoled the earl to part with large sums of money for projects for which, at the beginning at any rate, he had little sympathy. The foundation of Mount St Bernard in 1835 was a case in point. It had not raised enthusiasm from Lord Shrewsbury, rather the reverse. Ambrose anxious that the exercise be repeated in Staffordshire received a cool answer[41]: would not alms houses for poor old people be more useful 'than a regular monkery'; Brothers of Christian Instruction would be fitter for the purpose than contemplative monks.

Ambrose replied with some heat: one could not fix on a more serviceable class of men than Trappists; they sang the divine office, acted as missionaries (there was some misunderstanding on this score), attended to the corporal and spiritual needs of the poor and sick, could act as spiritual directors, and their houses were places of retreat and moved men to return to the religion of their ancestors. 'Besides which', he ended 'you may support half a dozen Trappists on what would satisfy one ordinary priest'. For some time the expenses of 8 individuals had come to only £1 a week. Then there was the benefit of masses said for a founder or benefactor.

By 1839 Ambrose felt that the monastery building which had been erected should be demolished and a new and more splendid one, built by Pugin, take its place. The earl at first replied that if their premises were unsuitable, it might be better for the monks to leave England and move to Italy. The effect on Ambrose was electrifying and such was the force of it that his benefactor capitulated on condition that the site be changed to one of which he approved (the present location). He provided £2,000 initially, with a promise of another £1,000 if the monks added the small sums which they had already collected (some begging expeditions had been made which to quote Ambrose's words had 'given umbrage to the secular clergy'). In a letter[42] to his father he communicated his joy:

> Lord Shrewsbury is going to build a new Monastery . . . under Pugin's directions. The present monastery, which you remember is a poor, unfinished building, is to be converted into farm buildings for their use and their present church is to be made into a great barn. Lord Shrewsbury is giving great sums to the Church in different parts of England, but his giving this princely donation to Mount St Bernard he told me he did chiefly from affection for me and to please me. Pugin gives all his time, drawings etc gratis: and charges no percentage on the outlay.

Materials were close at hand; some could be used again and the monks would do much of the work themselves. The letter ended with the monks' thanks for the strawberry plants despatched from Garendon.

The happiness which the prospect of a new and improved set of monastic buildings offered was short lived, for in Lent 1840 came a fresh problem: Bishop Baines, Vicar Apostolic of the Western District issued a Pastoral Letter to his flock in which he charged certain converts of impropriety. He insinuated that several types of persons who had turned to Roman Catholicism were implicated, and it was certain because it was made explicit enough, that Ambrose, although not mentioned by name, was under censure.

Chapter 7

Some Crises

BISHOP Baines's Pastoral of Lent 1840 was a remarkable document which drew upon itself long and bitter argument in England and Rome. John Bossy in his *The English Catholic Community 1570–1850*[1] has described it as the last full scale public manifesto of traditional English Catholicism, which gives it an importance of its own, quite apart from what was revealed of current attitudes towards converts and Ambrose in particular. The Bishop was obviously writing under pressure; he saw change where he did not require it; always a severe psychological test.

The Pastoral was spirited, outspoken and courageous; it sought to placate the English nation as a whole and the established Church against what the Bishop thought the ill-considered behaviour of certain new Roman Catholics. But there was lack of tact shown in it also and a failure to grasp what must be the consequences of what he had written. The subject he criticised most strongly was that of praying for the conversion of England.

When Spencer and Ambrose had initiated the Crusade for such prayers in Paris in 1838, all the Vicars Apostolic were made aware of it. Only the Bishop of the Midland District showed any interest; Bishop Baines immediately declined to co-operate. Nicholas Wiseman, still in Rome at the English College, drew up specific prayers in response to Spencer's request, and asked the Congregation of Indulgences to attach some spiritual privileges to their use. Wiseman made known his success on this score to Bishop Griffiths of the London District; neither he nor Bishop Briggs in the North were sympathetic. The fact that the suggestion had come from the man by whom the English Bishops did not care to be represented in Rome, was enough to prejudice the matter at the start.

Much of the beginning of the Pastoral Letter was concerned with drawing a comparison between the 19th century present and the days of the Roman Empire. The Bishop's text included the words 'the days are evil'. He described the converts made by St Paul who 'though strong in faith were often lax in practice . . . many of an enthusiastic turn of mind, not satisfied with the frequent and undoubted exhibition of miraculous gifts and prophecy, were perpetually hankering after new ideal wonders' and listening, as St Paul put it, to '*old wives fables* . . . about the approaching end of the world etc'. There was a second allusion to prophecy near the end of the document; to the attempt on the part of some of the present day 'to pry into the hidden councils of God . . . soon these idle speculations become to them realities and the peace of the Church is disturbed by . . . wild and wayward fancies'.

He regretted that some modern converts had begun openly to apply 'certain reproachful terms, such as "*heretics*" to our spiritual brethren, and to write in a style of asperity and harshness . . . Almost all the little divisions which exist among us – and thank God they are not many – may be traced to those who have been recently called to the faith'; and again 'the greater part of our difficulties in this country still originate in the same source, though the number of converts among us is a small number'. Moreover they were increasing the distance between themselves and those they had left. If there were practices of piety, he continued, which the Church tolerated rather than approved, which could be calculated to confirm the prejudices of Protestants, then those practices would be paraded 'in preference to the most approved, most ancient, most impressive forms of Catholic devotion'. What a contrast, he felt, to the reactions of St Paul towards his neighbours: he was always guided by the dictates of charity.

At the last came the matter of the prayers for the conversion of England for which efforts had been made to secure the sanction of bishops. Such a public display he thought would give offence and excite opposition; but more than that: a national conversion was 'a moral impossibility'. It was all wrongly phrased: 'We do and ought to pray . . . with the understanding that our prayers should be heard in the manner and at the time most consistent with the merciful but inscrutible providence of God'. The prophecies 'which some pretend to have been made on the subject and by which we suppose the promoters of the scheme in question must really be influenced', he thought fables. 'To give credit to them on mere hearsay without canonical investigation and proof of authenticity' he considered superstitious. 'So far therefore' he ended 'from approving this novel and extraordinary project, we disapprove it, and strictly forbid any of our clergy to offer up *publicly* in their churches and chapels the weekly prayers above mentioned'. He exhorted the faithful to pray for an increase of clergy 'to call unbelievers to the faith through the ministry of apostolic teachings'.

Giovanni-Battista-Pagani[2] wrote from Prior Park to the Rosminian Father General apprising him of Bishop Baines' attitudes. The Bishop had spoken to him several times of '"Mr Phillipps" as a famous fanatic':

> In the Midland District, Spencer, Phillipps and others helped by their Bishop, show a great urge for the conversion of England, they make and recommend *public* prayers for this object. They believe that based on some prophecies they are persuaded that the great event for the entire conversion of this nation is at hand. Our Bishop looks on all this as the effect of a kind of exaltation of mind, takes a stand against the conversion of Protestants, who from this campaign are drawn to deride, censure and persecute still more the Catholic Religion. In the Circular which published the Lenten Regulations, the Bishop expounds his view. He praises private prayer for this object. He forbids in his district public prayer for the same object .. It seems to me that the two Bishops of the Northern and London Districts, if not entirely, at least in part are with him.

Later[3] he wrote again, once more transmitting what he felt were Bishop Baines' views on Ambrose.

> I have noticed at times when mentioning Phillipps, he speaks of him as having too exalted a head. He (Phillipps) is considered the head of a party and everything that appears to smack of fanaticism is attributed to the 'Filippiani'. This party is up against three Bishops (to my mind) and a big section of the Missionary clergy. In my opinion Phillipps is one of those rare men who are animated in a special way by the spirit of Christ: this however does not take from the fact that he and his

adherents can commit some imperfections that allows others to
fix on and form a party against them, . . .

The almost immediate result of the circulation of this document was a summons to the Bishop from Rome. He left
England on 19 May 1840 and arrived on 9 June. On the 16th
he was received in audience by the Pope Gregory XVI who,
according to the Bishop, was displeased with the English
Vicars Apostolic: he accused them of a lack of devotion to the
Holy See and spoke disparagingly of letters which had been
addressed to himself or Propaganda by them, and by Bishop
Baines in particular. The Bishop assured the Pope of their
loyalty.

A list of the expressions which had given offence in the
Pastoral was drawn up and read to the Bishop of the Western
District on 2 July by Cardinal Franzoni, Prefect of the Propaganda Fide. A written explanation was required. It is unneces-
sary to describe in detail the procedure by which the Bishop
was examined; sufficient is it to say that it was lengthy and
that an adverse decision was reached. A declaration to disclaim
certain meanings imputed to his words was requested; this he
gave on 15 March 1841; the Pope wrote him a formal letter
expressing satisfaction and provided money to defray some of
his expenses. Bishop Baines returned to his District; he had
been away for over ten months.

The Bishops defence to Propaganda was not published, but
the contents leaked out[4] To support his contention that converts had been listening to unauthorised predictions the Bishop
had referred to 'the chief of the prophets' who was 'a Cistercian
lay-brother or oblate in a monastery of the Midland District.
This man had constant visions relating to individuals and the
nation at large'. Back at Prior Park Bishop Baines enlisted the
help of Emilio Belisy[5] in translating some documents into
English from the Italian. The latter passed on the above and
other information to his superiors[6]

Since the final letter of the Pope had not at that time been
made public, the question was left open whether there had
been censure of the Bishop at Rome, or as he was anxious to
maintain, he had not been called upon to retract anything,
only to explain the meaning of some of his utterances. In order

to make this clear he wrote two further pamphlets: one[7] was printed, but not published, a distinction which he defended, but in fact it is not difficult to find a copy: the second[8] was addressed to a prominent convert layman and circulated openly. In both he marshalled arguments to support what he had written. In the second he declared 'The Pastoral was denounced in Rome, by whom I repeat I know not'. It had been suggested that Henry Bagshawe, a convert of Ultramontane views might have been responsible, but the Bishop thought not; Gentili was another suspect, but he was not in Rome.

From the archives of the Propaganda Fide it would seem as if the culprit (if such he be) was Lord Shrewsbury. At that date he was spending much of his time in Rome since both his daughters were married to Italian husbands and he could give the money he saved on his English estate towards church building. A copy of the Pastoral Letter is on the files[9] having been addressed to the Rt Honble the Earl of Shrewsbury, Rome, from England, post marked 9 March 1840, by a sender whose signature has been effaced. (The writing was not that of Ambrose). It would seem that Shrewsbury had sprung to the defence of his old friend by passing the attack upon him to higher authority. This is corroborated by a letter from Gentili to Rosmini from Prior Park[10] to the effect that the case of Mgr Baines was more serious than had been thought. 'Lord Shrewsbury has written from Rome that the Pope wished to see a translation of the Pastoral ... The Shrewsbury family is quite disturbed and write that they are highly indignant'.

Bishop Baines's two further documents did not win approval in Rome: the Pope in a letter[11] to each English Vicar Apostolic warned against accepting Bishop Baines's version of the affair. In handing a copy of the explanatory pamphlet to Belisy, the Bishop urged him to read it 'But don't lend it to Mr Pagani, nor Dr Gentili. That is the very centre of opposition – that is where my greatest enemies are'.[12]

For Ambrose a consequence of this controversy was to draw wider attention to his confidence in the authenticity of visions and prophecies. This had important consequences in the future and caused men to be wary of his plans. The 1840 Lent Pastoral episode served further to divide hereditary Catholics and converts by polarising their attitude to it. The distinctions

between various wings of converts, the aggressive such as
Henry Bagshawe and Frederick Lucas, and the eirenic like
Ambrose, became more apparent. The substance of Digby's
letter[13] to Ambrose immediately after the Pastoral serves as an
illustration.

> I hear the Bath Catholics are chanting victory ... I only
> scribble this to entreat you to be 'sage' and engage Spencer and
> Pugin to be 'sage' ... Let us grieve and be silent. My impression
> respecting you was that you would only say the Dr [Baines] has
> now dished himself. So I think he has. Let us leave it to others
> to serve him up. I almost fancy that the poor man is *timbré* ...
> The thing is a slap on the face for us all four converts.
> However some there will be no doubt to express anger, but I
> think silent contempt is the proper treatment.

With the arrival of Gentili at Grace Dieu in June 1840, his
host had solved part, but only part, of his missionary problem.
He looked forward to a time when a large assemblage of
priests would minister in the villages surrounding his home.
Where would he find them? Every District was short of clergy.
Ambrose decided that they must come from the Orders. Antonio Rosmini had sent him one of his most gifted men; he
planned for more like him; for a noviciate in England in his
neighbourhood which would train English candidates for the Institute.

'I believe that the day will come' he wrote[14] to Rosmini
'when I can found more than one Mission of the Order of
Charity, but for the moment it is best to step slowly and
carefully. In the meanwhile, you know where my heart lies,
and that I have no greater desire than to see your Institute of
Charity well established in England. Apart from this I am
nothing, and we do not know if God wishes to do this through
me'. In addition, he had not entirely given up hope of help
from the Passionists.

Once again, Lord Shrewsbury was not at the start in agreement with the aims of his friend. He wrote from Rome[15] as the
result of having seen Lord Clifford, Father Glover S J, and the
Passionists. The first two had felt that it was an impracticable
scheme to think of working with the Passionists in England. Fr
Glover had remarked 'You will never get an Englishman into

that order, so what good can you do with them'. Dominic Barberi had spoken a little broken English, but could not understand a word of what Lord Shrewsbury said. Shrewsbury continued:

> You will only bring yourself and others into trouble with these good people and do no good. We must work in the large towns with *large* churches in which we can influence the people by the splendour etc of our service ... we are all against your Gentili scheme. It is beginning at the wrong end. Besides which, Gentili is not suited for England. We must have a new race of zealous English missionaries, such as [we] are now bringing up at Oscott, under the good Bishop and Pugin ... we must have *chapels*.

Lord Shrewsbury with his long experience of life in Rome was aware of practices and attitudes within Italian Catholicism which had no counterpart in England. Those Italian Religious whom Ambrose proposed should join the English mission had been nurtured in a system in which there was nothing corresponding to the concepts of trust, individual freedom and fair play cherished by English Roman Catholics. The burning zeal and total commitment of the missionaries to the cause of transforming the religious scene in England may well have made Lord Shrewsbury nervous. In the event, the achievement in terms of conversions, the creation of a new outlook and habits of devotion wrought by the Italians was very remarkable; they were remarkable men.

Gentili placed (at Ambrose's insistence) at Grace Dieu had need of his heroic qualities. His difficulties came to him from four directions: his superiors, his host (Ambrose), local conditions, and the complexities of his own nature. The circumstances which led to his withdrawal from Prior Park and the revision of his status, so that he was made subject to the jurisdiction of Pagani (Provincial of the Rosminians in England), have already been described. Pagani treated him with severity to the point of harshness, and lack of understanding of his unusual subordinate. Over a distance of 200 miles from Bath, consultation was required over trivial issues: oversight of Gentili's possessions, permission to spend even small sums of money and, of course, total obedience, were demanded. Rosmini wrote his customary sage letters from Stresa, but asked for full and lengthy reports at frequent intervals. Pagani's closely written minute scrawl in black ink filled ten to twelve pages of detailed information every few days. Much of it was devoted to doubts about Gentili; whether he was living up to the required ideals of poverty and so on. Gentili in Leicestershire was constantly in trouble for not writing often enough.

Ambrose made great demands. 'I know of no truly apostolical man in England. Oh! if God would only send us a Saint Augustine . . . or someone like St Francis de Sales' he had written to Rosmini[16]. It was a role to daunt the bravest spirit. Since there was no money for a chaplain's house, Gentili's base was a room near the chapel in Grace Dieu Manor. Each day he said the offices, celebrated Mass and held night prayers with the family. He was expected to visit the sick and poor in the neighbourhood and set up centres for preaching. On Sundays a procession with a good deal of ceremonial preceded a Mass sung to a Gregorian chant accompanied by the organ. The services of Vespers and Benediction took place in the afternoon.

At first relationships were smooth. Pagani reported that Gentili found Ambrose 'a most lovable person so that all is smiling around him'. He had asked for a second pair of shoes as his feet were perpetually wet in the English weather, and these had been provided. An early letter[17] of Gentili promised well, although there were hints of problems to come. He gave an assurance that he intended always to wear his 'ecclesiastical garb' (he was the first Roman Catholic priest in England to do so) and to practise poverty.

> This fine house with its decorations and conveniences which instead of pleasing me give me annoyance and disgust, makes me more and more despise and detest the greatness, the honours, and the riches of the world.

The inhabitants of the neighbourhood were for the most part poor: they needed to be given books of devotions, catechisms and 'explanations of our religion'. Unlike himself, Jesuits were not required to ask permission before spending money on their missions. Gentili then proceeded to elaborate on one of his most repetitious hobby-horses: 'the easy-going ways' in

England in regard to relations between men and women.

The presence of women as servants at Prior Park he had felt dangerous, as also the practice permitted there of hearing the confessions of nuns and giving spiritual counsel to women on their own. Later[18] he returned to the theme relative to his own circumstances at Grace Dieu. Ambrose thought nothing of leaving him for several days with his young wife and sister-in-law and staff of six young servants, all women; or even without the family. Gentili considered this most improper. He disagreed with mixing the children (all under the age of eleven years) at Grace Dieu school. As a result of his prompting, boys and girls were separated. The fear of the flesh expressed by the Italian missionaries with its accompanying practice of extreme mortification and austerity, gave rise to some new emphases in moral teaching in England. Pride, exemplified by private judgement and individualism, had long been considered the besetting English national sin. This undoubted Pelagianism[19] was now joined by another limitation: an incapacity to deal adequately and theologically with the claims of the instincts. It was to have lasting consequences.

Gentili was later criticised for the paucity of his reports to his superiors. For the first few months, however, he wrote much on his mission. He found only twenty-seven Roman Catholics in the vicinity, twelve of whom, some quite young children, were members of Ambrose and Laura's household at Grace Dieu. The chapel there was far into the country; the centres of population all some miles distant. The processions and other ceremonies which Ambrose had introduced 'and I have no hope of cutting them down' left Gentili with little time to preach. Those who came and who understood no Latin tended to leave for another chapel [Whitwick] where they found English prayers and things were shorter. It would be necessary to hire rooms in various villages and preach there, but the distance, the 'dreadful climate', the loss of time and the cost, all made difficulties. Ambrose's means were limited, Gentili wrote[20]; his fare to England had not yet been repaid. With many apologies Ambrose had explained that the stipend of £50 a year which had been promised could be only £30; he was obviously ashamed with the admission.

Ambrose and Laura had been kindness itself; 'they are the

most fervent set of Catholics I ever saw; their thought and desires always turn upon one subject, namely the conversion of England,' Gentili wrote to Frances Taylor[21]. But to Rosmini he confided that living with the English gentry could undermine the spirit: the complicated etiquette, taboos and proprieties, though innocent in themselves, were a waste of time. The reactions of Ambrose to his missioner were equally frank. He sent Rosmini £24 for Gentili's fare in September, and gave an account[22] of his activities. His health was improving, though he was not robust, and sometimes in low spirits. Gentili was extending his efforts beyond the immediate parish of Grace Dieu; preaching in the villages of Osgathorpe, Belton and Shepshed once a week in hired rooms. He had not heard many confessions, but these could mainly be left to the priest at Whitwick; Gentili should 'concern himself with conversions'. He was using an abundance of words in his sermons and in fact spoke English 'as if he were one of us'. His manner was impressive and he succeeded in finding his way to the hearts of his hearers, though 'he is sometimes a little too metaphysical for the common people who do not understand these philo-sophical subjects'. It would be necessary, Ambrose felt, for Gentili to make a careful study of the cases of conscience in Liguori[23] (the book that was followed in the diocese) because he would soon be having to hear confessions among the populace. It seemed to him that Gentili was rather a rigorist:

> I know of no greater trouble or more terrible danger than not knowing clearly the distinction between the precept and the advice of the Lord, between what is obligatory and that which pertains to perfection, between that which is useful for the development of Christian virtue, and that without which a man actually falls, ipsofacto, into deadly sin. I tell you this because not only myself, but also my sister Henrietta [Laura's sister], have noticed this same tendency towards rigorism in the good father, and because when he was at Prior Park, the same observation was frequently made in the college. An outstanding sweetness of manner is still most necessary, particularly when dealing with young people ... I have seen priests that have won the hearts of those little ones in Christ in a single moment, simply through a sweet word, or a smile. An arid, dry or reserved manner, on the other hand, does not please them, and

it does not win hearts. I am sure . . . that with advice from you, without mentioning, however, that I have said anything, Gentili would acquire that little which he lacks in these matters. I believe that he is an apostolic man who will do a great deal of good here.

By 27 October Ambrose was able to report progress: he told Rosmini that Gentili's missions in the villages were gaining support; 'he has aroused a great spiritual excitement about the Holy Faith'. Despite what Monsignor Baines had been saying, 'the whole of England is on the eve of its conversion'. Bishop Walsh had mentioned the provision of old Oscott (two miles from the new building) for the Rosminians as a noviciate house. This was no longer available. But during a recent encounter with the Bishop at Alton Towers (the home of the Shrewsburys) he had offered the mission of Loughborough to the Rosminians instead. There was a church and good house. Ambrose thought it ideal. (One reason was clearly that it was close to his own domain).

Gentili corroborated much of this activity to his Superior General the following day. He added that Ambrose had taken exception to a paragraph in Rosmini's *Maxims of Christian Perfection* (published in 1830). He saw '*rigorismo o giansenismo*' in a phrase. He would not recommend it to anyone as it was; the English and French translations should be altered to meet the doubt. Gentili suggested that Ambrose be conciliated. 'He is a man of wide influence, well connected politically . . . He is well in with the Bishops and has an extraordinary deference and veneration for Bishop Walsh'.

The year ended with a visit to Grace Dieu by Pagani in order that he might observe Gentili's deployment. Dominic Barberi who had been a guest in the house for a few days, had returned to France. His first visit to England had been a disappointment. He had found the students at Oscott lacking in enthusiasm; they had thought his appearance and poor grasp of English comical. Bishop Walsh had promised a house for the Passionists at Aston Hall in Staffordshire but Barberi had not been allowed to see it because the occupant, a secular priest, was disinclined to move. Pagani was present in Grace Dieu Chapel on Christmas day 1840 when fifty seven converts were received; the Rosminian mission in the Midlands seemed to have a future.

There were a large number of letters between England and Stresa in the years that followed. After his fortnight's stay at Grace Dieu Pagani had a great deal to report: his most important letter[24] in relation to Ambrose was one which gave the substance of a long conversation with him. Pagani had heard rumours of revelations received by the de Lisle family. 'I did not intend to give too much weight to these things, but to explore them'. Ambrose 'did not have great difficulty in responding candidly to my demand'.

The long account that followed traced the first visit of Ambrose to Italy; his illness in Florence and remarkable recovery; the strange visit to Mark Carricha, and the events that led to the foundation of Mount St Bernard. Last came the prophecies of Brother Simeon which were now related in great detail. Several of them had concerned the future of Everard, the second son of Ambrose and Laura; according to the lay brother, he was chosen by God to be General of the Institute of Charity and then Pope. Ambrose was inclined to give credence to the revelation because when Simeon spoke of God's plan for Everard he described the extraordinary manner of his birth.

Towards the end of her pregnancy Laura, quite alone, went into labour and found herself about to be delivered without assistance. She began to recite the Rosary and thought how the Virgin Mary had given birth to Jesus in similar circumstances, when suddenly her son lay new-born on the ground. The doctor, when summoned, was astonished that the child had survived his precipitated arrival. It was not thought possible for the monk to have been made aware of this event by natural means.

'The apostolical ministry on which Gentili is engaged has been singularly blessed by God. Every day he is away at one of the three missions from 7.a.m. to 8.p.m. to preach' Pagani reported[25]. He was walking great distances; many people came to hear him and ask for instruction in the Catholic faith. The number of those who hoped to pass from darkness into light by his ministry was '*grandissimo*'. Relations between Pagani and Gentili had improved; Ambrose and Gentili had experienced some '*urti*' (clashes): as a layman Ambrose, although much attached to the Institute, intruded too much in religious affairs and tended to restrict the liberty of priests. For example he had written to the Abbot of Mount Melleray in Ireland and asked him to change the Prior at Mount St Bernard!

Gentili's letters did not dwell on the difficulties of his mission so much as the low temperature and sad social conditions: the cold was so terrible that when out on a journey on foot, icicles appeared on eyes and nose which impeded his sight and breathing: 'I seemed to be one of those beings made of ice in the pages of Dante'. His concern was for the poor; 'many among my dear people . . . are actually starving . . . and I cannot help sometimes shedding tears of compassion at the sight of the utter destitution'. He was discouraged by his inability to help materially: many were without boots or hats; their clothes were torn which left them half naked; they could not go to church because they had not decent clothes. There was a shortage of work and those who did work could not earn enough for their keep. Ambrose did what he could and went without entertainment and lived as economically as possible; he appealed for funds to his friends, but it was not enough among the thousands of the poor. Laura provided soup, flannel petticoats and bedding for the sick.

Pagani's reaction was to take a sanguine view of the success of the missions; in fact Gentili endured severe psychological hardships in addition to the physical ones. Although he steadily gained their affection, the inhabitants of the Leicestershire villages were not at first inclined to accept his teaching: he was ignored, mocked and reviled, pelted with mud and refuse, burnt in effigy, before he began to gain a hearing.

Bishop Walsh, suddenly became anxious to replace Norbert Woolfrey[26] at Loughborough as a matter of urgency; he pressed Ambrose to encourage the Rosminians to accept the mission. Pagani, though eager to leave the Western District, and Prior Park in particular, disliked the manner in which the arrangement had been contracted through a layman. Moreover, Ambrose had sent an article to *The Tablet* of which Pagani did not approve; criticisms of it had not been well received:

> Among the beautiful gifts he [Ambrose] possesses, he is inclined
> to take up things with too much enthusiasm. He has been given
> a beautiful mind, but he lacks solidity. On the subject of the
> Institute he seems to me to be drawn to action and the
> assumption of a certain role of authority.

Ambrose had taken the original initiative in asking Bishop
Walsh for the mission at Loughborough before it had been
mentioned to him. This had caused him to feel he had a
prescriptive right not only to advise, but

> also to deliver judgement about things and to condemn those
> measures we take that are contrary to his taste ... He has a
> strong inclination to take an active part ... by declaring and
> almost dictating to his superior's disposition. I hope you will
> give me some advice to be able to proceed in peace with this
> gentleman without damaging our causes.[27]

On 13 May 1841 Pagani accepted the direction of the
Loughborough mission on behalf of the Institute of Charity,
with Domenico Ceroni who was in priest's orders, and Peter
Zencher a lay brother; they were joined a few months later by
another priest Angelo Rinolfi and Fortunatus Signini, a deacon.
Pagani arrived just in time to take part in a ceremony of some
splendour in Grace Dieu chapel on 3 June at the marriage of
Henrietta Clifford, Laura's younger sister.

> It was decidedly the most Catholick marriage that has been
> celebrated in England for three centuries, perfectly according to
> old anglo-Catholick [sic] custom

wrote Ambrose to Bloxam[28]:

> ... It is only in our marriage service that we English Catholicks,
> under the government of the Roman Diocese, have retained the
> use of the Sarum rite and even this we should have lost but for
> the energetick remonstrances of the late venerable Bishop
> Milner.

Ambrose gave away the bride; his eldest daughter, Philomena,
was bridesmaid. Amo and Everard knelt beside the bridegroom,
Henry Whitgreave; they had wept when told a few days earlier
that Henrietta was to leave the family circle. The wedding
dress of white satin, embroidered with gold, was appropriately
'in the style of the middle ages; nothing could be more interest-

ing or lovely than her appearance'²⁹ The marriage was performed by Nicolas Wiseman who also celebrated the pontifical
high mass and preached. Spencer assisted; Pagani was deacon;
Whitaker, the parish priest at Whitwick, sub-deacon; Gentili
master of ceremonies. The mass was sung to plain chant by
the Prior of Mount St Bernard, two monks and twelve singing
men of Grace Dieu chapel. The service ended with the *Te
Deum*. The chapel was crowded with 300 of the neighbouring
tenantry who had received tickets: 'Grandpapa' sat with Laura
in the organ gallery. The Henry Whitgreaves left at 1 before
the *déjeuner*, in a carriage with four horses, but it arrived a
few minutes too late at Loughborough railway station; Laura
(who as usual noted the train times in her diary) recorded that
they had to wait there till a quarter past four.

During the same month, Ambrose attended an even more
remarkable set of celebrations-lasting three days, at the consecration of the Cathedral of St Chad in Birmingham, designed
by Pugin. Their style and magnificence revealed once more the
changes that were taking place in English Roman Catholicism.
The bones of St Chad (which had only recently come to light
after centuries of loss) were placed under the High Altar
before thirteen Bishops, two hundred priests and three thousand lay people. Ambrose was greatly moved:

> I have seen a sight which . . . convinces me that the hour is not
> far distant when God will again raise up his afflicted Church in
> this Kingdom and overthrow all heresies under her feet.³⁰

The consecration began at seven in the morning and lasted
many hours 'and most tremendously solemn were the rites
used on the occasion'. Ambrose was in the organ loft 'as the
rubrics forbid any but the clergy to be in the body of the
church'. Various ceremonies followed on the subsequent days:
the opening of the cathedral as a place of worship was one,
when altars were hung with cloths of gold; hundred of wax
lights, garlands of flowers and little trees were placed everywhere, so that 'the church looked like a vision of paradise'.
Bishop Wiseman's sermon affected Ambrose and many others
to tears: 'he expressed the most confident hope that the English
would soon be reunited to the Catholick Church'. A dinner
followed in the town hall: peers, bishops, laymen and more

than 200 priests were 'crowded to suffocation'. 'I felt as though I had no more life in me, that is, as though life was only worth having to serve our holy Mother the Church'.

The provision of a Rosminian noviciate and its location were matters which occupied Ambrose and the members of the Order in England during the next two years. Cannington, in the Western District, was a possibility favoured by Bishop Baines. Ambrose offered a piece of land on his estate. It was hoped at one time that Sibthorp (who had a good deal of private money), now at Oscott, might provide funds for a building. Relations between the Institute and Bishop Baines deteriorated to such an extent that it became clear that the Rosminians would be wise to leave the Western District; to create a novitiate by extending the Loughborough house was the expedient then arrived at. It is only fair to Bishop Baines to point out that Bishop Walsh also regarded with alarm the increasing number of priests in the Central District who were not subject to his jurisdiction.

As he became more successful in the matter of converts, Gentili pleaded with Rosmini to send him help in the form of more Brothers;[31]

> There is a great deal of difference between the planting of the Lord's vineyard and its cultivation. In the first stage a man on his own can do a great deal, whilst in the second, a single man can do little . . . Converts who constitute the main part of my mission, remain untaught, they do not celebrate holy days, and they do not receive the Sacrament. Ignorant as they are of every principle of Christianity before being received into the Holy Church, and often ignorant even of the Creed and the *Pater*, they cannot, from what they were taught before abjuration, feed in those rich pastures necessary to make true Catholics of them . . . It seems to me . . . impossible to continue with the Mission if we are unable to attend to it as we should . . . I have to attend to four villages, with only one chapel that is a long way from any of them and all this without either material help, or the assistance of other people. It would take too long to tell you all my worries, and all my pangs of conscience. However, without the hope of somebody's help in the near future, I cannot continue to bear this responsibility without sin, for the damage that could be done to these souls . . .

Later he reinforced the request by suggesting that the remaining Rosminians at Prior Park should come to the Grace Dieu estate. Ambrose had asked for one of them as a teacher for his children; otherwise he was thinking of having a Jesuit. It would be helpful to be in harmony with Ambrose; he should be pleased if possible.

This eirenic outlook was severely tested at the end of May 1842 when a clash of considerable magnitude took place between Ambrose and Gentili. According to the report sent to Stresa (*'un caso assai serio'*)[32] Gentili had received Ambrose's permission to say a second mass at Shepshed on Sundays. A supply priest from Mount St Bernard, or Whitaker at Whitwick, would sing the 11 o'clock mass at Grace Dieu. So poorly attended was the Grace Dieu service, that Ambrose decided to join the Whitwick and Grace Dieu congregations together. The preservation of the ceremonial in his own chapel with its beauty and holiness was essential to him, and also, he felt to the spiritual well-being of others. Gentili opposed the plan. Ambrose became very heated and said 'I forbid you to say Mass at Shepshed'. Gentili remonstrated at the retraction of a promise, whereupon Ambrose declared 'From this moment you cease to be my chaplain'.

Next day he and Laura drove to Hinckley to see the Dominican Provincial. According to the tale as it reached Pagani, on their return Laura, ever the reconciler, went to see Gentili in his room. She told him that the Dominican had agreed that Ambrose had acted rightly; Gentili would in conscience be bound to do as he was asked. As to the dismissal, Laura excused it as issued in a moment of *'trasporto'*[33] and said that it was withdrawn. The new arrangements would, however, stand and saying mass in Shepshed was for Gentili forbidden. Gentili related the foregoing to Pagani who said he would call at Grace Dieu. Before he could do so, Ambrose and Laura appeared at the Loughborough Mission. Pagani, according to his own testimony, spoke for five minutes, Ambrose for two hours. Gentili was withdrawn from his chaplaincy in order to serve the Institute at Loughborough. In commending this arrangement to Rosmini[34] Pagani pointed out its benefits: with the help of his brethren and from this base, Gentili could give his work round Shepshed the stability it required; he could complete the conversion of his people.

One last major controversy between Ambrose and the Rosin-
ians remained before Ambrose bowed to the inevitable. The
Institute of Charity had its origins within a tradition where the
laity listened, obeyed, provided. A similar situation was about
to take root in England. The creation of a Rosminian noviciate
and school at Ratcliffe near Sileby, Leicestershire, (not eventually at Loughborough) was a domestic matter; it did not
concern Ambrose since it was far from his estate, beyond the
fact he was expected to contribute towards the cost, most of
which was supplied from Italy. But when it was proposed by
Bishop Walsh that the Rosminians should take over the Birmingham parish of St Peter, and most of the Loughborough
brethren be transferred there, Ambrose's opposition was immediate. He visualized once more the ruin of years of effort to
convert his neighbourhood. His letter[35] to Gentili (addressed
as 'my dearest Friend and Brother') described the protest he
had made to the Bishop:

> I have told his Lordship that in the event of this arrangement
> being persisted in, I shall be under the painful necessity of
> resigning into his hands the two missions of Shepshed and
> Whitwick . . . It is with the greatest difficulty that I can manage
> to do what I now do towards supporting them; but I am quite
> resolved not to embarrass myself for *useless* or *fruitless* under-
> takings, for *failures* – such as these missions will assuredly
> become if the priests on whom alone we could count for
> serving them either now or in the future, be removed. Of
> course Fr Pagani will not expect me to subscribe towards
> Sileby if this arrangement be persisted in . . . I am unwilling to
> remain connected with a religious Institute which I see I cannot
> count upon to aid me in carrying out my designs for the
> Propagation of the Faith in this county and on this estate. My
> duties are to this estate and the people on it, and if I endeavour
> to serve anything else, it must be in connexion with the pious
> claims of what is paramount in my mind.

Pagani who was on the verge of a nervous breakdown
because of the difficulties of the English scene, told Rosmini
what he thought of Ambrose's part in the affair:

> How sad it is to see lay people boldly enter the sanctuary and
> with abominable audacity make decisions, pass judgments and
> condemn the Lord's anointed Masters in Israel, and claim to

direct those from whom they should seek direction, and to make laws for those from whom they should think themselves fortunate to receive them ... This makes me all the more anxious to be independent of this gentleman, who has indeed a great zeal for religion, but it is not always according to knowledge.[36]

Pagani left almost immediately for Italy to try to restore his shattered health. The rigorous customs and relentless programme that had been adopted had caused a good deal of illness among the brethren; several had died; some had tuberculosis. Gentili received a severe reproof for his complicity in the opposition to the Birmingham plan: he had discussed it with Ambrose and taken his part. The pressures under which he laboured can be measured by the detailed nature of the criticisms. The mixed character of the Shepshed school came under censure. Gentili pointed out that whereas it accepted both boys and girls as pupils, they were separated, could not see each other, and were taught by master & mistress respectively.

The withdrawal of Gentili from Grace Dieu, far from imparing the relationship between him and Ambrose, in fact improved it. With various constraints lifted, they began a fresh association on a new basis. In October of 1842 Ambrose invited Gentili to accompany him, Laura, Amo & Ebby (Everard) on a three day visit to Oxford. They drove in the pony carriage; Gentili wore his religious habit throughout the visit. Although they had exchanged much correspondence, Ambrose and Newman had not met. On 19 October 1842 they came face to face for the first time. In Ambrose's latest letters[37] he had offered asylum on his estate in the form of land on which to build a monastery for Anglican clergy 'in case any change of position should be forced upon you'. Newman expressed himself grateful[38] but

> a distressing feeling arises in my mind that such marks of kindness as these on your part ... are caused by a belief that I am soon likely to join your communion ... I must assure you then with great sincerity that I have not the shadow of an internal movement known to myself, towards such a step. While God is with me where I am, I will not seek him elsewhere.

Newman's 'amiable manners' were only equalled by his 'gigantic learning and talents'. Ambrose and Gentili also visited Pusey 'and found him what we expected[39] . . . I think I never met with greater humility joined with such prodigious learning.' There is no record that they met again or corresponded. A meeting in W. G. Ward's rooms in Balliol which was to bear remarkable fruit, was with William Lockhart, a young friend of Newman. The intention to speak to John Dobrée Dalgairns prompted the party to drive out to Littlemore to visit him at Newman's 'monastery'; Dalgairns was out, so they did not see the interior as they had wished. Despite the disappointment caused by the termination of the Bloxam correspondence, Ambrose clearly still had hopes of effecting a reunion with the Oxford men and continued to cultivate them. His seriousness was reflected in letters of immense length which he addressed to Cardinal Acton in Rome on this theme. He pressed for an 'English Catholick Hierarchy':[40]

> If we go on as we are, we shall never do much, we are so dreadfully disunited (I mean we English Catholicks) and I attribute it in great measure to the small number of Bishops and the absence of antient holy hierarchical organisation.

Such was Ambrose's expenditure on furthering his religious ideals that he lived in perpetual financial straits. From time to time they reached crisis point of which the pages of Laura's diary provide evidence: bills could not be paid; loans had to be negotiated. It was often Laura who broached the matter of debts to her father-in-law: 'I spoke to Mr P after breakfast about the check for £360' was an entry in February 1840. They owed this amount to Dolmans the publisher. In March 1842 Ambrose tried to raise money through a loan. Laura wrote 'March 4. Mr E. Middleton called about a loan of money; March 5. Ambrose received a very disagreeable letter from Messrs Middleton' (his bankers in Leicester). Although economies were made, Ambrose and Laura found it unpleasant not to provide for their missions those improvements which they thought necessary. Thus at a time of financial stringency, Laura's diary reveals '7 April 1840 G. Kington the tailor from Ashby and a boy came all day to work at vestments'. In September there was a new boiler to heat the chapel: '£30 for apparatus and men's work 4/6 per day with board and lodging to put it in'; 17 Sept 1841. A new font was ordered for £5 'Kirk to put it up and charges for his pains'. On 27 July 1842 a new screen was placed in the Grace Dieu chapel; '11 Dec 1843. Our banner arrived'. In April 1844 'A new organ for the chapel arrived from London, 100 guineas, 5% interest if not paid for a year'. John Hardman, the Birmingham craftsman, received £20 towards an outstanding bill on 26 March 1842, with the promise of the remainder after 10 August. Items continued to be ordered, a record of which survives in the workshop's archives.

Ambrose gave a frank appraisal of his financial position to Lord Shrewsbury[41] in December 1842. The earl had asked for an explanation why it was that the monks of Mount St Bernard's Abbey had not moved into their new monastery building, much of the cost of which he had borne. Ambrose replied that it was because the abbey church was not finished; funds had run out. He explained that he could not stand security for the required amount to be raised by a mortgage; the interest would be beyond his means:

> You know that the allowance I have from my Father amounts only to £1200 exclusive of other advantages we have from him, not in money, as the Manor of Grace Dieu, fruit and vegetables from Garendon, the gamekeeper's wages, thinning of plantations . . . out of this I already pay £129 a year as interest to the Bishop for Mount St Bernard (the original purchase money). Then the Mission of Whitwick . . . costs me £70 p.a. including the expenses of the school and additional to £40 which you so kindly pay for the same holy object . . . There is our own chaplain here at Grace Dieu and chapel expenses; to which is now added heavy expenses connected with our Shepshed chapel and Mission and a school of 80 children there . . . Connected with all these undertakings I have taken up a very considerable sum of money, for which I have to pay interest, so that *inter nos* (pray do not tell a soul) we have not more left than £700 p.a. to live upon, so that we are obliged to live with great economy and if it were not for the fact that we are obliged to spend several months each year at Garendon, I am sure we could not get on at all. You will see from this that we have actually made ourselves poor and straightened in order to serve the cause of our holy Faith here . . .

By the standards of the time, the number of domestics engaged at Grace Dieu manor was meagre. During the Spring and Summer of 1840 two servants gave Laura their notice, in spite of the prevailing national shortage of employment. 'July 20', Laura wrote 'Hunt gave me notice to leave on account of the fewness of servants. She will remain, if I wish, until October'.

Ambrose and Laura were on one of their frequent visits to Garendon at the time of the 1841 census on 8 June. They had with them all their children and two of their own nurse-maids, Elizabeth Slater and Honorine Renard, a French girl who also acted as personal maid to Laura and accompanied her on the almost daily walks round the neighbourhood visiting the poor and sick. There were twelve other female indoor servants at Garendon and eight menservants. Outdoor men working on the estate who lived in various tied cottages, numbered at least twenty more. Most of the servants were still there in 1851 and some in 1861. In 1841 at Grace Dieu there were five servants recorded who were women, and two men: only one of the seven was still in Ambrose's employ in 1851. Honorine left to be a nun at Atherstone in July 1842 and was replaced by the Belgian Mlle de Beaune as nursery maid at the salary of £24 a year: cooks at Grace Dieu received between £16 and £20 with tea and sugar. Thomas Mullins the footman had £16 for the first year and £18 for the second, to rise to £20 if he gave satisfaction; together with two suits of common livery and one hat per year. The odd job boy and an assistant in the nursery had £6. A housemaid received £10. The size of the staff compared unfavourably with Uncle Edward March Phillipps' household at Hathern Rectory of fourteen indoor servants, of whom three were men, and corroborates the economies of which Ambrose wrote.

Towards the end of 1842 came the opening of Pugin's church at Shepshed, dedicated to St Winifred. (The foundation stone had been laid on 28 March by Everard, Ambrose and Laura's second son; Amo, the eldest, had fallen downstairs on the previous day and had so disfigured himself that he could not appear in public). Bishop Walsh arrived for the consecration on one of Ambrose's favourite feasts, that of St Elizabeth of Hungary. Five priests assisted at the High Mass. 'The

church was quite crowded and everybody behaved admirably',
recorded Laura. Ambrose took the opportunity of writing a
public letter of thanks to all those who had helped him build
St Winifreds; awareness of his proprietary duty to assume this
initiative lay in every paragraph:

> It is a great comfort to me to think that you, my dear Friends,
> will pray for my welfare and that of my Family. We shall also
> pray for your's and at all times do what lies in our power to
> promote the well-being of the people of Shepshed; and I ear-
> nestly hope that St Winifreds's church may prove a bond of
> everlasting union between us.

Bishop Walsh was taken ill in the evening and so serious a
view was taken of his condition that Wiseman came from
Oscott. He wrote[42] at once to Cardinal Acton in Rome: Bishop
Walsh had been 'seized by a painful affliction of the bladder in
consequence of the long function of consecrating the altar at
Shepshed church'; things did not look well. He had been sent
for, and felt it was his duty 'to call in the best advice'. Three
more priests came next day; a specialist from Nottingham
made numerous visits and gave his opinion that the Bishop
could not be moved for a month. However he left on December
1 'in our chariot. He bore the journey better than was expected'
was Laura's verdict. It had all involved a great deal of extra
expense. Bishop Walsh never totally recovered his health; the
District became increasingly dominated by Wiseman.

The removal of Gentili to Loughborough left Ambrose without a chaplain at Grace Dieu. A visit to Oscott to persuade
Monsignor Weedall to accept this assignment was fruitless.
The Dominican Provincial at Hinckley was more sympathetic
and agreed that the aged Benjamin Caestryck should come on
a temporary basis; he died in 1844. Ambrose made attempts to
combine this chaplaincy with the post of tutor for his boys;
negotiations with the Jesuits at Stoneyhurst to this end came
to nothing. Purcell in his life of Ambrose labours the point
that Bishop Walsh refused to allow a Jesuit Father as chaplain
at Grace Dieu.[43] The facts do not confirm this opinion. Bishop
Walsh wrote[44] to Fr Lythgoe, S.J. English Provincial, on 10
October 1843 with an earnest petition that he 'should give a
proof to Mr Phillipps and myself of your sincere desire to

oblige us by sending a Father of the society' to fill this need. It
was not in the Bishop's power to send a secular priest. 'It
would be a great advantage and would heal every wound'. It
was the Jesuits who had reasons for not complying with the
request. A worse crisis was to come.

In the spring of 1844 Whitaker, the priest at Whitwick, left
his charge overnight and absconded, taking with him some
parish funds. Ambrose wrote to Rosmini in desperation: the
missions he had created for which he had given up so much,
the converts who had been made, all were to be abandoned
through lack of priests. He implored the Superior General to
send help. It was to arrive through a new source. Monsignor
Forbin-Jansen, Bishop of Nancy, made a visit to Grace Dieu.
His friendship with Monsignor Mazenod, Bishop of Marseilles,
secured the services of the Society of the Oblates of Mary
Immaculate founded by him; Grace Dieu Warren, a sizeable
house on the estate, was placed at their disposal. A new set of
foreign priests, usually three, sometimes five in number, began
to minister in the villages surrounding Charnwood Forest.

More conversions took place; in May 1847 Bishop Walsh
confirmed two hundred and thirty two people at Whitwick.
The Oblates left at the end of that year. The difficulties of
understanding the English social scene were too great. Ambrose
thought the Frenchmen uncultivated and critical of the Rosminians; they found him autocratic:

> Il prétend régler l'ordre des cérémonies, le mode de chant, la
> longeur des offices etc. Il est évident qu'on ne peut souscrire à
> de pareilles conditions[45].

The mission of Shepshed had remained in Rosminian hands:
now Whitwick was added also. They had received reinforcements, some from Italy, others from Ireland and England. One
such was William Lockhart.

Lockhart was twenty two years old and had just taken his
degree when he became a member of Newman's 'monastery'
at Littlemore, and taught at the school. He was clearly unsettled from the start, particularly over the matter of certainty of
absolution. Newman realized this and told him he must agree
to stay for three years or not come at all; Lockhart made this
undertaking. His meeting with Gentili at the time of Ambrose's

second visit to Oxford prompted him to write to the Italian in the spring of 1843. Signing himself ARZ and from an accommodation address, he asked for advice on corporal mortification and where he could buy a hair shirt. When summer came, he took his mother and sister to Norfolk and Lincolnshire from whence he called at Loughborough to see Gentili. 'Don Gentili with his gentle attractive ways, began little by little to win the soul of the good young man'[46] Lockhart made a three days' retreat which ended in his being admitted into the Roman Catholic Church; three days later he entered as postulant into the Rosminian Order.

Newman felt the departure of Lockhart keenly; it caused him to resign his living of St Mary's: 'for I had been unable to keep my word with the Bishop'.[47] To John Keble, Newman wrote[48] of Lockhart

> He wanted something absolutely to take hold of him and use him, he felt the Church of Rome could do this and nothing else.

Ambrose on receipt of the news from Gentili, replied from his holiday in Barmouth that it was 'intelligence supereminently delightful'. (From this moment Lockhart became a close member of the family circle, often at Grace Dieu). He warned Gentili that whatever happened Lockhart must not be allowed to go near Oscott. Spencer had written[49] from there to Ambrose;

> He [Lockhart] is a man of property, and you may suppose he would have been acceptable here; but if he does attach himself to the Institute of Charity, and helps to finish their grand house at Sileby [Ratcliffe], we must be glad for them, and trust that by mutual charity we shall deserve all to be replenished from that fine source. I am sometimes oppressed with many sorrows, and among them is the necessity under which we still appear of being in a state of rivalry with our brethren. One college living at the cost of another, thriving in proportion to its loss; rivalry with men such as Gentili for it is above human nature to be insensible to the winning or losing for our particular body such subjects as Lockhart and the rest. Oh pray for the things that are for the peace of Jerusalem . . .

The activity of the Institute of Charity in Loughborough

was increased in 1843 with the arrival of Rosminian sisters. Mary Arundell who had offered to support them financially, decided to make Loughborough her base; she rented Paget House, Woodgate, to await the nuns' arrival. Ambrose and Laura saw a great deal of her and were much concerned with the plans. Two young Italian women of peasant background Sister Mary Francesca Parea and Sister Mary Anastasia Samonini, made their appearance in the autumn as founder members of the English branch of the Sisters of Providence. There were many problems at first: Sister Anastasia was only 22; neither sister spoke English and thought it appropriate to develop the convent on lines to which they were accustomed at home. This, with the unheated house and unfamiliar cooking, daunted early postulants, none of whom persevered. Gentili tried to effect some changes, but Sister Mary Francesca complained to Rosmini of his interference and it was withdrawn. In Italy the Sisters of Providence were sent to teach in village schools; Gentili's complaint that well-bred English ladies wishing to become nuns could not become itinerant teachers received short shift. Rosmini said he could make no provision for those who were not willing to mix with and teach the poor. A compromise was reached: a day school for the poor was established at Loughborough and a boarding school for the daughters of the more well-to-do attached to the convent, where several of the de Lisle daughters received their education. Gradually direction passed into indigenous hands and the Order prospered; the Sisters began to teach also in the schools founded by Ambrose and Laura in the Charnwood villages.

The joy caused by the reception of William Lockhart was short-lived. A month later came the news that R. W. Sibthorp, having been ordained priest in the Roman Catholic Church eighteen months before, had returned to the Church of England. Newman's opinion of him as unstable was justified; a view which was shared by Anglican authorities. Sibthorp was not permitted to resume his ministry until the end of 1847.[50]

Financial pressure and the many problems they had endured, encouraged Ambrose and Laura with Amo, Everard, Spencer and John Squires, a groom, to make a prolonged expedition to the continent in the summer of 1844. They left England on 6 July and returned on 11 October. Their own horse-drawn carriage was placed on the train, in the custom of the time, during much of the journey. They proceeded from Calais via St Omer and Tournay to Brussels where they met Monsignor Pecci, the Pope's legate, later Leo XIII. Visits to Malines, Louvain, Liège, Aix-la-Chapelle followed. Everywhere the party was received by ecclesiastics, even Archbishops; Spencer was able to urge the need for prayers for the conversion of England; Ambrose spoke much of 'the Oxford divines'.

One of the main objects was to visit Laura's relatives who lived in the Rhineland. It was a period when English opinion thought in terms of a 'good' Germany; to have German relations was to follow a royal precedent. Ambrose and Laura made a call at Cologne where the gothic cathedral entranced them. Everywhere ancient buildings were being refurbished; new paintings and choir stalls commissioned. The excellence of the plain chant impressed Ambrose:[51]

> I never heard anything better than the Vespers and Compline on Sunday. Two High Masses are sung every day . . . the whole of the chaunts are sung *in German* and between the chaunts devout prayers are recited by a priest in a surplice whilst the Priest at the altar says the Mass in Latin. It was one of the most edifying services I ever witnessed, more than 3 thousand people assisted at it and every individual of that vast concourse joined in the singing in the sweetest and most melodious manner . . .

At Königswinter, a small town on the eastern bank of the Rhine, just below Bonn, they were greeted by members of the family of Laura's mother, the former Henrietta von Lutzow. 'Aunt Weichs'[52], her mother's sister, with her nephew Conrad, and two cousins Antonia and Fanny von Lutzow had their home in Königswinter. Antonia (Toniton or Toni) had been close to Laura since childhood. She was a novelist;[53] fiction writing had a vogue among German women of the time. Laura's diaries record that they wrote to each other every month for the whole of their lives. Count Karl von Kurzrock, whose father had been first cousin to Laura's mother, was another Königswinter relative. His family had owned the castle of Drachenfels on the crag which dominated the town and still is a feature of the Rhenish landscape. Ambrose was delighted with everything and everyone he saw: the neat, clean, white-washed houses, each of them with their own small portions of land; the proliferation of vineyards, fruit-trees and vegetables; the response to religion; Laura's relations with their ancient chivalrous background; the Kurzrock's beautiful fifteen-year old daughter, Marie, who devoted her time to the succour of the sick and poor; Shepshed was a place of similar size.

> Oh happy country, it is enough to draw tears from one's eyes, when one thinks of the sad contrast our poor England affords to this bright picture.

All was attributable to 'the plenitude of Catholick benediction'. If some of Ambrose's contemporaries laid too great a stress on economic factors in their interpretation of events, he went to the opposite extreme; they did not enter into his calculations.

After some happy days, the de Lisle family set off via Mainz, Heidelberg, the Black Forest, Ulm, Augsberg, to Munich, home of the great Dr Döllinger, Professor of Theology. He gave Ambrose a good deal of his time, introduced him to librarians of the King's Library, university colleagues and friends. Chief among them was Alexis-François Rio, writer on Christian art, whom they met for the first time, with his Welsh wife (the former Apollonia Jones); they became frequent visitors to Grace Dieu. At the atelier of M. Eberhard, Ambrose and Laura ordered life-size figures of *Mater Dolorosa* and the Dead Christ[54] for a new chapel to be constructed near the Calvary rocks. They were to be completed in a year.

The journey home, entirely by horse-drawn carriage, led from Munich to Tegernsee, Innsbruck, Merano (where a large crucifix, price one hundred Austrian florins, was purchased for the Cistercians), Caldaro & other small towns to Venice. Here Ambrose renewed his acquaintance with the Armenian monks at San Lazzaro. Numerous introductions were everywhere taken up. A five day journey across Italy to Milan in August was extremely hot. After four days they were off again along the shores of Lake Maggiore to Stresa where Ambrose and Laura saw Rosmini's house and some Rosminians, but not the Superior General. Nor was he at his College at Monte Calvario near Domodossola at which the family called on their ascent of the Simplon pass. After a night at the Hospice on the summit, they descended to Turtman and 'the rather dear and worst beds in Switzerland'; on through France to Paris seven days later, and finally Boulogne where they saw the Digbys.

'All our darlings perfectly well and delighted to see us; the house in capital order' wrote Laura at Grace Dieu after three months' absence. But fresh crises were not long delayed: on 12 March 1845 came the first death among the children. After an illness of only two days, 'Our lovely boy Reginald taken unwell at ½ past 5 in the morning. Then slept till 10 when convulsions came on . . . They ceased about 1 but our darling boy never regained consciousness'. The doctor remained all day; Mr Woolfrey gave him conditional absolution and extreme unction at 11. 'Our darling Reginald breathed his last at 1 in the morning while Mr Woolfrey was reciting the prayer for the agonizing. He went off without a struggle to join the society of angels in Heaven aged 5 years and 8 months. God's will be done . . . I have one darling boy less' wrote Laura. Reginald was placed in a shell (inside lining of a coffin) and the family waited five days for the funeral until the vault under Grace Dieu chapel could be finished. It was Holy Week; the heaviest snow that year covered the ground 'a fit emblem of the purity of our beloved Angel Reginald'.

Ambrose was concerned not only for the loss of his son, but for the safety of his wife awaiting her next confinement 'overwhelmed with grief as I am'. To Montalembert he wrote:[55]

> It was a great affliction for us, for of all our children, nine in number, he was perhaps the most promising and the most pleasing . . . We had at least the consolation of feeling that he was snatched from the evil to come and that no past evil had yet stained the whiteness of his baptismal robe. I trust now we have a saved child praying for us in heaven and aiding by his prayers the poor efforts of his father on earth.

The not unexpected result of this sudden loss was a tendency to send for the doctor more frequently and at the first signs of ill health among the remaining children. He was called to the house thirty eight times before the end of the year; a considerable additional expense. Gwendoline, ninth child, was born on 2 April 1845 with Laura alone, apart from the midwife, Mrs

Squires. Almost at once she developed measles, caught from
her brothers and sisters.

There were other extra expenses: books to be bound; improvements made to the churches in Shepshed and Whitwick;
rooms for a priest to be hired in Shepshed; the drawing room
and library re-wallpapered; a new chapel built to house the
figures from Munich; Pugin appeared at 7 a.m. and walked
with Ambrose across the rocks near the Calvary to choose the
site for what came to be called 'the chapel of dolours'. He also
discussed plans for 'new offices'. Pugin's second wife died in
August 1844. Some months later he proposed to Mary Amherst
who at first accepted him. Her mother was cousin to Lord
Shrewsbury; they did not approve the match. The young
woman (who was only nineteen, Pugin was thirtytwo), was
drawn towards becoming a nun; this was the outcome: she
joined the Sisters of Providence at Loughborough, in time
became the first English Superior, and set the foundation on its
feet. Pugin was greatly distressed and at first at any rate
blamed Gentili for his disappointment. Pugin made two more
abortive attempts to become engaged before he married his
third wife in 1848.

Lady Mary Arundell died in Loughborough on 2 June 1845
after a short but painful attack of gallstones. Ambrose immediately took command of the funeral arrangements and wrote an
account for *The Tablet*[56] in the form of a letter to the Editor:

> It was probably the most solemn funeral that has been wit-
> nessed in England since the schism of the sixteenth century.

After the service of great length, a procession was made
through the streets of Loughborough to the railway station, to
the astonishment of bystanders. At the front were the boys of
the day school, preceded by their cross; each boy wore a black
cassock with crimson sash and skull cap; next, the girls of the
nuns' school in mourning for their benefactress; then the men
of the Loughborough Guild of the Immaculate Heart of Mary,
wearing white albs and blue mozettas, with blue sashes and
tassels. Another processional cross was that of the chapel of
Grace Dieu, borne by a chorister, followed by twenty-two
other choristers of that church in cassocks and surplices;
fourteen choristers from Loughborough chapel followed their

cross. Eight priests, including Gentili in black cope, preceded the coffin drawn by twelve men in long black cloaks. The Sisters of Providence walked before the family mourners with Ambrose and the Jesuit Provincial; finally came ladies, Laura and other friends of Lady Mary, and her servants, all in deep mourning;

> the clergy and choristers chaunting Psalms and Antiphons in a most solemn manner.

Ambrose could not resist the remark that the absence of offensive behaviour gave proof that the people of England 'can appreciate the venerable ceremonial of their ancient religion'.

Mary Arundell had willed her money partly to the Sisters of Providence and partly to Ratcliffe College. Since she had lent her brother, the Duke of Buckingham, a very large sum and he was bankrupt, little was forthcoming.

Ambrose had sustained his association with Dominic Barberi with letters and visits to the Passionist house near Stone, where the Italian had made his permanent foundation since his second journey to England in 1842. In the Spring of 1845 he made an attempt through Bishop Walsh to persuade the Order to man one of his missions. Barberi wrote to his Superior:

> I have refused the offer – for the reason that it involved our acting as chaplains to Mr Phillips (which does not seem in line with our rules) and other reasons[57].

Although the Passionists had not made the progress in England achieved by the Rosminians, Lord Shrewsbury's doubts had not been proved justified: converts were received and the lapsed reclaimed. Their finest hour was to come.

On 23 September 1845 John Dobrée Dalgairns wrote to Dominic Barberi that he intended to become a Catholic and wished to be received in some remote place. Barberi gave him directions for Stone. 'I hope it will not be difficult to find our house, since by the grace of God, you have succeeded in finding your way to heaven'[58] Dalgairns was received on 29 September; a further meeting at Littlemore was arranged. Newman saw in it the opportunity to make his own submission. He had been worn down by the current liberal forces in the Church of England and the University which did not

accept his interpretation of the nature of the Church. He had
begun his Essay on the *Development of Christian Doctrine* at
the beginning of 1845 and was near its end. He had satisfied
himself on the points which had so troubled him during the
Ambrose-Bloxam correspondence: that Transubstantiation,
and veneration of the Blessed Virgin were not explicitly set out
in the original deposit of the faith.

Dominic Barberi arrived at Littlemore on the evening of 8
October; Newman and his friends Bowles[59] and Stanton[60] were
received the next day. Later they recited the Office in the
chapel: the portion to be read contained the record of St Denis
after his martyrdom putting his head under his arm as he
walked[61]. Barberi stopped the reading as unsuitable for beginners. His use of the term beginners says much about him; also
much about Newman. Newman's reply[62] to Ambrose's warm
letter of congratulation[63] was equally significant; both of his
innate humility and of the lack of recognition of his stature, a
situation which was to endure.

> It gives me so much pleasure to receive such congratulations as
> yours that I hardly like to say what is too true, I am unworthy
> of them . . . Father Dominic told us that we were but babes in
> Christ, and that is the beginning and the end of it.

Dalgairns made a short visit to Grace Dieu at the end of
October; Newman went there for four days with John Moore
Capes[64] early in January 1846. He visited the monastery several
times; a poem of 1850[65] which referred to 'monks in midnight
choir or studious cell; in sultry field or wintry glen' was,
however, dedicated to a secular priest, St Philip Neri (to whose
Order Newman had pledged himself), and to whom the greater
admiration was given.

There was a further resurgence of financial problems for
Ambrose and Laura over these months, of a sort so sensitive
that even Laura's diaries refer to them by a series of blanks:
'16 March Mr Miles [the agent] called to see Ambrose about –
'. Several long talks with his father followed. Despite a new
loan which Ambrose had negotiated with Pagani, to whom he
had to send £50 interest every half-year, the situation was
clearly very serious. Doctors' bills had been heavy: forty three
visits in 1845; twenty-two in the first half of 1846. At the

beginning of July it was decided that the family should live temporarily in Boulogne in order to save money.

Ambrose, Laura, Robert Coffin[66], a convert from Oxford who was acting as tutor to the boys, all the children, two nursemaids, Hadley and Annah, and the midwife, Mrs Squires, crossed the channel on 2 July. After some unsatisfactory temporary arrangements, lodgings were found in the rue de Desille off the main street from the harbour to the Haute Ville, close to the church of St Nicholas; street and church exist today; a greater contrast to Grace Dieu with its gardens, rocks and expanse of Charnwood forest cannot be imagined. There Bernard, fourth boy and tenth child, was born on 22 July; no doctor was called, no doubt to save expense. Laura was unable to feed the child after 13 August; wet nurses were engaged until 24 April 1847.

There was no idleness in Boulogne, but the usual ceaseless activity: Ambrose wrote many letters; the boys had their tutor and extra French and music lessons; Mena went to an Ursuline convent. Expeditions, walks, visits, were made and received; ecclesiastics, including Dominic Barberi, came and English travellers. Parents and children bathed and played on the sands. The family returned to Grace Dieu on 22 October 1846. Charles March Phillipps agreed to alter the kitchen premises and build a new wing to the house. Ambrose had been pressing these needs for some years. It was not until 22 March 1847 that his father spoke of making a start (the first estimate for the kitchen department was £950). Work on the foundations began on 4 June.

A fresh need arose that spring. In May of the previous year, George Dudley Ryder[67] second son of Aunt Ryder and the Bishop, announced from Italy that he had become a Roman Catholic. A student at Oriel with Newman as his tutor, he had been ordained and in 1834 he married Sophia, youngest of the five beautiful daughters of John Sargeant, Rector of Lavington, Sussex[68]. The eldest, Charlotte, died as a girl in 1818; Emily married Ambrose's old school friend, Samuel Wilberforce later Bishop of Oxford, and died in 1841; Mary the third daughter married Samuel's brother Henry; Caroline, the fourth, was briefly the wife of Henry (later Cardinal) Manning. She died in 1837[69]. Sophia was as delicate as her sisters; George Ryder took her to the continent in 1845 to try to improve her health. They were accompanied by their three eldest children and George's youngest sister, another Sophia, who became Roman Catholic also.

George was the first of Ambrose's relations to follow his religious lead; he forfeited his livelihood thereby. There were five children and another expected. Ambrose felt compelled to help. He offered the Ryders Grace Dieu Warren and removed the Oblates of Mary Immaculate to a house in Thringstone. Ambrose asked no rent for which he was criticised by his father. Thereafter the two families saw much of each other. The Ryders moved to the Warren on 22 July; Cecilia Mary was born a week later on the 29th; she lived, a nun, until 1937; Ambrose and Laura were her godparents.

Laura's own next confinement came later that autumn. She thought it was upon her during an evening when her father-in-law and two of his brothers came to see the new kitchen wing, but 'the alarm passed off'. She gave birth to Osmond on 6 November 1847, fifth son and eleventh child. A most severe crisis in their lives was about to face the de Lisle family.

Although the delivery was straightforward and no doctor was called, Laura recorded (uncharacteristically) how weak it had left her. In early December she became seriously ill with jaundice, at first undiagnosed. By the end of the year she was better. In the first week of January came the first relapse; she rallied, but on 19th became worse again. One after the other the children developed mumps; Ambrose himself succumbed to it on that day. By 24 January it was thought Laura was dying. George Ryder fetched the French Rosminian, Nicholas Lorrain, from the Shepshed mission; he heard her confession and administered the *viaticum* and Extreme Unction. Laura spoke to the three eldest children and her father-in-law. Pagani's account of the scene to Rosmini survives[70]. Lorrain described Laura's extraordinary devotion; Ambrose was on his knees sobbing. The children came in and she spoke to them 'as a saint and heroine. She is gravely ill'.

Uncle Edward March Phillips, who acted as physician as well as Rector to his poor in Hathern, urged a second medical opinion; this was acted upon. The fresh doctor who disapproved of Mr Eddowes' treatment and changed it completely, said that 'I had had medicine enough to kill me if the disease had not'. On 27 January Fr Bernard from the monastery called and, Laura wrote, 'brought me moss from St Winifred's well which I took, after which I had no return of inflammatory symptoms and every other improved from then'. The doctors began 'to have hopes of me'.

By 4 February they found 'Everything perfectly healthy for the first time. The Novena to St Winifred ends today', Laura had been saved. Pagani told the Superior General that she was out of danger[71]: 'She is a treasure, a real woman, one in a thousand'.

Chapter 8

Clerical Victory

LAURA's recovery did not mark the end of problems for the de Lisles; some severe set-backs lay ahead, the family's share of a much larger sphere of controversy which engulfed the Catholic body in the decade of the 1850s. At its most profound level it concerned the form of government to be accorded to the growing community in England: the matter of the status of its bishops and the degree to which it should be subject to central authority in Rome, itself much disturbed by invasion and disorder. In practice there came to the surface intense disagreement on the matter of freedom of opinion, especially for lay people. Disparate views were expressed with considerable vehemence on what might have been considered largely matters of taste, in ecclesiastical art, architecture, religious literature, music and ritual. These were often based upon differences of tradition and nationality; principles were evoked and feelings ran high.

The 'old' Catholics who had endured the struggles of penal times, tended to possess an independence of spirit and resilience that precluded the easy absorption of ideas from, for example, the recently arrived Italian missionaries. Most of the Vicars Apostolic, with the notable exception of Nicolas Wiseman, were of this mind. More recent converts, on the other hand, welcomed all that was seen to derive from Rome itself: literary conventions, customs, Baroque architecture, or centralized methods of Church government. Men, like Wiseman, whose education had a Roman origin, seemed to find its influence pervasive for the rest of their lives.

Ambrose did not fit tidily into any of these categories. A convert who never wavered in his loyalty to the Holy See, he pursued a singular and unceasing determination to follow his own instincts because he thought they would produce what was best for the Church; he continued to proclaim his right to do so. He was swimming against the tide and it brought him unhappiness which only his buoyancy and sense of purpose helped him to overcome.

The feeling of Ambrose for all things Gothic was of long standing. To him it was a style intrinsically Christian, with ecclesiastical connotations which he thought important. Soaring naves and ogival arches spoke of a world beyond the temporal which would edify and transport the beholder. Roodscreens, found in gothic churches, were to Ambrose a vital ingredient, as they sheltered the most holy area. A move to dispense with roodscreens in England, as in Baroque churches on the continent, he viewed with horror. A particular controversy with Frederick Faber concerned such a suggestion; neither man kept a sense of proportion and the scenes that followed were ludicrous.

Following his conversion to Roman Catholicism at the end of 1845, Faber spent a few months in Birmingham where he and some companions formed themselves into a small community. A visit to Rome provided an approved Rule and he returned to England to set up his Brothers of the Will of God of the Congregation of St Wilfrid. Lord Shrewsbury gave them a mansion, Cotton Hall, on his estates in Staffordshire, and Pugin designed a church dedicated to St Wilfrid on the property. The relationship with Pugin, with his predeliction for gothic architecture was, however, to be short-lived. Faber began to turn his back on everything that was reminiscent of his old life and associations, and to embrace with exuberance devotions and styles of building that he viewed as essentially Roman.

In the Spring of 1848, Ambrose and Pugin paid Faber a visit at St Wilfrid's. Ambrose had visited Faber a few days earlier, while he was not well, during the course of a stay at Alton Towers with the Shrewsburys. Faber had recorded

> Ambrose was most pleasant today: screens were not the subject of our converse.

The second occasion was not so agreeable. Ambrose had asked why there was no roodscreen in St Wilfrid's church. Faber had explained that 'we are great people for Exposition', and that he would burn the screens of the 16th century. Whereupon Ambrose accused him of copying the Italians and setting himself up against bishops and old Catholics and introducing new usages; he maintained his right to utter his sentiments, although Faber was a priest: 'You are a Catholic of but a few months and I of twenty-two years'.[1] Faber, as he later explained[2], remonstrated. 'Mr Phillipps, you have no right to speak to me in this way.' According to Faber's account, Ambrose replied in the following terms, while standing opposite *Mama's image*[3]

> Father Faber, God for your pride destroyed and brought to naught your first effort. (*Stamp, fist to heaven*) He will curse and destroy your order and it will perish if you go on thus.

Although it was recorded that Ambrose remarked that he would 'never set foot in this place again', five minutes later the two protagonists shook hands and ate a meal of veal and suet pudding together; Ambrose 'talked kindly' and departed.

On his way home to Grace Dieu from Alton Towers on May 20, Ambrose called upon Newman in Birmingham at his recently formed community of Oratorians. Ambrose referred to the incident, but was not able to finish the conversation and therefore completed what he intended to say by letter.[4]

> I hope he [Faber] may become less violent and excessive in his ways and ideas. If he does he will render to the Church those solid services which his abilities and his zeal qualify him to render, but if he does not, I tremble for the result . . .

Faber in the meanwhile had written his deeply injured letter to Newman who immediately registered his regret to Ambrose[5] at what had passed between the two men. Newman's recent return from his period of formation in Rome inclined him to be more sympathetic to Italian ideas of popular devotion than was to be the case in his later years, but his first letter of reproach to Ambrose concerned his lack of tolerance rather than matters of taste.

> I could say much about the grief I feel at the neglect I see, of that so good and true maxim, *in necessariis unitas in dubiis libertas*. How is it, dear Mr Phillipps, that you understand this so clearly in doctrinal questions, yet are slow to admit in

ritual? . . . If Mr Pugin persists, as I cannot hope he will not, in loading with bad names the admirers of Italian architecture, he is going the very way to increase their number.

Ambrose replied[6] swiftly, anxious to refute all inferences that he might have Gallican[7] sympathies; his own estimate of his views emerged as he suggested that an incorrect version of the incident had reached Newman.

> . . . it would seem as though some one had represented me as having a leaning to Gallicanism or at least as being more tolerant of Gallicanism, than of opposition to church skreens and Gothick architecture. Probably I do not know myself, as I ought, but really I am not conscious of being a Gallican, or of being overbearing or intolerant to the opponents of *Gothick ideas* . . . my wish is to be neither Gallican nor Ultramontane but a simple Catholick . . . I have a strong conviction that Gothick is Christian architecture and Italian as Grecian Pagan, in their respective origin and destination, but I have no desire to *quarrel* with those who would build their churches on the model of a Pagan temple . . . But really I cannot plead guilty to a charge of intolerance even on ritual questions. In my own chapels I would certainly insist on Church principles being carried out, but if other people have other views on these questions I have no idea of quarrelling with them on that account. On the occasion before alluded to at St Wilfrid's I did not quarrel with Fr Faber because he had no skreen, but he shocked me by his awful expression in denouncing the skreen at Cheadle . . .

A large number of Catholics were critical both of Faber's books and of 'his whole way of going on'

> . . . yet we did not expect you or your disciples to preach a crusade against us, to denounce us as mere Puseyites (Faber's words to me) as Gallicans, or to divide the Catholick body, already too much divided, by throwing the weight of your talents your zeal and your piety in the scale against the noble efforts of that admirable man Pugin, who has been so evidently raised up by Almighty God to rebuild the material Fabrick of His Temple in this Land, as evidently as I believe that great and blessed Man to whom I am now writing is raised up for the restoration of the spiritual edifice. No, my dear Father Superior, *we* ought not to be severed from each other, in our

joint but different efforts, we ought to go hand in hand . . .

Newman did not leave the matter there, but wrote[8] again to express his concern that 'there should be a difference of opinion between the one I esteem and admire so much as yourself, and me' He would not let Ambrose say, without protest, that a crusade was being preached against him, or that Oratorian 'weight' was being thrown against Pugin.

> . . . Mr Pugin is a man of genius; I have the greatest admiration of his talents, and willingly acknowledge that Catholics owe him a great debt for what he has done in the revival of Gothic architecture among us. His zeal, his minute diligence, his resources, his invention, his imagination, his sagacity in research, are all of the highest order . . . But he has the fault of a man of genius as well as the merit. He is intolerant, and, if I might use a stronger word, a bigot. He sees nothing good in any school of Christian art except that of which he is himself so great an ornament.

Newman went on to explain that in only half Christendom had Gothic art prevailed; the other half Pugin ruled as Pagan; the Pagan half happened to include the see of St Peter himself, where his body lay:

> that earthly home of the Apostle, that treasure house of his merits, a building, be it grand or be it mean, which the creation of a succession of Pontiffs, this central monument of Christianity, is pronounced by him to be *pagan* . . .

The need for Gothic to be adapted to suit the living ritual of the 19th century occupied much of the remainder of Newman's letter. The Church had consolidated her Rubrics since the death of Gothic Architecture.

> Our Padre Ceremoniere tells me that the rigid observance of Gothic details is inconsistent with the Rubrics – that he must break the Rubrics if he would not break with Mr Pugin; which is he to give up, Mr Pugin or the Rubrics?

He ended by expressing what little sympathy he had ever entertained with parties, which trait had its origin in his Anglican days, and added a postscript

> I grieve indeed at your feelings towards Fr Wilfrid but hope time will change them.

Ambrose replied at length[9] in grateful vein for 'the beautiful and most kind (may I not say affectionate and parental) letter' which he valued and treasured. It was clear, however, that his views had not changed

> I venerate as much as any man the See of St Peter and St Peter himself in the person of his successors and I would to God I could conscientiously venerate all that they have done, but I find this impossible. We none of us venerate St Peter's denial of Christ, why should we venerate the indecencies of the Vatican. No place ever charmed and edified me more (taken as a whole) than Rome. I spent the greater part of 2 years there, and I know it better than any other town in Christendom, but yet I should not be honest if I did not say that I saw much that grieved and shocked me, much that was in flagrant contradiction to that blessed and glorious Catholicism, of which it is the centre and principal See ... My feeling for Rome is precisely what my glorious Patron St Gregory the Great wrote to our blessed St Augustine, that we should love things not because they were Roman, but because they were good, and that whatever he saw good in all the Churches, whether those of Gaul or elsewhere, he should collect together and transfer to the new Church of the English ... I have always thought that if we would revive Catholicism in this country, it must be by restoring in all its pristine life and beauty, what our people have always more or less loved and revered in a ruined state. Such were always my feelings and Grace Dieu Chapel was the first in England in which a rood skreen with the blessed image of Christ Crucified was restored after a lapse of these centuries ...

At the end of the year Ambrose and Faber made their peace. A message from Ambrose via Robert Coffin to Faber was well received, and in his reply[10] Faber wrote

> ... You do not know, my dear Mr Phillipps, how much I love and revere you, and have done ever since that visit to Grace Dieu wh so strengthened and fomented my catholic tendencies at ye[11] time ... Don't you think you have let my losing my temper with you when I was ill and in gt pain last Easter remain upon yr mind longer than you ought to have done, seeing how kindly you took my apology and consented to dine with us afterwards ... Pray do not be cast down about ye converts. If any great work is to be done, confusion and

scandal must accompany it, and we must not split among ourselves because of this. What lessons we have of this danger in ye lives of ye Saints! . . . It is a great token for good for us, my dear Mr Phillipps, that you speak with so much kindly trust in our dear F Superior.[12] Perhaps all ye Church will one day think of him wht we think of him now, who are daily and hourly witnesses of what he is.

The reference to the *Lives of the Saints* was to an earlier cause of controversy in which Ambrose was implicated, and which once more serves as an illustration of the tensions and lack of a sense of proportion, of the times. It came to a head as the result of the union of John Henry Newman's Oratorian community at Maryvale (old Oscott) and the Wilfridians under Frederick Faber. Faber had been writing, with the permission of Bishops Walsh and Wiseman, a number of *Lives of Modern Saints*. The question arose as to whether Newman, on behalf of the Oratory, would adopt the series. He asked for a year in order to make a decision. *The Lives*, which were translations in the main of continental sources, had caused a certain amount of stir since they differed materially from the devotional literature familiar to hereditary English Catholics: Faber had criticized Alban Butler[13] whose earlier volumes had been much used and revered, for not giving greater prominence to the supernatural aspects of the lives of saints; to miracles and prophesies as well as mortification, and declared that he wrote like a Protestant; secondly, Faber's references to non-Catholics as heretics, perverse persons, as on the high road to perdition, were considered impudent and uncharitable.

An attack in *Dolman's Magazine*[14] on *The Life of St Rose of Lima* brought the matter into prominence in that Faber had included fulsome accounts of her austerities and penances which, it was held, were unsuitable for the public eye; moreover her extreme devotion to images, as stated, practically guilty of idolatry. Bishop Walsh had already written to Faber a 'kind and fatherly letter', since he had been made uneasy by the *Life of St Gertrude*. This communication Faber answered[15] on the 8 December 1847

With regard to ye Lives of ye Saints and ye opposition to them, I had a long conversation with Dr W [Wiseman] in Golden

Square last Friday. Ambrose Phillipps has excited Lord Shrewsbury on the subject and so he wrote to Bishop Wiseman. It is
rather singular that just after Mr Phillipps (who has really no
acquaintance with ye progress of ye Oxford movement, and
who has retarded many, as I know) had told Lord S that many
were being kept back by ye Lives, I received a secret letter from
London conveying to me a picture with ye strongest expressions
of sympathy with ye Lives from Oxford, ye parties there not
daring to correspond directly with me because of ye authorities.

Shortly after his appointment to the Central District, Bishop
Ullathorne sent to other Vicars Apostolic to ask for their views
on the *Lives*. On 31 October 1848[16] he wrote to Newman

I find that the general opinion is still the same in whatever
quarter I enquire, viz. that the spirit of the *Lives* as given in
these translations is not adapted to the state of this country;
that even religious persons and nuns do not find in them a
wisdom according to sobriety, and that to the laity in general
they are the source of uneasiness as they are written.

Before receipt of this letter, Newman had decided that the
present series of *Lives* must come to an end; he felt considerable
sympathy for Faber when he wrote[17]

It appears that there is a strong feeling against it on the part of
a portion of the Catholic community in England on the ground,
as we are given to understand, that the lives of foreign saints,
however edifying in their respective countries, are unsuited to
England and unacceptable to Protestants . . .

Ambrose's views, expressed[18] to Bishop Ullathorne revealed
the dichotomy which existed

Lockhart brought us over yesterday a copy of the Tablet (for I
have long ceased to take it myself) [it had become an ultramontane periodical] to show us your admirable Letter on the
subject of Fr Faber's Saints' Lives. It exactly expressed my own
view of that publication. With the best intentions and an
ardent devotion, I must confess those lives did appear to me
wanting evidently in sound judgement, not altogether free from
that fictional vanity that seeks to make men stare as well as to
edify them, and claiming for their author a sort of reparti for
general orthodoxy and sanctity than '*the good common* run (to

use a phrase of Thomas à Kempis) of the Catholicks around
them'.

Newman's departure from Maryvale and the setting up of
the joint venture in Alcester Street, Birmingham (with Cotton
Hall as noviciate) took place early in 1849. But it soon became
clear that it would not be fruitful for him and Faber to remain
in the same community. Steps, particularly painful to Newman,
were taken towards the formation of a separate second English
Oratory, headed by Faber, in London. These experiences inclined Newman to recognise the wisdom of Ullathorne's standpoint. Plans for the London Oratory appalled Pugin who
wrote to Ambrose[19]

> They have got the most disgusting place possible [a temporary
> one in King William Street] for the Oratory in London, and
> fitted up in a horrible manner, with a sort of Anglo-Roman
> altar. These things are very sad, and the mischief they do is in-
> conceivable.

Lord Arundel and Surrey, heir to the Duke of Norfolk,
wrote to ask Ambrose to serve on the committee which was to
support the construction of a permanent church for the London
Oratory. He refused; and explained[20] to Montalembert

> Of course I declined taking part in such a work, it would have
> been absurd in me to have laboured all my life and sacrificed
> so much as I have in the cause of Xtian Art and Xtian
> Architecture and then to have played into the hands of an
> eccentrick set of men, who would identify the Faith of Rome
> with its abuses, and who would revive here in England, what
> mainly contributed to its decline on the continent during the
> last three centuries, the Pagan taste and ideas of the Renaissance
> ... really I could not appear on a committee for building a
> church in Pagan Architecture in the heart of London ...

Ambrose did not cease to use Pugin's gifts to his own account.
Laura's serious illness and recovery had inclined her father-in-
law to increase his sympathy towards Ambrose and his family
in a series of visible means. Laura wrote in her diary 24
February 1848 'Aunts Harriet and Fanny laid all our pecuniary
affairs before Mr Phillipps. He took it very well' and two days
later 'Aunts H and F told us that Mr P wished us to remain at

Garendon this year with all the children'. In the meantime, plans were drawn by Pugin, at Charles March Phillipps' expense, for an extra wing to Grace Dieu Manor. The work in fact took nearly two years, and it was March 1850 before Ambrose's family returned to their home. Extensions to the Chapel were made also.

At the time of the consecration of the alterations, Grace Dieu Chapel was at the height of its gothic splendour. In the diary of his *Pèlerinage en en Angleterre* of May 1847, Abbé Vandrival had recounted with awe and amazement the style, decorations and embellishments of the chapel: its stone high altar, carved stalls for the Celebrants, tabernacle, numerous candle-sticks of gilt copper, miraculous picture of Virgin and Child in the reredos brought by Ambrose from Italy, sanctuary lamp perpetually burning, the carved lectern and stand for Pascal Candle in oak, the stone pulpit, the elaborate processional cross. In front of two side altars, dedicated to St Philomena and St Joseph, were full-length statues of the saints. A rood screen of oak separated sanctuary and nave where the doors bore the inscription *Sanctus, Sanctus, Sanctus*; columns supported a cornice on which stood a crucifix, a statue of the Blessed Virgin and St John and four candlesticks; candles and flowers were placed there on feast days. In the middle of the nave, suspended from a beam by a red silken cord, was a blue and gold crown carrying six candles 'far removed from the drawing room chandeliers which degrade our churches'; no chairs, but carved benches with *Prie Dieux*; men on the Epistle side and women on the side of the Gospel. Inscriptions above two doorways were painted 'in gothic characters in harmony with the place'.

A carved font and confessional of ash, stood at the back of the church; the organ to the left. The choir was three steps higher than the nave, was narrower and had a lower ceiling and less light. The effect, enhanced by draped curtains behind the altar, added much to 'the mysterious appearance of holy things' and contributed 'to contemplation and the spirit of prayer'.

Abbé Vandrival's description did not include the windows: the four on the south of the nave filled with stained glass, the gift of John, Earl of Shrewsbury and representing patrons of the family standing under celestial crowns supported by angels, two lights in each window: St John Baptist and St Ambrose; St Winifred and St Bertha; St Aloysius and St Charles Borromeo; St Osmund and St Francis of Sales.

The enlargement of the church in 1849 consisted of a new aisle to the north to provide a chapel of the Blessed Sacrament with an elaborate stone canopy 'one of the handsomest works of Pugin'; a good deal of extra seating was thereby created for congregations increased in size. The interior decorations were also renovated; Ambrose and Laura made frequent visits from Garendon to supervise the choice of new carpets, curtains, and cloth of gold vestments. (Most of the features of Grace Dieu chapel were repeated, on a lesser scale, in the two other churches at Whitwick and Shepshed built and maintained by Ambrose; moreover all were heated by coal boilers). Bishop Ullathorne spent five days at Grace Dieu in July consecrating various altars of the renewed chapel with scenes of considerable splendour; he administered confirmation to 63 adult converts and 4 children, of whom Philomena de Lisle was one.

It can be no surprise that the chapel created so profound an impression upon visitors and worshippers. Apart from the unusually rich decorations, incense, candles, a further sensation of the numinous was provided by the music; always plain chant, sung by a substantial choir and cantors, led by Ambrose himself[21]. He chose, trained, and paid them from among his tenants, servants and the children of his schools. Services were long and frequent, with special ceremonial and festivals on Saints' days. Regretting that plain chant was no longer heard elsewhere in England, Ambrose wrote[22]

> At the present day in our English Catholic chapels and churches the antient Church Musick has been almost totally abandoned, and instead of it has been substituted a light and indecorous style of singing far more calculated to express the feelings of earthly passion than the grave and solemn effusions of true Christian devotion.

The robes worn by Cantors were of cloth of gold richly decorated with Pugin's designs and crimson hoods; choir boys and acolytes were clothed in scarlet cassocks, sashes and skull caps. But it was the vestments worn by the clergy which were the most remarkable features of the chapel at Grace Dieu, and the adjacent ones at Shepshed and Whitwick. Long, wide, flowing chasubles, in the main of one colour, (not usually ornamented with flowers or patterns) bore silk braiding bearing Christian symbols. Dalmatics and tunics were also soft and flowing. Pugin devoted much of his time and skill to such designs, in strict contrast to the straight, short, stiff, decorated vestments in common use.

It was the fact that they were based upon liturgical garments used in earlier times, that caused most of the furore which was to last well over a decade. It formed the basis of some of the most bitter of the arguments that divided Catholics because the wearing of these 'gothic' vestments was seen as a declaration of independence from the wishes of the Holy See. The anguish which this lack of acceptance by ecclesiastical authority created in Pugin, pushed him, already over-worked and suffering from stress, into mental illness and eventually death.

By the early 1850s his record was remarkable, but signs of strain were apparent. The ecclesiastical buildings which he had designed *in toto* included the Roman Catholic Cathedrals of St Chad's, Birmingham, (1841), St Barnabas Nottingham (1844), and St George's, Southwark (1848); the churches of St Mary's Uttoxeter, St Marie's Derby, St Wilfred's, Hulme, St Mary's Southport, St Mary's Warwick, Bridge, Cumberland, St Giles', Cheadle, St Marie's, Rugby, St Mary's Dudley, St Winifred's Shepshed and St Augustine's Ramsgate. Those in Ireland were some of the best constructed and largest. He was also consulted in the restoration and rebuilding of several Anglican churches of mediaeval origin. Pugin's buildings for communities ranged from Mount St Bernard and the Convent of Mercy, Handsworth, part of Oscott and Ushaw, to the chapel of St Edmund's, Ware. His secular commitments varied from Alton Towers, Staffordshire, English home of Lord Shrewsbury, and Scarisbrick Hall, Lancashire, to plans for an extensively rebuilt Garendon, which did not materialize. Everywhere he based his structures on the styles of 'ancient ecclesiastical architecture' with rich development of his own.

In addition, Pugin was constantly in demand for designs of furniture, objects in metal work, vestments, carving in wood and stone, and interior decorations of all kinds and for such

locations as the House of Lords. He wrote various treatises
and articles and eight books which achieved publication on the
subjects of his enthusiasms: ornaments of the 15th and 16th
centuries; two on contrasts between the art of past centuries
and the present which claimed to show decline in taste; the
principles of gothic architecture; an apology for its revival; a
glossary of ecclesiastical ornament and costume; floriated ornament; and at the end a treatise on chancel screens and rood
lofts, their antiquity, use and symbolism. Ambrose, who was
not above criticism of Pugin in some of his most excessive
moments ie. in his suspicion of Jesuits, nevertheless remained
loyal and close, and wrote[23] of the last book

> . . . a most triumphant and admirable production . . . we were
> all enchanted with it here . . . This feeling would be universal, I
> am convinced, if it were not for the unfortunate spirit of Party
> that has grown up of late in our Body which warps men's
> minds and blinds their judgement to a lamentable degree . . .

The controversy over vestments first broke out in 1839.
Pugin had designed gothic sets for his new churches in the
Midlands. Bishop Walsh received instructions from Propaganda Fide in Rome that their use be discontinued since they
offended against authorised length and shape. Pugin was
heart-broken and expressed[24] his outrage to Ambrose

> The Bishop showed me . . . a Letter he had just received from
> Propaganda censuring his proceedings and denouncing me in
> no very measured terms . . . the only Bishop in England who
> has really advanced the dignity of religion. Dr Walsh found the
> churches in his district worse than barns; he will leave them
> sumptious erections. The greater part of the vestments were
> filthy rags, and he has replaced them with silk and gold. For
> this he has been censured!!!! . . . He was accused of innovation.
> He should therefore have been firm; but he has suspended the use
> of the vestments everywhere. Thus the wretched old things are
> actually used in the new Derby Church while Lord Shrewsbury's
> splendid donations are shelved. I feel cut up beyond measure,
> but I do not mean to let this business drop. I will set forth the
> antient Glories of Catholicism and leave people to judge why
> the service now performed in the modern Catholic Chapels is
> not a ghost of the antient rite . . . You are a marked man for the
> vengeance of those who do not like *to be put out of the way* . . .

Since to write in Latin was beyond him, Bishop Walsh replied in French[25] to Cardinal Franzoni at Propaganda, expressing his desire to maintain the unity of the Church and obedience to the Holy See. He protested that the vestments used in his District represented no innovation (his letter enclosed numerous drawings of the offending vesture). Chasubles of this sort had been in use four hundred years ago. Apart from other considerations, it was of great importance at the present time to identify Protestants who had considerable veneration for antiquity, with the forms and customs of the pre-Reformation Church in England. The beauty of the vestments and the solemnity of ceremonies had done much to encourage conversions. He asked for a prudent person in whom there was confidence to examine what was being done in the District and report to the Sacred Congregation, since he wished to give proof of his devotion to the authority of the Church. The Bishop also wrote to Nicholas Wiseman, then at the English College in Rome, to make him aware of the problem[26]; perhaps he thought Wiseman would be chosen to mediate.

In the early 1850s the matter was raised once more, at a time when circumstances, soon to be related, had persuaded the Holy See to seek a uniformity and standardization which Ambrose maintained had never been known in mediaeval Christendom. He put[27] his point of view to Montalembert in relation to Pugin's 'terrible affliction[28]'

> . . . I for one have a hard battle to fight. It was in England . . . that we first revived the grand old mediaeval chasuble and now I am told that some of your Bishops are introducing it in France, but alas in London the Catholics are taking up the idea that the only orthodox thing is the hideous Roman chasuble . . . It was the Oratorians who commenced this frightful fashion, and it has been taken up by others. However, the movement in France will help us greatly, especially as the generality of our Bishops are in favour of the grand old mediaeval vestment. I hope . . . later to do more to advance the great cause of Christian art in England, if I ever live to succeed to my Patrimonial Estates, but meanwhile I assure you that I am far from idle, and as long as God gives me life and health, I am determined to go on contending for our glorious principles.

It was an accurate summary of his attitude and activities.

Ambrose called upon Bishop Ullathorne in Birmingham in September 1852. Writing to Laura at Grace Dieu from London on 14 September he described the meeting in his own terms, which may well not have been an exact repetition of those of the Bishop. There had been another letter about vestments. Bishop Ullathorne had said that 'most certainly this odious recommendation from Rome should be utterly disregarded. He spoke of it in terms of the greatest displeasure. He thinks it is as much the Cardinal's fault [Wiseman] as that of the Oratorians, tho' mainly due to Father Faber's influence'. Strangely enough, while Ambrose was as yet unaware of it Pugin had died on that day in Ramsgate. His output had been prodigious and he was only forty years of age.

There were a number of deaths in the later 1840s and early 1850s which were of significance to the Church history of the period and the de Lisle family in particular. The first of them in August 1847 was Bishop Griffiths, Vicar Apostolic of the London District for fourteen years; he was viewed with reserve in Rome, even to the point of being considered a Gallican[29], for he had shown unacceptable degrees of independence and had been suspicious of Regulars, especially the Jesuits, particularly when it was proposed that they should build churches without recourse to the Bishop. Bishop Wiseman, co-adjutor to Bishop Walsh in the Central District, was immediately appointed Pro Vicar Apostolic for London on a temporary basis. It was not a move that was popular with the majority of the clergy; in fact a certain hostility was to remain. Since it was intended in Rome that a hierarchy be established in England with bishops in ordinary in place of vicars apostolic, a year later in August 1848, Bishop Walsh despite his protestations as to his frailty, was sent to head the London District since the intention was that he should eventually be the first Archbishop. Wiseman remained as Co-adjutor. Bishop Ullathorne of the Western District moved to the Central Vicariate. Bishop Walsh died six months later on 12 February 1849, mourned by his friends in the Midlands, Ambrose and Laura in particular whom he had supported in their various enterprises so long and so faithfully without display or outward show. A gothic monument was placed over his grave in St Chad's Cathedral, Birmingham; his portrait in a Pugin mitre and chasuble still hangs in the hall at Oscott. Wiseman succeeded to the London District.

In the family, various young cousins fell victim to tuberculosis; among them in March 1849, Emma Phillipps, daughter of Uncle Edward, vicar of Hathern, aged 25. Ambrose and Laura had paid her several visits, 'a mere skeleton'. At Grace Dieu Warren in March 1850, the same disease carried off Sophia, wife of George Dudley Ryder, aged 35, one of the last two remaining fateful Sargent daughters and mother of seven, the youngest a year old. Laura, at George's request, cut Sophia's hair and helped to 'put her into her shell'[30]. Only Mary, wife of Henry Wilberforce was left alive. Mrs Sargent and Samuel Wilberforce, now Bishop of Oxford, widower of Sophia's sister Emily, arrived at 2 a.m. and departed by nine the same morning, such was the feeling of religious separation. Newman preached next day at the funeral in Grace Dieu Chapel at which they were not present, and not a word, nor it is said a glance, had been exchanged between the old friends, so much had happened to divide them. Henry Manning, widower of the former Caroline Sargent, did not appear. Ambrose recorded having met him, supposedly for the first time, shortly after Manning's reception as a Roman Catholic in the Spring of 1851, while they were both staying in London with William Monsell. 'He really is a most striking person. What I have seen of him charms me'[31]. Their relationship was never to be close, though they met and corresponded; it endured for Ambrose's lifetime, and beyond it with his family.

Laura's sister Henrietta died in Pau 14 February 1852 aged 37 from 'inflammation of the lungs' leaving two small children. Since Mary Lucy Clifford, her other sister, a nun in Dublin, did not long survive her and died in August 1860 at the age of 46, Laura outlived them both by thirty six years, despite her many sorrows and constant child-bearing.

Dominic Barberi, never a robust figure, had been worn down by his austerities and the intensity of his labours over several years. In March 1848 he wrote that he could scarcely stand. 'I am ill from the crown of my head to the soles of my feet'. It was said that he looked more like a man of eighty than sixty. The work of his Order in England had progressed; numbers had increased. Spencer had been clothed as a Passionist in January 1847; this did not preclude visits to Grace Dieu, which though fewer, continued. Besides the base at Aston, a House at Woodchester in Gloucestershire and a site in Hampstead were acquired by the Passionists. On his way to the opening of the church at Woodchester, Barberi became so ill on the train from Paddington in August 1849, that he was forced to alight at Reading. There at the station hotel he died a few hours later.

Among the pioneers of the Catholic revival also to finish his course in these years was Gentili; not old, but exhausted by toil and effort. Using the Loughborough Mission as a base, he had endured months of unremitting travel as he preached, gave missions and retreats, heard confessions, all over England on an alarming scale while still pursuing his own frugal way of life. At last, his resilience spent, at the age of 49, he died in Dublin of a prevalent fever on 26 September 1848. Laura was much affected and wrote in her diary of the death of 'our holy friend' and 'may our end be like unto his'. Pagani gave her Gentili's cloak which she continued to wear. Ambrose thought 'his career was rather beginning than ending'. Certainly during the last months of his life Gentili had been more highly regarded and more was demanded of him than ever before. Propaganda in Rome had entrusted to him, in collaboration with Pagani, a difficult and delicate commission; to report on the state of the Vicars Apostolic and clergy in England with a view to the establishment of a hierarchy.

The progress of this measure has been told many times, but not from the viewpoint of a Roman Catholic layman. This is a fitting point to introduce the history of the proposition in these terms.

Ambrose showed himself in favour of a diocesan hierarchy in England from the start, and for his customary reasons: he considered it would benefit various aspects of English Catholicism. First, as he wrote to Lord Shrewsbury,[32] this kind of Church government would be more dignified and appropriate

> As long as we have Vicars with outlandish titles, Catholicism *here* will appear only in the character of an exotic, timidly contending with the adverse influences of a foreign and ungenial climate.

Secondly, he was anxious that the role of the laity be more clearly defined; that the episcopate should take take steps

> ... to heal the deplorable divisions that reign amongst the members of our Body and to *lay down* some solid and intelligible principles of action which may serve as a guide of conduct for us laymen in our endeavour to serve our Pastors and under their direction to promote the Church's cause by such means as come *within our sphere* ... Once that our Hierarchy shall be established, and that the Canon Law shall become operative amongst us, all will know their respective Rights and Duties: but in the absence of positive laws there is necessarily a confusion of ideas, and consequent collisions of the most unseemly character in practice[33].

It would appear that he did not forsee the eventual outcome of his pressure: a restriction on much of his former activity. It was because they feared for the independence which they had enjoyed under the rule of the Vicars Apostolic, that many of the hereditary Catholics opposed not only plans for the establishment of a hierarchy in England, but its eventual introduction. They were more realistic than Ambrose, with his ideas of partnership between Bishops and laypeople, and cannot have failed to be more aware than he that it was their own firmly held views which were adding to the divisions.

In 1838 the Vicars Apostolic had drawn up what came to be called a *Statuta Provisoria* for submission to the Holy See concerning ecclesiastical government in England; the matter of a hierarchy *per se* was not mentioned. Later that year Propaganda sent to the Vicars Apostolic a document called the *Statuta Proposita* drawn up by Cardinal Antonio De Luca, one of the consultors; it acknowledged the inexpediency of bishops in ordinary, but made a series of other suggestions. This was debated by the English Vicars Apostolic in November 1838, together with requested answers[34] to two decrees issued by the Holy See and sent to them in September, regarding their relations with the Regulars to whom had been given a certain degree of independence of their Bishops.

In August 1839 the Sacred Congregation for the Propagation of the Faith met to discuss the English ecclesiastical scene. Before them was a series of documents arranged in the form of a *ponenza* or *ristretto* prepared by Cardinal Mai, with a commentary or *votum* thereon, prepared by Cardinal De Luca[35]. Three English peers, Lords Shrewsbury, Stafford and Clifford, he said in his introduction, had given verbal evidence as they were in Rome. Submissions, numbering A to V, included documents from the English Vicars Apostolic, members of Religious Orders and clergy, and as enclosure M extracts made by Dr Rock from letters addressed to Lord Shrewsbury; number N was a copy of a letter[36] to the same by Ambrose, the only enclosure from a completely lay source. The Sacred congregation expressed general dissatisfaction with the Vicars Apostolic: their answers to the *Statuta Proposita* were regarded as thin, the frequency of their consultations inadequate and their independence regrettable. Their reputation was not enhanced by a *votum*, at Propaganda's request which had come in later, from Gentili and Pagani who gave as their opinion that the English clergy, infected with Gallicanism and dominated by a spirit of ambition and national autonomy, did not show the respectful submission and dependence on the Holy See that was required.

Only one major change was made; as previously recorded, the number of English Districts was increased from four to eight. There the matter rested for some years, although one further document must be mentioned, in view of disclaimers in later years. A different file in the Archives of Propaganda[37] reveals a letter sent by Lord Shrewsbury on 22 January 1839 to the Secretary. In it he refers to the honour done to himself, and two other Catholic peers in being asked for their opinion on the *Statuta Proposita*. They had not alluded to the desire which they knew 'to be very prevalent for the Restoration of the Hierarchy because that question did not appear to him to form part of the intended amelioration in the ecclesiastical government of England'. But they felt that the establishment of Bishops in Ordinary, if not absolutely necessary, at least infinitely more desirable, and pointed to the precedent in the United States of America.

At a Low week meeting in 1845 the English Vicars Apostolic decided that Bishops Wiseman and Baggs should draw up a petition that the hierarchy question be reopened, and take it to Rome. The deaths of both Bishop Baggs and the Pope, Gregory

XVI, caused delays. Early in 1847, Propaganda itself decided
to take action. Cardinal Franzoni, the Prefect, wrote to Rosmini to ask whether Gentili might be entrusted with 'a religious
mandate of the highest importance'. Upon his assurances,
Gentili had begun to send reports[38] on the state of English
Catholicism. He did not hesitate to be critical; there were
many obstacles to the conversion of England as he saw them;
disunity between Seculars and Regulars, between priests, between priests and bishops and between Districts. Training of
clergy was inadequate among both Seculars and Regulars;
religious spirit was lacking among the Regulars many of whom
were opposed to the claims of the bishops. Pastors did not
know their flocks and there was leakage from the Church. The
Restoration of the Hierarchy he saw as the only remedy and
he gave his suggestions as to how this might be achieved.

The decision was taken, ahead of the arrival in Rome of the
representatives of the Vicars Apostolic (Bishops Wiseman and
Sharples in the event), that an English hierarchy be created;
papal sanction was given on 1 November 1847 for briefs to be
prepared. In the meantime, Ambrose continued his correspondence with Lord Shrewsbury on its desirability;

> I am delighted that you enter into what I say about the
> Hierarchy; it is impossible to overrate the importance of that, I
> firmly believe . . . there is not any real difficulty . . .[39]

More delays had two causes; doubt as to who should head
the new hierarchy was the first. Ambrose saw the appointment
of Wiseman to the Pro Vicariate of London as 'very judicious';
that he should be the first Archbishop of London 'prepared to
assert for the Catholic Church of this country the respect due
to it from Englishmen and from their Government also'. Their
past association would be of considerable advantage to Ambrose in the pursuit of his own enterprises. In Rome, Bishop
Walsh the senior bishop was favoured; his move to London
was the direct result. Still the process hung fire; the Vicars
Apostolic sent Ullathorne to help with the last details and it
was in the final stage of the negotiations in the autumn of 1848
that the second and more serious cause for delay occurred:
revolution broke out in Italy; the Pope was forced to flee
from Rome. All thoughts of revised Church government for

Catholics in England were shelved for two years; the incident was to have a lasting effect on the outlook of the Pope.

The election in June 1846 of Cardinal Mastai Feretti[1] former Bishop of Imola as Pope, with the title of Pius IX, was well regarded in England. Unlike his predecessor, Gregory XVI, who had caused many Italians to react unfavourably towards his extreme conservatism, Pius IX had an early reputation for more liberal ideas. To a disturbed collection of Italian communities he brought promise of a less oppressive future. He began with a general amnesty for political prisoners and in response to popular demonstrations in the Papal States (as elsewhere) granted a constitution and parliamentary government, save that discussion of religious questions was not permitted. He initiated some moderate administrative reforms such as admitting a few laymen to offices; he accepted newspapers with a political bias; the lifting of an embargo on railways in the Papal dominions became a possibility. '*Chemin de fer, chemins d'enfer*' was a remark attributed to his predecessor.

In 1848, the forces of revolution, prevalent throughout Europe, reached Vienna; Count von Metternich[41] fled. Austria whose authority had preserved the status quo against the desire for political freedom within the Italian states, became immediately vulnerable. It seemed a golden opportunity to end Austrian domination: Piedmont under its ruler Charles Albert, seized it and declared war. But they were not strong enough, nor well enough supported by the kingdom of Naples and the Pope; the battle of Custozza was an Austrian victory. The leadership of an Italian national movement passed, as a result, to a more extreme republican party headed by Guiseppe Mazzini, an ardent young patriot of the Society of Young Italy, who had returned from exile in France and England. As the result of the uprising a republic was declared in Rome; the Papal States were removed from papal rule. The Pope fled for refuge to Gaeta. Charles Albert and the forces of Piedmont made one more bid for power, and denouncing the Armistice, crossed the frontier into Austria but were rapidly defeated at the battle of Novara in March 1849. France, anxious to demonstrate against Austrian power in Italy, took up the cause of the Holy See, and against the troops of Giuseppe Garibaldi, another Italian popular leader, put down the nationalist insurrection and restored Rome to the papacy in July 1849. Many of the followers of Mazzini and Garibaldi fled to exile in England. A rigid purely clerical regime, reminiscent of the immediate past, was re-instated in Rome. In fact, absolutism returned to the Italian peninsular as a whole and the events of the previous two years became memorable for their bearing on future events and attitudes, English ones included.

Pius IX never forgot the experiences of the revolutionary period. From 1849 onwards he did all in his power to shore up the papacy against the forces of democracy, liberalism and freedom of expression, and to promote a centralized and authoritative form of government. The States of the Church he regarded as particularly significant and their restoration to him in 1850 highly symbolic, as the base of the Church's power in the world. Their eventual loss was inevitable, and when it came in 1860, the blow was deeply felt. Ambrose took the first loss (in 1848) of the temporal power very calmly. He expressed his views to Newman[42]

> ... now that the temporal sovereignty is put down by the Roman people themselves, and this act in this respect does but agree with what is going on everywhere else, the separation of Church and State ... But on the other hand I believe as that temporal power of the Pope expires, his spiritual power will be more and more recognized, in *the sphere* and *according to the measure* that Our Lord intended it should be exercised in the Church.

Ambrose wrote in much the same vein to Pagani. For some time the temporal sovereignty of the Pope, he thought, had been a source of unpopularity rather than of power to the Papacy. The time had passed when the Pope could not exercise the Primacy unless he were himself an independent Prince; the Supreme Vicar of Christ did not need the poor bulwark of an earthly sceptre. 'The transition may be terrible but I am persuaded the Church's grandest day is coming'. Extreme ultramontane opinion in England was far from agreement with Ambrose; the temporal power remained a burning issue.

The Pope's return to Rome from exile in April 1850 removed the last reason to delay any longer the reactivation of the Briefs which had been prepared in 1847 for a hierarchy in

England. It would appear, however, that there was hesitation up until the last as to who should be its head. A decision does seem to have been taken to create Wiseman a Cardinal which, at that time, would mean leaving his native land to reside permanently in Rome. Some of the disadvantages of Wiseman's return were clearly apparent; in the event, this indecision was justified. Gentili had favoured Bishop Ullathorne as the first Archbishop of Westminster. Wiseman himself, determined not to run the risk of exile, decided to enlist the help of Monsignor George Talbot,[43] an arch-manipulator with whom later Ambrose was to have dealings, who had the ear of the Pope. He sent Talbot a confidential memorandum[44] which set out his achievements in the London Vicariate and suggested that a change of leadership would threaten further progress.

Wiseman left London in August 1850 on a summons from the Pope. He arrived in Rome on 5 September after a visit to his family. The apostolic letter which established the English hierarchy and nominated Wiseman as Archbishop, was dated 29 September. Next day a Consistory named him a cardinal. Talbot, who had made some enquiries in England as to the reception of a prelate of this rank, had achieved what had been asked of him. Wiseman's entreaties had done the rest; he had been permitted to return.

No doubt elated by the success of his endeavours, Wiseman rushed into print with his famous Pastoral Letter[45] 'From the Flaminian Gate' to English Catholics, announcing the establishment of the hierarchy in terms ebullient, unwise, tactless and lacking in diplomacy. He despatched it to England with the request to his vicar general, Robert Whitty, that it be read immediately from all pulpits in his archdiocese. This was done on 13 October. Meanwhile Wiseman planned a gentle itinerary round Europe before his return to England. The most inflammatory part of the Pastoral Letter concerned his own role, with use of the royal plural

> ... his Holiness was ... pleased to appoint us, though most unworthy, to the Archiepiscopal See of Westminster ... giving us at the same time the administration of the Episcopal See of Southwark, so that at present, and till such time as the Holy See shall see fit otherwise to provide, we govern and shall continue to govern, the counties of Middlesex, Hertford and

Essex, as Ordinary, thereof, and those of Surrey, Sussex, Kent, Berkshire and Hampshire, with the islands annexed, as Administrator with Ordinary jurisdiction.

Some words as to the departure of England's religious glory, that Saints of our country 'must bless God who hath again visited his people', also managed to create sorrow and outrage. The response to the Pastoral Letter in general was indeed violent and immediate; unhappily, from both political and religious sources, Anglican and in some cases Roman Catholic.

The national hysteria, for such it was, as the result of taking Wiseman's words far too literally, derived from various bases. One was the inference that the Pope seemed to be claiming exclusive rights which ignored the Church of England. The letter[46] presented by the Anglican bishops to the Queen is representative of this reaction.

> This our Country, whose Church being a true branch of Christ's Holy Catholic Church, in which the true Word of God is preached and the Sacraments are duly ministered according to God's ordinances, is treated by the Bishop of Rome as having been a heathen land, and is congratulated on its restoration, after an interval of 300 years to a place among the Churches of Christendom.

The letter of Bishop Edward Maltby, Bishop of Durham, to the Prime Minister, Lord John Russell, set off a chain of intolerance and anger. Moreover, the nature of spiritual authority exercised by the Pope was held to inhibit academic freedom and scholarship; corruption of dogma became a possibility. A rival claim to allegiance and a threat to the constitution, was a third area of criticism which would be heard again. English opinion, in addition, was sympathetic to the aspirations of the colourful exiled 'freedom fighters' Mazzini and Garibaldi, and decried authoritarianism. Lord Minto, whose abortive mission to the Pope in the interests of establishing diplomatic relations took place in 1847, had given the impression that a Roman Catholic hierarchy would not be unwelcome in England. But as EEY. Hales has pointed out[47], in 1848 there was sympathy for a liberal Pope under threat from insurgents; yet by 1850 he was regarded as a tyrant[48] and his decrees correspondingly suspect.

Wiseman was in Vienna when he was first made aware of
the force of the storm that his Pastoral Letter had aroused in
England. Copies of *The Times* reached the Austrian capital
bringing with them indications of the wrath to come. A
leader[49] stated

> ... however reluctant we may be to add fresh elements of
> discord to the present agitated condition of Europe, we are not
> disposed to submit with perfect tameness and indifference to
> the wanton interference of a band of foreign priests in the
> affairs of our country.

Wiseman at once wrote[50] to the Prime Minister, Lord John
Russell, to try and persuade him that 'erroneous and even
distorted views' had been given in the English papers of what
the Holy See had done in regard to the spiritual government of
the Catholics in England. 'With regard to myself I beg to add
that I am invested with a purely ecclesiastical dignity; that I
have no secular or temporal delegation whatever'. He then
made immediate plans to come home.

Meanwhile, much disturbed by what he read in the newspapers of unfavourable English reaction to the idea of the hierarchy, Ambrose, in the space of two days, produced[51] a twelve-
page pamphlet which was printed at once. It took the form of
an open letter to Lord Shrewsbury, as a return of compliments
for the printed open letters which Lord Shrewsbury had addressed to him 'on the present posture of affairs' in the 1840s.
Ambrose intended to give the impression that this was a
measure to which all Catholics in England had looked forward

> the glad event for which we have been all so long and so
> earnestly labouring for which our most devout prayers have
> been poured forth to the Throne of Grace, has at length taken
> place.

The importance of the event, he considered, was being
witnessed by its effects upon the organs of public opinion in
the form of leading articles, pouring out upon 'the Spiritual
Chief of Christendom all the vials of their wrath and sectarian
prejudice'. It appeared to him the 'sacred duty of the English
Catholic Laity to speak out at once' which he proceeded to do
with enthusiasm by way of trying to minimize the measure of
innovation that had been involved.

And now, after all the bluster and stupid violence of the press, what has the Pope done?

He had simply abolished the office of Vicars Apostolic and placed the English Catholic Church under the government of '*ordinary bishops*'. Ambrose urged that the sacred principles of religious liberty, which were being flouted in certain other Kingdoms, should obtain in England, where Catholics had never swerved from a course of 'exhibiting a stainless pattern of loyalty to our Sovereign and Constitution'. He sent a copy of his pamphlet to Newman who acknowledged,[52] with approval, 'your noble Protest against the present outcry. It is just what all who knew you would expect from you'.

Bishop Ullathorne clearly viewed certain aspects of Wiseman's Pastoral with dismay. He wrote two letters to *The Times*, the first on 22 October 1850, pointing out (he might have added, contrary to the Cardinal's precise words), that the transaction to create the English Catholic hierarchy was simply a matter of internal re-organisation and church administration; there was no intention to rule the English people. Ullathorne then made preparations to compose an explanatory pamphlet. Nicholas Wiseman arrived in London as Cardinal Archbishop of Westminster on 11 November 1850, took over Ullathorne's material and by 20 November his 'Appeal to the English People'[53] emerged; a good deal more reasonable a document than his last, and one that had a calming influence.

Ambrose, in the role of eirenic layman, hearing that 'your Eminence is happily and safely arrived among us,' offered[54] his 'most dutiful homage of respect and congratulation'. He also draw Wiseman's attention to his recently published Letter to Lord Shrewsbury on 'the glorious restoration of our Hierarchy'.

Meanwhile Lord John Russell had on 4 November given an answer to the letter of the Bishop of Durham; *The Times* published it in the edition of the 7th. His government was at low ebb (it fell the following year) and it may well be that he was partly minded to create a diversion and to rally his countrymen by so doing. For he attacked as well as the Pope's 'insolent and insidious action' with his 'assumption of power' and a 'pretension of supremacy over the realm of England', the outlook and usages of those who had come to be called the 'Puseyites', 'unworthy sons of the Church of England herself'. They were an easy target: the attitude of this group of Anglicans towards the state connection provided an irritation and a threat to those of more Erastian ways of thinking. Overall this was an undignified document, deliberately provocative, and demonstrated the illiberality of Russell's Liberal position.

Ambrose conteracted with a further pamphlet, written on 18 November, addressed to Russell,[55] in which he showed that he recognised the hysterical nature of the recent outbursts and questioned the motive of those who were spoiling for a fight. What was its aim, he asked. No doubt he felt that the attack on the 'Puseyites' weakened his own position, for it was upon them that he depended in the Church of England for the development of the cause closest to his heart – the reunion of the Churches.

In one particular, Ambrose's own assertions came to be challenged: that the new hierarchy had been keenly desired and fought for by the Catholic laity. Illustrations of the contrary were now to come to the fore. *The Times* commented[56] that although Cardinal Wiseman had been among the Roman Catholic laity for six weeks, he had remained 'wholly ungreeted and unwelcome'.

> Ever and anon have appeared in our columns letters from Roman Catholics seeking to vindicate themselves, their religion and their Pontiff, but almost always ... concluding with a most undutiful and irreverent denunciation on the folly, vanity and ostentation of the new-made Cardinal ... at public meetings ... the tone of the Roman Catholics who have addressed the people have been anything but complimentary ...

There is evidence of the truth of these allegations and some curious disclaimers as to personal involvement, because of the way it had taken place.

Lord Shrewsbury's first letter[57] to Ambrose after the event showed that he considered Wiseman's return *as Cardinal* 'ill-judged'. He clearly blamed him personally for the unfavourable reception of the news; Pius IX had wanted Wiseman to remain in Rome. Lord Shrewsbury went on to question how the Pope had come to say that the laity had solicited the establishment of the hierarchy:

How or when was this done? I have no recollection of anything of the sort . . . It is a hard case to put the responsibility upon us when (as far as I know) we have had nothing to do with it.

Whether there was provision for the rights of the lower clergy concerned Lord Shrewsbury. 'If they do not get their rights, they have been scurvily treated'. In fact, no mention was made of a changed status for the clergy, who remained as missionaries, their lives regulated by their bishops. It was partly on this account that many of the older priests were as critical of the event as lay people. Neither was there, as Ambrose had hoped, any mention of the place of the laity.

Lord Shrewsbury was prompted to write his own printed answer to Russell; that of Ambrose he 'liked extremely'. He continued to correspond with Ambrose on the subject for much of 1851, in a vein critical especially of Wiseman, whom he termed *Wiseacre*. Though he deplored the violent reaction in England to the Pope's action, 'certainly ill-advised things have been done by us to provoke much of it'; 'the pompous Pastoral from the Flaminian Gate' was one of them: 'The Hierarchy would have been everything that is right had it been wisely managed . . .' But he was critical also of the extreme nature of the attitudes of some of his fellow Catholic peers. A sharp contrast exists here between the freedom of expression on the part of powerful Roman Catholic laymen up to and including 1850, and that of most of their counterparts (with a few notable exceptions) in the period following about 1860. At the time of the original vestments crisis of 1839, Shrewsbury himself had written[58] to (later Cardinal) Acton at the Vatican, of Propaganda's 'abominable letter to poor Bishop Walsh'; 'a scolding letter on a subject of which they knew nothing'. In 1850, Lord Beaumont was equally scathing[59]; Catholics had been placed in a position where 'they must either break with Rome or violate their allegiance to the constitutions of these realms'. Lord Camoys took up a similar attitude. The Duke of Norfolk went further: ultramontane opinions were 'totally incompatible with allegiance to our sovereign and with our constitution[60]'. He left the Roman Catholic Church[61] and began to make his Communion as an Anglican.

Twelve sees had been created; seven had been filled by the

former Vicars Apostolic; five remained vacant. Newman commented[62]

'We are not ripe ourselves for a hierarchy. Now we have one, they can't fill the sees, positively can't. We want seminaries far more than sees. We want education'.

It was an opinion that was to be debated a good deal in the next decade and bring its own crop of problems. Wiseman suggested[63] Newman as a candidate for the new See of Nottingham; Newman struggled successfully to avoid consideration. Ullathorne supported his appeal. He respected Newman, but as he wrote to Rome[64] 'he had neither the will or the tact to manage others'. By the summer of 1851, all the appointments of bishops had been made; the furore that had been stirred up had subsided. Ambrose, his household, his chapels and any projects he might devise, became the concern of Joseph William Hendren[65] newly appointed Bishop of Nottingham. Ambrose, Laura and their two eldest daughters attended his enthronization on 2 December 1851; Ambrose with three other laymen carried the canopy over him and dined with him afterwards at the Palace. Ambrose had ridden the storm with calm; his pamphlets had tried to reduce tension and been well received. Unlike some of his compatriots, he had exhibited continued demonstrations of loyalty to the Holy See; the increased dimunition of his influence and initiative, was, therefore, to become all the more a hard burden to bear, as will be apparent in the next chapter. It was not the establishment of the hierarchy by itself which effected these changes, but the personalities and outlook of those in high places who drew afresh the boundaries of power.

In the years following the recovery of Laura from her illness, the lives of the de Lisle began to take on a new impetus. It was as though they were conscious of having been given extra time together which might have been snatched away: they needed to put it to good use. Particularly after the move back to Grace Dieu in March 1850, there were more visits, more visitors and a good deal more time spent in London. There were additional reasons why this should have been so: the wish to provide education, entertainment and friendships for their many children; Ambrose's responsibilities following the death of the Earl of Shrewsbury which took him often away from Leicestershire. The extra wing at Grace Dieu obviously made more simple the offer of hospitality to over-night guests; the enlarged and newly decorated chapel drew visitors from near and far. During the 1850s, Ambrose it would seem, sensed that he must extend the range of his activities; there were restrictions on what he could achieve as a layman in relation to his local missions and the Monastery. As time went on and ultramontane views began to predominate in the English Roman Catholic Church, he was made to feel increasingly aware of the limitations of his station. The sphere of the laity had been left undelineated with the arrival of the hierarchy; the inference was that it should confine itself to listening and the supply of funds. For those who, as Ambrose, liked to take initiative, it had to be an idiosyncratic path. He did not hesitate to take it. As a result his home and surround-ings became increasingly a centre both for those who had changed their religious allegiance in the way he had, and those interested in relationships between the Churches. There was nowhere else quite like it, nor like him.

Aubrey de Vere, an Irish peer and Cambridge contemporary who visited in October 1853, wrote[66] to his sister

> The people here are the most delightful . . . you can conceive. You would think it a lovely image of a Christian household. There is choral service in the Chapel morning and evening, the younger children, dressed in red soutanes and acting as acolytes, until displaced by a still younger batch. There are already twelve children. You would delight in this house and feel nothing in it to make you uncomfortable. Ambrose Phillipps is called by some of his friends 'a tremendous *Puseyite*', the fact is that he is a great lover of theirs and of all their doings, and a great believer that the whole Church of England is some time as others to come back *as a body*. The consequence of this is that, though 1,500 people in this neighbourhood have become Roman Catholics, he is less anxious to make converts than any religious Roman Catholic I ever met in my life. He and his wife are overflowing with charity and hopefulness, and seem to believe that all parties are trying to do right, and will sure to be guided some day into union.

Already in 1849 from Garendon, Ambrose and Laura with

their three eldest girls, Philomena, usually know as Mina or Mena, Alice and Mary, had carried out the most extensive tour in England so far, of two entire months. The object would seem to have been to meet those members of the 'old' Catholic gentry who lived in Yorkshire, many of whom were related to Laura, to see the extent to which he could depend on their help in his causes; also to be in touch with 'Puseyites' and visit their churches. Towards the end of the itinerary Ambrose summed up his experiences in a letter[67] to Bishop Ullathorne; he had much very interesting information to report on the 'Puseyite movement' of which he had seen a great deal during his visits

> ... that in my judgement is the main hope of England's conversion. You will be greatly astonished to hear what I shall have to tell you. The more I see of the *old Catholick Body* the less do I expect and hope from them ... though there are great and glorious exceptions to be found here and there.

The hereditary old Catholics included members of Laura's own family of Clifford and those related to them: the Vavasours[68] of Hazlewood Castle where they met also Stonors[69] and Langdales; at Allerton Park, home of Lord Stourton[70] a fellow guest was Joseph Weld into whose family Mena was to marry. Ambrose's appreciation of the 'very magnificent house' under construction may well have contributed towards his need to extend Garendon when he inherited it. Described a curious Elizabethan building with a large central Gothic lantern lighting the staircase, Ambrose admired particularly the proportions of the proposed Great Hall; to be 80 feet long and 35 wide and 60 feet high. The Constable Maxwells[71] of Everingham Park entertained them also; 'delightful and *saintly* people ... the service is splendidly done in their chapel, which is a magnificent thing of *its kind*. but not to be compared with Gothick'. Sir Clifford Constable[72] of Burton Constable was their host for several days 'though very silent, pleased us very much by his kindness to our little girls'. There were 36 horses in the stables; 'all of them splendid animals'. The final visit was to Myddleton Lodge, near Bolton Abbey; home of the Middleton family, connections of the Maxwells. Houseparties in each place had provided numerous introductions and reunions, but Ambrose was dissatisfied by the lack of initiative or energy, 'Catholicity in Yorkshire seems in a very slumbering state, few signs of activity or progress'.

For their part, the de Lisles showed remarkable determination; bathing in late September at Whitby despite 'very cold and tremendous winds'. At York they visited the prison (75 inmates) and went all over it; also a Blind Asylum and convent and a host of other sites of historical and artistic interest. A day was spent at Ushaw where they saw a 'most perfect church by Pugin'.

On the 'Puseyite' side he was encouraged: Ambrose recorded churches 'fitted up in quite a Cath way'. During some days spent with his old friend Dean Erskine of Ripon, Anglican guests included the Bishop, Charles Thomas Longley, later Archbishop of Canterbury, whose relations with the followers of Pusey were more relaxed than many of his brethren on the episcopal bench; also William Wilberforce, son of the great philanthropist, who invited them to Markington Hall. He and his wife and Lord[73] and Lady Campden, whose acquaintance the de Lisles made there, were 'Catholickly disposed to a degree that is quite wonderful'.

Although Ambrose had his sights on corporate union, he rejoiced in the conversion of the more illustrious whom he thought would lead others as part of a wider movement; he worried when such acts were sporadic, as did Lord Shrewsbury: the Gorham judgement[74] he felt, had displaced more than had the establishment of the hierarchy. Gentili had been of the same mind: conversions in England came 'not because of our efforts, just a wonderful disposition of God's grace without our ministry'. These opinions may have been true of the more educated, but the progress of the missions supported by Ambrose among the inhabitants of the Leicestershire village owed a very great deal to the Rosminian and other clergy.

Many of the converts of the 1850s found their way to Grace Dieu. Newman had been right when he suggested that Ambrose understood tolerance in doctrinal questions, yet not in ritual. For the visitors who came embraced very varied viewpoints. For example, W. G. Ward who had adopted extreme ultramontane views, came with his family to Grace Dieu for a week in January 1851. Sir John Acton[75] who was to oppose these opinions so stringently particularly at the time of the Vatican Council, was a visitor in May of the same year, in the company of Ignaz Döllinger, Professor at Munich, as his tutor. Döllinger left the Roman Catholic Church in 1870 as the result of a decree of that same Council. Lord[76] and Lady Feilding who had become Catholics in Rome shortly before, were guests in October 1850; they overlapped with a visit by the Nightingale family. Lord Feilding 'pitched into Florence' as he put it later, with a view to her conversion, on a walk to the Chapel of Dolours which Ambrose had built among the rocks near Grace Dieu.

The visit of Charles Robert Scott-Murray[77] and his wife came later the same month; this relationship was put severely to the test when he and Ambrose became joint executors of Lord Shrewsbury's Will. The circle of acquaintances of the de Lisles became however widened as the result of it. At Danesfield the 1,600 acre estate of the Scott-Murrays near Maidenhead, Ambrose and Laura in November 1850 found a large and distinguished house party. Unlike many of its counterparts at Grace Dieu, it was an entirely Catholic gathering. It included, among others, Pugin who had built the chapel, Thomas Allies[78] and his wife, Lord and Lady Feilding, Bishop Wareing of Northampton, Lord and Lady Camoys, Lady Georgiana Fullerton an author and person of austere habits quite unlike her exuberant grandmother, the celebrated Georgiana, Duchess of Devonshire, and last but not least, Cardinal Wiseman and his entourage. Reasonably frequent opportunities for meeting occurred over the years, since the Cardinal sent Ambrose regular invitations to his soirées in London.

William Monsell, MP for Limerick and later after some government appointments created Lord Emly, a friend of Newman, grew even closer to Ambrose with his reception as a Roman Catholic in Grace Dieu chapel in December 1850; (this association was to prove particularly significant at the time of the 1st Vatican Council). Others who had recently changed their allegiance, Lord and Lady Campden, Henry Wilberforce[79] and his wife Mary, Robert Wilberforce,[80] his brother, and R. R. Suffield,[81] became guests also. Old friends returned throughout the years; Spencer, Digby, Anglican clergy, neighbours and many relations. A momentous visit was made to Alton Towers in August of 1850, for Lord Shrewsbury had as fellow guests his son-in-law Prince Borghese with his second wife, and daughter Agnese. Painful collisions were in store for Ambrose with this family.

The early years of the 1850s saw Ambrose, with an even larger circle of friends and acquaintances, starting to pursue new avenues. They are the subject of the next chapter when his activities can be seen to antagonise, in particular, members of the Catholic body in England. Some fresh departures were dictated by increasing shortage of funds. Family demands were greater than ever. The affectionate letters exchanged between Ambrose and Laura, if they were parted, give evidence of their continued happily married life. 'It seems quite an age [it was in fact four days] dearest Amber, since we parted' she wrote on 1 June 1851 when her husband went to London for a short visit.

'What an awful affliction death must be when a married couple love each other *as we do*. It makes me pity poor G Ryder more than ever. The chicks send their love. Ever your devoted wife'.

It is therefore no matter for surprise that a week after Ambrose's return, Laura gave birth to the first child after her illness; she was forty years of age and it was her twelfth, a boy who received the name Francis. His sponsors were William Monsell and Mrs Scott-Murray. Mary Lucy Clifford, Laura's sister, wrote from her convent in Dublin to ask whether the family was now complete.

I remember many years ago your saying you would like to have a dozen children, so as you have now got your wish, I suppose you mean to stop and spend the remainder of your life in preparing your dear ones for their happy home that they may be worthy of re-joining the most happy and enviable of them all, dear Reginald, in praising and blessing God . . .

But this was not to be the case. Almost exactly a year later in June 1852, Edwin was born during a lengthy visit to Grace Dieu of Bishop Hendred of Nottingham. The birth of Edwin, seventh son, secured the continuation of the family, since he was the only member on the male line to provide descendants to the present generation.

A few days after Francis' birth, Ambrose decided that he must re-deploy his financial resources. The further embellishment of Grace Dieu chapel, and building a new house for the priest at Whitwick, had exhausted the money which could regularly be set aside for the maintenance of churches at Whitwick and Shepshed. Almost every letter for two years, addressed quarterly to Bishop Ullathorne and to the Provincial of the Rosminians, in respect of monies borrowed, enclosed cheques not to be presented immediately as his accounts were overdrawn. All that could continue were those repayments of interest on long-outstanding debts and support for the Loughborough house. Financial maintenance of the missions of Shepshed and Whitwick would have to be found elsewhere. The Rosminians were dismayed, but hardly astonished; Fr Fortunatus Signini, the priest at Whitwick, had written[82] earlier to his Provincial, G-B Pagani, of Ambrose

> '. . . [he] has a way of giving money even when he has none and that so long as he may live he will always squander his money and if he does not give it to us he will give it to somebody else.'

Certainly Ambrose and Laura continued most imprudently to supply what they considered necessary for their chapels. In her diary for 1851 Laura noted that the chapel of St Winifred at Shepshed needed 82 yards of material for hangings: 67 yards round the church; 11 yards round the windows and 4 yards round the statue of the Blessed Virgin; no doubt she supplied them. On their return from France going through London, in November 1852, at a time of financial stringency, she wrote

> Amb and I and the girls went to Mr Burton's shop to settle about orphreys for cloth of gold vestments.

The following day, still in London, just before they watched the funeral procession of the Duke of Wellington, they heard from Lord Edward Howard[83] of the death of Lord Shrewsbury. Back at Grace Dieu came letters urging Ambrose to return to the capital on account of Lord Shrewsbury's will, of which he and Charles Scott-Murray were executors and residuary legatees. It seemed as if each would receive a considerable amount; perhaps as much as forty thousand pounds, a large sum in contemporary terms. At last, not only was it likely that long-outstanding debts be paid, but endless other possibilities swam before Ambrose's delighted eyes. He would like to help build the Cardinal a Cathedral, he wrote[84] to him on 28 May 1853. The exaltation was, unfortunately, to be short lived.

Chapter 9

The Association for the Promotion of the Unity of Christendom

THE funeral of John, 16th earl of Shrewsbury was not on the scale of that of the Duke of Wellington, but in its own sphere not devoid of splendour. Ambrose and Laura were back in London by the 22 November for the numerous formalities concerned with the duties of executor. The body of Lord Shrewsbury, on arrival in England, was taken to St George's Cathedral, Southwark. There, according to Laura's account, his coffin was placed under a pall and cataphalk [sic] in Edward Petre's chantry chapel. A Requiem, with music by Mozart (clearly not one of the arrangements made by Ambrose) was sung on Monday 29 November; Bishop Thomas Grant[1] preached. The coffin was then transported to Alton Towers where the spectacular part of the obsequies began.

Alton Towers, the scene of so many pleasant visits by the de Lisles, was not an ancient seat of the Shrewsbury family, although the site had been acquired by the first Earl, created 1442 (the 'Grand Talbot')[2], Henry V's principal successor in command of the English forces in France, by marriage with the heiress to the barony of Furnival. Heythrop in Oxfordshire had been the family home until it was burnt down in 1831; but before the fire, the 15th Earl had in 1814 begun to create the exceptional gardens of Alton. The landscape of the estate provided much scope with its undulating countryside, steep valleys and cragged promontories. Before he died in 1827 he had converted an ancient hunting lodge, then the only habitable building, into the beginnings of a stately home.

John Shrewsbury, the 16th Earl, continued the process of development; from 1835, with the help of Pugin whose stamp was everywhere. As a result, at the time of the funeral Alton Towers represented a set of castellated and turretted buildings of considerable size and elements of fantasy. The steps of the main entrance tower were flanked by two giant talbot hounds. A blind Welsh harper (who had a thatched cottage in the grounds) was employed by the earls to sit here and provide a mediaeval atmosphere with his music. Galleries lined with armour and arms, divided in two by a screen of halberds, extended north for over 600 feet. At the far end was the octagon hall, modelled on the chapter house at Wells Cathedral with a central shaft supporting the lath and plaster vaulted ceiling. A great equestrian statue of the Grand Talbot, in full armour, dominated the scene; Pugin had difficulty in obtaining such as would be sufficiently authentic. The Talbot gallery, 100 feet long, continued from the Octagon. Over 700 pictures, many of which would have hung here, were placed in the sale of 1857, including a Velasquez Philip IV, a Van Dyck full length portrait of the Earl of Arundel, a Virgin and Child attributed to Raphael and Bellini's Circumcision, now in the National Gallery. A conservatory gallery led to the state rooms and Great Hall with high painted roof and windows filled with glass bearing heraldic emblems. It was the large chapel dedicated to St Peter adjoining this block, where the decorations revealed much that was typical of Pugin: stencilled designs and lettering with gold stars on the roof and the prolific use of tracery. The roof was supported by painted and gilt plaster figures of angels kneeling on floriated corbels as they read books in Gothic binding.

Here John Lord Shrewsbury lay in state for some days during the week beginning 12 December 1852. Ambrose and Laura with Alice and Winifreda[3] arrived at Alton Towers on the following day and in the evening attended 'Mattins and Lauds for the Dead at 8; very solemn. We were in the body of the Chapel. It was a very impressive scene'.

Next day the funeral took place. All natural light had been excluded from the windows by black drapery; the altar was hung with black velvet, bearing a white cross in the centre. In the centre of the chapel a large and ornate catafalque had been erected. It resembled a richly decorated baldichino. The late earl's coffin lay on a raised plinth under the catafalque which was cruciform in shape supported by twelve pillars of carved wood; eight had gilt coronets surmounting shields and at the summit talbots bearing candelabra each with seven long candles; on the floor were more standards carrying branches of lights, altogether the tapers numbered between three and four hundred.

The coffin and pall, made by Hardman of Birmingham a craftsman much patronized by Ambrose, were likewise ornate and elaborate. (Ambrose, as one of the executors, tried in the autumn of 1853, to give the pall and catafalque to Bishop Ullathorne for use in St Chad's Cathedral at Birmingham; the offer was repeated by Charles Scott Murray, but not accepted).

Masses on the 14 December began at six am. and carried on until eleven o'clock when high mass began with Bishop Ullathorne as celebrant, his vicar-general deacon and the Vice-President of Oscott sub-deacon. The Bishops of Northampton, Shrewsbury and Clifton were present, together with a number calculated at one hundred and fifty secular priests and the representatives of the Religious Orders in England. The choir of St Chad's Cathedral, Birmingham led the singing. After the mass Monsignor Weedall preached the panegyric. The Bishops pronounced the Absolutions and censed the coffin and a procession formed up headed by the cross-bearer and bearers of torches out of the chapel; Bishops, the choir, monks and priests, a servant carrying the late earl's coronet, the hearse drawn by six horses with his coffin, the chief mourners, servants, tenants and workers on the estate, many hundred in all, went slowly through the far-famed gardens to the perimetre of Lord Shrewsbury's domain. Carriages took a smaller gathering with the hearse to the Chapel of St John on a rocky eminence overhanging the river Churnet. The coffin was laid in a vault beneath the sanctuary. It was a significant moment for there passed from the scene an English Catholic layman of substance who was not afraid to express his opinions in public.

His legacy to his friend was to prove an almost intolerable burden. Ambrose in 1854 wrote[4] to Bishop Ullathorne . . . 'this odious executorship has been a new trial, for without benefitting me a single farthing it has earned me the most terrible abuse'.

Thus, criticism became increasingly heaped upon Ambrose as he entered fresh fields of activity. First, the acrimonious process of executing Lord Shrewsbury's will hung over Ambrose like a cloud for fifteen years; the final visits and letters to solicitors were in 1868. Secondly, the interest which he kept in affairs on the continent of Europe took an upward trend with a visit to France and a series of conversations and letters with Liberal thinkers; some of whom paid visits to Grace Dieu. The gap between him and the growing tendency towards ultramontane thinking in English Catholic circles widened thereby. Thirdly, Ambrose's long standing preoccupation with prophecy which resulted in a published work[5] in 1855, received short shrift in periodicals such as the *Dublin Review* and its reading public. Fourthly, an even less generally favourable reception in England, and in Rome, greeted his pamphlet of 1857 *On the Future Unity of Christendom* and the formation, with Ambrose as one of the founders, of the A.P.U.C.[6] in the same year. A few of his Anglican friends supported him; but enthusiasm was sporadic and criticism more widespread. It was on his part a prophetic stand for which his contemporaries were not prepared. Money problems continued to plague him and put a brake on his initiatives. Finally, the relationship of Ambrose with the local Catholic clergy who had tolerated the so-called interference because it was he who provided support, deteriorated when he could no longer do so.

The establishment of the Roman Catholic hierarchy in England had not given securer bases for the clergy in relation to their bishops, but the status of the clergy did change in relation to the lay people. Gone for the most part were the days when chaplains resided in the homes of the gentry and ministered from those points of vantage as members of a close knit community. Now priests lived in, paradoxically, more isolated circumstances, in clergy houses in towns; their apartness reinforced by concepts that they had chosen a more perfect way and that it was their duty to keep the laity in their places; a clerical caste hitherto unknown in England, was to emerge.

At first, the terms of Lord Shrewsbury's will seemed almost too good to be true. The recent visit to Alton Towers and vivid reminder of its splendour, its pictures and precious objects, no doubt helped to convince Ambrose that not only were his own domestic financial troubles and his debts at an end, but he could begin to devote funds to fresh ecclesiastical causes and improvements to his property. His immediate actions indicate that he was so convinced: during the first few months of 1853 he gave further evidence of the ever-hopeful and impulsive nature of his character. He asked Hardman of Birmingham to call upon him on 7 January and ordered 6 stained glass windows for Grace Dieu chapel: the two large ones were to be £60 each and the 4 small ones £35. On 14 February two men arrived to put up a new fence for the grounds abutting on to the Ashby Road and Ambrose received a design for the Lodge gate posts: £150 for them and £40 for an adjoining wall. On 4 April he went to the Monastery with Edward Pugin 'in order to settle about the church being completed.'

His letter[7] of 10 January 1853 to his son Everard, then in Paris, set out his expectations at that juncture. Lord Shrewsbury had left to him and his co-executor Charles Scott-Murray a sum amounting in total to one hundred and thirty thousand pounds; it was not known how much would be required to be paid out of this sum, but it was expected to be not less than thirty five or thirty six thousand each; perhaps as much as forty. Some mistakes had crept into newspaper accounts of the legacy, he wrote: 'It is quite untrue that it is left for Church purposes, it is left absolutely to our own use and benefit'. The papers had made a mistake too about Alton Towers having been left to the de Lisles: '. . . it is true that Lord S has left *Alton Castle* to us and the beautiful Hospital, though the Bishop has a lease of each of these for 90 years'. Ten had expired, so the fee simple on the two properties and also of an estate at Farley of about 200 acres would eventually go to Ambrose's heirs.

'But the most remarkable part of the will is, that in the event of Bertram Talbot [a young man of twenty, living abroad in poor health], the present Earl dying without male issue, in that

contingency the late Lord has left the whole of his vast estates
to be equally divided between Mr Scott-Murray and myself . . .
the late Earl did this by a power he inherited from the Duke of
Shrewsbury, and to prevent his property falling into Protestant
hands, for if he had not made this will, and the young Lord
had died without male issue, it would have been claimed by
Lord Talbot of Ingestre. Lord Talbot has already given *us*
notice that in the event of the young Lord's death, he intends
to contest that part of the will with us. But our lawyer says he
would fail . . .'[8]

Everard was urged not to let any of this get into the French
periodical *L'Univers* which had already published an article
about the will. His father advised him to call on Jules Gondon,
an old friend who was concerned with English affairs on that
paper, and assure him 'he was quite mistaken in saying Lord
Shrewsbury meant it all for the Church . . . he has left it
absolutely to our own discretion and use'.

The Shrewsbury case, as it came to be called, was of
extraordinary complexity and one that it is by no means easy
to unravel at this distance, since many of the most significant
papers have failed to survive, either in England or in Rome,
and often only one side of a correspondence. Newspaper
reports are tantalisingly obscure or brief. But an outline of the
affair must be attempted because it affected the de Lisles so
materially and reveals the lack of bitterness and innate resilience of Ambrose in the face of what must surely have been a
series of outstanding blows which put an end to many hopes,
but failed to quench others.

What is clear is that when the copy of Lord Shrewsbury's
will reached London from Italy in January of 1853 and was
received by Jackson the solicitor to the Executors, it was
placed in the hands of Edward Bellasis[9] without consultation
with Ambrose. He was kept in ignorance until 2 March of the
existence of what has been referred to as a 'secret paper' which
had accompanied the will, purporting to have been drawn up
by Lord Shrewsbury, setting out that the legacies were to be
devoted to certain church purposes. Unhappily this document
is now nowhere to be found. It led to considerable trouble and
bitterness; there was even a suggestion that it was a forgery; so
it was alleged by Robert Belaney[10] who had lived in the

household of the Countess of Shrewsbury as tutor to the young Earl Bertram, and who communicated this allegation to Ambrose.

The death of Lord Shrewsbury had seriously affected a number of institutions which he had supported. He had helped Ambrose with repeated sums of money; for the maintenance of the Roman Catholic Schools he had started on the estate, for instance. No one suffered more than Bishop Ullathorne whose financial situation became so precarious that he and the President of Oscott, Dr Moore, spent ten days in Warwick Gaol in April 1853 on account of inability to raise the money for a debt incurred as shareholders of a company that had become bankrupt. He had inherited a parlous situation from Bishop Walsh who had been generous with loans for good causes, many of which had not been repaid (Ambrose was one of his debtors). Lord Shrewsbury had made regular contributions to the upkeep of numerous churches in the Midlands and to Cotton Hall where the Passionists had their noviciate.

Bishop Ullathorne therefore made a request to the Executors of the will to make up this short fall and provide funds out of the Estate. This Ambrose declined to do, thinking the 'secret paper' irregular, even illegal and that he would not be able to swear that he had received his legacy as set out in the will if, in fact, he had not. He sought a good deal of legal and priestly advice (from the Rosminians, Bishops Hendred of Nottingham and Brown of Shrewsbury) which assured him of the propriety of his stand on legal and moral grounds.[11] But there were many critics who spread around the rumour that Ambrose was defying the last wishes of his benefactor. 'I am quite aware of all the atrocious abuse that has been lavished on me by a large number of Catholics in London and elsewhere. Such calumnies will not intimidate me' he wrote to William Monsell.[12] The chief instigators of the criticism, from their correspondence, were clearly Bertram, Lord (John) Shrewsbury's cousin and heir, his mother and step father Captain and Mrs Washington Hibbert, and the late Earl's widow, the Countess of Shrewsbury.

'There is not the slightest shadow of foundation for the abominable statement that I intend to devote a Farthing of the Fund you refer to *to any purpose of my own whether secular or religious.*'

In deference to the strong feelings that had been expressed, Ambrose had decided not to use any funds he might receive to pay off 'any ecclesiastical debts', but to devote the money 'to the building of churches where they are likely to be conducive to God's Glory, but not on my own estates nor for the benefit of my own tenantry', but in doing this he did not intend to transgress the law of the land, 'nor yet to put myself or the property bequeathed to me within any kind of risk of . . . legal penalties'. This was not sufficient for Bishop Ullathorne who, whilst recognizing that he was a plaintiff in this matter as well as private adviser, wrote to tell Ambrose 'the subject fills the whole of catholic society'; that he would 'never attribute to you a wrong intention but I do feel that your conscience is wrongly instructed'.

By 1854 it became clear that the whole question was largely academic: the liabilities of the late Earl's unsettled Estate (the entailed estate had gone to Bertram as his heir) were greater than the Estate itself. As Ambrose pointed out to Ullathorne, he had received only £200 of his legacy by that date.[13] Had he been rash enough to authorise any claims which the Bishop might have presumed he had, Ambrose would have been required to refund the money from his own pocket.

Upon the death of the 16th Earl, his descendants in Italy began to make their claims. Three children had been born to him and the Countess of Shrewsbury: a boy John who died aged four months and two daughters, Lady Mary Talbot to whom Ambrose had been so attracted many years before, who had married Prince Filipo Doria Pamphilj in 1839 and Lady Gwendoline who in 1835 had married Prince Marc'Antonio Borghese. According to contemporary engravings extant in Rome, both Princesses were much beloved by the Roman populace for their work to relieve poverty. One such depicts Princess Doria ministering to the sick; Princess Borghese's extraordinary devotion to the poor caused her to join a charitable association whereby distinguished ladies divided between them the different quarters of the town; each member had her own district where she went from house to house; also from shop to shop to beg alms. Princess Borghese worked in the parish of St Roch. She changed the bedclothes of sick people, swept their rooms, saw to their dressings and listened to their troubles.[14]

What caused her to be a legend in her time was that she died in 1840 aged 22 after a short illness probably contracted during her ministrations. Memories in Rome attribute her death to plague; certainly her body, very unusually, was burnt and it was her ashes which were taken for burial, but from the evidence scarlet fever would seem to have been more likely. Extraordinary scenes occurred as the carriage passed through Rome to the church of Santa Maria Maggiore where she was interred in the Borghese chapel.[15] Forty young men with top hats and frock coats unhitched the horses and themselves, with long ropes, drew the carriage through the streets. An escort of dragoons headed the column and a great assembly of rich and poor followed. It was said that half Rome was there. From the windows overlooking the route inhabitants threw down the petals of flowers as the cortege went past. Verses were composed in her honour. Within a short time Princess Borghese's three sons Camillus aged three, John-Baptist two and Francis a few months, were dead also, of the same disease; only her daughter Agnese aged four, though she became ill, did not succomb.

It was this same Agnese who laid claims in 1853 on the Estate of Lord Shrewsbury as his grand-daughter and sole descendant of her mother. The proceedings carried over many years during which Agnese married and became the Duchess of Sora. Two separate petitions were lodged; one for payment of amounts outstanding, with interest, on her mother's dowry; only half of the sum prescribed, it was alleged, having been paid. Secondly, for a portion of the dead Earl's Estate, as an heir, under the terms of the same marriage settlement. Princess Doria made similar claims on her own behalf.

The death of the young 17th Earl, Bertram, in August 1856 at the age of 24 and still unmarried, added to an already tortuous situation. He named James Robert Hope Scott[16] and Edward Bellasis as his executors and left all his freehold estates to Lord Edmund Bernard Fitzalan Howard[17], an infant of thirteen months, second son of Henry Granville 14th Duke of Norfolk. Henry John Chetwynd, 3rd Earl and 5th Baron Talbot[18] then claimed the Earldom of Shrewsbury. While protracted legal proceedings were taking place in the Committee for privilege of the House of Lords with a bevy of Counsels, the executors of the 17th Earl's Estate saw fit to hold a large sale at Alton Towers of all the contents. Periodicals of the time devoted space to fulsome descriptions and elaborate drawings of the items.

Mary Alathea, Princess Doria Pamphilj and Agnese, Duchess of Sora then placed their claim to the honour and dignity of Earl of Shrewsbury and opposed the petition of Earl Talbot, and as co-heiresses at law maintained that they were entitled to the entailed estate; the legality of the sale was also challenged. Major Talbot of Castle Talbot, in addition, was an Irish claimant to the Earldom.

Finally, after a very large number of hearings in Committee, the House of Lords on Monday 31 May 1858 delivered judgement in favour of the claim of Earl Talbot to the dormant peerage of Shrewsbury. The title thereby left Catholic hands; the new 18th Earl had strong Anglican connections, and was the descendant of a former Bishop of Salisbury, Oxford and Durham. The recovery of the title did not necessarily involve that of the estates. The second round of the litigation started with an action of ejectment in the Common Pleas for the recovery of Alton Towers, which succeeded. Earl Talbot gained revenues which were then estimated to amount to £47,000 per annum. The trustees of the 17th Earl's will appealed to the Exchequer Chambers on behalf of the infant Lord Edmund, where in February 1860, the matter was again decided against them, although certain issues were left open. Finally in July 1867 judgement was given by the Lord Chancellor, Lord Chelmsford, who sat with two other Lords Justices, in favour of the trustees in the case Howard v Shrewsbury. A considerable portion of the entailed estate was recovered for Lord Edmund as a minor.

In the meantime the Princesses, unsuccessful in their claim in regard to the Estate of Bertram, Lord Shrewsbury, pursued the petitions filed in regard to that of the 16th Earl, in which Ambrose was so much concerned. The matter of the payment of the remainder of the dowry was not in doubt, as was that of the Princesses' entitlement to the unentailed estate. It was not until 13 November 1860 that Vice Chancellor William Wood in the Chancery Court gave a summing up on that issue that lasted $3\frac{1}{2}$ hours. The question he said, turned on the construction of a single clause in a preliminary contract made upon a treaty of marriage. Every word and even the punctuation of that clause had been most minutely discussed, as also matters of foreign law; a mass of evidence, embodied in several folio volumes containing conflicting opinions of the most eminent Roman lawyers had been presented. The plaintiff's claims could not be sustained, he ended, and although the bill was dismissed, the executors of Earl John (the principal defendants) did not receive costs which, with six counsel in attendance, were enormous. The outstanding dowry payments, with interest since the 1830s, were made by Ambrose and Charles Scott-Murray on 7 February 1861. The exact amount which Ambrose himself received of the legacy willed to him is not mentioned at all in any of the papers that remain. A sole reference is in E. S. Purcell's life of Ambrose[19], which has so many inaccuracies that it may not be correct; it puts the sum at £11,000 after more than ten years of litigation. By that time he had come into his own inheritance on the death of his father, and although there were always to be debts, the lean years were over.

In the Autumn of 1852 Ambrose had decided to make a visit to France with Laura. He had several objects in mind. He had translated Montalembert's Letter to Abbé Gaume[20] on his *Ver Rongeur* ['Thorn in the flesh'] for the *Catholic Standard* and appended others from Donoso Cortés[21] and Cardinal Gousset Archbishop of Rheims. His old friend Jean Baptiste Henri Lacordaire, who had in 1840 become a Dominican and thereafter not only a well-known preacher but member of the Constituent Assembly after the revolution of 1848, had been to England and visited the de Lisles at Grace Dieu in the Spring of 1852 with conversation full of interest. Ambrose explained to Montalembert[22]

> I felt very anxious that some of our very *dull and routine* English Catholics, especially of *the Oratorian species*, should see what the Leaders of the Catholic Church on the Continent

think on these matters. I can assure you, my dear Friend, that while the Principles which you and I have all our lives been upholding, are every day triumphing in France, and in England too amongst the Anglicans, amongst our English Catholics they are quite at a discount, I might almost say *in disgrace* . . . most of the English Catholics are very much in the rear of the Great Christian Renaissance of the present day . . .

Ambrose wanted to speak to some of the French writers whose work he admired.

A further reason for the French visit concerned the education of the two eldest children. One of the most serious problems which faced the de Lisles as parents of a large family was to find suitable careers for their sons which fitted their station in life (so great a concern for Victorians), but which required little or no outlay in financial terms. (A similar problem lay a few years ahead in relation to suitable husbands for their daughters). Amo would one day inherit the estate and he could therefore be allowed to continue his country pursuits and learn to be a good landlord; a broad general education was best for him; Everard had shown signs of wanting to be a soldier, but to buy a commission in a good English regiment was out of the question. He would need to join the Indian Army which was possible with small private means. A good school of Oriental languages existed in Paris where he could learn Hindustani.[23]

Mena and Alice accompanied their parents with Amo and Everard, and they set sail from Folkestone on 30 October 1852, Laura and the young people visited churches, galleries and gardens: Notre Dame (recently restored in 1845), the Sainte Chapelle, the Madeleine, the new 'beautiful gothick' church of Ste Clotilde still being built (which Montalembert much disliked), Ste Sulpice, Notre Dame des Victoires, Ste Genevieve, the Pantheon which was shortly to be opened as a church, St Germain l'Auxerois, Chapelle des Martyres, St Vincent de Paul, Notre Dame de Lorette, St Rock, the Cathedral at Amiens, the Louvre, Versailles, the park at St Cloud, the Luxembourg and Tuilerie Gardens and the Opera. Ambrose meanwhile made visits in order to learn more of the state of French religious opinion. He saw much of his old friend Alexis-François Rio, his family and his circle. Montalembert

who, as a frequent correspondent was one of Ambrose's greatest sources of news, was at his country home, but a number of
Liberal Catholics were in the Capital.

The period before the revolution of 1848 in France had been
one of religious revival and religious peace. Montalembert had
made his influence felt in calling on Catholics to claim their
rights in relation to the state, especially in the area of education. Since the revolution had not been hostile to the Church,
it appeared as if the freedom which Catholics wanted would
come; but within a few years the democratic ideas which had
been unleashed frightened many and secured allegiance for the
Second Empire under Louis Napoleon, which offered protection. Ultramontane elements in France led by Louis Veuillot.[24]
more greatly alarmed than the rest, became increasingly extreme, criticized Montalembert, Lacordaire and Bishop Dupanloup of Orleans as lukewarm, not true Catholics, and sought
inspiration increasingly from Rome. Although Ambrose had
ceased to subscribe to *L'Univers* when it had begun to attack
Montalembert (in spite of having been a contributor many
years before), he had two meetings with the Editor in Paris. He
spoke on several occasions to Jules Gondon whose acquaintance reached back to 1840 and who dealt with English matters
on the paper. (*L'Univers* was censured by the French bishops
in 1853; Veuillot appealed to Rome; the Pope replied with his
encyclical *Inter Multiplices* and the bishops were forced to
withdraw; M Gondon left *L'Univers* in 1857. Divisions were
created in the French Church as in England).

Ambrose spent many hours with Louis Félix Danjou,
founder and editor of *Revue de la musique religieuse, populaire
et classique* and with Adolphe Napoleon Didron[25] an archeolo-
gist and writer on Christian iconography; his atelier received a
visit; with Donoso Cortez whose writings he had wished to see
noticed in England, and Père Xavier de Ravignan, S.J. .[26] Some
members of the diplomatic circle were included in the round of
calls; the former Piedmontese Ambassador, and Augustus
Craven of the British Embassy whose French wife, Pauline de
Ferronays a writer, was a close friend of the Rio family, and
known to the de Lisles also.

The interest which Ambrose continued to maintain in Continental writing on subjects close to his heart was shown in his

desire to meet and speak with Abbé Jean-Joseph Gaume. A prolific writer, his work under the title *Ver Rongeur des Societes modernes ou le Paganisme dans l'Education* found in Ambrose a sympathetic reader, The Abbé's view that pagan classics tended to dominate over those by Christian authors in the teaching of the young, with detrimental results, was exactly what Ambrose wanted to hear with his own strong views on pagan art. He had written[27] to Lord Clifford in 1851

> I rejoice at the Holy Father's reform of the grossly improper statues and pictures of Rome . . . would to Heaven I could live to see the Sixtine Chapel cleansed of its semi-pagan frescoes, and that same type of Xtian purity and sanctity beaming within the Chapel of St Peter's successor that adorned it before the unchaste hand of Michael Angelo obliterated the heavenly art of the Blessed Angelico de Fiesoli.

The meeting between Ambrose and Abbé Gaume led to a ten-day visit to Grace Dieu during the following year.

An arrangement was made through a recommendation from the Jesuits, for Amo and Everard to live at the Institut de l'Assomption in the rue Faubourg St Honoré. Everard was placed at the School of Oriental Languages in part of the former Palace of Cardinal Mazarin, under the supervision of M Garcin de Tassy, for 22 years Professor of Hindustani. The rest of the family left Paris for their return to Leicestershire. But the results of the tour, intensive as usual, were not forgotten: some of the ideas he had conceived as a result of his conversations, Ambrose brought to bear on his next published work on prophecy.

It would be a mistake to regard the mere fact that Ambrose had an interest in this subject as in any way strange in the mid 19th century. Preoccupation in the language and interpretation of prophecy, perhaps abnormal to late twentieth century secularized society, was familiar, common-place and orthodox, one hundred and fifty years ago. Where he differed from the rest of scholars and private persons who tried to unravel prophetic writings and sayings, lay in the rather general application he gave to these terms. Any unusual happening he would regard as a sign or prediction; to the words of a particularly holy or gifted man or woman he would attribute a special significance as to the future. As discussed earlier, he was particularly sensitive to alleged evidence of the supernatural breaking into the realm of the natural. In his attempts to interpret the prophecies contained in the sacred scriptures, a more widespread serious study, he was not alone in taking a historical view: but he approached apocalyptic writings (so-called as giving knowledge of divine mysteries through revelation) with not merely the hope, but the certainty that he would find in them references to events of his own day which would disclose what was to come.

This measure of certainty was characteristic of all that Ambrose said and did. *Mahometanism in its Relation to Prophecy* with the subtitle An Inquiry into the Prophecies concerning Antichrist with some Reference to their Bearing on the Events of the Present Day, was no exception. It was published in 1855, though much of it had been written twenty years earlier; the subject had been of continuous interest, and much discussed with a wide circle of friends. There was an element of fervour in the work because Ambrose was putting a case: first the ultimate triumph of the Roman Catholic Church and, secondly, in refutation of the extreme Protestant view that Antichrist was the Pope. He proceeded from the two fixed points: one, that at the end, in the fulness of time, in the glorious period of the Church's reign according to the principles of St Augustine's *City of God*, 'all kings and nations will then do homage to the Apostolic See, and the Pope father of the Gentile nations as well as of the converted Jews, will rule over the earth, and gather the peoples into one happy sheep-fold';[28] second, that Antichrist was Mahomet.

Ambrose's reasoning was not deductive, but argued from a conclusion towards its proof by appeal both to passages in scripture and events in history. He saw in the contemporary scenes of revolution and unrest and acceptance of the Turkish empire, signs of imminent predicted catastrophe. The destruction of Antichrist, as personified by the forces of Islam, he thought to be at hand, probably as a result of a struggle with 'that great northern potentate, the Russian emperor'. But first there would take place the restoration of the Jews to Palestine and their conversion; then 'the glorious period of the Church during which St John tells us that Satan will be bound in chains, is to last for the space of a thousand years'.[29] Upon the much debated question whether the second coming of Christ would precede this binding of Satan (usually referred to as the millenium) and the period of the Church's earthly triumph, he did not voice an opinion. He did not need to do so; he had done what he had set out to do: to provide 'a fitting compensation to the Catholic Church, even here on earth for all her previous trials, sorrows and persecutions;' and as for his identification of Antichrist with Mahomet, 'that is all I want, to overthrow the Protestant misinterpretations of the prophecies relating to Antichrist and to establish a solid Catholic theory in its place', he wrote to Dr Pagani[30].

In the issue of June 1855, the *Dublin Review* had an introduction to the effect that

> these wonderful events have been wrapped up in language so obscure and imagery so enigmatical, that a serious attempt to penetrate their meaning would seem the most hopeless enterprise in the world.

Five books were examined on 'the Turks in relation to prophecy'. That of Ambrose was one; J. H. Newman's *Lectures on the History of the Turks* was another. Ambrose's work was not enthusiastically received.

> We must not conceal that there is part of his theory which we think untenable on principles of merely human criticism.

There were several features that incurred censure which, it was inferred, were present in the book: 'the system of private interpretation of the Scriptures' and 'the pre-existence in the commentator's mind of the theory to which it is sought to fit the text'. The review continued

> We cannot help observing that in the strength of his own profound convictions, he has too often proceeded upon arbitrary constructions and unsupported assumptions; and that he frequently accepts as undoubted proofs what we are sure he never would have allowed to an adversary, or never would himself have admitted, had he for a moment placed himself in the position of an adversary.

There is a hint that more of Ambrose was being criticized than his book on prophecy.

He sent a copy of the work to Newman who replied[31] that
he had read it 'with great interest': he seemed to disagree with
the *Dublin Review* that the subject should be left alone,
particularly by laymen:

> It is important, over and above the sound views you put forth,
> that Catholics should handle the Apocalypse ... My only
> difficulty in following you absolutely and altogether is, that
> Catholic tradition seems to teach that Antichrist will come
> shortly or immediately before the coming of Christ. That
> Mahomet is our most special type of him, I do not at all doubt.

W. E. Gladstone could be calculated to be more interested in
Ambrose's treatise since he read it in 1876 at a time of crisis,
and wrote[32] of having been 'exceedingly struck with the force
of your interpretation in that part of it which refers to the
Mahometan powers'; he added

> I rejoice to be in sympathy with you on this subject. In some
> other parts of your work you would hardly expect me to
> follow you. I have a lurking doubt indeed whether if you now
> had pen in hand you would rewrite the whole of them, after
> the recent events in your Church.

The two were by this time closely associated in the campaign
to rally public opinion against Turkish atrocities in Bulgaria
and elsewhere. Although a life-long Conservative, Ambrose
reacted violently against the pro-Turk foreign policy of Disraeli
in the 1870s. He not only gave Gladstone considerable support
and tried to lobby Roman Catholic opinion in this cause, but
he engaged in a spirited correspondence with the Cardinal
Archbishop of Westminster[33] on the alleged pro-Turkish sympathies of Pope Pius IX.

Thus, Ambrose's convictions on this issue did not change
and although he did not publish again about prophecy and
millenarianism, the subject comes up a good deal in his correspondence. It was, after all, as already mentioned, of considerable contemporary interest. In England a good deal of it was
confined to Anglicans, although it must be said that the
Rosminian Pagani at Loughborough wrote a book[34] published
also in 1855, on the Second Coming, to Ambrose's great
delight. On the continent, Catholics were concerned in

scholarly activity to a greater extent; Döllinger, for example, loaned Ambrose books from the royal library at Munich. Sources of earlier date, some of them quoted by Ambrose, were receiving renewed notice: Joachim of Fiore[35], a mediaeval millenarian of great influence, Bartholomew Holzhauser of Bingen[36] whose apocalyptic writings Ambrose found particularly compelling, and Manuel de Lacunza y Diaz[37] a Chilean Jesuit living in Italy. His *La Venida del Mesias en gloria y majestad* of 1790, Ambrose discussed with Henry Erskine, Dean of Ripon, although it had been banned in Rome for its 'moderate millenarianism'. 'A wonderful and sublime book' wrote[38] Ambrose to Pagani

> ... it seems to me to afford a clue towards solving the mysteries of God's present dealings with unhappy Christendom more than any other book I ever read.

The de Lisle family found no dichotomy between theological matters of eternal significance relating to a world beyond this one and happenings in this world for which there seemed no rational explanation. Keen attention continued to be paid to signs[39] and wonders and was devoted also to the practice of table-turning, in order to attempt to receive messages purporting to come from beyond the grave, which became of general interest in the 1850s. Alongside advertisements in the *Guardian* (a Church orientated newspaper) for lectures on the Apocalypse by well-known theologians, were descriptions of table-turning sessions, particularly popular in Germany. Lord Dunraven, a convert friend of the de Lisles, investigated[40] the phenomena of spiritualism and declared it genuine. He took a simultaneous interest in the works of Lacunza, probably at the instigation of Ambrose.

On 31 July 1853 Laura's diary showed that with a group of friends 'We had table-turning a spirit answering, Joseph a Buddist'; among other occasions, on 15 November after dinner 'there was table and spirit raising by Mr Wyse' (a secular priest, temporarily at Shepshed). In 1855 further attempts with the help of some of the servants as likely intermediaries, are recorded. On 21 July 1858 at the Warren, Lawson, one of the grooms, was put into 'a mismeric state by 60 passes. Lawson remained in this state 3 hours and during it performed all sorts of strange things'.

As the 1850s passed it was becoming increasingly difficult to maintain a lay role according to an older pattern. There had been warnings that this would be so. Bishop Hogarth[41] of the Northern District wrote to Wiseman in London

> There never was a time when it was more necessary to admonish the laity to keep within their own sphere of action. The ardent zeal of converts and the want of prudence in many, often induces then, with perhaps the very best intentions, to meddle with matters purely ecclesiastical and produces the worst consequences ... I am glad your Lordship had administered to all such a solemn warning which they can neither mistake nor forget.

In his own domain Ambrose had problems as a layman. He spent many hours in the chapel at Grace Dieu which he had done so much to provide and beautify; he wrote[42] to F. G. Lee[43], explaining what took place at Christmas.

> Our services at Grace Dieu commence at about 9pm when we sing the Matins of the Nativity. They finish at Midnight when the High Mass commences which is followed by Lauds – which is over by about 3am – when we retire to rest. The second High Mass is at 8am and the third at 11am. Vespers at 4pm after which I generally feel pretty well done up – as you may imagine.

Easter was the same; Ambrose told[44] the same correspondent

> Next week we are greatly occupied with the lengthened services of our Church and every day of it I myself have to sing no fewer than *6 entire Hours* at the Lectern, so that you may imagine one has not much time for other things, but what a sublime occupation is that, and when once a man has learnt to relish the interior sweetness of the Gregorian song allied as it is with the inspired words of Holy Scripture one never tires, and one has some faint notion of the chief occupation of the Triumphant Saints in that Heavenly Jerusalem, which is above, and to which as S Augustine says the steps of our Pilgrimage are bending.

But his sphere was circumscribed. Two incidents reveal some of the difficulties.

The first concerned a Corpus Christi procession at Grace Dieu, which had become an honoured custom of eighteen

years' standing. The Bishop of Nottingham had given permis-
sion for the occasion to be delayed for a few days on account
of the weather. On Sunday 24 June 1855, a number of guests
had joined the de Lisle family, who included M. Abbadie, an
Oriental traveller, Charles Montalembert, Lord and Lady
Campden, Lord Dunraven; George Ryder came from the
Warren. Three Rosminian priests took part: Fr Pagani, Fr
Mitchell, Fr Nicholas Lorrain, a Frenchman, chaplain at Grace
Dieu; Fr Ignatius Sisk[45] and some of the monks attended from
the Monastery. Fr Lorrain had issued 400 tickets, mainly to
Catholics, for entry into the chapel itself. Vespers over, a
procession with choir, candle bearers, schoolchildren and congregation, emerged from the church with Fr Pagani bearing the
Blessed Sacrament; Montalembert, Lord Dunraven, Lord Campden and George Ryder carried the canopy over it. As the
peregrination through the grounds began along the 'rhododen-
dron *allées*, charming green swards and rocky woods'[46], the
route was lined by hundreds of local people.

Fr Mitchell, put out that few knelt or removed their hats,
made what Ambrose called 'a stupid attack' on their lack of
respect. At this point it would appear that Fr Pagani expressed
his opinion that Ambrose was at fault for not restricting
admission to the grounds, to witness the procession, to Roman
Catholics. Ambrose lost his temper at this criticism of a
ceremony initiated in the locality by him and much treasured,
designed as a means of encouraging Catholic devotions. He
remonstrated publicly with Fr Pagani, which was ill-received.
The incident blew over and the protagonists later expressed
their respect for each other, but it was not forgotten by the
clergy. Ambrose's anger was, as usual, short lived. Fr Lorrain
wrote[47] to Fr Pagani three days later that he had seen Ambrose
that morning: 'He was in good spirits . . . I believe he has by
this time entirely forgotten the past, and that he does not keep
in his mind any feeling of rancour'. Fr Lorrain went on to
explain 'how painful the situation of a priest must be here'. He
found Ambrose 'excitable and wanting in judgement'; by this
he probably meant independent.

A letter Ambrose sent[48] to Fr Pagani gives an explicit summary of his views on the attitude he felt should be adopted
in relationships with non-Catholics, and is therefore worth

quoting. He was convinced that processions in general did exceeding good in England

> 'but they do good in proportion as we leave Protestants to themselves, without constraining them to make outward acts of reverence, which would not agree with their prejudices – as their standing and wearing their hats *out of doors* was not meant for *irreverence for Christ*, I do not think that Our Lord would be offended with it.

He went on to maintain that when Jesus was on earth proclaiming His messiahship

> 'we do not read that even His apostles knelt or bowed down to him on all occasions . . . But here not only His Divinity, but His Humanity is hidden . . . nothing is seen but a morsel of Bread. This outward form the Protestants regard as *a mere figure of Christ*, and so we can hardly expect them to fall down and adore . . .'

He went on to explain that it had been found over the years that those who were permitted to witness 'our glorious processions' were affected by them. He cited times in the past when Bishops had taken part and had made no comments such as had flawed this occasion.

A second episode concerned Fr Lorrain personally. He recounted[49] the event to his new Provincial, (Fr Angelo Rinolfi; Rosmini had died and been succeeded as Superior-General by Pagani who left for Italy). Due to the departure of the organist Prinns, Mena played for chapel services. At Vespers in December 1856, Ambrose did not sing the Antiphon after the Magnificat as usual because he did not think Mena would be able to manage her part. So there was a silence

> 'So, at last the good Mr Ambrose, whether through holy zeal, passion or silliness, or perhaps all three together, shouted *Dominus Exaudi . . . Dominus Vobiscum Oremus*. Then naturally I felt indignant and ready to undress myself at the Credenza and to withdraw instantly both from the Chapel and from the house altogether.'

Later he had spoken to Ambrose in French.[50]

> I hope and trust you will never more do what you have done today in the Church. Remember that no one is allowed in the

house of God not even the Kings of the earth, to sing *Dominus Vobiscum*, but the officiating priest, or deacon. By doing so wether [sic] through zeal, ignorance, passion or presumption, you have painfully violated the most strict rules or Rubrics of the Church, insulted your officiating minister in the performance of his sacred duties and thereby you have given a great scandal to those present.

Few indeed, he felt, after this would want to stay as chaplain, and he would not wish to continue to sleep at Grace Dieu moreover, if he did not love and respect Ambrose more than he did himself that evening. A few days later Lorrain completed his letter: Fr Pagani had been aware of the difficulties he faced; but had said 'it is well for the Institute to be on good terms with Ambrose Phillipps ... He may do us some good by and by; for I quite expect he will help us in building a church in Loughborough, when in better circumstances'.

Aware of his lack of support from the clergy, Ambrose expressed his sense of isolation to John Hardman when he wrote[51] of 'our one only remaining friend in the Hierarchy, our learned and truly illustrious Bishop Ullathorne' with whom they

> should stand firmly together and work on all the more vigorously in proportion to the discouragement we meet with on all sides, looking forwards to a great day of triumph, which is to come, but the advent of which depends in great measure on the zeal with which it is laboured for, or laboured against.

His expectations of the Bishop were somewhat misplaced, for Ullathorne was to write to Rome expressing his opposition to de Lisle's ecumenical activities a few years' later. Neither would Ambrose's stand in the matter of the Shrewsbury legacy have done anything to soften the Bishop's attitude. It would be a reaction beyond the comprehension of Ambrose; he was hot tempered, but the storms were soon over.

Nor was Laura exempt from censure. In the 1860s, Henry Collins[52] then a monk at Mount St Bernard and her spiritual director, upbraided her for her lack of respect for the chaplains who had served the Grace Dieu chapel; more reverential treatment was required, and a more correct mode of address than that of 'Mr'. Accommodation too, had not been adequate.

The de Lisle family increased twice more in the mid 1850s. Rodolph,[53] so named after Lord Feilding, his sponsor, was born in November 1853. Laura cannot have failed to know that Theresa Eliza Vaughan mother of the future Cardinal,[54] a connection by marriage, had died giving birth to her 14th child four months before. Perhaps that was why the doctor and midwife were called early and he remained all night but was in fact absent when the birth took place. In 1855 Laura's 15th child, a daughter whom they called Margaret Mary, was born on 31 May, ten days after the arrival of the midwife. She was baptised next day; Lord Dunraven and Mrs Constable Maxwell were her sponsors. In the following December, Bernard aged nine years who had been born in Boulogne, slipped as he was sliding on some ice in a rut in the ground; most of the winters of the 1850s were very severe. Ambrose wrote to a correspondent at the end of the year that he feared that the child had injured his spine 'and we greatly fear he will die. Our grief is intense . . . He was such a fine clever little boy'. Bernard died on 11 January 1856; he had shown signs of recovery on the 2nd, but relapsed on the 7th; he was buried in the crypt under Grace Dieu Chapel.

There were departures from home by other children: Everard, back from Paris, sat an examination in Hindustani at Addiscombe near Croydon early in 1854; Lord Edward Howard had used his influence to secure the offer of an Infantry Cadetship for him. Everard left for India on 17 October. It was a painful parting; Laura took him up to the Chapel of Dolours in the rocks above Grace Dieu early in the day where they said the prayers for the indulgences which the new Abbott had recently brought from Rome. Ambrose and Laura went with him and Amo to Loughborough where the boys boarded the train for London. 'Dear Everard bore the parting from us with great courage', Laura wrote, 'tho' he seemed a good deal affected'. He was only nineteen years old and the family did not see him again for he was killed in the seige of Delhi three years later.

Mena and her governess Mme Brabender spent some months in France in order to attend lectures at the University in Paris prior to her 'coming-out'. Fr Lorrain informed his Provincial that Ambrose and Laura had not accompanied her; *non ce danaro.*[55] It was arranged that Alice, Winifreda and Mary should go to the Loughborough Convent as boarders, as their governess wished to retire; another governess, Mlle Olive, taught the younger children.

Laura agreed in 1852 to become the first secretary-general for England of the Association of Holy Childhood, founded by Bishop Forbin-Janson of Nancy; she continued with this work 'for the redemption of pagan children in China and India. It is one which every year saves thousands of poor babies from an eternal as well as (with some) temporal death'. Despite her own continued childbearing, she persisted with her sick visiting in the nearby villages, and teaching in the schools (now 93 girls and 110 boys at the Grace Dieu school). In the Autumn of 1858 at the suggestion of Fr Ignatius Sisk who was acting as parish priest at Whitwick, she helped to found a Society for Young Women in the village and attended their meetings month by month, often on foot and in bad weather, for many years. The signature at the bottom of business letters was increasingly hers. When she attended a Retreat at the Loughborough Convent in 1854, she wrote to Fr Pagani of her husband, 'It was very good of him to let me come here'. She recognised his dependence upon her, as that of her family, though seemed to accept it.

At Christmas 1856 Laura scalded her left foot with some boiling water, having upset a kettle at Shepshed where school-children 'were reciting their pieces'. Next day a doctor came to cut the blister, 'three inches long and three wide', but it did not prevent her travelling immediately by pony carriage to Husbands Bosworth from where, the day following, she and Mena went with post horses to Market Harborough for Mena's first ball; 'she danced every dance except walzes'. Back at home, Laura's foot was so injured[56] that she did not leave her bedroom until 14 February when the doctor allowed her to walk to her boudoir, except to hobble down to the drawing room on one occasion to receive Cardinal Wiseman who was on a visit to the Monastery. He was to have stayed, but was fortunately prevented by the weather and shortage of time.

Amo's majority on 10 May 1855 was marked merely by the fact that the younger children stayed down for dinner and went to Benediction. Finances did not allow for any more

ambitious celebrations. The shortage of funds was more acute
than ever; no money had come from the Shrewsbury bequest.
Ambrose was bound to appeal to his father and lay his cards
on the table. Some re-settlement of the estate was able to be
made on account of Amo's coming-of-age and two substantial
loans, one of £5,311 to Bishop Ullathorne and another of
£2,000 to the Rosminians, were paid off. There were others
that remained; the experience had been humiliating and Ambrose had not told his father the whole story. He wrote[57] to
the Bishop and asked him

> when my father's sollicitor [sic] Mr Davidson, pays you the
> money, not to give him any idea whatever that there is anything
> due beyond that sum, or anything contingently due on my
> succession ... My arrangements with my Father, ... from the
> large amount of them, have been a very heavy affair. P.S. Mr
> Davidson must not on any account see the Deed I signed at
> Princethorpe.

To Pagani Ambrose wrote[58]

> I have scarcely enough to pay the necessary weekly bills ... To
> which must be added that my Father has been unecessarily
> *fussy* and fidgetty in looking into every item, not to say very
> cross at my having incurred such heavy responsibilities for
> Religious objects foreign to his own Religious views.

Charles March Phillipps had given substantial amounts of
pocket money to his grandchildren on many occasions: to
Amo and Everard in Paris, to Mena and Alice (and ball
dresses); also to the younger ones. He paid school bills at
Oscott; for a holiday in Wales for the entire family; but it is
clear that he intended to keep the disposal of his money
strictly in his own hands and not to be coerced, nor pay for
anything of which he did not approve. Ambrose felt keenly, so
he expressed to Bishop Ullathorne in an attempt to gain
sympathy when his payments were overdue, that his work for
the Church had not only greatly impoverished him, but had
'drawn upon me much ill will from my Father and consequent
witholding of much that he would otherwise have done for
me'. It was more likely that his father deplored his irresponsible
handling of money.

1856 was a sad year: the death of Bernard; Ambrose was ill

shortly after; bad news from India which caused the family to worry over Everard; lack of funds and stalemate over the Shrewsbury legacy; unfulfilled lay aspirations; Laura's incapacitating injury. So it was with especial enjoyment and interest that Ambrose regarded the unexpected arrival in his post on 11 February 1857 of a periodical named the *Union Newspaper*. It set off a chain of events that were balm to his mood of frustration; that were to absorb him for many years to come and with which his name is particularly associated.

Ambrose at once wrote[59] to the Editor, expressed sympathy with his political and religious views, asked to become a subscriber and to receive back numbers. He then immediately launched into a rendering on unity which put his own outlook and hopes, if not in a nutshell (never a possibility), at least within a reasonable compass. Though 'a member of the English branch of the Roman Catholic Church', he had never sympathised with the feelings or policy of those who desired the destruction of the national Church of England and who

'in their just and holy abhorrence of Ultra Protestantism draw no distinction between that Church as the original Ecclesiastical organisation of this country, and the Ultra Protestant Principles forced upon her in an evil hour by a corrupt court and by time serving Erastian statesmen'.

He looked forward, he continued, to the ultimate re-establishment of Religious Unity, not only in England, but throughout Christendom, and hailed with intense interest and 'the most affectionate cordiality every attempt to restore Catholic Principles in the national Church'. When a majority of intelligent members would have learnt their value and their truth, the day would not be far off 'when the divine Truth of God shall triumph in this great country'.

The correspondence soon developed on a frequent basis. The Editor revealed himself as Frederick George Lee, curate of the Berkeley Chapel in London whose inheritance of Nonjuring descent[60] and interest in books of Roman Catholic theology and devotion, had given him a desire to see different Christian Communions draw more closely together. Hence his establishment of the *Union Newspaper*. Lee's earlier letters have not survived, and it is only through those of Ambrose

that the process of the development of their combined ideas
can be discerned. But they are sufficient to provide a fair
background to the formation by the two friends (for so they
soon became) of the Association for the Promotion of the
Unity of Christendom. The creation of the movement has been
described elsewhere[61] in a general way, but with few glosses.
The first and most important comment that needs to be made
concerns Lee's extreme youth. He was born in 1832. Therefore
unless his birthday fell in January, was only twenty four years
old and within little more than a year of his ordination,
following theological training at the new Cuddesdon College
near Oxford, when he and Ambrose began their plans. He had
limited experience in his own Church and his knowledge of
Roman Catholicism was restricted to books. Neither did his
views, nor those of Ambrose, reflect main stream opinion in
either of their Communions; their opinions carried no weight,
in fact were ridiculed. The whole enterprise was designed by
two idiosyncratic devotees for reunion whose enthusiasm exceeded their grasp on reality. But it must also be said that they
were alone in the field because few others had the courage to
discuss, let alone to embark upon, such a remote possibility as
the reuniting of the Churches. Their ideals were noble and
moreover prophetic; a little more than a hundred years hence
and most of the leaders of Christendom would be engaged on
a similar pursuit, carrying many of their members with them.

An understanding of Ambrose's outlook on the question of
reunion can come only by way of comprehending his view of
prophecy. In the preface to his book on this subject he had
referred[62] to God having revealed to men the secrets of the
future:

> 'Sometimes these revelations . . . have come direct from God,
> sometimes through the instrumentality of inspired men, that is
> of men speaking as the mouthpieces of God'.

Thus it was that Ambrose was apt to place more weight on the
words of Holzhauser, who had in the 17th century predicted
the coming conversion of England to Roman Catholicism, and
those of Mario Carricchia in Rome in 1831, than upon the
opinions of men current in the mid 1850s. But it was this
visionary element in his make-up that was also the undoing of

Ambrose; Cardinal Wiseman commented unsympathetically upon it when he wrote on the subject of the APUC to Propaganda Fide at the end of 1857.

It was not long before Ambrose presented Lee with his views on prophecy: there had been 'some remarkable Catholic predictions about what would be done in your Church in the way of restoration about this time'. He claimed to have had conversations with eminent Prelates and Cardinals on the continent on this subject 'in which they fully concurred in the abstract possibility of such a thing and even promised their concurrence and aid, should events even so far ripen as to lead to a negociation between the Church of England the Holy See'[63]. It transpired[64] that he referred partly to a conversation of fifteen years earlier with the Papal Nuncio in Munich, Monsignor Viale da Preta, now Cardinal Archbishop of Bologna.

The importance of reunion being corporate was another issue Ambrose raised early; it was a cornerstone of his thinking. Before the time of the Council of Florence, he maintained, the Popes did not call upon the members of the Oriental Church to join that of the West individually, but in 1539 did so corporately. Moreover, Bossuet (whom he quoted a great deal) 'was prepared to deal corporately even with the Hugenots, who had no pretensions whatever to Apostolicity of descent'. Ambrose's outlook was essentially eirenic. He had no doubt that 'God would have us Catholics aid . . . whatever tendencies they witness amongst their separated Brethern towards orthodoxy and unity'. He deeply disapproved 'of the sneering way in which such tendencies are met with amongst us'. He singled out 'the more recent converts' as particularly culpable and had no doubt that 'in so doing they deeply grieve the Holy Spirit of God'.

Encouraged by Lee, Ambrose was soon committing his ideas to paper in the *Union* and equally quickly reactions began to appear; and from the expected source, the recent converts. Edward Healy Thompson[65], wrote at length in protest to the editor of the *Weekly Register*[66] (Henry Wilberforce) 'We do not take the same view as Mr Phillipps of the character and prospects of the National Church'. Healy Thompson apprised Newman who was a friend, of what he had written. Newman replied[67] with the comment that he considered Ambrose's action, as a Catholic, 'a great impropriety'.

Ambrose retaliated by explaining to Lee that he had for some six weeks subscribed to the *Weekly Register* after the present editor had taken over, but gave it up as soon as he perceived the line he took in regard to movements in the English Church and 'the great Question of Reunion . . . I shall never retract either the expression of the one, or the hope of the other'. Capes of the *Rambler* was also contemptuous of the prospects of Reunion, Ambrose explained to Lee and talked of persons like himself as little better than maniacs for ever considering such a possibility. On 12 March 1857 Ambrose intimated that he had written[68] to Cardinal Wiseman, believing 'that he will go along with us'. In this he was much mistaken.

By the end of March further decisions had been made: Ambrose announced that it was his intention to write a pamphlet[69] on Reunion (which he had completed by the beginning of May). Lee came to stay at Grace Dieu and introduced some fresh initiatives; he brought to the notice of his host the name of Bishop Forbes[70] of the Scottish Episcopal Church who was likely to be sympathetic to their cause; also another Scottish Episcopalian George Boyle,[71] later Earl of Glasgow. Most important of all, it was resolved that Ambrose should write to Rome; it would seem abundantly clear that the drafting of the letter owed nothing to any pen other than his own. Addressed to the Cardinal Prefect of Propaganda, Alessandro Barnabo, in Latin, on thick vellum headed by the family coat of arms painted in colour, it was Ambrose at his most expansive.[72]

> There is at this moment a large party in the Established Church of this Realm (called the Anglican Church) which have conceived the idea of reuniting their national Church with the holy Mother Catholic . . .

With breath-taking wishful thinking and lack of realism, he estimated the party concerned to number two thousand priests and ten bishops. It was as yet, he wrote, a minority in the National Anglican Church, but 'I am of the opinion that we can, not without reason, hope for a happy issue . . .' Some encouraging word uttered by the holy Apostolical See would assist the work already done. Ambrose was repeating the mistake he made in the case of his involvement with the Tractarians: that to teach (what he considered) Catholic doctrine automatically led to a desire to seek the jurisdiction of the Bishop of Rome.

Cardinal Barnabo replied[73] with 'thanks over and over again and I shall pray for all things to turn out favourably according to our wishes'. He indicated that he would send Ambrose's letter to the Pope, as soon as he returned to Rome. Ambrose, greatly elated, chose to see this response as 'his heartiest approval to the project, as explained most distinctly and faithfully by me, for the Reunion of the National Church of England'.[74] 'You and your friends may now know' he continued 'that they have the approval and authority of the Highest Representatives of the Visible Church of God on Earth for boldly continuing the work which we have mutually undertaken . . .'

But far from having secured 'the approval of the See of Peter', Ambrose's letter had so alarmed Cardinal Barnabo that he wrote[75] to England to Thomas Grant, Bishop of Southwark, to ask for confirmation of the facts which had been presented. If his biographer[76] is to be trusted, Grant's was a somewhat wounded character, tortured by scruples, (he made his confession daily) and the suffering of those in purgatory; he found it difficult to look his contemporaries in the face. But during his tenure of office as Rector of the English College in Rome he had won the approval of the Cardinal for his straightforward opinions. In reports of great length in formal Italian in the third person (which has been described as 'elegantissimo') despatched to Rome, he commented upon Ambrose as one full of zeal and charity, but did not hesitate to criticise him also.

In the first seven-page report,[77] Bishop Grant sought to give the Cardinal an account of *il partito dei Puseyisti* and of the *Union* newspaper. He had obviously consulted other English Roman Catholic bishops, as a result of which one of the faults levelled at Ambrose was that of acting independently of his own bishop who had, it was said, not been apprised of Ambrose's activities until 20 June. This was unfair, since he had told Lee on that date that he had received cordial letters from the Bishops of Nottingham, Beverley and Salford in response to his sending his Unity pamphlet.

Bishop Grant then turned to Ambrose's pamphlet; he considered it would discourage individual conversions and greeted with disapproval his suggestion for calling a General Council of the Church in order to heal the divisions of Christendom. He sent two further long reports[78] before the end of July. In the first, he relayed some comments of Faber of a kind which would have caused Ambrose to exclaim yet once more 'was there ever such a troublesome set, as our recent converts'[79]; in the second, he quoted Wiseman as being of the opinion that Ambrose's pamphlet should be put on the Index. Immediately Cardinal Barnabo called for a copy of the pamphlet and asked Fr Smith, an English Benedictine, and one of the *Consultori* at Propaganda Fide, to translate it and make comments. Bishop Grant sought to establish corroboration of his statements to Rome by writing to Ambrose; a somewhat evasive answer was the result[80]

> I believe there are solid grounds for hoping that something will be done . . . towards bringing about reconciliation . . .

His letter to the Cardinal had faithfully communicated *the Facts*, which 'I was entrusted to lay before the Holy See what those facts are, I am not at liberty to mention'.

A feature of difficulty in tracing the history of the APUC lies in the disparate, even conflicting evidence presented by the personalities concerned. Ambrose and Lee were so overwhelmed by the significance and excitement of the enterprise that they took a view of prevailing circumstances which was not so much unduly favourable as based upon fantasy. A considerable measure of exaggeration was attached in particular to reports of the opinions of those in authority. Ambrose's description of the response of the Bishop of Nottingham[81] to his visit[82] hardly tallied with the Bishop's reactions to Bishop Grant. Ambrose and Lee by the beginning of July 1857 were completing their plans to launch their association of prayer for the unity of Christendom and debated on the choice of petition. Ambrose told Lee[83] he could rest assured

> There will be no difficulty I am sure in getting the approbation of the Bishop of Nottingham for that beautiful prayer which you suggest for our association and if you would prefer it I think I could get an imprimatur for it from the Cardinal of Westminster.

Wiseman's replies to Ambrose's letters at this period have not survived, but it would seem that they were low-key rather than condemnatory; his wish was they should remain 'strictly confidential'.

On 3 July Ambrose and Laura went to London. Amidst a number of other engagements, Ambrose had a series of meetings with Lee. On the 4th he saw the Cardinal by appointment at 11, Lee again at 2 and at 8pm Ambrose met 'a large body of Anglo Catholics in Lee's chambers. Wiseman's account of his interview given six months later,[84] was that he spoke critically to Ambrose about his pamphlet and 'made him see the indecency and the scandal of a prayer approved both by a Catholic bishop and a Protestant one'. Wiseman was to insinuate that he had not given his approval to the proposed association. Yet he permitted Roman Catholics to become members for the next seven years and made no public statement against it. It may well be that some English Roman Catholic bishops, unaware as yet of what would be the reactions of Propaganda Fide towards these initiatives, did not initially display quite the firm attitudes which they later claimed (in order to show their loyalty to the Holy See) had been theirs since the beginning.

Ambrose went on to his evening gathering where to his great delight, he met for the first of many meetings, A. P. Forbes, Bishop of Brechin; it was the start of a considerable friendship. The formation of the APUC was put in train and a suggestion of Ambrose was adopted: that a chalice and paten of Australian gold studded with jewels be presented to the Cardinal Prefect 'as a token of our grateful regard towards His Eminence for the kind way in which he has taken up the work and as a harbinger of the future renewal of Communion'. Bishop Forbes and George Boyle put forward some suggestions as to a paper on Anglican Orders, which it was proposed be circulated with a view to their acceptance by Roman Catholic authorities.

Another great Latin letter to the Cardinal Prefect from Ambrose followed on 3 August[85] setting out the resolutions passed at the meeting a month earlier: first the desire to present the gifts as a sign of esteem and gratitude, secondly the determination to bring about the declared reunion; to be achieved 'after a few years'; fourthly a history of the question of the validity of Anglican Orders would be sent to Rome by the leaders of the party; fifthly a select body of preachers would be organised to announce 'a holy reunion with our Holy Mother, the Catholic Church; and lastly it was the intention of the perpetrators to form a society for the promotion of these ends, 'having the sole religious obligation of reciting, every day in private, a prayer from the Roman Missal'. He concluded with a description of 'solid progress amongst Anglicans of Catholic principles': communities of nuns and churches with 'a wholly Catholic appearance'; the wearing of chasubles and dalmatics which had formerly fallen into disuse and so on. Ambrose enclosed a copy of his pamphlet *On the Future Unity of Christendom* 'privately examined and approved by some Catholic theologians', now submitted 'to the judgement of the Holy See'.

By the time Cardinal Barnabo received this document he had read all Bishop Grant's three reports, but not, it would seem, Fr Smith's translation[86] of the pamphlet on Unity, nor his observations[87]; for Barnabo indicated that the copy being translated was that which Ambrose had sent. He listed, however, various accusations against it. Apart from the reports mentioned and the later one of Archbishop Cullen, no documents containing comments on the pamphlet can currently be found on the files of Propaganda Fide or the English College in Rome, although it must be added that the correspondence between Manning and George Talbot, formerly in the archives of the latter until the second world war, no longer seems to be there. In his biography of Ambrose of 1900, E. S. Purcell made it clear that he considered both Manning and William Ward responsible for influencing the opinion of Propaganda Fide in 1857[88]. Manning, whose years in Rome in the early 1850s brought him close to Pius IX (whom he saw nearly once a month) and Talbot, became Provost of Westminster Cathedral in April 1857, at their personal instigation. He was therefore an interested party in relation to religious associations formed in his area. Moreover, the last of the accusations against Ambrose was that of gallican sympathies, a term much used by Manning and not contained in the reports of Bishop Grant. But evidence of such complicity in that year does not exist in the documents that have so far come to light.

Ambrose was angry that his work should have been attacked on account of hearsay.

> I had heard again from the Cardinal Prefect[89] and ... our enemies had not been idle, but had lodged various complaints against my Pamphlet ... I hope therefore that when he gets my answer and compares it with the Pamphlet itself, he will see the thing in this light ... I suspect Cardinal Wiseman is the person who has thus represented my Pamphlet. And if so, I fear it may prove a great hitch in the affair.[90]

He sent[91] back a strenuous refutation of the charges held against his book: that the question of reunion had been discussed as if it were 'between equal parties' and that he had asserted that Anglicans follow the same rule of faith as Catholics; that the sin of the original schism was treated too lightly; the proposals for reunion too visionary and by advocating a General Council to treat of reuniting divisions, the authority of the Supreme Pontiff was arrogated. As for gallicanism, he protested it was 'something furthest from his thoughts'.

The fact that the pamphlet was not placed on the Index can be attributed partly to the Cardinal having been adequately satisfied by Ambrose's answers; he certainly replied fairly amicably on 16 November. But it may owe more to its examination[92] at the end of September by Archbishop Paul Cullen of Dublin (later Cardinal) who was another of the Consultori at Propaganda Fide, and who happened to be in Rome. Although he drew attention to some of the same faults already mentioned, he considered the work to be of little value and would be forgotten in a few weeks. To condemn it would cause a stir and alienate those who might draw closer to the Church.

In England the *Rambler* and the *Dublin Review* added their disapprobation. *The Rambler* wrote of 'this mischievous pamphlet ... scandalous to the very highest degree'.[93] 'Mr Phillipps is not content with setting up a theory of his own' wrote the *Dublin Review*; 'he calls in the Church to endorse it'.[94] Even the faithful Montalembert thought that Ambrose was mistaken

> 'in point of *fact* on the *extent* of the good dispositions of so large a body of the Anglican clergy as you suppose'.[95]

Ambrose explained that he had been guided by the large number of Anglican clergy, 9,000, so he said, also 16,000 Anglican ladies of High Church principles, who had signed a petition against the Bill then in parliament which would facilitate divorce.

Ambrose had sent a copy of his pamphlet to Newman who on 1 July 1857[96] expressed his appreciation of 'that gentleness and affectionateness, which it not only requires, but which it gains from you on all occasions'. But in common with other critics, he took up the point that while waiting for corporate reunion, men and women would be risking their souls. Ambrose had recognised the danger and had earlier suggested[97] a way out of the difficulty which would remove from individuals the responsibility of schism, as an interim measure. In the course of several further letters Newman added a postscript

> If England is converted to Christ, it will be as much due (under God) to you as to any one[98]

He had commented adversely[99], however, when he received from Ambrose the detailed plans for his association of intercessory prayer for reunion, on the absence, as having nothing to do with the work, of Pusey, Isaac Williams, 'or of dear Keble'. It was to be a serious weakness of the association that these vintage Tractarians did not join. Lee had earlier asked them to subscribe to the *Union* newspaper and they had declined (Keble cancelled his subscription after a few editions).

When, therefore, the Association for the Promotion of the Unity of Christendom finally had its inaugural meeting, at Lee's chambers in London on 8 September 1857, it was a less influential gathering than the initiators had hoped. There was only a sprinkling of Roman Catholics at this stage, one of whom was William Lockhart; H. N. Oxenham[100] and Henry Collins who were present, were received a few weeks later. Several of the Anglicans were clergy from London parishes, C. F. Lowder, A. H. Mackonochie, A. H. Stanton. Others hung back because they felt they were already united in a bond of intercessory prayer as members of the Church. The vast majority took no notice: the reunion of Christendom was simply not on their agenda. Ambrose declined Lee's offer of the chairmanship 'as naturally nervous and in many other respects

ill-qualified for such a post'. It fell to E. B. Knottesford-Fortes-
cue, Provost of St Ninian's, Perth, though it was Ambrose who
proposed (surely for him a crowning moment) that the Association be formed.

For the next seven years membership grew to probably
about 8,000, of whom about 1,000 were Roman Catholics, 300
Orthodox and the rest Anglicans.[101] Cardinal Wiseman on
Christmas Eve 1857 despatched a long memorandum entitled
Relazione intorno al partito della 'Unione' nella setta Anglicana
(in Italian) to Propaganda, on the APUC. It had obviously
been copied and was not in his handwriting, though signed by
Wiseman. Wilfred Ward included a great deal of it in his *Life
and Times of Cardinal Wiseman* of 1897, but the extent of the
omissions was not recognised by his contemporaries. Comparison with the original shows that nearly all of them refer to the
Cardinal's estimation of Ambrose and his part in the movement.

Features to which he drew attention in the version in Rome
described

> ... good Mr P's fanaticism ... He has always believed himself
> to be under the influence of a supernatural power, and studied
> the strangest illusions in the form of revelations, visions and
> prophesies. He believed, and still does believe ... that his
> children enjoy divine inspiration, and that they are constantly
> seeing visions of the Virgin ... With fiery looks and the most
> enthusiastic manner, he said that he was quite convinced of the
> imminence of the national conversion of England. For many
> years, despite his own unworthiness, the Lord had shown him
> that he would play an important part ...

Ambrose was always inclined, wrote the Cardinal, to maintain
the validity of Anglican orders;

> ... were he on the point of death, he would receive the
> sacrament from an Anglican minister rather than dying without
> it. Never, however, would he take it from a 'dissenter'.

After many of the classic criticisms already lodged by various
quarters against the pamphlet on Unity, the APUC, the *Union*
and Ambrose himself, Wiseman ended by assuring the Holy
See that were there ever to be an approaching national conversion, the Bishops 'would hasten to announce it to the Supreme
Pastor and would not leave this part of their duty to a

layman'. He did not recommend any action on the part of the Holy See. So for the time being there the matter rested.

Throughout 1857 Ambrose's letters to various correspondents gave evidence of growing anxiety for the safety of Everard in India. Though his family were filled with pride at his exploits, many of Everard's letters[102] home which described them, added to the alarm. He was at first acutely homesick; then greatly enamoured of his Colonel's daughter, Agnes Rutherford, whose family did not want her to marry a Catholic; perpetually short of money and since May, in conditions of great danger. He was at Meerut when the insurrection began there on 10 May and was required to address captured sepoy rebels of his regiment, the 11th National Infantry, since he was known to have a good grasp of the Hindustani language. Colonel Figgis was killed by his side, although Everard remained in that engagement unhurt. In Ghazee-Deen-Nuggur on 31 May he had his horse killed under him and he was slightly wounded, but as the result of his gallant conduct, Lieut-Colonel Jones of the 60th Rifles wrote an application to the Duke of Cambridge for a Commission without purchase in the Queen's Army in that regiment. On 5 June the death of a young officer created the required vacancy.

The march on Delhi, held by the insurgents, began at the beginning of June; Everard's unit joined the Commander-in-Chief on the 7th after three marches, one of seventeen hours without tents or food. For the next three months attempts were made to seize and occupy the city. The final storming of the defences took place on 14 September when Everard having been the first to scale the Water Bastion, helped to clear the enemy amidst tremendous firing. On the 17th, after protracted street fighting, Everard was hit in the head by a gun shot whilst erecting a small breast work to protect his men. He fell unconscious and died ten minutes later. The news did not reach Grace Dieu until 15th November, contained in a letter from Colonel Jones. It was a devastating blow, particularly to his mother whose favourite child he had been. 'The news of his untimely end, cut off in the midst of a bright career well nigh overwhelmed us', she wrote to one of Everard's brother officers. 'God's Holy Will be done' she wrote in her diary. It was the greatest tragedy of her life and one she clearly never forgot, for she continued to mention it.

It was a consolation for Ambrose to see his son as a martyr in a Christian cause against the forces of Islam; Everard had died a hero which had been recognised by a recommendation that he be awarded the Victoria Cross[103]. The correlation between soldiering and the old concept of chivalry was one which both Everard's parents held dear and it supported them in their loss. The younger children were filled with grief; Mary at school at the Loughborough Convent wrote stricken letters to her mother: 'How shall you be able to live without Ebby? As for me my happiness is gone with him'.

During the next months one hundred and ninety nine letters of condolence were received at Grace Dieu, as a measure of the de Lisles' wide circle of acquaintances and its sense of sorrow; the death of Everard coloured the remainder of the decade. There were also problems in the neighbourhood: Ambrose was drawn into the unsettled conditions at the Monastery. The new Abbot, Bernard Burder, had seen fit in 1856 to establish a Reformatory for Catholic boys to be run by the monks on Monastery property some half a mile from the Abbey. It was a warm-hearted gesture for the reclamation of boys who were victims of prevailing bad social conditions, but in practice adequate supervision was often lacking; gangs of boys began to roam over the countryside, although Ambrose never mentioned occasions which filled the pages of local newspapers with indignant letters. He and his family made visits to the Reformatory the occasion of many afternoon walks and watched its progress.

Affairs in Leicestershire occupied a prominent place in the English file at Propaganda for the years 1857–8. In addition to the matter of reunion already mentioned, and that of the Reformatory and its troubles, a long correspondence, in which Ambrose took part, concerned a wish by Abbot Burder for the Monastery to cease to belong to the Cistercian Order, but become Benedictine. Originally Ambrose had been opposed to this suggestion; he had founded the Abbey specifically for Trappists. But gradually he conceded that whatever the Pope should decide he would agree to. The number of choir monks was small, the conditions hard; there was no mitigation of the Rule for different parts of the world at that time, to suit variations in climatic conditions. There was long correspondence

as to whether one of the monks, Fr Ignatius Sisk, who had
been acting as parish priest at Whitwick, should be permitted
to remain there. One specific complaint to Rome from the
Abbot concerned Ambrose particularly. He had protested when
the Vicar General had ordered that the screen between choir
and secular congregation in the Abbey church, of open fret-
work, be replaced by curtains fixed and nailed, at all times.

> This regulation so much displeased Mr Phillipps, our patron
> and founder, that he threatened never to enter the Church
> again, nor to finish the church as he had intended . . .' our
> secular congregation has been greatly distressed by not being
> permitted to see the High Altar[104] . . .

All Ambrose's achievements seemed at one time or another to
run into difficulties.

Despite the underlying misery, there was one interesting
development in 1858. On 16 June Ambrose and Laura were
invited to Norfolk House by the Duke; all the state rooms
were thrown open. 'The only party he ever gave' Laura commented in her diary. As the result of an introduction, Mr
Gladstone who had long before been aware of Ambrose's
existence but had never seen him face to face, invited him to
breakfast the following day. It was a meeting that was to have
important consequences.

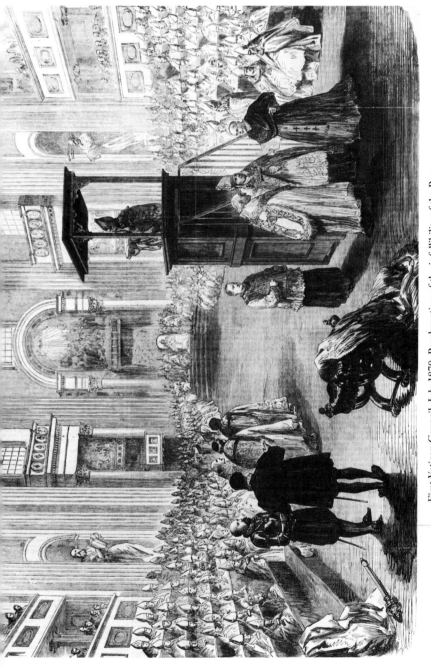

First Vatican Council, July 1870; Proclamation of the infallibility of the Pope.

AUGUSTUS PUGIN
in the later 1840s

LUIGI GENTILI
of the Institute of Charity (Rosminians)

IGNATIUS (George) SPENCER, C.P.
after his profession as a Passionist

BLESSED DOMINIC BARBERI, C.P.

Chapter 10

The 1860s

THE life of Ambrose de Lisle in the 1860s was dominated by domestic concerns, though the claims of family and faith remained closely knit and neither was neglected for the other. Moreover, the tensions he underwent and his aspirations reflected in microcosm the tensions and experience of the wider Catholic community, both in Rome and in England. All were taken up with the part that Catholics should play in the world and nation.

So far as the Papacy was concerned, sovereignty over the Papal States with the exception briefly of Rome itself, was lost in 1860 after years of unrest and disturbance. The removal of Austrian protection which alone had kept the peace, was responsible for the final rift. Catholics divided on the issue of whether this was a misfortune or a blessing. Pius IX took the first view and as a consequence issued the Syllabus of Errors in 1864, part of a process that was to culminate in the events of the first Vatican Council. The Syllabus did not consist of a new set of propositions; its components had been published before, but to string them together was a fresh attempt to show how strongly the Pope opposed liberal, democratic, socialistic, modernistic ways of thought which he regarded as destructive of the capacity of the Church to maintain its authority over society and Government. There were 80 propositions which rejected various aspects of contemporary thinking. The last denounced the thesis that the Pope 'can and ought to reconcile and adjust himself with progress, liberalism and modern civilisation'. The message which issued from the Curia was that Catholics should withdraw from participation in modern society, thought and scholarship.

Ultramontane elements in England reacted by interpreting

that it was incumbent upon them to increase and extend their loyalty and dependence upon the Holy See. The Pope, correspondingly, developed a more personal form of rule. Whereas at the beginning of the 19th century almost all episcopal nominations were locally initiated, now Pius IX began further to exercise his own choice, as was to be the case with the appointment to Westminster in 1865. Moreover, authority from sources in Rome began to triumph over detail, made possible by improvements in communications during the past two decades.

English Roman Catholicism after 1860 became increasingly affected by the poor health and waning powers of Cardinal Wiseman coupled with differences of opinion between him and his Chapter, with the coadjutor chosen to lighten his load, and with most of the English bishops. An autocratic style had rubbed off on Wiseman during his days in Rome and with growing infirmity this natural tendency became exacerbated in his attempts to deal with the many issues that confronted him.

The first concerned the division of property consequent upon the creation of the diocese of Southwark out of the archdiocese of Westminster; cool relations between Wiseman and Southwark's Bishop Grant were the result. A second problem was presented by the status and control of the ecclesiastical colleges (Ushaw, Oscott, St Edmund's Ware and up until 1856, Prior Park). Although located within diocesan boundaries and therefore the responsibility of the diocesan bishop, they were used to train for the priesthood candidates from dioceses which did not possess their own seminaries. It was felt by many that responsibility, especially over teachers and finance, should be shared. To the difficulties which persisted, since personal feelings ran high, have been attributed the further impairing of Wiseman's health.

St Edmund's Ware, which served Westminster and Southwark, was a case in point. In 1855 Wiseman appointed Herbert Vaughan, not yet 23 years old and who had been befriended by Manning during his training in Rome, to be Vice-President of the College. At once Vaughan faced opposition from his colleagues. This became intensified when he joined the Oblates of St Charles, a community of secular priests set up by Manning. Three further members of the Oblates were placed at St

Edmund's and the fear was that the affairs of the college
would be managed from outside. It was at this stage in April,
1857 that Manning was appointed Provost of the Westminster
Chapter. The position of the Oblates at St Edmund's was
further entrenched.

It was not a position which pleased Archbishop[1] George
Errington who, in 1855, had reluctantly become coadjutor to
Wiseman to assist him in the administration of his diocese.
Monsignor Talbot had complained[2]

> I do not think he is Roman in spirit. He has a great deal of
> what they detest so much here, Episcopalianism, that is, think-
> ing that a bishop ought to interfere with everything in his
> diocese.

The coadjutor was supported by the Westminster Chapter
who initiated an investigation into the place occupied by the
Oblates at St Edmund's. It was maintained that Manning's
community was independent of the Ordinary; an issue which
was not as trivial as it might seem, since it affected the
freedom of the college to manage its own affairs. When
matters came to a head, Wiseman asked to see the Chapter
books and this request was refused; copies of the resolutions
only were produced. He was convinced that Errington had
played a part in what he considered a conspiracy against him.
The young Vaughan was of the same opinion and fanned the
flames in a letter to Talbot to the effect that whereas it was
formerly the laypeople who had tried to remove the Cardinal
from England 'now it is Dr Errington, Grant and [the] Westminster Chapter'[3]. By the Spring of 1859 Wiseman decided that he
could no longer work with his coadjutor and asked the Holy
See for him to be removed.

Wiseman and Errington (followed by Manning summoned
for assistance by the Cardinal) were called to Rome in the
autumn of 1859 for resolution of the many current problems.
Bishop Grant also appeared since it was the Southwark property matter which was deliberated first and decided almost
completely in his favour. But Wiseman, supported by Manning,
had his way over the removal of Errington. (Wiseman had
already secured the resignation of John Maguire his vicar-
general, and chief opponent on the Westminster Chapter).

Talbot added his weight to the indictment by declaring Errington an enemy to converts in England and animated by a Gallican and Jansenist spirit. The Pope bowed to the inevitable and released him from his coadjutorship with the right of succession at Westminster.

Before the prelates left to return to England another matter for consideration reached Rome. J. H. Newman had written an article in the *Rambler*,[4] of which he was briefly editor, entitled *On Consulting the Faithful in Matters of Doctrine*. Bishop T. J. Brown of Newport and Menevia had considered some passages sufficiently heretical to justify delation to Rome. By reason of his presence there, Wiseman's assistance was sought; he was heard to say that he would help Newman in his difficulty. But the Cardinal failed to make the required list of so-called offending passages, as he had been asked to do, and opprobrium continued to rest on Newman for his failure to defend himself against accusations which had never been formulated.

In the autumn of 1861, Bishop Ullathorne and the Bishop of Clifton, William Joseph Clifford[5], made a visit to Rome to represent the majority of the English bishops in their complaints against Wiseman's handling of affairs, his disregard of their views. They appealed for a more democratic procedure at Low Week meetings. They received a sympathetic hearing, but Ullathorne's resignation from the see of Birmingham was not accepted. Monsignor Talbot, as usual, was responsible for the creation of much ill-feeling: his condemnation of the English clergy and bishops as 'insular, national, narrow-minded, Anglo-Gallican, anti-Roman as they may be'[6] was particularly unfortunate from one who had the ear of the Pope. Cardinal Barnabo, Prefect of Propaganda, was led to wonder whether there was danger of schism from bishops who had 'little veneration' 'for the wishes or even decisions of the Vicar of Christ'[7]

This kind of alarm gave rise to the request from Rome that first the *Rambler* and then its successor, the *Home and Foreign Review*, the property of Lord Acton and Richard Simpson,[8] should be discontinued. Both periodicals had published articles considered dangerous on such subjects as education and the temporal power, and were the mouthpiece of Catholics like Newman who felt that there was a place for the discussion of contemporary issues; a process not considered wise by their detractors. Wiseman had the support of his bishops (already alive to the problems) in the suppression of the periodicals and was to gather further co-operation before his death in two areas: the banning of the APUC and university education for Roman Catholics. Wiseman's position was not so greatly threatened as Rome had been led to believe. Differences of opinion existed among Roman Catholic bishops in England certainly, but there was loyalty too and a knowledge of what had always been the extent of Wiseman's expansive dedication.

Ambrose, true to form, added his voice to the *Rambler* debate in a series of letters to (then) Sir John Acton. He was far from wanting to silence the right to free speech 'I am certain that no two men are more agreed in their hatred of tyranny than I am with yourself', but he was concerned that the word 'Church' had been used in an article in a loose way 'injurious to the Catholic cause'

> I should be very unhappy if I thought 'the Church' had any blame whatever to bear for Papal mismanagement in Rome. You might with equal justice talk of the blame due to the Church for St Peter's denial of Christ! I must draw a broad line of demarcation between 'the Church' and the faults of Popes, whether in their individual capacity or in their civil and secular one, as sovereigns of their own Dominions.

The temporal power of the Pope, now almost entirely lost since 1860, was one of the subjects where English Catholics sought most to exercise freedom of expression. Newman let it be known that he would not let his name stand as a member of the Academia founded by Wiseman, if it were used as a platform to promote the temporal power of the Pope as dogma to be held by all Catholics.

Ambrose did not hesitate to give his views[10] to his old friend George Spencer, now Father Ignatius and a Passionist,

> I consider all attempts to bolster up the Papacy quite useless; out of loyalty to the Holy Father I put my signature to the address that went to him from the Laity of England, but I do so in love, *not in hope*.

Again, in a letter to Montalembert,[11] Ambrose spoke out

> I cannot go along with you in your admiration and love of the Temporal Rule of the Papacy or in your regrets for its downfall.

> I believe the Temporal sovereignty of the Popes was equally injurious to Xtianity and to sound government: at the time of its first institution it tended to enervate the piety and virtue of both Popes and clergy, wherever its influence was felt . . .

He added, for good measure, his dislike of coercion; a change of view since his youth.

> My notion of Catholicity is altogether your own in one respect at least. I associate it with the ideas of free, spontaneous, ardent Faith . . . I abhor anything like force applied to the consciences and the Free will of men . . .

In the summer of 1863 Cardinal Wiseman made his last visit to Europe. He had been invited to address a large Congress called in Malines on the position of the Catholic Church in the modern world. One of his fellow-speakers was Charles Montalembert who chose as one of his subjects a Free Church in a Free World. His doctrines, wrote Wiseman to his secretary, 'made terrible, though silent confusion'. W. G. Ward wrote an attack on the speech intended for the *Dublin Review*; it was not eventually published but the rumour reached Montalembert that it had found its way to Rome after it had been privately printed and that the speech was about to be placed on the Index through the influence of Cardinal Wiseman and the Oxford converts. Montalembert wrote[12] for sympathy to Ambrose who instantly sent a letter[13] to the Cardinal. He felt, he said, that the report was 'pure calumny', but he took the opportunity at the same time to plead for toleration of differences of opinion upon open questions:

> . . . nothing can be further from your mind than to render a reconciliation between the Church and the 19th century impossible.

In his reply[14] to Ambrose, Wiseman did not try to hide his disagreement with the 'political principles and tendencies' upheld by Montalembert, but denied that he had denounced the speech to Rome nor given any authority to anyone to speak unfavourably of the text. His own address, given in French, standing for two and a half hours, had related the progress of Catholicism in England over the past thirty years. He applied to it a motto, familiar to Belgians, *L'Union fait la force*.

It was in the interests of such solidarity that a move was made which created one of the most searing blows in Ambrose's life: the banning, in 1864 by the Holy Office in Rome, of Catholic participation in the membership and activities of the APUC. The first ruling was contained in a Letter of the Holy Roman and Universal Inquisition to all the [Roman Catholic] Bishops of England, dated 16 September 1864[15]. A report had reached the Holy See, so it read, that certain Catholics and also ecclesiastics had enrolled themselves in an Association for promoting – to use their own expression, the Unity of Christendom. It was not easy to understand either the nature of the Society or the object in view; the belief was that it had been directed by Protestants and moved by

> the very spirit which it openly professes, to wit that three Christian Communions, the Roman Catholic, the Schismatic Greek and the Anglican, although separated and divided from one another, claim nevertheless by equal right the name of Catholic ... that the faithful of Christ and ecclesiastics under the guidance of heretics, and what is worse, according to an intention most grievously polluted and infected with heresy, should pray for Christian Unity, can in no way be tolerated.

'The very constitution on which the Society rests' it was maintained, 'turns the divine constitution of the Church upside down'. The result was

> that pestilential indifferentism in matter of religion which especially in this age creeps abroad to the ruin of souls.

Speculation as to the identity of the originator whose efforts led to the condemnation, has not ceased. E. S. Purcell in his biographies of Manning and Ambrose, does not hesitate to put the blame on Manning. The files of Propaganda Fide in Rome suggest otherwise. Manning was not idle in letting it be known in Rome that the *Union Review*, with which 'some lay Catholics and priests, but not many, are associated', had published articles 'which are gravely erroneous and scandalous'. But according to the documents, the instigator of the enquiry which had re-opened scrutiny of the APUC after Wiseman's advice, seven years earlier, that the matter should be allowed to rest, was clearly Bishop Ullathorne.

The issue of the APUC was raised at the annual meeting in Low Week of the English bishops in the Spring of 1864. According to his account given later[16], Bishop Ullathorne was deputed by Cardinal Wiseman and the others present, to write to the Cardinal Prefect of Propaganda Fide on their behalf to ask for a ruling as to what should be their attitude towards the Association. Ullathorne duly sent two letters[17] in Latin which now lie in the files of Propaganda.

In the first, he attributed the origins of the APUC to

> that famous Protestant group informally called the Puseyites; this governs its life and from whose teaching it develops for the main part ... The Association comprises some English Catholics, among whom, though it is hard to believe, even bishops. It never stops hinting in its private sessions, that there are connections, albeit indirect, with some Roman prelates who are thought to represent the thinking of the Holy See ... The Association is formed with the specific aim of uniting the Roman Catholic, Greek and Anglican Communion, by prayer and intercession as those who claim to have inherited the name of Catholic and priesthood 'quae sibi vindicant haereditatem sacerdoti [sic] et nominis Catholici' ... Therefore this said society is founded on the theoretical assumption that the *Anglican Sect is part of the true Catholic Church 'qua assimitur sectam Anglicanam esse veram Ecclesiae Catholicae partem'*.

Bishop Ullathorne enclosed the prayer and rule of the APUC; also its manifesto. He also made mention of the *Union Review*, the fact that free discussion was suggested as profitable on certain topics such as the use of the vernacular in the Liturgy and singled out articles 'which do not make edifying reading'. Among them was one by E.S. ffoulkes[18] on the division and varied viewpoints between Catholics, and a dissertation by 'a famous Catholic, Phillipps de Lisle', 'On the Question and Hope of Union', where the phrase *Filioque* had been under review. To dissuade conversions was mentioned as a practical aim. The Bishop ended by asking two questions: should Catholics be permitted to join the Association described and secondly, should priests be allowed to worship in harmony with it and to celebrate Mass for the furtherance of this Society.

The response was the Holy Office Rescript of 16 September 1864. Ambrose in particular, was deeply wounded by it.

Unfortunately, his 186 letters addressed to F. G. Lee during the years 1857–74 which have survived, have a gap between the Spring of 1864 and 1865, so the reactions of Ambrose to his chief collaborator are missing. But William Lockhart, also a prominent Roman Catholic member of the APUC, while a guest of the de Lisles gave Lee his version of the situation.[19]

> I have had a great deal of conversation with our friend Mr de Lisle on the subject of the Cardinal Prefect's letter. I find him in very low spirits about the prospects of the APUC. I have done my best to encourage him. I do not by any means share his forebodings and feel more confidence than I ever had in the good cause. Because all opposition is so far a sign of the work being of God that no good work ever succeeds without it.

In a letter of February 1865, addressed to Newman[20] on another matter, Ambrose gave an insight into his feelings when he sympathised with Newman having been forced

> to yield to that imperious and inexorable despotism that crushes all free action even in defence of the Faith – the same overwhelming force has compelled me to withdraw my name from the Association for the Promotion of the Unity of Christendom . . . what the end of all this, and of the Encyclical[21] proclaiming the duty of State Prosecution at a moment when Catholicism itself lives everywhere only on the Tolerance of its opponents, will be- it is hard to say . . .

Newman replied[22] agreeing that it was 'one's duty to submit'.

> For myself, I did not see my way to belong to the Union Association – but I think its members have been treated cruelly.

In an earlier letter[23] to Ambrose he had written in the same strain

> Certainly, to my mind one of the most affecting and discouraging elements in the action of Catholicism just now on English Society, is the scorn with which some of us treat proceedings and works among Protestants which it is but Christian Charity to ascribe to the influence of divine grace.

Soon, Ambrose's misery began to turn to renewed activity; he went to see his Bishop (Nottingham); Lee, ffoulkes, Fr

Henry Collins, and as already noted, William Lockhart, came to stay in Leicestershire to discuss future plans. Ambrose resolved that some form of answer must be sent to Rome. He despatched a spate of letters in the direction of the now dying Wiseman. The first[24] rejected any suggestion that he had held, or for one moment dreamt of holding, any of the principles condemned in the Rescript. The clauses of the APUC had been very carefully worded; the case had been misrepresented to the Holy See. He thought the whole event deplorable 'just when a powerful section of English Churchmen and English politicians were looking at Rome with longing eyes and earnestly desirous of a better mutual understanding'.

A few days later[25] he wrote again. 'A humble and concilia-tory letter' to Cardinal Patrizi of the Holy Office had been drawn up by the Anglican leaders which was being circulated for signatures. Wiseman's approval was sought; as also his willingness to despatch it to the Holy Father himself with an earnest appeal

> to his generous and loving heart not to despise the humble effort which is being made in all sincerity to reconcile the English with the Roman Church.

Wiseman played for time[26], though he had little left

> I think it would be better for you to do nothing personal in the Union matter, till what you have already mentioned to me shall have taken place ie. the address by Anglican clergy etc.

In the meantime his aide, Canon Morris, was asked by the Cardinal to reply to an enquiry as to whether it had been Manning who had obtained the Rescript from the Holy Office as the result of representations. The answer was in the negative. Ambrose was able to secure an interview with Wiseman on 1 December, but in the event the Cardinal was too ill to see him. Not to be daunted, he returned the following day, 2 December, and spoke with Wiseman at 11 am for an hour. At midday a group of APUC members appeared by appointment, but Wise-man's strength had gone and he sent messages via Ambrose. It was their last meeting, though Ambrose continued to write him letters. Permission to be exempted from the Holy Office ban, as a special case, was a request in one of them. When it began to be rumoured that Ambrose had refused to comply, Lockhart advised that he should make a public show of resignation *under protest*. This he did in a letter to Lee on 20 December 1864[27]. Cardinal Wiseman died on 15 February 1865.

While signatures were being collected for the reply to the Holy Office Letter, Bishop Ullathorne wrote a long pamphlet[28] of forty-three pages in the autumn of 1864 on the APUC affair that was to become the first of several published during subsequent years on the subject of reunion. The formal censure which had been passed upon the APUC, he wrote, could come as no surprise to any Catholic acquainted with the spirit and drift of that society; its principles were heretical; the censure had not come a day too soon. Catholic bishops were entreated to be instant in exposing the errors which were embodied and in repelling the evils with which it was fraught. The struggle would be against

> a novelty which is the most dangerously delusive, as it comes with a fair colouring upon its features of piety and with an expression of solicitude for the Unity of Christendom.

It had been inferred that the Association was approved by the Pope and Catholic Bishops[29] whereas the Cardinal Prefect of Propaganda had told the writer 'in no other way can Anglicans return to the Church than as erring children'. The chief defects of the Society were attributed to false ecclesiology; the so-called 'branch theory' of three great divisions of Christendom; the invitation to the members of 'the three Communions' to come proffering the condition 'that they may drop from notice their distinctive doctrines and habits of discipline' for 'they are not expected to compromise any principles which they, rightly or wrongly, hold dear.' What was lost, Ullathorne maintained, was the Church. Terms such as 'unhappy divisions' and 'loss of visible unity' he found unacceptable, as also the concept of prayer in common. It was a feature of the Church's unity and integrity

> that her members do not communicate in prayer with those beyond her pale.

With the information as to the origin, constitution and operation of the Association, Ullathorne made mention of the leading part played by 'a distinguished Catholic layman'.

A reply to both Ullathorne's pamphlet and the Holy Office Letter came in the shape of *Unity and the Rescript*[30] from Dr R. F. Littledale, an Anglican member of the APUC, who maintained that the programme and principles had been misrepresented to Rome and misunderstood there. The Roman Catholic members could not and did not hold the 'branch theory'; the manifesto had been so worded as not to commit them to it. The second half of the essay devoted itself to defending the APUC against Ullathorne's presentation of the Catholic teaching on strict visible unity. Lockhart thought the pamphlet 'glorious'.[31]

> In the most courteous way he was *wiped out* the good Bp. of Bm in all he says in defence of the Cardinal's [Patrizi] Letter and against the APUC.

Cardinal Wiseman had given Ambrose de Lisle an undertaking to present the Anglican reply to the Rescript to the Pope. After his death, Ambrose rather unwisely, but intent that it should reach Pius IX in person, enlisted the help of Monsignor Talbot. It became a matter of crucial importance, with the news at this juncture, that Henry Manning was to become Archbishop of Westminster. Wiseman had not seen fit openly to make known his wishes as to a successor. The Westminster Chapter duly submitted three names in the *terna* to Rome: Archbishop Errington, former co-adjutor, and Bishops Grant and Clifford who subsequently withdrew. Talbot was later to allege that Pius IX appointed Manning, not because Talbot had persuaded him, but because Talbot had tried to be subtle and continue to speak against other possibilities. This is clearly a simplification. There was considerable opposition to the appointment of Manning in Rome; the Pope chose his own candidate.

Ambrose was quick to address[32] his new Archbishop 'to express my own hearty devotion to you'. He referred to an earlier visit to Grace Dieu and was rash enough to make a comment on the APUC which he had been forced to leave, and his belief that the Holy Ghost was working in the Anglican Church, 'not only for the conversion of individual souls, but

for that of the whole Body itself'. Archbishop Manning commented to Talbot[33]

> Mr de Lisle wrote to me the other day saying that there are I
> know not how many who desire to be reconciled to the Pope. I
> had rather hear of one who will submit to the infallible voice
> of the Church. This is the one point which they do not hold or
> see.

Here clearly was a new leader of decided views. To what
extent he would stretch his concepts of infallibility was less
certain; when they became clearer a further source of division
was created. But whereas Manning gave every indication of
strictness with bishops, clergy and lay people, his social attitudes towards the poor and disadvantaged of England, with
special regard to the impoverished Irish elements, were more
highly developed than those of most of his contemporaries.

Talbot was urged in several letters[34] from the new Archbishop of Westminster to see that the reply to the Anglican
letter on the Rescript be expressed as clearly as possible. There
had been no misunderstanding. The APUC

> is part of a system which is deceiving many Catholics, and will
> give us much trouble if we do not cut down to the bone.

Talbot agreed that in relation to the use of the word '"Catholic", Mr de Lisle encourages the error',

> but I think that there are many persons in England who think
> they are Catholics because they hold Catholic views, whereas
> they know very well that the most ultra-Puseyite until he has
> made his abjuration, is no more a Catholic than the most
> bigoted Evangelical.

The Holy Office reply to 198 Anglican members of the
APUC was despatched in November 1865. F. G. Lee had anticipated, as had Ambrose, to be able to attach a far greater
number of signatures to their letter, but it would seem that the
nature of the appeal, as of the Association itself, was limited
to a few enthusiasts on the Anglican as well as on the Catholic
side. The reserve with which it was regarded can be gauged
from a letter of Pusey[35] to John Keble

> I wonder whether, when you are better ... we could put that

> Society on a better footing, if we were to join it; ie, not to leave
> it so entirely in the hands of the Secretary [F. G. Lee].

The Holy Office reply reiterated, but at greater length, much of what had been said earlier on the nature of the one true Church.

> All ecclesiastical bodies separated from the external and visible
> Communion of the Roman Pontiff cannot be the Church of
> Christ. nor in any way at all belong to that Church.

The clerical titles of the 198 signatories were omitted and they were addressed as *Honorabiles and Dilectissimi Domini*. Ambrose did not hesitate to express himself forcefully to Talbot.[36]

> I care not how I am individually calumniated for speaking my
> mind and stating what are simply facts. In doing so I am doing
> my duty. For it is always a duty to speak what one behoves to
> be the Truth and it is no use to deceive the Holy Father by
> telling him that there is a great prospect of numerous *Individual
> Conversions*, when there is no such prospect at all.

He went on to express the opinion that by ceasing to look hopefully at opportunities for achieving corporate reunion. the Holy See was driving Anglicans into a connexion

> with the Churches of the Greek Separated Rite and a Union
> will be formed of all who think evil of the Papacy on a larger
> scale than any which the world has hitherto beheld.

Talbot's reaction was to ask Ambrose for a donation towards the restoration of a church in Rome; such, he implied, was the proper duty of the laity.

Manning wrote to Talbot 'I had hoped for more, but it will do'. In a letter[37] to Ullathorne he spoke of the need for caution 'de Lisle has some letters of the Cardinal's [Wiseman] which imply more tolerance of the union than could be wished'. By way of explanation of his doctrine of the Church, Archbishop Manning wrote an open letter to Dr E. B. Pusey on the *Working of the Holy Spirit in the Church of England*.[38]

> In denying the Church of England to be the Catholic Church or
> any part of it, or in any divine and true sense a Church at all,
> and in denying the validity of its absolutions and its orders, no

Catholic ever denies the workings of the Spirit of God or the operations of grace in it.

Yet, he went on to say

The Church of England, so far from being a barrier against infidality, must be recognised as the mother of all the intellectual and spiritual aberrations which now cover the face of England.

The publication of *Essays and Reviews*[39] by a group of Anglican clergy who believed in free enquiry into religious issues, had shocked many, doubtless Manning among them. The censure of the book in 1861 by the Anglican bishops, followed officially by the Archbishop of Canterbury, and synodical condemnation in 1864, did not remove the threat posed by critical forces at work and at large to those who mistrusted the process. Darwin's *Origin of the Species*, first published in 1859, was a further threat; the theory of evolution as put forward is known to have been unacceptable to Manning. The presence, within the Roman Catholic Church, of scholars such as Dr Döllinger, who had presided over an assembly of German Catholic academics in Munich in 1863, was an additional hazard. They had argued for freedom for scholarship from the interference of ecclesiastical authority. A papal brief had repudiated this principle, but the danger remained.

Pusey answered Manning's open letter in the autumn of 1865 with his *Eirenicon*[40] which he addressed to John Keble; he having suggested that Pusey should write it. Pamphlets by those who eschewed, or attacked, the APUC began to proliferate. Had it not been for its formation by Ambrose and his friends, the only Association of its kind, the subject of reunion would have received no attention whatever.

Pusey proceeded to take Manning to task over his view of the Anglican Church and proclaimed that it was innovatory. Earlier Catholic writings on reunion had not found such dichotomy between the two Churches; he listed similarities. The position of the Bishop of Rome had been subject to change: the English Church was not more independent of Rome than Africa had been at the time of St Augustine. A particularly controversial element then entered the pamphlet. Pusey described some tendencies in doctrine and devotion among Roman Catholics which he suggested were barriers to reunion. He singled out the writings of Frederick Faber and W. G. Ward as giving vent to what might be thought extravagances in regard to devotion to the Blessed Virgin Mary, and the extent and nature of Papal Infallibility.

More pamphlets followed in response, notably another from Ullathorne[41] and one from J. H. Newman; but since this latter was accompanied by a series of letters between Newman and Ambrose on the subject of corporate reunion in 1867, it would seem that the broad national scene should be left at this point and rejoined later. The microcosm – Ambrose's individual activity during the early 1860s – demands attention.

But first, one further issue of national concern must briefly be touched upon. An account of the complexities of the long drawn-out arguments as to whether Roman Catholics be permitted by their authorities[42] to attend English universities, is not called for in a study specific to Ambrose; beyond the fact that he showed himself concerned in the struggle and wished for a positive outcome, with his large family and hopes for their future and that of other young Catholics.[43] Once again, E. S. Purcell makes assumptions that he does not substantiate with documents; he writes in his biographies of Ambrose and of Manning that Cardinal Wiseman shared Ambrose's enthusiasm for attendance by Roman Catholics at Oxford and Cambridge and declares that letters on this subject (none extant) passed between Wiseman and Ambrose (as also between Ambrose and other bishops), in order to prove his point. Manning is seen as the villain who caused changes of attitude, whereas it seems clear that the English bishops became united over the issue of University attendance during Wiseman's lifetime.

He had called a special meeting of bishops in December 1864 and all had signed a letter to Propaganda that Catholic Colleges at existing universities could not be opened and that Catholic parents were to be dissuaded from accepting university education under the present system for their sons. Newman had bought a plot of land for an Oxford Oratory; he dutifully cancelled his plan. It may well be that Newman's publication of his *Apologia*[44] during the crucial year played some part in forming the decision of some of the bishops.

The most significant single event which affected Ambrose in

the 1860s was his inheritance of the whole of the Garendon – Grace Dieu estates and ownership of the mansion and parklands of Garendon, on the death of his father, Charles March Phillipps, in April 1862. It led to his greatest folly: the alterations to the house under the direction of A. W. N. Pugin's son, Edward Welby Pugin[45]. Such architectural merit as the 18th century house had possessed were removed; the cost impoverished the family for several generations. Intermittently, up to the end of the century, and beyond to 1907, the house had to be let in order to recover debts. Why the transformation was undertaken in the first place was a particularly 19th century matter: it was one of status, prestige and position in society which affected the family as a whole: the future of Ambrose and Laura's sons, their choice of brides and the possibility of marriages considered good by contemporary standards for their daughters. Most of the family money was tied up in property. Charles March Phillipps left little apart from it.

In addition, Ambrose undoubtedly felt that he could carry more influence in relation to his religious schemes if he could be seen as a considerable landowner. In his defence, it must be said that Garendon was badly in need of repair. There had been no mistress of the house since 1817, for Charles March Phillipps had been a widower on his inheritance. The top floor and one wing needed restoration, but the scheme that was adopted was radical and designed to a great extent to serve purposes of grandeur.

Ambrose had earlier attempted to improve his social lot by searching out the possibility of reviving a Lisle barony that had been in abeyance since the reign of Edward III. It was a process engaged upon by a number of Roman Catholic families with varied success. A long correspondence, and several visits had been exchanged with F. J. Baigent, an amateur genealogist from Winchester who tried to promote the cause. Even as late as December 1863, Ambrose persisted[46]

> If ever we could recover some of the old family honours, we shall be deeply indebted to your friendship for the result.

The attraction of the connection with the de Insula, Lisle, family, proved so strong that on gaining his inheritance Ambrose changed his name from Lisle March Phillipps to March

Phillipps de Lisle. This F. J. Baigent was able to effect in August
1862.

The fundamental problem posed to Catholic parents launching their children into the 19th century world was that of
education. Ambrose and Laura tried to solve it initially with a
series of tutors and governesses who were nearly all from the
continent, French or German. The supply of suitable English
Roman Catholic candidates was very limited. Bishops or superiors of Religious Orders were loath to spare a priest to be
chaplain and tutor in a lay household. There were a few
schools maintained by Religious: the Jesuit Stoneyhurst, for
example. In addition, Ushaw, Oscott, St Edmund's Ware and
(until 1856) Prior Park, as well as providing seminary training
for candidates to the priesthood, also acted as boarding schools
for boys. The fees of the latter helped to supply financial help
to the former. (The schools accepted boys from eight to
eighteen years of age; since attendance by Catholic boys at
English Universities was, as has been recorded, frowned upon
at the least by the bishops, their higher education was a
serious problem to those who considered it important).

For Ambrose and Laura payment of the fees and the cross-
country journeys to school were further inter-related difficulties. In February 1846 they had accompanied Amo to St
Edmund's Ware for the first time by taking the train to
London. A detour enabled them to see Mena who had, six
months earlier, gone to the convent of New Hall where Laura
herself had been educated. The journey on to Ware by carriage
took four hours. The new Pugin church at St Edmund's they
thought 'beautiful', it was certainly a contrast to the chapel of
Ambrose's own youth. Ambrose and Laura were overnight
guests of W. G. Ward[47] and his wife who had a cottage in the
grounds. It was a longer, though easier, journey than one three
days earlier to take Everard to his first term at a school run by
the Dominicans at Hinckley in Leicestershire. There had been
a heavy fall of snow and the roads so bad that having left
Grace Dieu at three in the afternoon by carriage, they lost the
way and did not arrive until nine at night; a journey of just
over twenty miles.

Everard joined Amo at St Edmund's the following year and
in 1849 they both left for Oscott where their brothers were

educated in turn; seven in all. It was considered a more 'gentlemanly' school and had an easier journey by train to Birmingham from Loughborough. Grandfather, Charles March Phillipps, had paid some of the fees.

Mena left New Hall the year before, which had been one of extreme financial stringency, and with her sisters shared the schoolrooms at home with two governesses; one for the older and one for the younger children. In 1854, Alice, Winifreda and Mary became boarders at the Sisters of Providence Convent in Loughborough, where Bertha and Gwendoline and eventually Margaret also, were pupils in due course. A move to send some of the girls to a convent school at St Leonard's in Sussex was the result of a long acquaintance by Ambrose and Laura of the remarkable Cornelia Connelly[48]. An American, wife of Pierce Connelly[49] who had been ordained into the Orders of the Episcopalian Church of the USA, they both became Roman Catholics and travelled to Rome in 1836. Their fifth child was born in 1841. Her husband felt a call to the Roman Catholic priesthood, and in order to enable him to proceed, she agreed to give up her children and became a nun. After some months of uncertainty as to where her vocation lay, she went to the Convent of Mercy in Birmingham at the suggestion of Cardinal Wiseman in the summer of 1846. She moved to Derby in the Autumn and began her own foundation of the Society of the Holy Child Jesus; its object the education of Catholic girls. Here she received visits from Ambrose and Laura and so impressed were they that it was decided to send Winifreda and Mary to her school, which by 1858 had moved to St Leonard's. Charles March Phillipps had refused to pay the fees, but since Winifreda was suffering from what a specialist in London had called 'consolidation of the upper part in front of the left lung', Sussex was thought more healthy than Leicestershire, at whatever cost.

Mother Connelly's strength of character was put severely to the test in two main ways[50]. Her husband revoked his priesthood and tried to claim back his wife in 1849 with a writ through the courts. An appeal to the Privy Council was decided in Mother Connelly's favour in 1851, but her problems were not over, for the educational tradition she established did not find favour in some quarters, notably with Bishop Grant of

Southwark who was one of those who found her too powerful.
Picnics and games, school plays, whist and dancing were part
of the curriculum. Bishop Grant 'afraid of the evil effects of
these recreations' wrote to her in 1865[51]

> It is said in one of your houses girls are taught the polka and
> waltz as well as whist. If you discover this to be true, stop it
> quietly.

And after the nuns had enjoyed a picnic

> I am glad you have had your day at Fairlight, as I could not
> have agreed to it if you had asked for it . . . I am sorry that I
> cannot hold out any hope that the Church will relax her rules
> in this particular.

Bertha and Gwendoline de Lisle joined their sisters at St
Leonard's in due course.

The beginning of the decade of the 1860s found young
members of the de Lisle family poised on the threshold of
adulthood, and by reason of their circumstances facing a
future more uncertain than that of their contemporaries.

For one of them at any rate, a happy outcome had been
painlessly achieved. In late January 1859 Frederick Weld,[52] son
of a cousin of Laura's, came to stay at Grace Dieu; it would
seem for the first time. After walking out with Ambrose when
no doubt permission was sought, on February 2 'before night
prayers and Benediction, Fred Weld proposed to Mena and
was accepted'. The marriage took place a month later.

Fred was the third son of Humphrey Weld of Chideock
Manor in Dorset who had married a daughter of the 6th Lord
Clifford. He was one of many children and a member of a
junior branch of the Welds of Lulworth; there was little
money. At the age of 19 Fred had gone to New Zealand by
sailing ship on a voyage of six months with three friends, two
of them relations, a bag of sovereigns and a land order from
the New Zealand Company of 100 acres, and another in a
town lot in what was to become the city of Wellington. After
some years of struggle and privations in establishing a sheep
farm and helping to quell a Maori rising, he became a Member
of the Legislative Council. Mena and Fred would seem to have
been well suited. She was fond of outdoor life, was a good

horsewoman and showed herself calm and stable under conditions of danger and difficulty far from home. Charles Weld writing to Laura about his brother[53] described Fred:

> You will easily find witnesses to his public character throughout his early struggles and rise into influence and independence in the country where he has been living and if ambition forms any part of Mina's [sic] hopes for her husband I know no one more likely to realise them, but there is no living testimony who can speak so well as I to those personal qualities of delicacy, honour, affection and virtue which are the daily enduring sources of a wife's happiness for life. There is not one of his brothers and sisters who does not gladly admit his superiority and repaid him with unqualified love and respect . . .

Since there were no religious impediments, the wedding was conducted by Bishop Clifford, who was related to both bride and bridgeroom, in Grace Dieu Chapel before a large congregation of tenants and neighbours. A local paper, clearly surprised at the lack of disturbance, commented

> 'We saw a solitary police-constable present, but there was no need of his services, as a more orderly and quiet assemblage could not have been witnessed.'

Tickets had in fact been issued to regulate numbers. There was further comment on the bride's 'exquisite moiré antique dress', the presence of the Dean of Ripon, Henry Erskine, and John Lambert[54] (who shared Ambrose's passion for plain chant) who played the organ: 'The Imperial Mass in the 6th tone' had been chosen. Alice, Winifreda, Mary, Bertha, Gwendoline and Fred's sister were bridesmaids. As well as 'a sumptuous breakfast consisting of all the delicacies of the season' at Grace Dieu, Laura had supplied tea and supper in the villages of Whitwick and Thringstone. The Welds sailed for Australasia at the end of the year; in 1860 Fred became Minister for Native Affairs and in 1864, Premier of New Zealand. The first of Mena's thirteen children was born in Wellington in June 1860. In the meantime, Laura had given birth to her 16th and last child, Gerard Lisle, at the age of 48 in January 1860.

The next few years were to provide some domestic stress to accompany the disappointments caused by failure of reunion plans. To find a husband worthy of Alice their second daughter, was of major concern. It was not to prove easy, partly because her parents had set their hearts on nothing less than a brilliant match for Ambrose's favourite child. The social round became greatly increased and accelerated. As well as many balls in the neighbourhood, house parties at the great houses of Leicestershire and beyond, Belvoir Castle, Elton, Stanton Harold and so on, were open to Ambrose, Laura and their two older girls. There were picnics, archery meetings, afternoon calls and much riding and hunting. Young men from good regiments stayed at Grace Dieu. Ambrose and Laura endured the long rides home by carriage in the early hours of the morning over frozen roads for the sake of the cause.

And then there were the activities in London. A house was rented at least once a year so that Alice and Winifreda could enjoy the London season. Laura presented Alice at the Queen's Drawing Room in 1859 and Winifreda in 1860; Ambrose attended levées. As soon as they reached the capital, Laura would set off in a hired carriage to leave cards in order to apprise hostesses of their arrival; sometimes as many as 25 calls would be made in an afternoon. Invitations flowed in; the girls, with their parents as chaperones, would sometimes attend three balls one after another on a single evening.

In the midst of this daunting programme, Ambrose and Laura carried on their usual activities: visits to their own churches and services to hear preaching by Faber or Manning with whom Ambrose lunched on several occasions. Expeditions were made to what were named 'Anglican sights', Dr J. Mason Neale's Sackville College and convent of St Margaret at East Grinstead; to Harriet Monsell's Sisterhood and House of Mercy at Clewer; to F. G. Lee's church of All Saints' Lambeth where Ambrose and Laura did not baulk at attending a service; 'the Revd Mr Liddon[55] preached a magnificent sermon'. Their circle of acquaintances during these London weeks was wide: Roman Catholic and Anglican clergy, members of both Houses of Parliament, especially Monsell, MP for Limerick and Lord Edward Howard, MP for Arundel; Lord Dunraven and Lord Lovat, Catholic peers. Sir John Acton was often in their company. Among old friends would be Digby if on a visit to London from France, though identity of opinion had lessened during the years. Peter le Page Renouf[56] was a friend with whom many theological attitudes became shared. Spencer died suddenly on a country road in the autumn of 1864.

Laura's terse diary comments tell much: '800 invitations sent out, very handsome supper', 'heat and crowd immense'; 'capital ball, the best of the season; we stayed to the end'. Ambrose commented chiefly upon his daughters; he wrote to his father in July 1860[57] on how much they had been admired: 'Alice looks more lovely than ever I saw her'. He passed on the news that he had 'heard people saying "Have you seen the beautiful Miss Phillipps from Leicestershire?"'.

It looked at one time as if the Duke of Rutland had taken an interest in her, as he paid Alice a good deal of attention. He was twenty five years older than she and died a bachelor in 1888. Ambrose clearly liked the idea of Alice as a duchess: moreover, he thought, a mixed marriage might do much for relations between the Churches. He continued to his father

> You need not think the Vatican would interpose any obstacle, if anything came of it. Every rule has its exception and our Bishop . . . who had heard rumours, said there was nothing he more earnestly desired.

Ambrose had also heard tell that the young Marquess of Hastings was in love with Alice, but that ill-fated romance lay still in the future.

It was during the course of the de Lisles' enjoyment of the London season of June 1860 that a telegram came from Mother Connelly: Mary was in danger and spitting blood. Laura hastened to St Leonards and eventually brought Mary back to London to a convent in Harley Street. She became so excitable and violent that the nuns asked for her to be moved again. With a nurse. Laura went with Mary into lodgings in St John's Wood. During their separation warm and affectionate letters passed between Laura and Ambrose, some of which have survived. They show not only the enduring strength of their relationship, but the anguish which was the common lot of Victorians in the face of young death and of illness in which there was not only no cure, but no relief. Mary's illness had brought back memories of Everard. Ambrose replied[58] to 'your most affectionate and truly beautiful letter'

> I quite feel my darling Laura all you say about our darling Everard: he was your special darling and he was worthy to be

so and in taking him from you, God laid on you a trial of inconceivable heaviness: but you must look forward to the thought of meeting him again and of being with him thro' blessed eternity.

After a week in St John's Wood the landlord 'told me he wished us to leave the house as Mary disturbed some of the neighbours'. Eventually with two nurses, Laura took her by train to Leicestershire; to Garendon rather than Grace Dieu; Grandfather was in Cheltenham. None of her sisters saw Mary until late in August and another month had passed, and Amo not until 30 September. On the first of October she was clearly dying; she could keep nothing down and was wasting away. Her father saw her for the first time since she had come from London. Whether this was because of the risk of infection or to spare Ambrose pain was not made clear. Mary's condition would have been very similar to that of his mother fifty seven years before. Early in the morning of 8 October 1860, Mary repeated a committal said by Alice, and died a few minutes later, aged 17 years. It was a considerable blow to her parents. Laura revealed some of the problems of a large family when she confided to Pagani in 1855[59] her special love for Mary 'who is, I fear a great *pet* of mine, tho' I always try *not* to show it'. She reminded Laura of her two brothers Reginald and Everard.

> I cannot disguise from myself that I cling to her more than to the others. Besides which, she has always had a very extra-ordinary love for *me* just as these two brothers of hers have always had.

The next marriage was not, as earnestly expected, of Alice but of Amo who in August 1861 announced his engagement to Frances Amelia Victoria Sutton[60] who became known as Fanny. She was an excellent horse-woman which had greatly endeared her to Amo who lived for hunting. Ambrose expressed his pleasure in a letter to F. G. Lee.[61]

> My son's Intended is still a member of your Communion, but of very Catholic principles. She is a beautiful girl, very elegant and accomplished and just of age. She inherits a very handsome fortune from her Father who left her nearly £2000 a year. My son has long known and admired her . . .

The wedding took place in London in October: there were two
services; the first at the Roman Catholic chapel in Warwick
Street where William Lockhart was the celebrant; the second at
St James' Church, Piccadilly conducted by the bride's brother
Augustus, a Prebendary of Lincoln. The reaction of her two
clerical brothers (Frederick Heathcote Sutton was in holy orders
also) to Fanny's reception into the Roman Catholic Church in
August 1862, clearly worried Laura, who warned F. G. Baigent[62]
that both Fanny and Amo wished to keep the fact secret for this
reason. Several attempts were made by Ambrose and the family
solicitor, Davidson, to persuade Charles March Phillipps to
increase Amo's allowance on his marriage. He firmly refused to
do so, but paid for the whole family to stay in London for the
wedding 'except for the carriages'. He was also generous in
paying for ball dresses for the girls, made in Ashby de la Zouche.

In September 1862 Fanny and Amo's first child was born at
Garendon which had become their home. (Charles March
Phillipps spent most of the time in Cheltenham). At Laura's
request the child was baptised Everard; the fact that the day of
his birth coincided with the anniversary of the death of his
Uncle made the choice especially appropriate. Fanny had a
second son in July of the following year who survived less
than a day. In the summer of 1864 she gave birth to a third son
to whom the same name, Bernard, was given, and in 1869 to a
daughter who lived only half an hour and who was baptised
by Amo. Laura recorded that there was neither doctor nor
nurse in the house and that 'Fanny herself never did better'.
But her mental health was soon to deteriorate severely; she
died at the age of thirty one in the Spring of 1871.

Henry Weysford Charles Plantagenet Rawdon Hastings,
fourth and last Marquess, began to visit Grace Dieu sporadi-
cally from the winter of 1860 when he was eighteen years old.
He had lost his father at the age of eighteen months and his
mother when he was sixteen, was wealthy, dissipated, undisci-
plined and full of charm. His hobbies were gambling, cock-
fighting and bear-baiting; he had a penchant for the lowest of
life in the East End. Tenants who had rented Donington Hall,
his family home, gave up their lease in 1861. From then
onwards Lord Hastings moved into the social scene in the de
Lisles' neighbourhood; he and Alice met at various functions.

In January 1862 he came to stay for the Loughborough Dispensary Ball; on the 18th he 'proposed for Alice to Ambrose and spoke to her after dinner'. Their engagement was made public in the newspapers in February with the news that the wedding would not take place until after Lord Hastings' majority the following year. Henry Collins, as Laura's spiritual adviser, later took her and Ambrose severely to task over the Hastings affair which they had appeared so anxious to promote. Clearly they were dazzled by the prospective bridegroom's lengthy entry in *Debrett*; some of his waywardness must have been known to them, but the popular view 'if only you will let him have your daughter it will be the making of Hastings',[63] obviously influenced their decision. It was soon reversed when a fuller extent of his character and activities became known. Amo played a part in rescuing Alice from this disastrous union. On 30 March he called to tell his father of reports his friends had given him about Hastings. It may have been of an escapade in which Hastings had turned out the gaslight and released a sackful of rats he had acquired loose at a dance in London. Ambrose and Laura had already received 'disagreeable' letters from Earl Howe, Hastings' guardian. On 8 April the engagement was broken off. Poor Alice entered somewhat of a decline for a while and reduced her social whirl, but recovered, and attended the Fancy Dress Ball at Donington for Hastings' Coming of Age in July 1863 as a Watteau shepherdess; he, appropriately enough, was attired as Charles II.[64]

No sooner had the Hastings affair been brought to a close than news came from Cheltenham that Charles March Phillipps was dangerously ill with angina. (His brother Samuel had died a month before in March). Ambrose and Laura hurried to Gloucestershire, followed closely by Ambrose's brother Charles. They took turns to sit day and night beside 'Grandpapa' who died on 24 April with his family kneeling round his sofa. The full observances of Victorian mourning were then set in motion. First, 'a funeral of unusual splendour attracted much attention'. A cortège of 'a stately hearse drawn by four horses', four funeral carriages and other private carriages bore the family, servants and friends to Swindon Church five miles outside Cheltenham where the burial took place next to Aunt

Harriet who had died in 1859. In the afternoon the Will was read: the personal estate was under £20,000. Ambrose was residuary legatee and one of the Executors. Amo received his grandfather's horses and saddle room equipment; the servants at the Cheltenham house had legacies amounting to £850. March Phillipps had leased Vallombrosa near Pittville circus in Cheltenham since 1853; it had become a fashionable resort and considered particularly healthy (Aunts Harriet and Fanny had acquired Lisle villa in Clarence Square). The upper servants at Vallombrosa as also those at Garendon and Grace Dieu, 18 in number, received £10 each with which to buy mourning; the lower servants were given black dress material, bonnets, shawls, gloves, black pins, cotton and hooks and eyes, with which to make their own; or if men, livery.

A stone cross was ordered for the grave before Ambrose and Laura left Cheltenham which, with the railings, cost £70. The extraordinary speed at which it was possible to execute business is remarkable. Within a fortnight the lease of Vallombrosa had been disposed of, the furniture sold and pieces they wished to keep returned with them to Grace Dieu on 10 May for the cost of four pounds twelve shillings. Two days later Ambrose began to talk to his agent on the alterations he intended to make at Garendon; a subject that was to absorb them for the next two years. Meanwhile Laura and her daughters were distributing copies of Charles March Phillipps' monument to all his tenants; on some afternoons forty calls were made in the villages.

The futures of three more daughters, Winifreda, Bertha and Gwendoline, became settled as the 60s passed. The wife of Lord Edward Howard who had long been suffering from consumption, died in the summer of 1862. Ambrose writing to Laura from Scotland in September of that year where he had accompanied Alice and Winifreda for two Scottish weddings, pondered on Lord Edward's new burst of interest in their family. Some would say he was anxious to marry one of their daughters.

How I wish this might ever be. What a comfort it would be for us!

The marriages had gone off charmingly; there had been no crying or fainting after the dejeuner. Alice had 'looked *divine* and threw all the other bridesmaids into the shade'. A guest had told him that 'she could not keep her eyes off her Madonna face'. Winifreda had been admired also.

It was Winifreda whom Lord Edward asked to marry in the summer of 1863. The marriage took place at Grace Dieu on 16 July on a somewhat reduced scale. Ambrose explained to a correspondent that on account of Lady Edward's still recent death and forthcoming anniversary, few guests were invited. No doubt there was relief at the necessity for economy. The Abbot of Mount St Bernard performed the ceremony in place of Bishop Grant who was prevented from doing so. Shortly after, Winifreda had her 'first reception by the children; very satisfactory'. She became stepmother to six survivors: the elder son and heir, Charley, had died the previous year, a few days after the birth of the youngest of the five girls. It was a role which she performed with great success, no doubt armed with her experience as one of the older members of a large family. She also became a notable hostess in London; 19 Rutland Gate was a haven for de Lisles on visits to the capital. Lord Edward was created a peer in 1869 as Lord Howard of Glossop and for the next eight years he was Chairman of the Catholic Poor Schools Committee; an interest he had long pursued. His presence as member of the family was a considerable help to Ambrose, many of whose concerns he shared. His political influence replaced that of Ambrose's uncle by marriage, Sir George Grey three times Secretary of State for the Home Department during the period 1846–66, whose relationship to Ambrose had been cool since his pamphlet on the establishment of the Roman Catholic hierarchy in 1850.

Bertha had also 'disposed of herself' as her father put it, by choosing to be a nun. She entered the Order of the Good Shepherd, formed by a French woman, Mary of Saint Euphrasia Pelletier at the beginning of the 19th century, for the rescue of the many prostitutes of the times and young women in moral danger. The first house in England was founded in 1840 and filled so great a need that soon houses were set up in Bristol, Liverpool, Finchley, Manchester and Hammersmith.

When George Dudley Ryder's sister, Sophia, decided to become a Religious in 1849, Newman's opinion was sought as to where she should go; his decision[65] favoured the Good Shepherd Order at Hammersmith. It was into this house that

Bertha went as a postulant to join her cousin Sophia and Apollonia[66] cousin of Fred Weld in May 1863. On 14 July following she received the habit of a novice from Cardinal Wiseman; she wore round her head since she was, as was custom, dressed as a bride, the circle of orange blossom which Winifreda wore for her marriage two days later.

Gwendoline announced her wish to join the Sisters of Mercy at Limerick during August 1867. A certain amount of ill health, the contemporary ailment of 19th century young women, a lung condition[67], followed and it was not until the Spring of 1869 that she went, not to Limerick, but to the Benedictine convent at Atherstone despite the doctor's advice that 'Ireland would be healthier than Leicestershire'. The fact that the Reverend Mother was Laura's cousin, and the shorter distance may have governed the choice. Her response to the Religious Life was to be less easy than Bertha's, who on family visits was pronounced to be 'the picture of health and happiness'. There was a good deal of illness, though she survived till 1908 and the age of sixty three.

A member of the family who suffered from the lack of educational opportunities open to Roman Catholics was Frank who left Oscott in 1868, to compete as Robert Ornsby[68] put it 'in the unequal struggle of native powers against disciplined skill'. After two desultory years at home, he joined Fred Weld and Mena in Australia and thereafter in the Straits settlements, but his lack of purpose clearly gave his parents some anxieties throughout his short life.

Admidst the paradoxes of the rulings on Roman Catholics and their education, Rudolph, born three years later than Frank, fared much better than he. After only a year at Oscott, Rudolph left in the summer of 1866 at the age of twelve and in October went to 'Dr Burney's Naval Academy' at Gosport. Uncle Samuel Phillipps' son Alfred had procured the Navy Exam papers. The following April, Rudolph passed out sixth out of the 65 successful candidates from a total complement of 105, to join the *Britannia* at Dartmouth. In August 1868 he gained a first class certificate with rating as a midshipman and twelve months sea time allowed, and proceeded via HMS *Victory* at Portsmouth to HMS *Bristol* at Spithead. A year later, the personal intervention of his naval great uncle, Henry

March Phillipps caused Rudolph's posting to the much sought after Flying Squadron Cadmus; he sailed for South America, Australia and the Far East on a four-year engagement.

Ironically enough, the close proximity and power of influence over him of men other than Roman Catholic throughout this period, and at a younger age, was infinitely greater than it would ever have been at an English University. Yet Oxford with its connotations was regarded as the more dangerous. That Rudolph encountered challenge to his views is illustrated by a letter home in 1876.[69] He asked for some pamphlets, including those of his father, to be sent to him

> ... There having been once or twice rather bitter arguments upon the impossibility of Catholic loyalty on board here.

Throughout his naval career he showed himself well able to defend his position.

For the remainder of the decade of the 60s, Ambrose and Laura were faced with increased commitments: some of their own choosing, others forced upon them. The affairs of the newly acquired estate came into the latter category. While with the urgent repairs there was no choice, the decision whether to make the large mansion of Garendon their primary home was not reached for two years. In regard to Corporate Reunion, Ambrose's involvement did not cease with the ban on his membership of the APUC. Though his loyalty had caused him to resign, he chose to regard his continued support and writings for the *Union Review* as exempt from the interdict and a separate issue.[70] His championing of the rights of the Catholic laity in the face of Ultramontane opinion which extolled the increase of centralized power in Rome, at the expense of local Churches, did not wane. Ambrose was not afraid to make public pronouncements in this field; some of which documents ie. those which concerned the whole matter of infallibility, belong to the area of the first Vatican Council and will be treated in the next Chapter under that head.

Laura's commitments increased also, as the neighbourhood in which she visited, taught, consoled, became larger with the acquisition of the Garendon estate. The sixties was a time of expansion in the Roman Catholic parishes initiated by the de Lisles, with crowded chapels, increased number of confirmations and flourishing schools, But there is plenty of evidence to show that conditions of life in the Leicestershire countryside for the poorest remained very harsh. Laura's distribution of food and petticoats, though doubtless appreciated, were but a drop in the ocean.

During the autumn of 1863, Edward Pugin took measurements of Garendon and drew plans for alterations. They were not quite so radical as those made earlier by his father, the second of which turned the mansion into a mediaeval Castle, complete with moat, and large separate church. The chief change was to re-style the west front to create a huge picture gallery ninety four feet long and a dining room of a length of forty feet. Since the following winters were extraordinarily cold, with oil frozen in sanctuary lamps and snow so deep as to make a carriage unusable, the discomfort will have been considerable. The motives which led the family into such an enterprise have been discussed. It may well be that the disappointments of the Shrewsbury inheritance and forfeiting of property at Alton had something to do with it; as also the marriage of Winifreda to the son of a Duke (Norfolk). Ambrose may have felt the need to keep his end up.

He did not proceed without the opinion of Brother Simeon[71] who was summoned from his seclusion at the Monastery and in whose prophetic powers Ambrose had such faith. It is presumed that his was a favourable reaction to the move to Garendon as the chief family home, for in April estimates for the work began to arrive. The lowest by far from Gascoignes of Leamington was accepted, with a deduction of £600 made by altering some of the proposals, to save money.[72] The sum agreed in the contract was £5,838 for which a new roof, attic floor and indoor chapel, as well as west front were to be provided; the work to be completed by July 1865. When the Abbot from Mount St Bernard's Abbey had blessed the building operations, Gascoigne with twenty men of his own and twelve more engaged from the neighbourhood, began 'the work of destruction'. Furniture in the house was sealed up in rooms that were to be spared.

8 May was Ambrose and Laura's last Sunday at 'dear Grace Dieu, where we have lived for twenty nine years and three months'. It had been decided that they should live at Longcliffe

Lodge, a large farm house on the estate, until Garendon was finished. Amo, Fanny and the infant Everard moved into Grace Dieu.

The work at Garendon did not advance swiftly or smoothly; some of the walls were found to be in poor condition for which a further £100 was allowed. In addition family visits to the site on an almost daily basis were made as the destination of afternoon walks; alterations were the result. By October, Edward Pugin pronounced that the work was being well done, but too little of it. It was clear by the spring of 1865 that the dead-line would not be met and not until St Ambrose's day (7 December) were the de Lisles able to leave Longcliffe Lodge after eighteen months, for their new home. Inevitably Gascoigne presented an additional bill of £2,500, which by negotiation over several months it proved possible to reduce to 'a present of £700'.

The enlarged house provided additional scope for entertaining (though guests had never ceased to be invited during the Longcliffe period). Particularly noticeable from the pages of Laura's diary was the greater number of clergy, both Anglican and Roman Catholic, with whom Ambrose was in touch; several were incumbents of neighbouring Anglican parishes who came to meals and to whom the de Lisles were invited. Bishops Ullathorne, Grant and Roskell stayed at regular intervals. During a visit by Bishop Forbes of Brechin, Bishop Roskell was a guest also. Ambrose escorted them for a walk together in the shrubbery; a most unusual occurrence in the contemporary ecclesiastical climate. William Lockhart, H. N. Oxenham[73], and E. S. ffoulkes who had all been members of APUC, and George Nugee[74] and F. G. Lee who were still associated with it, were probably those guests who conspired with Ambrose in the next move in the context of reunion. On 26 April 1866 a 'private meeting' took place in the Architectural Hall, 9 Conduit Street, in London. F. G. Lee opened the proceedings by saying that there was no connection with the APUC. This was purely a meeting of friends favourable to the Reunion. Since 467 persons were present, this was a far-fetched assumption. H. N. Oxenham was the only Roman Catholic who spoke. There was a speaker from the 'Russo-Greek' Church and the remainder were Anglicans: three laymen: Colin Lindsay,

CARDINAL WISEMAN,
Archbishop of Westminster

WILLIAM EWART GLADSTONE

CARDINAL NEWMAN,
painting by Emmeline Dearne
(detail) 1889

CARDINAL MANNING,
painting by George Frederick Watts RA

Garendon after alterations by Edward Pugin, drawing by A. de Lisle.

President of the English Church Union, a surgeon on its Council, George Boyle; and a handful of clergy. The proceedings lasted four hours until midnight, Laura commented 'I would not have missed it for anything'

The papers of the *Union Review*[75] for this period present some remarkable contrasts to the writings of the Ultramontane school of thought, and show that Ambrose did not stand alone among Catholics. Some Roman Catholic contributors wrote anonymously: *Presbyter Catholicus* commented on the 'sickly sentimentality and strange songs' then prevalent, which 'would have made my dear friend, the late Bishop Baines very, very sorrowful'[76]. 'I for one shall continue to labour and pray for peace and the removal of divisions' he wrote in another edition[77]

> I could name many who watch with interest all that our brethren of your Church do in spreading Catholic views, and who hold that the two Churches are just coming to agreement on essential matters, though my opinions about the wisdom of altering several of our disciplinary customs, eg celibacy, prayers in a dead language, the right of loyal Churches to settle their own internal affairs without the interference of the Roman Curia, gave offence in some quarters, they were received with approbation in others.

Catholicus Dunelmensis[78] wrote as one whose ancestors had always been Catholics, of the converts who

> serve to make our religion now as different from what it was when I was a boy, as the religion of the Church of England is to Wesleyan Methodism.

'Wild extravagancies and foreign eccentricities' were deplored on the part of those converts who 'in undue haste had turned into sentimental unmanly priests at Clapham, at Bayswater and at Brompton'.

> As for corporate reunion, he must be a short-sighted student of Church history who can deny that corporate reunion of separated Churches has continually taken place, and will take place again . . . whenever the Church in her wisdom shall find people prepared for the same.

Ambrose's contributions to the *Union Review* included a long essay[79] *On the present prospects of Reunion*. It contained comments on Pusey's *Eirenicon*, some material on explanations concerning the Immaculate Conception, on Bossuet, and the See of Peter as the centre of unity. He sent a copy of the 1866 edition containing his essay, to Newman.

Response to one another's writings was the subject of current letters between them. Newman had written earlier[80] to thank Ambrose for his reactions to the *Apologia* in terms which would suggest that he gave his approval to the way in which Ambrose was trying to minimise differences and difficulties between the Churches.

> . . . it pleased me very much to find what you thought of my late volume. It was a great trial to me to write it, and it is a great compensation to have favourable remarks upon it, such as yours I assure you, I esteem your approbation very highly, as coming from so good a Catholic and so true an Englishman and lover of England. The mixture of good and bad, which makes up the Protestantism of England, is a great mystery; He alone whose infinite Intelligence can understand the union of the two, can also dissolve it, and set the truth and the right free: but, if any human agency is to be much His instrument in any part of this work, surely it must begin by acknowledging, not denying, what Protestants have that is good and true, and honouring it in them as coming from the one source of all light and holiness . . .

Newman's pamphlet[81] in reply to Pusey's *Eirenicon* was published the same month as that of Ambrose. He had been driven, albeit unwillingly, to write it by the necessity to refute the views of such as Faber, Manning and Ward as being the only ones tenable by Catholics. His preference for English habits of devotion to foreign ones and rejection of exaggerations newly introduced, won him approval of Anglicans and 'old Catholics' alike. He showed a desire to remove obstacles to unity similar to Ambrose's whose congratulations he welcomed[82]

> It is a great encouragement. I have been full of anxiety about my pamphlet, there being so many parties and persons whom I had to keep in view, and to avoid offending. I have an especial desire to act considerately towards the Catholic movement in the Anglican Church because they have been severely handled, and because kindness seems a better way of dealing with them.

He commented, as Ambrose had done so, on the letters he had sent him twenty years before, and had been published in the *Apologia*.

> There were some too which were written and did not go ... from the shifting circumstances of the time ... I am now getting old[83] and tired – and have difficulty in laying out work for myself in prospect. You must not forget me in your good prayers.

Ambrose had written of the 'immense impulse to the Reunion movement' Newman's work on Pusey's *Eirenicon* had given.

In receipt of Ambrose's pamphlet, Newman wrote[84] of his pleasure

> ... in finding how very much I had in my own pamphlet run along the same lines as you. But it was not merely this personal gratification that I felt in reading it, for everyone ... must admire the spirit and tone of the whole composition.

To Ambrose's comment on the 'harsh and repulsive' tone of Archbishop Manning's recent Pastoral on the *Reunion of Christendom*[85] Newman tried to defend the motives, if not the utterance: an Archbishop must be 'faithful to his trust'. Pressed further by Ambrose on the *object* of his pamphlet, the corporate reunion of the Anglican Church with the Catholic Body, Newman provided[86] an answer of great length. 'Nothing is impossible to God' was his starting point. What would be needed to bring the Anglican Church into a condition capable of union could be done in a succession of ages, but not in any assignable period; however, he could not conceive 'the Establishment running into Catholicism any more than I can conceive the Thames running into the Wash'.

Newman's Oxford plans were revived in 1866 by the personal initiative to Propaganda Fide of Bishop Ullathorne. Eventually an agreement was achieved whereby the building of an Oratory at Oxford was to be permitted, but a secret clause disallowed the presence there of John Henry Newman. The influence of such as Manning was obvious, with his strong fears as to what the effects might be. Bishop Ullathorne embarrassed by the course of events, hesitated to make the embargo known to Newman who began once more to circulate his friends for funds for the Oxford Oratory, Ambrose among them.[87] The true facts leaked out in the pages of the *Weekly Register*.[88] A group of English Catholic laymen incensed by the insult offered to Newman wrote him an open letter[89] of support. Ambrose's name was one of the signatories, as were those of many of his friends; William Monsell was the chief perpetrator.

> We, the undersigned have been deeply pained at some anonymous attacks which have been made upon you they may be of little importance in themselves, but we feel that every blow that touches you inflicts a wound upon the Catholic Church in this country. We hope, therefore, that you will not think it presumptuous in us to express our gratitude for all we owe you, and to assure you how heartily we appreciate the services which, under God you have been the means of rendering to our holy religion.

Newman was deeply touched, but Talbot's reaction in Rome did not augur well for the future, when he wrote to Manning[90]

> ... I look upon the address of the English laity as the most offensive production that has appeared in England since the times of Dr Milner, and if a check is not placed on the laity of England they will be the rulers of the Catholic Church in England instead of the Holy See and the Episcopate ... Dr Newman is the most dangerous man in England, and you will see that he will make use of the laity against your Grace. You must not be afraid of him. It will require much prudence, but you must be firm, as the Holy Father still places his confidence in you; but if you yield and do not fight the battle of the Holy See against the detestable spirit growing up in England, he will begin to regret Cardinal Wiseman who knew how to keep the laity in order.

The flow of letters that continued to pass between Ambrose and Lee reveal unremitting efforts towards the cherished objectives: Lee's reprint with commentary, dedicated to Ambrose, of Franciscus a Santa Clara (Christopher Davenport's) 17th century treatise[91] on the 39 Articles seen in a light acceptable to Roman Catholics; a book on the validity of Anglican Orders[92]. From Ambrose came an essay in a collection[93] on Reunion, with Introduction by E. B. Pusey' and one on the

Filioque clause[94] (for which he derived help from E. S. ffoulkes), to mitigate misunderstandings with the Greek Church.

In March of 1867 came a proposal that Ambrose should accept nomination to stand as a Member of Parliament for the Northern division of the county of Leicestershire, since Edward Hartopp was proposing to resign. He declined, but accepted the office of High Sheriff in 1868 when he chose F. G. Lee as his chaplain. A decree from Rome in 1866 further to dissuade attendance at other than Catholic churches, the de Lisles chose to ignore. When in London, or away from home, after their own church services, they might hear Liddon preach in St Paul's or accompany Lee to churches of his choosing: the interest in 'Anglican sights' did not flag. On a stay in the Close at Lichfield as guest of Archdeacon Moore, Ambrose had no scruples in attending the Cathedral. Still active in many ways (60 years of age at the end of the decade) he was capable of 13 mile walks. Rheumatism, particularly in his hands, drove him to Wiesbaden and Hamburg to take the waters at the suggestion of his doctor, in 1868. In 1867 there had been a visit to Paris for the exhibition and to keep in touch with his French friends. Other holidays were spent in bracing resorts such as the familiar Whitby.

Strenuous outdoor pursuits and self-denial were practised by the de Lisle family for reasons of health, economy and spiritual benefit. Though probably not quite as severe as during the 1840s, conditions among the inhabitants of Hathern, Shepshed, Thringstone and Whitwick which encompassed the Garendon estate, still gave rise to much involuntary deprivation, sickness and poverty. Laura recorded cases where women gave birth on bare ground without clothing, food or warmth. Men without food or work who poached for game received one month's hard labour, unable to pay the fine of twenty shillings. Laura made frequent excursions into the villages in all weathers; 'soaked through' or 'my boots filled with water'. Her child-bearing and rearing over, she intensified her works of mercy. After mass at 8 am at Shepshed, she 'staid' until 7 pm at night offering relief of various kinds[95], not only to Roman Catholics. At the request of the vicar of Hathern (who had married Ambrose's cousin Betsy Phillipps) she became a member of the Mothers' Meeting and made regular attendances.

The dying was her especial concern: 'sat with old Jelley who is going; he asked to kiss Margaret'; 'to Mrs Sheehan who is dying; she took leave of us imploring every possible blessing on myself and all the family'; 'Coates died at nine very happily; Margaret and I had seen him at three'. Some serious accidents received primitive treatment. 'Green, the dog doctor, had his foot cut off in the threshing machine'. The following day Laura called with Gwendoline; he was 'getting on wonderfully well'. Later Margaret read to him. Rudolph read to Isaac Bond, a groom 'hurt by Flirt falling on him'. The injury proved fatal. When babies were thought to be dying, Laura would regularly be sent for to baptise them. Henry Collins, her spiritual director, clearly was of the opinion that time spent on these village expeditions was excessive; he urged Laura in her relations with the poor not to stay long on visits, advantage could be taken. 'never make them feel they had anything to offer' was his advice; what she had to offer was what counted and must be accentuated. It was strange counsel and seems to have been largely ignored.

When there was smallpox in the villages Laura went alone; otherwise her sons as well as her daughters helped to teach in the schools on Sundays. The family became depleted by the return of Mena and her children, plus Frank, to the Antipodes in 1869, on the appointment of Fred Weld as Governor of Western Australia; also by the death the same year, of Osmund, fifth son at the age of barely 22 years, of typhoid fever after a fortnight's illness, at the Agricultural College at Cirencester. Six weeks later on 8 December 1869, Laura wrote in her diary

Vatican Oecumenical Council opened by Pope Pius IX.

Chapter 11

The First Vatican Council –
Last days

THE event of the first Vatican Council in the years 1869–70 and its significance, is a field so large that it will not be treated in a general but restricted, and therefore inevitably partial, way; what will be considered is that part of it which concerned Ambrose de Lisle; the letters and documents he wrote in relation to the Council, its possible agenda and consequences; the letters and documents written to him by his friends, and their contributions to the whole debate.

A General Council of the Church was a phenomenon to which Ambrose had looked forward certainly since his early conversations with the Oxford Men in 1841. He visualized a Council, the highest ecclesiastical authority, as able to remedy the evils of the disunion of Christendom, and to advance an era of concord and brotherhood. He had run into censure by his suggestion of the expediency of calling a Council in his pamphlet of 1857 *On the Future Unity of Christendom*: such was the prerogative solely of the Pontiff. So the initial news of the impending assembly in Rome found him full of hope, he even imagined that it might prove possible for Orthodox and Anglican bishops to attend. As others began to formulate their aspirations as to the agenda, Ambrose began to have fears also. All these manifestations are revealed in his correspondence.

The timing of the preparations for the Council were as follows: two days after the publication of the Bull *Quanta Cura* and the Syllabus, 6 December 1864, Pope Pius IX spoke to the Cardinals alone on the possibility of his summoning a Council. He asked them, under strictures of secrecy, to study the matter and send a response. Of the 21 replies, two were negative; six expressed doubts and hesitations; the majority were in favour and sent in some suggestions for the agenda: clear statements of Catholic doctrine where it had been challenged were suggested as needed; thought given to improvement in the education of the clergy and the re-invigoration of mission to the heathen. Several Cardinals mentioned the possible role of the Council in the return to Catholic unity of those separated[1]. Two Cardinals referred to the definition of the Infallibility of the Pope. A Commission was set up of five Cardinals to make preparations; in April 1865, again under conditions of secrecy, a letter was sent to 34 bishops chosen by the Pope, of whom Archbishop Manning was one: later, there were included certain Oriental Uniat bishops.

Talbot's departure from Rome divested Manning of his influence; nevertheless the Pope allowed him access to the central [preparatory] commission, and certain of its papers, which put him in a further strong position. While he and the Bishop of Ratisbon were in Rome for a large gathering to celebrate the centenary of the death of St Peter in 1867 they made a solemn vow[2] that they would do all in their power at the forthcoming Council to secure the definition of Papal Infallibility.

Newman and Pusey speculated by correspondence in the Summer of 1867 as to why a Council was to be held. Newman wrote[3]

> There has been talk of it for years – first I heard the wish from such Catholics as Mr de Lisle – then from our own Bishop – and from Rome.

Bishop Ullathorne had suggested that the modification of the canon law, at the wish of the French bishops, and confirmation of the dogma of the Immaculate Conception, might be discussed. Newman agreed it was a point he had insisted upon himself, showing that the *normal* mode of deciding a point of faith was a Council, not the Pope speaking *ex cathedra*.

> That there is a party who would push for the Pope's Infallibility, and be unscrupulous in doing so, I can easily believe too – but this to me personally is no trouble – for they cannot go beyond the divine will and revealed truth.

Bishop Ullathorne had written[4] to Ambrose also on his return from Rome from the centenary celebrations; 'half a mile of mitres in pairs in the procession formed the episcopal contribution'. He confirmed that an Oecumenical Council was to take place the following year [It was in the event delayed twelve months on account of the war between Prussia and Austria]; the Pope had so announced to the assembled prelates. 'It intends' Ullathorne wrote 'chiefly the revision of the Canon Law and discipline of the Church', to adapt it to the exigencies of present conditions[5]. Ambrose had not hesitated to speak his mind before Ullathorne's journey[6]. It was utterly out of the power of Churchmen to stop the onward progress of ideas, he thought. If there were to be a gathering of Bishops in Rome that Summer

> I hope a strenuous effort will be made to reconcile those at variance, and, by a judicious acceptance of accomplished Facts without approving what was evil in accepting it, to prove that Catholicism is fit for its new Mission *to sanctify the modern world.*

He referred, of course, to the lost temporal power, but in so doing presented in broad terms what were to be his hopes of the eventual Council.

Ambrose's dislike of the position adopted by the Ultramontanes grew as 'the party' (so he referred to them) became increasingly outspoken. 'I am not of the number of those who would confound the Infallibility of the Catholic Church with the modern claims of the Papacy and its officials', he wrote[7] to Montalembert. He associated the words of extremists in France such as Louis Veuillot, formerly of *L'Univers*, with those in England of W E Ward who took over the *Dublin Review* as editor in 1862. In 1866 Ward published in book form[8], a series of articles which had appeared first in that periodical, and which put forward a view of papal prerogatives which greatly increased their scope: for example, encyclicals and allocutions issued by the Pope he held to come within the sphere of infallibility, a distinction easily determined by men of fair ability from the authoritative tone of the Pope's own words, that he was speaking *ex Cathedra*.

Newman told Pusey that he thought Ward's notions

preposterous[9], and permitted Fr Ignatius (formerly Henry) Dudley Ryder[10], a member of the Birmingham Oratory, to write a pamphlet in response. (In the event he produced three, for Ward wrote two more, and Ignatius Ryder tried to provide replies to them all). His salient points concerned the 'means of assistance', the theological advice, the consulting the Church, the influence of the episcopate, the Convention of Councils, with the aid of which the Pope defines; and the competence of the *Schola Theologorum* alone in the determination of the force of his utterances. Ambrose congratulated 'dear Cousin Harry Ryder'[11] on his 'able and reasonable words' and added his own in that he believed Infallibility to be a conjunctive and collective attribute of the whole Catholic Church. He had used much the same language in an answer[12] he had given Charles Langdale earlier in 1867, who had written on behalf of a group of English laymen to solicit the signature of Ambrose to an address destined for Pope Pius from the Catholic laity of England, on the centenary celebrations. Ambrose suggested that the formula he had received to be signed was faulty at various points: he was therefore unable to add his name.

> The Personal Infallibility of the Pope has never been an article of Catholic Faith, and when assumed has a tendency to discredit the claim of the Church herself to this great prerogative.

He hoped that another address, 'no less expressive of devotion to His Holiness', and 'more in conformity with Catholic Orthodoxy', could be presented.

The next piece of writing relevant to the Council by one close to the de Lisles, was by Peter Le Page Renouf who made regular visits to Leicestershire. His appointment as Inspector of Catholic Schools from 1864 brought him yearly, at the least, to the schools Ambrose had founded at Shepshed and Grace Dieu; fundamentally a scholar, he had set his heart on teaching at a Catholic College at Oxford. Renouf had already published an essay on the subject which he knew had Ambrose's sympathy, *University Education for English Catholics*[13]. Renouf with Newman's approval, in the Spring of 1868 published a short paper entitled *The Condemnation of Pope Honorius*[14], in which he gave a historical survey, without polemics, of the case of the seventh century pope who was censured for heresy.

In a letter of considerable interest and importance Newman told Renouf[15] he 'found it to have the completeness and force which I had expected in it'. It had not 'seriously interfered with my own view of Papal Infallibility'.

> I hold the Pope's Infallibility, not as a dogma, but as a theological opinion . . . [it] must be fenced round and limited by *conditions*.

Honorius had acted without consulting his natural advisers.

Ambrose, already alive to the problem posed by Pope Honorius, made further reference to his own views on the Infallibility question in a letter to Renouf[16] much on the lines pursued earlier in regard to its collective, corporate nature;

> It is a gift promised to the Body in its corporate action but not personal to any one as *distinct* from that Body . . . Thus the Roman Bishop as successor of St Peter whom all Antiquity calls Prince of the Apostles would have the highest personal share indeed in the collective gift, but this would not exempt him from the possibility of error, and would account for those occasional facts of erring in the history of the Papacy – and all other Bishops would have a personal share also, equally compatible with personal errancy . . .

The correspondence that survives between Ambrose and his Anglican friends such as Bishop Forbes, suggests that much as he wanted to see the Council break down the barriers between the Churches, he did not take much active part in the attempt, though he approved it, to secure Orthodox and Anglican presence. Ambrose certainly, with his knowledge of the French scene, furnished Bishop Forbes with an introduction to Montalembert, when he went to France in February of 1868, and suggested that he should see the Archbishop of Paris, Monsignor Darboys, who was a moderate and likely to be sympathetic; also the Emperor and the Cardinal Archbishop of Bourges.

> It would be well to get some letters from *them* to the Pope. Let me hear from Paris.

A year earlier, an exchange of letters had shown Bishop Forbes' hopes of the prospects of the Council, as expounded by Ambrose, shortly after the first public announcement. He urged[17] Ambrose to put himself 'into communication with

Propaganda, or the proper influential quarter in Rome' and suggest

> That the Council which would really seek to heal the wounds of Christendom would either draw in Anglicans or leave them without excuse. Whereas such a Council as merely registered foregone conclusions would but perpetuate the wounds of the Church.

Ambrose who had suffered too many rebuffs at the hands of Propaganda lightly to expose himself again with so little chance of success, did not take up this suggestion, though he wrote to the Bishop[18]

> It will be no less beneficial to us than to their own Churches that their [non-Roman Catholic] bishops' voices should be heard in the Council . . . It is at Rome that the learned men of all the Christian Communions should set before the whole Christian world, whether united or not with us, what are those things which they believe to be faulty in our system . . .

The attempts made in the correspondence between Bollandist Victor De Buck, SJ in Brussels,[19] with Richard Simpson in London, Dr Pusey in Oxford and Bishop Forbes in Dundee, to further the possibility of Anglican participation at the Council owed nothing, therefore, to Ambrose. It may just have been he who urged Forbes to send a copy of his Commentary on the 39 Articles to Dr Döllinger in Munich (but more likely to have been Dr Pusey). In response[20] Dr Döllinger express his wish that Anglicans had brought out more distinctly the errors of the Popes and their advisers.

> The Ultramontane party (particularly in France and England) refuse to see the beam in their eye, and talk constantly as if they were invulnerable and immaculate and as if the Oriental and Anglican Churches had only to say with contrite heart and mien 'mea culpa' and to submit unconditionally to every error in theory and every abuse in practice.

The approaching Council, Döllinger maintained, filled many 'reflecting sons of the Church with anxious dismay'.

> . . . for there is a mighty power at work, which intends to use the Council as an engine for the corroboration of their favourite views. My hope and consolation is that a small but resolute

knot of Bishops, who will make resistance, is quite sufficient to frustrate their designs, but there must be some moral courage.

Döllinger was referring to the invitation to the Bishops of the Eastern Church to attend the Council, which was issued in September 1868 after previous comment in the press. The Patriarch of Constantinople having stated that the only basis of reunion was that the Church should revert in doctrine and practice to the form which existed before the schism, giving up all added since that time, handed back the envelope. Ambrose 'deeply regretted the blunders committed by the officials of the papal court'[21].

The three so-called Jansenist bishops in Holland were not included in an invitation, nor the Anglican bishops on account of their Orders not having been recognised. A letter in September 1868 to all Protestants and other 'non-Catholics' exhorted them to 'reconsider their position and return to the fulness of Catholic Faith and to Catholic Unity from which their Fathers had broken away'. So disappeared the hopes of Ambrose and his friends in several Communions, of what the Council might have been able to achieve in terms of reunion.

Pusey who had, until that moment, struggled for some kind of Anglican representations to be made to the Council, the subject of correspondence with Newman over several years, said that recent comments had put him 'quite out of heart as to any negotiations'[22]. He told Forbes[23] that explanations were needed before talk of union; the sending of written propositions 'were a much more systematic way than verbal discourse'. Dr Döllinger, Pusey reported, feared that the Pope's Infallibility would be decreed; Archbishop Manning being the mouthpiece of the party.

Montalembert's last two letters[24] to Ambrose referred to Manning's 'exaggerated doctrines about papal authority which was the rock on which the Catholic Church in England shipwrecked three hundred years ago', and of his 'fanatical spirit' which Montalembert thought would prevent any real progress of Catholicism in the United Kingdom. How 'unfathomable' he found the designs of God in allowing such as Dr Ward, Herbert Vaughan[25] and others to be representative of Catholic intelligence in England. On the eve of the Council Ambrose gave his views[26] to Bishop Forbes

> The propositions of Archbishop Manning will never become
> the faith of the Catholic Church; at present I believe them to be
> repugnant to it. On the other hand, there is too much of
> rationalising tendency on the side of those who oppose the
> extreme party, too little of ascetic piety and Christian humility
> ... *We* all feel that in our own Communion the abuses are
> enormous, our shortcomings numberless, our sins awful, we
> need an immense reform, but this reform must come from the
> Holy Ghost speaking through the Church, not through clever
> and learned, but crude and ill digested writings ...

William Monsell, who had been received as a Roman Catholic in Grace Dieu chapel in 1850 and still a visitor and good
friend, identified himself closely with Ambrose's views in 1869.
As a Member of Parliament he had not baulked to criticize
papal attitudes in foreign policy.[27] A friend also of Newman,
he wrote to him in August 1869[28] after a visit to France. He
had been staying with Bishop Dupanloup of Orleans, one of
the most prominent of the Inopportunist party which was
developing as the result of writings and rumour. The Bishop of
Orleans, he reported, was much alarmed at the efforts which
were being made to get the personal infallibility of the Pope
defined at the Council. To which of the English bishops could
he speak and rely on him and his efforts to defeat the project?
Newman suggested Laura's cousin, Bishop Clifford, who had
made his views clear also. Monsell continued: he had been
given a confidential document in French, clearly a translation
of a memorandum addressed to German bishops, of which the
author was Döllinger. Monsell felt it should be sent to English,
Irish and American bishops also. Newman agreed; he would
have it translated, printed and circulated.

Newman's own attitude to the possibility of this definition
is contained in the many letters he wrote to his friends,
particularly during the Autumn of 1869. A succinct resumé[29]
was written on 20 September of that year:

> Why is it, if I believe the Pope's Infallibility I do not wish it
> defined? Is not *truth* a gain? I answer because it can't be so
> defined as not to raise more questions than it solves.

They were to be prophetic words of considerable sagacity. It was the enlargement of the scope of Infallibility that he discouraged most. Manning's Pastoral Letter to the clergy, *The Ecumenical Council and the Infallibility of the Roman Pontiff*[30] did nothing to cheer him. Ullathorne, as ever in the middle ground, spread oil on troubled waters with his pastorals[31] as with his expectations of the Council; a good chapter drawn up on 'the status, sanctity, and obligations of the pastoral clergy'. Newman recorded his approval of the Pastorals;[32] Ullathorne's biographer commented that he was trying to keep Pope and bishops together, whereas Manning was trying 'to keep bishops out of it'.[33]

The good relationship which Ambrose enjoyed with his own Bishop of Nottingham, was exemplified by Bishop Roskell's letter from Rome, two days after the Council had begun, dated 11 December 1869. He commented on the de Lisles' recent loss of their son Osmund and of the holiness of life which the boy had attained. He then gave an account of the opening of the Council. The procession had started at nine in the morning punctually, and the ceremony had ended at three in the afternoon. The spectacle in the transept of St Peter's especially put aside, was very imposing. Next week, he reported, the election of the twenty four members of each of the particular deputations, on the Faith, Discipline, the Orders and Oriental affairs, would take place.

> 'As far as one can see the question of the infallibility will not be mooted. It is generally considered as inopportune. Dr Manning's letter to the clergy of the Arch-diocese is regarded with disfavour by all. I do not know the number of Bishops present but including the Cardinals they are more than 700.'

Dom Cuthbert Butler's definitive book on the Vatican Council[34] records with censure the successful attempt (by Manning and others) to arrange that the deputation on Faith contained twenty four bishops who were in favour of the definition on papal infallibility, and none of the opposition party; and wrote of it as 'a serious blot on its [the Council's] doings'. The English bishops were displeased at the manoeuvre; apart from Robert Cornthwaite of Beverley for whose appointment Manning had been responsible, none held the extreme views of the Archbishop of Westminster. So sure was he of the justice of his

cause that he brooked no opposition. Acton, who had gone to
Rome to observe the proceedings, noted in his journal words
spoken to him by Archbishop Darboys of Paris[35]. Archbishop
Manning had been 'trying to convert him'

> He thought Manning very absolute and trying to make up by
> exaggeration for the short duration of his Catholicism.

Ullathorne wrote home using the word 'intrigue'.

By a process of petitions, counterpetitions and a special
commission, beyond the scope of this book, by 1 March the
Pope had confirmed that the matter of infallibility was to be
discussed; five days later came the public announcement. In
April, having read two letters in the press by Newman, Ambrose addressed to him[36] a long letter in connexion with what
he called the 'ill-omened question of the separate personal
infallibility of the Pope' which he felt, to quote the Bishop of
Orleans [Dupanloup] not only had thrown the Catholic world
into a state of perplexity and alarm, but that 'it is rekindling
extinct animosities between Catholics and our Separated Brethren of other Christian Communities.' He drew attention to
what he called the 'unequal and imperfect' representation of
the Catholic Church, as that of England in the unreformed
Parliament of 1831, which could overrule and set aside 'the
principle of moral unanimity' and 'a truly ecumenical pro-
nouncement' for a more nominal majority of episcopal votes.
He referred, of course, to the large number (276) bishops
present from the Italian as compared with the lesser number
from England, France[37] and Germany. Ambrose felt himself on
the eve of what might be a third tremendous rending of the
Church. He had hoped, rather, that the Council had pressed
for the reunion of divided Christendom and 'the consolidation
of Catholic piety and faith among ourselves'. Instead, it might
yet be seen dividing and convulsing the small remnant of
God's people.

Newman in his reply[38] explained his letters to the press. He
had written to Bishop Ullathorne to Rome[39] one of the most
confidential of his life; copies had somehow been taken; they
had travelled to London and reached the English papers in a
partially inaccurate form. (Although he did not mention it to
Ambrose, what had not been inaccurately rendered, was that

part of Newman's criticism of the Council's apparent intentions which included the phrase 'why should an aggressive insolent faction be allowed to "make the heart of the just to mourn, whom the Lord hath not made sorrowful"'?) He hoped the letter 'had wriggled into public knowledge for some good purpose'; he wished that a strong lay petition might reach the Bishops to beg them use their influence 'to let matters alone'. He ended on a calm note

> Anxious as I am, I will not believe that the Pope's Infallibility can be defined at the Council till I see it actually done. Seeing is believing. We are in God's Hands, not in the hands of men, however high exalted . . . when it is actually done, I will accept it as His act; but until then, I will believe it as impossible.

It was a duty to act strongly and vigorously, in the matter, to be full of hope and of peace, and to leave the event to God.

On Wednesday 13 July 1870 the dogma on Papal Infallibility was decreed in the Council. Archbishop Manning had spoken for one hour and fifty minutes (in Latin) during the general discussion, but had failed to achieve the definition in the extreme form that he had wished. On 21 July Ambrose and Laura called to see Newman at the Oratory in Birmingham, obviously in need of his guidance. A few days later Newman drafted a letter[40] to Ambrose which he then decided not to send; he had suffered enough from misrepresentation to risk his views being once more spread abroad. But that he changed his mind on the substance is most unlikely, since he used the material at a later date[41], it is therefore worth repeating.

Newman had seen the new Definition since the de Lisles' visit; he was pleased at its moderation. The terms were vague and comprehensive. Personally he had no difficulty in admitting it. The question was, did it come to him with the authority of an Ecumenical Council? The Council had been legitimately called, prayers had been said. On the other hand, it could not be denied that there were reasons for a Catholic, till better informed, to suspend his judgement on the validity. Ever since the beginning, there had been opposition to the definition of this decree; when it was actually passed more than eighty fathers had absented themselves. If the fathers were not unanimous, was the definition valid? As at present advised, he thought it was. But whatever was decided, 'the scandals which had accompanied it will remain'. It seems probable that it was his talk with Newman, a week after the publication of the definition, that led Ambrose who had been so strong an opponent, to agree to accept it and on Newman's terms.

Critical events, especially those within the family circle such as the death of Ossy in 1869, further increased Ambrose's already heightened sense of apprehension. His correspondence during the early 1870s was full of foreboding, his own life-expectancy nothwithstanding. 'If I live "to bring Margaret out"', he wrote in his mid sixties, with no sign of illhealth, and Margaret's first season a mere few months ahead. Laura described in a letter[42] to her youngest child Gerard, at school at Oscott, Ambrose's reactions to news from Atherstone Convent that Gwendoline was ill. Laura had gone over immediately, found her very unwell, but nothing dangerous; Laura had been able to return to Garendon for the night:

> I determined for several reasons to go home, one of them being to reassure your Papa, for he had immediately made up his mind that all would soon be over.

In relation to national and international news, Ambrose tended to take a dramatic view: his letters[43] to Monsell contain references to 'the obscurity of the present world-wide cataclysm', 'this blinding chaos', 'the horrors of modern history'. He was particularly affected by the murder of Archbishop Darboy of Paris during the rising of the 'Commune' in the Spring of 1871. Ambrose's belief in the trustworthiness of signs and portents as a guide to the future remained with him and was never buried deep; it rose to the surface at times such as these. An optimistic view of world events was not precluded. He did not cease to repeat his wish that Catholics paid as much heed as other Christians to Biblical prophecies. A time would surely come of 'unbroken peace between all nations'; of the 'eternal reign of Christ and the last Resurrection'.

In spite of his premonitions, Ambrose's decease, so long anticipated, did not occur until 1878. During the first seven years of the decade, the customary activity did not flag, with new schemes almost up to the end. Domestic events included the long-awaited marriage of Alice and the terrible accident to

Amo's wife Fanny, which placed her two children in Ambrose and Laura's care. The upbringing of their own sixteen children almost over, they now assumed daily responsibility for two grandsons, clearly regarded as an enrichment. Alice's health in the winter of 1870 gave her parents great concern; severe headaches and 'pains all over' were diagnosed as 'gastrick fever' and treated largely with 'mustard plaisters' at the back of her head and down her spine. The doctor was called almost daily, and on two occasions twice in a day, during the course of a fortnight. But on her recovery, which was complete but slow, there was a more serious problem in the family in regard to Amo's wife, Fanny, who began to behave very strangely: 'very nervous', 'very full of delusions', 'a return of her highly excited state' were Laura's comments. At midnight on 26 March 1871 just as Laura was getting into bed, Amo's pony carriage came to fetch her to Grace Dieu.

Fanny's tarlatan dress had caught fire as she was lighting a candle for her two boys to go to bed. She rushed from the passage to the drawing room where Amo was fast asleep. He threw her on the ground, rolled her over and put out the flames with his hands, which became badly damaged. A doctor came at once and slept in the house; next day a specialist came also and pronounced that although Fanny was 'a good deal burnt', he had great hopes of recovery. Two nuns from a French Order arrived to nurse Fanny who seemed gradually to improve; as also the burns on Amo's hands. But just over a month after the incident her state deteriorated and she died in the small hours of the morning of 28 April, her family round her. Ambrose wrote in a letter to Rudolph 'She, poor dear, made a very edifying end and her funeral at Grace Dieu was a very solemn one'.

Edwin, Alice and Winifreda had decorated the chapel. Lockhart sang the Mass with three assistants in copes. Four monks including the Abbot, from Mount St Bernard attended; one of them, Fr Collins, preached on the text 'All souls are mine'. Wyvers, the organist from St Chad's Cathedral in Birmingham, played and singers from the same formed the choir. All five of Fanny's brothers who were Anglicans were present, with two sisters-in-law 'who assisted in the gallery'. A requiem was sung for Fanny on subsequent days in the chapels of Shepshed, Whitwick and Mount St Bernard.

The current craving for memorials was not denied; a window to Fanny's memory made by Hardmans of Birmingham. was placed on the west wall of Grace Dieu chapel and a painting commissioned of Fanny on her favourite horse 'Sultan'. As a consequence of her death Amo, who had taken his bereavement 'much to heart', went abroad for a year. Laura after a stay of nearly two months, and having arranged for Grace Dieu to be let, moved back to Garendon with Amo's two boys, Everard and Bernard and their governess; an arrangement which persisted until Amo's remarriage in 1880. From now on Laura's diary entries were filled with the exploits of her grandchildren.

There were happier family occasions in the 1870s, one of them the marriage of Alice to Arthur Strutt, second son of Lord Belper. The two families had long been friends, as also Arthur and Alice; the difference of religion which had seemed to provide a barrier against marriage, was eventually resolved, though problems remained which were to increase in the future. Alice had been to stay at Kingston-on-Soar, the home of Lord and Lady Belper during January of 1873; she returned home on the 28th, Arthur Strutt had proposed marriage and she had accepted. It was agreed by the bridegroom's family that there should be a Roman Catholic marriage service, but Lord Belper was adamant that any sons must be raised as Anglicans. Ambrose and Laura called to see him by appointment;

> We had a confidential talk with Lord Belper in the study about Arthur's future prospects which are better than we had expected, but he does not give in about the boys.

Ambrose wrote to Lee about his prospective son-in-law.

> He is a member of your Church but pious and very moral and good and high Church in his principles, the marriage is to take place (DV) in our private chapel ... He has been attached to my daughter for several years, and she has returned the attachment for some time, though at one time we rather opposed it. It is a very satisfactory marriage from a worldly point of view, as the family are very wealthy, and in other respects it is also most satisfactory for he is personally all we could desire, and the family are most amiable and delightful people and they have been for many years among the number of our most

intimate friends. The young people are to reside only 20 miles from hence, so that is some alleviation for me in parting with my darling Alice, who has always been, as you know, my pet child, and the pride and joy of my existence – but I do not know what I shall do without her, especially in the celebration of the Divine Offices . . .[44]

The wedding ceremony took place on 22 April 1873; a dispensation from the Bishop of Nottingham for the mixed marriage had been obtained, but it did not permit Bishop Clifford to preside, nor for there to be a mass. Lockhart officiated and preached. A chef from Brunetti's of Lower Grosvenor Street had arrived four days earlier and prepared the wedding breakfast. The Yeomanry who had been exercising in the park, escorted Arthur and Alice to the lodge gates in their carriage. Thereafter the couple made their home at Milford House on the outskirts of the large industrial village of Belper on the banks of the river Derwent, dominated by the mills which had brought the Strutt family their style and prosperity.

Their rise from humble beginnings, was a particularly Victorian phenomenon, and originated when Jedediah Strutt, a journeyman wheelwright turned farmer, solved in 1756 the problem of adapting the 150 year old mechanical knitting frame to ribbed hosiery. After perfecting the invention, Jedediah from his farm started as 'a putter-out' of hosiery in his district. In 1762 he moved to Derby with his equally enterprising wife, the daughter of his landlord, with whom he had grown up during his seven years of apprenticeship from the age of 14. By 1769 and the age of 43 he was a prosperous man. With the help of his three sons to whom the empire passed, he built up one of the largest cotton businesses in England, celebrated for its size, its exceptional buildings and equipment, and for the welfare of its 2,000 workers. The inventions of Richard Arkwright received financial backing, as did the Derby Infirmary. In 1813 the brothers William, George and Joseph Strutt were held to have a million pounds between them.

William was Arthur's grandfather. He bought the 1200 acre estate at Kingston from the Duke of Leeds in 1796 and left it to his son Edward, Arthur's father. Determined that Edward 'should make the fullest use of opportunities which he had

never himself enjoyed', William Strutt sent Edward not into
the firm of W. G. and J. Strutt whose management passed to the
hands of cousins, but to Cambridge; he then studied law in
London and was admitted to Lincoln's Inn and the Inner
Temple. He became Liberal Member of Parliament for Derby
in 1830 and subsequently for Arundel and Nottingham, Chief
Commissioner of Railways and Chancellor of the Duchy of
Lancaster. In 1837 he married the daughter of Bishop Otter of
Chichester; in 1856 he was raised to the peerage as the first
Lord Belper. They were not the achievements of a man who
could be persuaded easily to change his mind, so Alice was to
discover to her cost.

Alice gave birth to a son at Milford House during the
following year; Laura who went to be with her, commented

> One bottle of chloroform was used and a second begun which
> had a most marvellous effect on her and her baby was born
> without her knowing. She was wonderfully well and the baby
> too. [Alice was thirty four].

Three days later the child was baptised by the vicar of the
nearby Anglican church at Hazlewood, as Lord Belper had
decreed, and given the names Edward Lisle. Laura recorded 'I
did not assist'.

Nearer home, Laura faced problems in the schools she and
Ambrose had founded many years earlier, in which her guiding
hand was constant. The 1870 Education Act had provisions
consequent upon the introduction of compulsory education.
Denominational schools were to be supported by voluntary
subscription and assisted by government grants which were
doubled; non-denominational or board schools were to be
maintained by an education rate. Some grants for denominational schools had been operating since the Education Code of
1862, provided the school reached a certain standard. Payment
was by results of examination by Government inspectors. The
maximum amount provided fourteen shillings per child; four
shillings for a minimum of two hundred attendances and eight
shillings for passes in all the three basic subjects of reading,
writing and arithmetic. Two shillings and eight pence were
deducted for each failure.

The principle of denominational inspection of schools was allowed by Archbishop Manning to lapse in return for increased Government aid. 1870 was the last year in which the Grace Dieu school at Turry Log on the road to Whitwick, and the school at Shepshed, were inspected by Renouf; he pronounced the standards satisfactory. In May of 1871 Laura drove to Shepshed to meet Blakiston, the newly appointed Government Inspector for the greater part of Leicestershire. Under the new Code he could only examine children who had two hundred and fifty attendances in the past year; this amounted to a mere 40. Next day she drove the Inspector to Grace Dieu, where only 85 children were eligible for examination out of 252 on the roll. During the following month Laura presented the schoolmaster at Grace Dieu with the Government report:

> ... most unsatisfactory. No grant to be given this year on account of 252 having been at the school, whereas only 142 ought to have been.

It fell to Laura's lot to tell one of the schoolmistresses at Shepshed she would have to go on account of the consequent lack of funds. In the following year, 1872, results were better at Shepshed: of 63 children examined there were only 7 partial failures, but the Inspector insisted on the provision of a mistress for the Infants. With only 35 pupils left to teach, the schoolmaster wanted to leave. At Grace Dieu Laura was told that no grant would be forthcoming unless 'Old Needham' ceased to teach the younger children.

In 1873 matters were much the same. Laura wrote in her diary:

> At Grace Dieu 200 present in both parts of the school; Patrick Edwards Schoolmaster; only 26 passed in reading; 34 in writing, 36 in arithmetic out of 68 presented. In the Infants' School under Miss Fogarty 87, all that were examined, passed capitally. Edwards is to have notice given to him.

Shepshed presented a rosier picture

> In all 130 present; 35 older children and 38 under 7 examined. All passed except one boy in arithmetic and another in reading.

Laura confided in Renouf by letter (though he was no longer responsible) about the problems, which were two-fold:

first, children were frequently placed in factories soon after the age of 11; second, English schoolmasters were hard to find; Irish ones such as the master at Grace Dieu, were not so popular, even among Irish children; all the children at Shepshed school were English. Should she try and find nuns as teachers, she enquired, as a way out of her difficulties?

The education of the de Lisle children was drawing to an end; Gerard, last son, went to Oscott in 1871. Ambrose and Laura took him to Birmingham, called at the Oratory to see Newman, who was out, so they had tea with Ambrose St John and then left Gerard at school.

> Poor Gerard kept up capitally until the fly drove up to take us away when he cried much.

Edwin left for good in 1872, having won a number of prizes. He had at one time considered the priesthood, but now his future was uncertain; Laura wrote to Rudolph

> I am so disappointed that Edwin does not intend being a Priest but perhaps Gerard may have that grace. I should much like to have one dear boy a Priest.

Edwin later attended various European universities for short periods, but not, it would seem, for any prescribed course of studies. Clearly had it been permitted, the mental discipline of an English university would have been of benefit to him. Subsequently as a writer and Member of Parliament, he did not find it any easier than did his father to express himself without exaggeration.

Archbishop Manning, unchanging in his attitude towards university attendance, made in 1874 an unsuccessful attempt to establish a Roman Catholic College for higher studies in Kensington. Newman found himself, without consultation, on a list of members of its Senate. He suggested alternative names.[45] 'Why not Mr de Lisle?' he wrote to correspondents.

From the sale of various personal possessions, it seems apparent that another financial crisis threatened Ambrose and Laura in the 1870s. In May of 1870 the representative of a London silversmiths came to weigh the plate; he pronounced it was worth £950 and offered £1000, which was accepted. It was carried away in three large chests. Three years later

Ambrose told Gerard at school that the carriage horses were to be sold; he rationalized the sacrifice by pointing out that they were unreliable animals; other neighbours of rank and substance such as Lord John Manners had told him they were doing likewise; it was cheaper and better to hire post horses. He told Gerard of the 'charming little villa at Nanpantan', some four miles south of Garendon, which he and Laura were shortly to make their home, and of the boring for coal which had reached a critical stage.

Ambrose had been attempting to dig wealth out of the ground for many years at various sites on the estate. Successful excavation by neighbours spurred him on. Mining for lead in Tickow Lane near Loughborough had seemed promising in 1866, but there were no takers for shares in a prospective lead mining company. Trace of alabaster had been found near the obelisk in Garendon Park, but the possibility of exploiting it was short-lived. The search for coal was of longer duration. All through the later 1860s into the 1870s surveys were made, shafts sunk, specimens examined. There were law suits also in respect of bad advice and what Ambrose called 'chicanery' in a letter to Gladstone.[46] After boring to a depth of 801 feet and 7 inches and the expenditure of much money and effort over many years, the enterprise was abandoned.

Generous hospitality was one of the causes of the financial straits; old friends continued to be entertained at Garendon and new guests added. It remained one of the chief ways in which Ambrose could exert his influence. John Patrick Crichton-Stuart, 3rd Marquess of Bute,[47] for example, made his first appearance in 1871. An idiosyncratic Scotsman with a predeliction for monasticism and gothic styles in architecture and decoration, he married Gwendoline Howard, stepdaughter of Winifreda, the following year. With this connection and many interests in common, it was not difficult for Ambrose to secure Bute's cooperation in the campaign mounted by Gladstone in 1876 in support of the Bulgarians under attack from the Turks; Bishop Thomas Joseph Brown of Menevia and Newport, and Bishop Herbert Vaughan of Salford, eventual Archbishop of Westminster, also made their first visits. The most influential guest of all arrived at Garendon on 7 October 1873. Ambrose and Laura postponed their move to Nanpantan Lodge in order to entertain him in more style.

William Gladstone, at the time Prime Minister, arrived during the evening; Ambrose drove with him in a carriage from Loughborough station. Henry Fearon, Archdeacon of Leicester, a frequent visitor, dined with a few others; all except the hosts, Anglicans. 'Much conversation with Mr de Lisle' wrote Gladstone. Next day he was escorted in very good weather over the Charnwood hills to Longcliffe and walked on the rocks. The party then drove to the Reformatory and Mount St Bernard. Gladstone's diary commented[48];

> We went over the whole [Monastery] and I had some conversation with the monks and with an Italian Benedictine. Mr Ottley[49] dined; he said the graces as did Archdn Fearon yesterday ... My conversations in the day with Mr de Lisle were wound up with one at night wh only terminated at 2.15pm [sic]

The last day of the visit was also fine. Ambrose and Gladstone walked and talked in the garden; finally, as Gladstone wrote,

> At Loughborough after further conversation bid farewell to my kind, devout and liberal-minded host; a very interesting person.

Laura wrote[50] enthusiastically to Rudolph of the visit of one whom she persisted over the years in describing as Mr *Glastone*.

> Mr G is the most charming, agreeable man I ever saw in Society. His conversation is perfectly bewitching. He knows everything and speaks upon every subject in so pleasant a manner. Nothing dictatorial about him and his voice is [a] most agreeable, pleasant one. Margaret[51] is now quite delighted she did not go to Dorlin because she has made the acquaintance of Mr G. She says she would not have missed such an intellectual treat.

Newspaper accounts of the visit were both scurrilous and inaccurate: it was said that Gladstone had invited himself; that the visit lasted ten days; that it had something to do with 'the politics of Rome at this remarkable crisis of affairs'. The call at the monastery received the worst abuse in relation to 'this strange excursus to Mr de Lisle's place'. The *Pall Mall* spoke of Gladstone 'about to assume the cowl of a monk'.

From consequent correspondence,[52] the extent to which

Ambrose and Gladstone had been drawn together by the days and discussions at Garendon becomes clear. Moreover, on Gladstone's side there were signs of what was to come: glimpses of intention, attachment, distaste, loyalties. Where these ran counter to Ambrose's own sense of allegiance, opinions and prejudices, he did not hesitate to say so. The fact that he was addressing the Prime Minister did not inhibit his capacity for speaking his mind.

At first the letters contained pleasantries and exchange of views on such subjects as literature; for example, on Dante and Homer. Ambrose and Laura were bidden to stay at Hawarden. Then books were presented: from Gladstone the works of Abbé Blosius[53] (to whose writings Ambrose had long been attached) translated into English by the Attorney-General; followed by W. F. Wilkinson's tract on *Special Providence and Prayer*.[54] Ambrose sent his own book on prophecy; he was clearly disappointed at Gladstone's lack of comment at this stage; also his translation from the Italian of *Il Diario Spirituale*.

Early in 1874 the mood of the letters changed. Gladstone dissolved Parliament and went to the country; he proceeded to lose the election that followed. A Conservative government led by Disraeli swept in. How much Gladstone was affected is hard to gauge, particularly in the light of a subsequent letter from Ambrose[55] which indicated that Gladstone had hinted of this possibility during the Garendon visit and that 'these events in some respect will not have been unwelcome to you'. Gladstone responded[56] the following day.

> Convinced that the career of strife, and tension in strife which alone my political position offers me, is not the right food for the latter stages of my existence upon earth ... I have ever desired that a way of escape might be opened for me ... I do not say I shall disobey calls of political duty, indeed I am pledged to the contrary, but they will be obeyed if at all with great reluctance, and I hope they will not come.

Gladstone's motives in engaging in his next undertaking do not appear to have been to any major extent governed by disappointment or need for retaliation, though his loss of popular support may have heightened the emphasis he placed on loyalty. He was a man of strong religious cast who thought in moral terms even on secular issues. Finding himself freed from political responsibilities, it should have been no surprise that he turned to campaigns which had a religious and moral base. He needed a new cause; two emerged to which he felt constrained to draw public attention. They followed closely upon one another and had several elements in common: the threat to civil allegiance posed to English Roman Catholics by the recent Vatican Decrees, and the atrocities committed upon Eastern Christians in Bulgaria by the Turks. Ambrose became involved in both.

Attempts have been made to account for Gladstone's writings on the first of these issues by suggesting that the conversion of his sister Helen and certain friends of his youth, namely Manning and James Hope-Scott[57] to Roman Catholicism, followed by his former Cabinet colleague the Marquess of Ripon in 1874, prompted him to react as he did. Although it must be admitted that there was to be an overwhelmingly emotional element in the pamphlets Gladstone wrote at this point, that the intellectual basis was weak and this caused inconsistency and lack of sustained argument, it was not Roman Catholicism *per se* that he attacked. Gladstone had a regard for *Catholicity* and for the faith and practice of the early Church. His friendship with Ambrose surely had its basis here; what drew them together was the sharing of views in this area. It was what he saw as '*Romanism*' that he deplored, considered growing and therefore dangerous. (He thought in particular that it had caused Roman Catholics to go back upon undertakings made earlier, in order to secure political advantages, which it was alleged, had denied belief in Papal Infallibility). As a corollary, Gladstone admired the Eastern Churches, and the stand taken by them, by the Old Catholics and by the recently excommunicated Döllinger, in opposition to such trends. Newman had recognised that it would be difficult for the precise, and restricted, nature of the Vatican decrees to be understood; Gladstone illustrated this difficulty by drawing exaggerated conclusions, but he was encouraged by contemporary ultramontane writings to do so. Manning's *Caesarism and Ultramontanism* written in the spring of 1874 suggested that papal infallibility was unlimited.

These various facets of Gladstone's thinking emerged during his correspondence with Ambrose during that year, with the latter trying to redress the balance when he thought he saw excess of strong feeling. On 10 April[58] Ambrose saw fit to comment on the recent visit of two of his sons to Rome and reception by Pius IX, of whom he realized Gladstone did not approve.

> His Holiness made them a most striking address both in point of wording and manner, and they were all charmed with their visit. He is really a wonderful man to be able to do all he does at 83 and after having suffered so much and so long.

In a subsequent letter he added,

> We are not bound by his [the Pope's] political views.

Ambrose asked whether Gladstone had seen the remarkable Pastoral from the Bishop of Orleans (Dupanloup) on supposed visions and miracles. It had been published in the *Correspondant*; he would send a copy. Ambrose commented later[59] on Gladstone's intention to visit Döllinger at Munich. He referred to his own acquaintance with Döllinger but added, 'I never think of him without pain'. Ambrose drew attention to his newest article in the *Union Review*, *On the present condition of Christendom*.

> It takes my view of the German schism and adverse therefore to that of Dr Döllinger.

Gladstone extolled in a letter of 26 April, an article on Bishop Samuel Wilberforce which had just appeared in the *Quarterly Review*. Ambrose took the opportunity in his reply[60] to comment on the sympathy which members of the Church of England in general showed (as did Wilberforce and Gladstone) for the Eastern Churches

> in the same breath in which they denounce the errors of Rome. Unless they are prepared to accept every doctrine of Catholicism except the Pope, all the rest are held in a more pronounced form in the Eastern Churches, than in the Western.

Gladstone accepted the comment.

Your remark about the Eastern Church raises some most interesting points. Let us try and touch them when we meet.

Ambrose had drawn close to anticipating what was to be Gladstone's main premise: the political danger of what he saw as the imperialistic outlook of the Papacy, which had recently derived new strength.

Ambrose and Laura's visit together in the summer of 1874 was postponed by Gladstone on account of the death of his wife's brother, to whom Hawarden belonged; but the correspondence continued. Ambrose expressed his pleasure[61] that Gladstone was intending to oppose the Archbishop of Canterbury's Bill for the Regulation of Public Worship and the importance of such a stand for the future prospects of reunion. Gladstone was preparing an article on *Ritualism and Ritual*, but before its publication in the *Contemporary Review*, he turned his attention to attitudes towards the Papacy in Germany. Bishop Forbes of Brechin who was close to the Old Catholics, came to stay at Hawarden; Gladstone in September went to Munich to speak with Döllinger. The visit was not without effect. On 20 October Ambrose wrote to comment on the Ritual article.[62] Whilst commending it in general, he drew attention to a paragraph 'not less eloquent than the rest' which 'wounded the feelings of your Catholic friends'. Gladstone had strengthened the force of his argument since his visit to Döllinger and attacked English Roman Catholics for their placid reaction to the Vatican decrees (though this was not the point to which Ambrose took exception). He wrote,

I have no wish to Romanize your church, but she must be Catholicised or her doom is certain and inevitable.

Ambrose added that he would not wish to achieve union 'by forcing uniformity on the Anglican or any other separated branch of the great Christian tree, a uniformity which is not necessary for unity'.

If we ever renew the conversations we commenced at Garendon they will be in the interest of mutual peace and not of an internicine war discreditable to Christianity and fatal to its grandest hopes.

He was to have his opportunity sooner than he expected; on

25 October Ambrose received a summons to visit Hawarden within the next few days, without his wife. Gladstone had drafted his pamphlet *The Vatican Decrees in Their Bearing on Civil Obedience: a Political Expostulation* and wished to have Ambrose's opinion.

Ambrose wrote to Laura from Hawarden on the 28th, having arrived on the 27th.[63]

> All this morning I have been busily engaged with Mr Gladstone in reading his forthcoming Tract 'on the civil relations of R Catholics under the Vatican Decrees etc'. This at least is the substance of the title of the work which will probably soon see the light, and I doubt not draw forth the Oratorian lion from his den. I haven't time to tell you the details of this work, the ability of which is incontestable, and the effect of which may be to elicit from our Authorities some useful statements, which certainly seem to be needed at the present moment.

He gave Laura a picture of Mrs Gladstone, pleasant, agreeable and kind; 'quite different from what I took her to be'.

> She is a most motherly person and interests herself just as you do in the condition of the Poor and of the inhabitants generally of Hawarden estate . . . You must go on praying that my visit may be productive of some good. Hitherto all has gone most satisfactorily.

Next day he wrote again at length. The whole of the previous day, with the exception of a walk with Gladstone of an hour and a half to see the old ruined Castle of Hawarden, had been spent in reading and discussing the long Pamphlet which had been prepared 'in explanation and in vindication of the paragraph in the article on Ritualism which gave us all so much offence' [the evil deeds of the reign of Mary Tudor].

> It is certainly a most masterly and eloquent production, and though I induced him to soften down some of its expressions, it is impossible to conceive anything more strong than the way in which he inveighs against the Vatican Definitions. Of course it is only from that point of view he either views it or impugns it. The Tract will of course enrage a great many Catholics . . . I am really glad that it should be published, as it will make it absolutely necessary to produce an adequate satisfactory answer . . . I have had conversations also of immense interest on other topics.

Sir Arthur Gordon[64] had appeared and Lord Acton also; 'with each of these', wrote[65] Gladstone, 'and with Mr de Lisle I had a great deal more of conversation on the MS and kindred subjects ... Mr de Lisle's decl [aration] on finishing was 'There are things in it wh I could wish altered, but as a whole I think it will do great good.'

The day following Gladstone recorded that all his guests had now read his article and he had had varied conversations at length.

> They all show me I must act mainly for myself.

Acton wrote to Simpson.[66]

> Objections in detail were attended to, but to all political, spiritual and other obvious arguments against publication he was deaf.

But Ambrose had an important private message to convey to Laura at the end of his letter; he had been able to achieve a private triumph.

> As soon as his Treatise is printed he [Gladstone] is going to send me a *proof* copy *before it comes out*, so that I may send it *to Father Newman for his inspection.* But mind you do not mention this to any one.

Nothing is clearer than Ambrose's determination throughout the visit to Hawarden and sight of Gladstone's pamphlet, that Newman should answer some of the points raised. Ambrose had maintained relations with the Oratory in readiness for moments such as these. Newman had come to his help in his crisis immediately after the promulgation of the Vatican Decrees; here was another such.

He had paid Newman a visit at Edgbaston in July 1874. Then, the joint visit to Hawarden having been cancelled, Ambrose and Laura had journeyed in August to Dorlin in Scotland to stay with Winifreda and her husband, now raised to the peerage as Lord Howard of Glossop. They found Newman's old friend Ambrose St John acting as tutor for the holidays to young Frank Howard, son of their host, a pupil at the Oratory School. Newman had warned St John not to take risks boating. A ferry had recently been sunk, he reported; it

took four hours by dog cart to reach Dorlin. Winifreda
Howard had the reputation of being 'a great danger-seeker
and likes the roughest seas immaginable'. 'Be on your guard'
wrote Newman.[67] An invitation was given for St John to visit
Garendon and its surrounding sights. (It had proved possible
to move back there after a period of exile and financial
stringency at Nanpantan Lodge). He came for a few days in
mid October, shortly before Ambrose's stay with Gladstone; St
John wrote[68] later to Laura

> I suppose that which struck me in all I saw must strike
> everyone; viz the amazing work one single man, devoted to his
> work, can achieve in a life time.

The proofs of Gladstone's pamphlet duly arrived and were
passed to Newman during the first week of November. Ambrose had written on the 2nd[69] describing the circumstances of
the Hawarden visit.

> ... it seems desirable in the interests of Peace and Truth that a
> satisfactory answer should be given from a moderate point of
> view ...

Gladstone had agreed to send a proof. 'He thinks, however,
that it would be better for you not to correspond with him
about it, in the first instance at least'. Extravagant articles by
Ward, Monsignor Patterson and Lord Robert Montague[70]
giving 'extremist and most offensive explanations' of the Syllabus and the Vatican Definition had produced 'a sense of
irreconcilable discrepancy' when seen with the views of non-
Catholics. Ambrose anxious to secure Newman's co-operation,
resorted to his customary exaggeration: the repeal of the 1829
Catholic Emancipation Act was in the offing; the only thing
that could prevent it was reasoned explanation of the Vatican
Decrees. Gladstone had referred most favourably to Newman,
Ambrose added for good measure.

A few days later he wrote[71] again; every sentence designed
to encourage Newman to respond. What was being written
was a caricature of the Catholic Faith. Warming to his subject,
he added it was possible that 'Mr Gladstone maybe won to the
Church of God though at this moment he partakes a little of
the spirit of a Saul'. Ambrose varied his approach once more

as he began to describe the holy living of the Gladstones: they
and their family went over a mile to church each morning at
seven whatever the weather; they had done so twice in pouring
rain during Ambrose's visit. Such attempts to interpret and
commend the religious outlook of others were part of Ambrose's nature; they appear throughout his life. He continued

> Mr Gladstone has promised me, when once these tangled
> questions are cleared, to devote all his energies for the rest of
> his days to corporate reunion.

There was a final entreaty, once more typical of the man: 'I
commend all my hopes and the great work, the dream of my
whole life, to *you* and to God'.

Though at first cautious, it was not within Newman's
nature to yield to effusiveness, Newman recognised the force
of the argument behind it. Other voices joined that of Ambrose
to persuade him that he must act. Not solely to Gladstone
must a response be sent, but to the perpetrators of the extremist
views which had caused his outburst. Ostensibly, an answer to
Gladstone would provide the opportunity.

Newman's first reaction[72] to Gladstone's pamphlet was,
therefore, not antagonistic, on account of the scope it offered.

> I am not at all sorry that he is publishing such an expostulation
> as this; it must turn to good. Today's papers say that Arch-
> bishop Manning is going to have a great meeting and to bind
> us all to certain propositions.

He thought Gladstone had been misled in his interpretation of
the decrees of 1870 by judging the theological wording by the
rules of ordinary language. Bishop Fessler [who had been
Secretary of the Council][73], Newman commented, had toned
down newspaper interpretations, both Catholic and Protestant,
without one hint from the Council itself to sanction him in
doing so.

But as the pressure placed upon him by Ambrose and other
friends, to write himself grew more insistent, Newman began
to have reservations.[74]

> You know it won't do to write unless one writes well. It would
> do more harm than good. I will write if I can, but I am not sure
> I can. And anyhow, if I write, I am sure kind friends will

expect too much of me and will be disappointed. I could not write anything long.

Ambrose replied next day.[75]

> I hear constantly from Mr Gladstone and I am sure his object is truth and justice. He too is looking forward earnestly to what you have to say on this very important subject.

At first the anticipated difficulties of writing almost defeated Newman and his progress was slow; gradually they were overcome. His answer to Gladstone in the shape of *Letter to the Duke of Norfolk* was completed during the last days of December 1874. He wrote to Ambrose[76] to tell him to expect one of the first copies.

> I have gone into most of the subjects which came into controversy – and have all through said all I think – so I am not sure to please everyone – perhaps not in all this any one.

At the same time, Ambrose had elicited the help of Laura's cousin, Bishop Clifford (who came down to stay at Garendon in January 1875), in writing his own commentary on Gladstone's *Expostulation*. Ambrose's article appeared in the *Union Review*'s February edition. In it he expressed the opinion that the Vatican Definition, 'far from amplifying what was previously held by all orthodox Catholics is rather a Definition of *limitation*. Some ultra-zealots . . . had held before the Council that the Pope was *personally* infallible'. This could now be denied by the orthodox Catholic. He also went on to say that the Expostulation would not operate as a hindrance in the great work of 'Ecclesiastical reunion'.

Newman wrote[77] to thank Ambrose

> for your excellent reply to Mr Gladstone. It is clearly and persuasively written and should I think must please any one . . .

He was grateful for the kind reference to his own article: 'I esteem such a notice from you as a very great honour'. Ambrose was much consoled[78] since he had received 'the harshest letter' from his new bishop[79] condemning eight propositions in his article and rebuking him for having submitted his MS to Bishop Clifford and not to himself. Newman offered much support[80] and told him he was 'deeply grieved'.

It is simply shocking, but it really must not discourage you. Be of good heart, there is nothing more to come. It is impossible you can be touched. The Bishop of C is a good Roman Theologian and knows when a book is safe, and when it is not . . .

Ambrose was able to answer Bishop Bagshawe[81] in a conciliatory manner with Bishop Clifford's help, though he insisted that his remarks as to a prominent party with extreme views were by no means out of order, since the Pope himself had referred to such in a conversation with one of Ambrose's relations

adding that they did the Church more harm than even her professed enemies.

Congratulations on his own article continued to arrive: from Lockhart, Emly (formerly Monsell) and again from Newman himself.[82]

I hear many accounts of priests etc. who like your article, and not one of readers who dislike it. To me the question is, first is the *scope* and substance of the whole good? secondly, is the tone and object good; and thirdly, the opinions in it, do they transgress that liberty which the Church allows? This is what I think most candid men would ask, and would answer in the affirmative.

Later in February 1875 Ambrose sent Newman another set of proofs: those of Gladstone's second pamphlet *Vaticanism*, an answer to replies and comments. This time Newman decided not to respond[83]; Gladstone had said little about his own article; he had 'gone off on an attack on Archbishop Manning'. Ambrose, however, produced an essay in the *Union Review* of May 1875 entitled 'On the Perpetual Belief of the Catholic Church concerning the Office and Authority of St Peter', which earned Newman's approval as also that of Bishop Ullathorne[84]. He thought it 'singularly good and able and to the main point, and cannot fail to do much good in a circle of Anglican readers',

the remark that there must be some one to judge between Council and Council is very happy, and cuts through the whole question. I could almost envy you this remark, so brief, yet so full and so decisive . . .

He said he had been prepared to speak in the Council, in the interests of conciliation with the views of the Archbishop of Paris cited by Ambrose, but had been prevented by illness. 'I could not leave my room on the day when my turn came'.

During the years 1875–77, the last three of his life ironically enough, Ambrose was at the height of his potential influence since he was meeting and corresponding simultaneously with three great men of his age, Newman, Gladstone, and now, to a greater extent than heretofore, Manning.

The most important occasion at Garendon of 1875 was the visit in September of Archbishop Manning, a Cardinal since 15 March. Ambrose had seen him in London earlier in the year on at least three occasions. From subsequent letters it would appear that the matter of corporate reunion had been discussed as the result of conversations Ambrose had had with certain unspecified Anglicans. He reported to the Cardinal that he saw certain tendencies among 'the High Church body'; one seemed to favour the creation of an Anglican Uniat[85] Church with *sub conditione* ordination and an English Liturgy; the recognised policy of the Holy See in previous such transactions had been evinced.

Ambrose continued to visit Gladstone in London. After one such meeting on 16 April 1875 he wrote[86] to Newman

> . . . I spent a long morning with Mr Gladstone, . . . I have no doubt that eventually he will be a Catholic; *humanly* speaking, but for the two new Definitions 1854 and 1870, he would have been one now, and the only thing he does not see is the harmony between the present and the past of the Catholic Church, as it is represented by what *he* calls Rome- the Eastern Church is evidently his beau-ideal of of Catholicity . . . He thinks you, me and many others of our Communion excellent Catholics, but bad Romanists – and Romanism or Ultramontanism he thinks a system that vitiates the mind . . . He has a great veneration for you, and if there were more like you to rule the Latin Church, he would soon be one of us.

A considerable family wedding had taken place the previous day in Brompton Oratory, between Ambrose and Laura's step-grand-daughter Angela Howard[87], and Marmaduke Constable

Maxwell, Master of Herries, a relation of Laura's. Cardinal
Manning officiated. It was followed by a notable gathering of
'old' Catholic families, at which Ambrose and Laura were
present, and Winifreda hostess. A few days later Laura was
called to Alice who gave birth to a daughter at Milford. On
Arthur Strutt's instructions, Laura wrote to Ambrose for him
to bring one of the monks from Mount St Bernard to baptise
the child, as he wished her to be brought up a Catholic; she
received the names Laura Mary.

Six weeks were spent in London that summer, Margaret's
first season. Laura called on Mrs Glastone [sic] 'by appointment'. The usual pattern of social and ecclesiastical engagements was followed, often with useful purposes in mind; for
example Ambrose had used his influence to secure a new post
for his son-in-law Fred Weld; he wrote to Emly

> Lord John Manners has received a favourable answer from
> Lord Carnarvon[88] as to our application for Fred Weld of the
> Tasmanian Governorship.

Mena set sail with eleven children, two nurses and several
ponies on a ship of only 90 tons, during the course of the year.
According to an account of the voyage given later by one of
her daughters, the ship's officers were often drunk and the
storms violent; Mena, at times of danger, gave orders to the
sailors and took command.

Rudolph, whom they had not seen for four years, returned
to England during the stay in London.

> He was looking particularly well and much grown, extremely
> tanned and a great quantity of whiskers, beard etc. the same
> affectionate, light-haired boy he always was.

For the Cardinal's visit in the autumn 'a man cook from
Gunters' was imported from London, although Manning himself was a man of austere habits.[89] But a large house party had
been invited also: the young Duke of Norfolk, his two sisters,
William Lockhart, some Clifford relations of Laura's and Lady
Flora Hastings, who lived at nearby Donington and in 1877
married the Duke; Lord and Lady Belper and Archdeacon
Fearon, who were, of course, Anglicans, completed the house
guests, though some Roman Catholic priests from the villages

were invited to meals. The weather was exceptionally beautiful for the entire three days, as Manning was escorted round the estate. The culmination of the visit was his preaching to two thousand people in the park on Sunday 12 September from the Greek Temple built by Ambrose's name-sake in the 18th century, which he had converted into a chapel. Later the Cardinal preached at Shepshed 'after the English Compline which he liked much'. He drove back in a closed carriage while most of the party walked to Garendon on the warm evening. Flora Hastings impressed Laura when she left by driving away 'in a carriage of four horses, two postilions and two powdered footmen behind'. Bishop Bagshawe of Nottingham made the first of many visits next day; it was a sign that reconciliation between him and Ambrose had been effected.

Opportunity to continue to write to Cardinal Manning was offered to Ambrose later in the year, and in 1876, over two issues: the first was a published proposal for the formation of an Anglican Uniat Church. It was anonymous, written under the pseudonym *Presbyter Anglicanus*, had the title *Christianity or Erastianism*, and was dedicated, by permission, to the Cardinal. Few of Manning's letters to Ambrose at this period have survived. In those which have done so, he did not offer much encouragement. He pointed[90] out that he did not believe in Corporate Reunion;

> I am convinced that the greater part do not see the principle of Divine Faith. If they did they could not delay.

Ritualism in Oxford he had found intensely anti-Catholic. 'In this form it is like Donatism or the Photian Schism'.

Ambrose took the proposition very seriously; it represented so closely what had always been his dream. It is unlikely that he was aware of the stature or qualifications of *Presbyter Anglicanus* or he might have been disabused of the success of the scheme somewhat earlier. As it was he wrote[91] with great enthusiasm to Cardinal Manning on 12 January 1876.

> With you under God it rests to gather in the magnificent harvest, which the Lord has been preparing outside of us . . . if the snowball is favoured by the Holy See, it will gather round it even millions – all who care for Christianity in our very dear old England – and of one thing I am perfectly certain that WE

with our *countless encumbrances* and our *frightful burden of abuses* from *one end of the Earth to the other* shall never win England or any other nation again, but shall continue to lose every day more and more the few that remain to us. But behold the Lord sends us an offer of new Life, which may be a germ of moral regeneration for the whole earth under the fostering care of the Holy See . . .

Manning's answer has not come to light. It did not prevent Ambrose's further exhortation[92] as to the great opportunity that had been created.

This under God rests with you. If you give it a valiant support the movement will embrace all who are needed, from the Prince who is destined to rule us, to the peasant who waits upon the landlords of England . . . I have advocated and defended this corporate reconciliation of England for 40 years, and every year has rendered it less improbable if not more likely . . .

As had earlier been the case, Ambrose chose greatly to exaggerate the numbers of Anglicans, clergy and laity, who were likely to respond.

He sent a copy of the pamphlet to Newman who replied[93] that he found it remarkable that it had been dedicated to the Cardinal, *by permission*. It seemed to him a plausible scheme, but 'I am told few will feel inclined towards it of the ritualists'. He was more realistic than Ambrose whose hopes had been high, yet were soon to be dashed. The scheme had collapsed already, he told Newman on 22 January. He had arranged with the Cardinal the previous June that it should be published in its present form, but 'powerful influences more weighty than the Cardinal have intervened'; 'the infant was already strangled'. It might have succeeded, he still maintained.[94] Newman sent Ambrose two supportive letters.[95]

Nothing will rejoice me more than to find that the Holy See considers it safe and promising to sanction some such plan as the pamphlet suggests. I give my best prayers, such as they are, that some means of drawing to us so many good people, who are now shivering at our gates, may be discovered.

And later

I grieve indeed to hear what you tell me about Church matters and for the severe pain it gives you.

Such information as remains on the Uniat Scheme is contained in the pages of the short lived anti-Erastian, pro-Tory, Anglican periodical, *The Pilot*. *Presbyter Anglicanus* was one of the contributors. Ambrose was another; he wrote at length on the need for corporate reunion and on unity. The unsympathetic response by the Church press to *Presbyter Anglicanus* and his pamphlets (he wrote a second), was the subject of comment. Though he seems to have kept his anonymity, certainly in *The Pilot*, it transpires he was the curate of St Paul's Church in Brighton by the name of Edmund Samuel Grindle. Scholar of Queen's College, Oxford, he was ordained deacon in 1864 and priest in 1865; therefore presumably only about thirtyfive years of age in 1876. He had a restless record of curacies; the present was his fourth. He had been in the archdiocese of York and written some earlier pamphlets; one of which 'Episcopal Inconsistency, or Convocation, the Bishops and Dr Temple' tells its own story. Grindle may have been a man of ideas, but not of substance nor of influence.

What is significant within the pages of *The Pilot*, however, is that another enthusiast for a Uniat Scheme, Charles Walker,[96] who wrote at length on the merits of a Uniat proposal, chose to present his case in the form of four letters addressed to Ambrose. At the start he referred to the formation of the APUC in 1857.

> You, sir, from the very first sympathised most warmly with our object: in fact from your previously published treatise 'On the Future Unity of Christendom', the Association may be said to have taken its rise. As one of its earliest members, I feel that I can address present remarks to no one so fittingly as to yourself.

It seems clear that Ambrose had, as no other, established a reputation of sympathy across denominational boundaries.

1876 was quiet, and mainly spent in Leicestershire. Ambrose and Laura did not go to London at all until June, when he saw both Gladstone and the Cardinal.[97] Letters had continued to be exchanged with Gladstone and were shortly to be much intensified, as with Manning also on the same account, for

Gladstone was on the verge of mounting the second great campaign since his departure from office. 'I cannot tell you how intensely I feel about these atrocities of the Turks, and that England should seem to be implicated in them', Ambrose wrote[98] to Gladstone on 22 August 1876. It was just what Gladstone wanted to hear.

Riots in the Balkans against Turkish overlordship began in Bosnia and Herzogovina in 1875. A Turkish force sent in to quell the uprising was defeated. In May 1876 some Bulgarians, spurred on by this example, defied the orders of certain Turkish officials and killed them. A large contingent of regular soldiers of the Turkish army was despatched to the site; incidents took place in which some undisclosed thousands of men, women and children were put to death. Gladstone's motives for his campaign of the autumn of 1876 to bring attention to the event, were similar to those in his course of action of 1874 in relation to the Vatican Decrees and they have already been indicated. He was dedicated to the idea of a moral crusade; the fact that the victims in this case were predominantly members of the Orthodox faith created an extra dimension. Historians have added other contributory factors: that he was seeking, for instance, to conciliate Nonconformist opinion. The grounds of the campaign were 'our common humanity'; it was designed to appeal on a wide front certainly, but that it was directed towards a particular branch of the public is less convincing. Gladstone's request to Ambrose to secure Roman Catholic support would appear to sustain the former view.

Gladstone's reply[99] to Ambrose of 26 August took in a wide range of subjects; he ended

> But I have room in me to feel about the Bulgarian horrors. I wish *you* could keep the Pope straight in that Turkish matter.

On 3 September Gladstone wrote again.[100] He urged Ambrose

> to write to Rome and induce the Pope's advisers to bring him back from the wretchedly false position into which they have betrayed him, and with him the Roman Church . . . in regard to the Eastern Question.

The Turk, he maintained, had two special allies, the Pope and the English Government. 'Do not, I beseech you, omit to consider it . . . Do not, at the most solemn moment of religious offices, forget the Bulgarians'. Ambrose agreed to write to Cardinal Manning at once: the *Osservatore Romano* and the *Civilta Cattolica* had strongly defended the Turkish view of things. He would do his utmost to carry out Gladstone's suggestion and rejoiced that he was taking up this case in such an energetic manner. Gladstone's pamphlet[101] was published on 6 September 1876 so that Manning had seen it when he first replied[102] to Ambrose.

> I think Mr Gladstone's intervention and pamphlet to come at this crisis a simple disaster. It will heat men's passions and blind their understandings . . .

He was not aware, he said, of any position 'wretched' or otherwise taken up by the Pope and therefore had no grounds to communicate with Rome. If the British government proposed to liberate the Christians in the East from Turkish rule, either by a Protectorate or Confederation, he would be happy to help it forward, but 'the present clamorous and vituperative agitation seems to me to be blind, and without an intelligible policy'.

Ambrose was unwilling to let the matter drop and persisted with several more letters, 'disappointed at the sentiments expressed on the Eastern Question'. Manning's responses castigated Gladstone for his 'insolent and slanderous accusations' as to the Holy Father. Ambrose attempted to put the record straight: Gladstone had pointed out that *his advisers* had betrayed the Pope and put him in a false position. Moreover, the Catholic press of Europe had much to answer for. He ended

> I have never shrunk from expressing my convictions and if I continue to serve the Church as I have served her for 50 years, I must do so as a free and outspoken Englishman.[103]

As Gladstone toured England making speeches on the Bulgarian issue, Ambrose continued to ply him with support, and after several reminders, persuaded Gladstone to read his book on *Mahometanism in its Relation to Prophecy* which he had sent several years earlier. In Gladstone's company Ambrose met Liddon, of whom he was a great admirer as a preacher,

who was active in the promotion of a Sick and Wounded Fund
for those in combat against the Turks.[104] Ambrose made the
cause his own, circulated his friends and served on the Committee, 'the most active leading spokesman of self-consciously
English Roman Catholic feeling'.[105] House parties at Garendon
were made aware of the issues: Ambrose reported on one such
which included his friend of long standing, Lord John Manners,[106] 'we were 25 at dinner for three days and I had very
interesting conversations with him on the Eastern Question'.
Bute, no doubt as a result of pressure from Ambrose, sent
Liddon a hundred guineas.

Ambrose by the summer of 1877 had nine months of life and
one reunion scheme left. The year had begun tragically, Alice's
husband, Arthur Strutt, had been to show his niece the great
wheel (which his grandfather had invented) in the family mill;
his foot slipped and he fell between the large wheel and a
smaller one and was killed instantly. His funeral had been at
Kingston on 10 February, pronounced by Laura as 'One of the
most miserable days I have ever spent', Ambrose told Gladstone that it was 'one of the greatest afflictions of my life'. A
great deal of time was now to be devoted to Alice and her
children. In April, after calls in London on Cardinal Manning
and Gladstone, who dined with them later that same week,
Ambrose and Laura made a long stay on the Isle of Wight
where Alice had taken a house. The opportunity was offered
to renew acquaintance with W. G. Ward, to whose views on
papal prerogatives Ambrose had been so much opposed, Ward,
his wife and three daughters, lived at Weston Manor on the
Island. The fact that the two families met on such numerous
occasions during this visit says a good deal as to the magnanim-
ity of all parties.

At dawn on 2 July 1877, a strange ritual took place on the
steps of St Paul's Cathedral in London. A document, called a
Pastoral Letter, was read on behalf of three so-called 'bishops'
of the newly created Order of Corporate Reunion: F. G. Lee,
with the title of 'bishop of Dorchester', T. W. Mossman (an
incumbent in the Lincoln diocese) as 'bishop of Selby', and J. T.
Seccombe a doctor from the parish of Terrington St Clement
in Norfolk, who called himself 'bishop of Caerlon'. They
claimed to have received episcopal orders by the hands of

consecrators belonging to Roman and Eastern jurisdictions; 'three distinct and independent lines of episcopal succession'; their aim was 'promoting the grand and most necessary work of corporate reunion, the highest and greatest need of our time'. The three men set out with the idea of conditionally 're-ordaining' clergy on a wide scale, thereby bringing them all into Communion with the ecclesial bodies from whom their own alleged Orders had been derived.

Examination of the OCR in a life of Ambrose de Lisle must be confined to three areas of search: for the prime mover in this extraordinary scheme; for the identity of the consecrators; and into the accuracy of the accounts which maintain that Ambrose was most certainly involved. The strict secrecy which accompanied the setting up of the OCR, and especially the 'consecrations', create difficulties for the investigator. Lee told those he 're-ordained' that his Orders and credential were locked away in a safe; at his death all his papers were destroyed. His wife and sons were anxious to protect his posthumous reputation, as Edwin in particular was to prove concerned to protect that of Ambrose. No letters of his which contain any mention of the OCR now exist; two letters addressed to him on the subject appear in Purcell's *Life*; they are both from Aubrey de Vere: the first, dated 24 September 1877,[107] asked for some copies of the Pastoral, expressed interest in the OCR and denigrated the disparaging tone of the Church press in its regard. In the second,[108] dated one month later and of great length, he thanked Ambrose for the Pastoral and appeared to be inclined to take the OCR seriously. These tenuous associations of Ambrose with the 'Order' prove little, beyond the fact that he had knowledge of it and possessed some of its literature.

Various attempts to unravel the mystery surrounding the OCR 'consecrations' and the originator of the scheme were made during the earlier part of this century.[109] In answer to an enquirer,[110] G. Ambrose Lee gave as his opinion that Murano in the Lagoon at Venice was the place where his father had been 'consecrated'. 'I know positively that my father never went near Naples' [a suggestion that had been made]. It was likely, he wrote, that the consecrator was a Bishop in Catholic Communion. There had been no 'movement' whatever. As soon as his father started the OCR, nearly all his clerical friends 'cut him absolutely, for years he was almost entirely isolated'. George Nugee had been one of the first deserters. His father had admitted that the OCR had been a failure. Only the mystery which had never been formally cleared up could account for what Ambrose Lee considered 'the unmerited notice it obtained'.

The treatment by the Society of the Holy Cross of T. W. Mossman who was a member of this Association of celibate priests in the Church of England, by expelling him when he appeared as a so-called bishop, confirms these statements. 'The assumed jurisdiction of the Order of Corporate Reunion is without any lawful foundation', was the expressed opinion of the Society.

In 1921, Canon S. L. Ollard, who was a specialist on reunion movements, then a residentiary Canon of Windsor, began a correspondence with G. Ambrose Lee in relation to the OCR. Ollard enquired in particular as to his father's relationship with Ambrose de Lisle. Ambrose Lee wrote[111] of the voluminous correspondence over the years.

> Most of A de Lisle's letters – there were hundreds of them, I lent to Edwin de Lisle who never returned them . . . I did not read them all, but read enough to see that de Lisle was in the habit of coaching my father as to plans for bringing about Corporate Reunion, pointing out who – here and abroad – might be looked upon as friendly and who hostile. I do not think anybody who had read as many of these letters as I did could help concluding that de Lisle did as a matter of fact commit himself to the attitude which was condemned by the Holy See . . .

In a subsequent letter[112] Ambrose Lee, pressed by Ollard, referred to Ambrose de Lisle again. To the best of his knowledge and recollection, he wrote, the correspondence between Ambrose de Lisle and his father 'practically ceased by sometime before the OCR began'. He continued

> 'Certainly there were no letters amongst my father's papers from de Lisle for a long time before that event. In the late sixties and early seventies letters came *very* frequently . . .'

In 1939 Ollard had a long correspondence with H. R. T.

Brandreth[113], then a layman, who was gathering material for his book on Lee[114]. In a letter dated 22 January, Ollard wrote about the OCR:

> I became more and more convinced that the one hope of discovering the answer to these various puzzles was in exploring the manuscripts of A. P. de Lisle. I am sure that he was the effective originator of the OCR. Indeed Mr Ambrose Lee told me as much, though he did not know the details. He was the godson of A. P. de Lisle.

That Ollard should have come to this conclusion is puzzling; those letters of Ambrose Lee which have survived do not appear to provide corroboration for such an assumption. Moreover, Brandreth was later to discover a letter of Ambrose Lee of 29 June 1921[115] which stated

> the whole idea of the OCR, I am positive, was my father's. I recollect the initiation of it and his journey to Italy perfectly well.

He maintained in the same letter that his mother 'was one who knew everything. She never corrected my reference to the Venice consecration and always led me to believe that she concurred in my attribution of this event to that city . . .'

Brandreth in his completed volume on Lee came to the conclusion that Mossman's 'consecration' may have been carried out by a Bishop of the Ambrosian rite, connected with the Archbishopric of Milan; though research into records have revealed nothing. A consecrator of Armenian Uniat origin has been considered likely in the case of Lee. So the episode remains a mystery and the involvement of Ambrose de Lisle, likewise. One last search must be made: that is for opportunities when the scheme *could* have been hatched by Ambrose and Lee. Diary sources show that Ambrose saw Lee once only in London in 1875 and then at a dinner party in the company of others. Ambrose and Laura called on Lee in June 1876 (their sole visit to London that year) and he was not at home. In the spring of 1877 they met for two hours on 14 April and again on 19th, at luncheon at Lee's home with two of their children, Edwin and Margaret. There was a breakfast meeting on 22 April but not alone. Lee's son had suggested to Ollard that letters had ceased to be frequent. Complicity in a broad sense in a reunion scheme would seem to have been unlikely with this intermittent degree of contact.

Ambrose knew of the plans, so much is clear; the most likely part that he played, and this must remain conjecture, would have been in suggesting the names of possible 'consecrators'. Lee's son had drawn Ollard's attention to the role of Ambrose de Lisle as distinguishing who was friendly and who hostile; he had a large circle of foreign acquaintances. In November 1850, for example, Archbishop Nakar 'Bishop of Keriatium on Mount Lebanon' arrived at Grace Dieu with his interpreter, and said several Syrian masses; his See was in Communion with Rome.

Brandreth considered Seccombe's 'consecration' to have been carried out by Julius Ferrette, so-called Bishop of Iona, one of the *episcopi vagantes* of whom he had written in 1947.[116] Ambrose had entertained Ferrette also at Grace Dieu, in November 1866. That Ambrose would have agreed to any consecrations by Ferrette is highly unlikely, since he was not impressed by him and wrote to Lee in a critical vein[117]

> I am not sorry he came here, much as I wondered at his vulgar audacity in saying what he said in a Catholic House, . . . But it was well to find out something of the characteristics of a man who has passed through so many phases of religious profession, that one wonders he has not at last found out a little more moderation in the expression of his opinions. In a Protestant publication *Christian work*, I see two articles by him when he was a *Protestant Missionary* in Syria in 1864, 1865, so that his transition into the Monophysite Communion must have been rapid indeed, when we find him (if it be so which I much doubt) ordained a Bishop by the Monophysite Patriarch of Syria in June 1866 . . .

It may be that it was in order to avoid participation by Ferrette that Ambrose helped to find alternative 'consecrators'. There, in the present lack of further evidence, the case must rest.

During the course of the de Lisles' visit to London in June 1875 they paid a visit to the church of St Etheldreda, Ely Place, formerly the London chapel of the Bishops of Ely, recently acquired by William Lockhart, with some adjoining land, as a

London Church for the Rosminians. There on a subsequent visit in April 1877 they met for the first time Cesare Tondini de Quarenghi, an Italian priest[118], member of the Barnabite Order[119], who was acting as assistant to Lockhart. Tondini had been ordained in Italy in 1862, whereupon he was sent to the Order's Paris House which had been founded by Gregorij Petrovich Suvalov[120], a Russian aristocrat who had become a convert to Roman Catholicism in 1843 after the death of his wife. In 1856 Suvalov joined the Barnabite Order and in 1857 was ordained priest in Milan; he was then transferred to France after having expressed to Pius IX the wish to dedicate himself and his Order to the reunion of the Russian Church with Rome. Suvalov died in 1859; Tondini did not, therefore, have a personal acquaintance with him, but made Suvalov's ardent desire for the reunion of Christendom his own. The Barnabites proceeded to found an 'Association of Masses'; in 1872 Pius IX granted[121] a plenary indulgence to all who should assist at the Mass for the reunion of Christendom to be celebrated once a month in the Chapel of the Barnabites in Paris. Tondini in England was working to spread the influence of the Association and to extend those privileges. He also wrote a number of pamphlets, including one consequent upon those of Gladstone on 'Vaticanism'[122], which concerned both the union of Christian episcopal Churches and 'the religious question of Russia'.

With this background, it was not unexpected that Tondini and Ambrose soon formed an acquaintance; the progress of it can be seen in the letters which Tondini sent to his Superiors in Rome, sometimes in French and sometimes in Italian[123]. On 1 June 1977 Tondini wrote that 'an illustrious convert whose life has been closely linked with the history of the religious movement in England and who is also personally in touch with the leaders of the Ritualists', wanted him to spend a few days at his home. 'My health needs it and talking to him I shall learn more than by reading several books. His name is Mr de Lisle whose daughter, Lady Howard, was one of those who took part in the pilgrimage[124].'

After his visit to Garendon (which followed one to Newman at the Oratory), Tondini reported on a suggestion by Ambrose that he might provide the Barnabites with a House on the

Estate; Tondini had been cautious. Later, when Ambrose became pressing, Tondini wrote[125] again; another suggestion had been that he should spend a few months at Garendon, study the situation and report to his superiors

> What pleases me in this proposal is that Garendon Park is one of the main centres of action of the movement which is operating in the bosom of the Anglican Church today to become reunited with us. I know that people of great authority attribute to Mr de Lisle a considerable role in the religious events of the last forty years, and I know also that very reliable people do not hesitate to call him a real saint. If the deepest humility, in addition to constant union with God and great merits are signs of sainthood, it is indeed the case with Mr de Lisle. His parish is as well regulated as a convent and Mrs de Lisle is a person whose virtue and piety are above normal.

He went on to describe what he would do at Garendon: to practise his ministry in the neighbourhood, render service to the family, giving Latin lessons to Ambrose's grandsons, and studying the work of Suvalov.

> I shall be treated as a friend by the de Lisles ... Allow me to add that it is by contact with the society that meets at Garendon (and this includes Gladstone) that I may be able, with God's help, to do something useful for the work of Father Suvalov, the union of the Churches, the work which finds the most echoes in England.

Tondini's superiors agreed to the plan that he should go, and he duly arrived at Garendon in September, having made it quite clear in his letter of acceptance that he was not to be described as tutor to the grandsons. He wrote to Ambrose[126]

> Your friendship made you desire to give an establishment of Barnabites on your estate for the double purpose of providing for the spiritual welfare of its inhabitants and of furnishing me with valuable opportunities to promote the great work of reunion. For this, and only for this, I have been allowed to make a temporary sojourn at Garendon, during which I shall be happy to do something on behalf of your family, in the persons of your grandsons.

It was agreed that Tondini should stay six months. He wrote contentedly of the household, the district, the amount of time available for study and the progress of his Association. 'I am treated with the greatest respect'. The Bishop of Nottingham had expressed anxiety that 'heretics might be approached to belong'; Tondini made it clear that it was an 'Association for Masses'. He wrote of the Order of Corporate Reunion with which he was clearly familiar; an article from his pen had been requested for their quarterly review on the subject of his own Association.

> Allow me to inform you of the assurances I have been given on the intentions of the bishops (validly consecrated) and others who make up the Order of Corporate Reunion, on the subject of the Catholic Church.

It can be established through the record of Laura's diary, that Ambrose had effected a meeting between Tondini and Lee; a likely source of this assumption. In October, Tondini went to Oxford and according to his report, successfully managed to form a branch of his Association there: 'The Church was full and there were a good many from the University'; there had been lectures and conversations with Anglicans. He explained to his superiors why and how he took the part of 'the Ritualists'. In addition he had been corresponding with Mr Gladstone.

On 7 January 1878 Tondini sent news to Rome of Ambrose's grave illness. He had become unwell on Christmas day. Ambrose had chanted a *Nocturn* and *Missa Cantata* at midnight, and again the third Mass at eleven in the morning, with his customary vigour. He went for a walk, which was his usual practice, but fainted during the afternoon and was not well enough to attend Vespers. He did not enter the chapel again. In the beginning, the main location of his complaint was in one of his feet where gangrene was soon diagnosed; the sickness and pain then spread to other parts of his body. Tondini continued

> I asked to be allowed to watch over him last night, thus allowing Mrs de Lisle and the rest of the family to have a good night's sleep ... The patient has now received the Final Sacrament. I only wish that I might be as pious as he. He is perfectly aware of his condition, and thoroughly prepared. He is an example of every one of the monastic virtues. Thanks be to the

> Virgin Mary! . . . I wish to omit nothing that might hasten the ascent of that soul to heaven, beauteous in its similarity to the soul of our divine Saviour, *if this is God's will.*

The letters to Rome proliferated, for some of Tondini's writings had been submitted to an examiner; criticisms had been made and he had given up the idea of publication. He referred to 'that kind of moral tyranny exercised upon opinions and conscience in the name of Rome, although Rome has no part in it . . .'

> If I were tempted by martyrdom, it would be for the just liberty of the sons of God. I have studied various of the champions of temporal power, and the experience has certainly not been edifying. However, this is not a question of personal experience, but of principle. Ah, dear and venerable father, I have little difficulty in understanding the battle against the Church, and the triumph of atheism. How much strength is lost in the battle?

A fortnight later, Tondini wrote again.[127] He thought Ambrose could die at any moment.

> I myself have undertaken a novena, of which we have reached the fifth day. I have applied a napkin that has touched the bones of Our Lord, to the forehead of my patient. He has great faith in the outcome of my prayers . . . I am learning the most uplifting prayers from him. I have found nothing in the account of the deaths of various saints more enlightening than that to which I am witness. The patient does not omit the Holy Father from his prayers . . .

Laura had written to Cardinal Manning, then in Rome, to ask for a Papal Blessing for Ambrose. Manning's reply, in his own hand,[128] told of the Pope's own weakness and that he was 'keeping to his bed'.[129] He sent the blessing 'most willingly'.

Tondini's letter of 7 February spoke of having been called to Ambrose every night for the past week; once he had been at death's door; his hands already chill, his breathing low. 'It is a dry gangrene which has already nearly reached the knee and internally seems to have made frightening progress'. The attitude of the sick man was giving edification to all; there had been a visit to him by the Bishop of Nottingham. Throughout February so Tondini reported, Ambrose continued 'to hover between life and death'. He begged Tondini not to leave him. Finally, on 6 March he wrote: '*C'est hier matin que M de Lisle rendit son âme à Dieu.*'

Chapter 12

Epilogue

PRAYERS for the repose of the soul of Ambrose began shortly after his death. His children arranged an altar in the room where he had died; Vespers for the Dead were chanted each evening; Matins and Lauds each morning before Mass. On 8 March a solemn Requiem was sung in the chapel at Garendon, the first of the ceremonies planned by Ambrose himself down to the smallest detail. Fr Aloysius (Henry Tatchell) from the Abbey, was celebrant; Fr Tondini preached a sermon on the text 'He was a man simple, upright and fearing God' from the Book of Job, in which he spoke particularly of the composure Ambrose had shown in the months of his illness and the patience with which he had accepted his sufferings. Next day, his remains left Garendon at half past four in the morning for Mount St Bernard. E. S. Purcell maintains[1] that Ambrose was laid out in the habit of the Third Order of St Dominic to which he had belonged 'since the year 1831'. Since an elaborate certificate, recovered from the Archives of the Nottingham Diocese, records his admission to membership of the Third Order of the Passionists on 3 May 1831, the latter habit would seem to have been more likely.

At the gates of the Abbey lands, the Abbot and community of choir monks, headed by the cross bearer, stood waiting, attended by acolytes carrying torches, incense and holy water. While the Abbey bells tolled and the *Miserere* and other psalms were chanted by the monks, the coffin was carried by lay brothers into the Abbey church which had been draped with black. A hatchment representing Ambrose's coat of arms, painted by one of the community, had been fastened to the rood screen. The coffin, covered by the monks' pall and a large cross, was set in the centre of the choir.

At 11 am, Matins and Lauds for the Dead were chanted, after which the solemn Requiem Mass was celebrated by the Abbot with three assistants, according to the Cistercian rite. The Garendon and Shepshed choirs sang *Dies Irae* and *Jesu Salvator*. Fr Augustine (Henry Collins) in his sermon preached on a text from the Epistle to the Hebrews: 'He looked for a city whose builder and maker is God'. He referred to the sensation caused by the conversion of Ambrose; it had become the animating spirit of the whole of his life.

After ablutions over the coffin by the Abbot, it was carried to the south-west aisle of the church, where a grave had been prepared in front of the altar of St Stephen Harding. The long and solemn Cistercian Burial Service was chanted by the Abbey monks and the many secular priests and other Religious who were present. All the principal tenants had come, which pleased the family, as no invitations had been sent out. Men sat inside the monks' choir and roodloft; women were placed in that part of the church assigned to lay people. At the end Laura and her children threw into the grave some of the flowers which had come from neighbours, tenants and servants. The ceremony had lasted until nearly two o'clock in the afternoon.

Of all the letters received by Laura following Ambrose's death, none was more telling than that of Newman. He realised that beyond all the condolences, criticism would continue to be expressed of the roles which Ambrose had adopted, most particularly of his attitude towards the views of the Ultramontanes. It continued to be suggested, as his family became only too aware, that he had been disloyal to the Holy See; that in some respects he had never shed his Anglican outlook. Newman recognised the circumstances as being close to his own. His letters to Ambrose had been more sympathetic during the past decade, than in the 1840s and 1850s, as he saw him challenged as a layman; for example, by such as Bishop Bagshawe. Some of Newman's letters to Henry Wilberforce spelt out his own frustration in the face of officialdom in Rome.

> ... there has been a tradition among the Italians that the lay mind is barbaric – fierce and stupid – and is destined to be outwitted, and that fine craft is the true weapon of Churchmen.[2]

When his *Grammar of Assent* ran into problems, he retaliated[3]

> I think it will be stopped after my infinite pains about it.

He felt that the theological philosophers 'move in a groove and will not tolerate anyone who does not move in the same'.

> ... they think they do the Church of Rome good service by subjecting her to an etiquette as grievous as that which led to the King of Spain being burned to cinders.

Newman reassured Laura[4]

> ... None can forget him or his great virtues or his claims on the gratitude of English Catholics who knew him even by name, much more personally. He has a place in our history, and a place altogether special. Nor has he ceased to be our benefactor now that he has left us, but, as I believe most fully, we profit, and shall profit by his prayers.

Earlier, during Ambrose's illness, Newman had written[5] in an equally comforting vein:

> ... As to him, there are few men who are so sure of heaven, as he. And when he leaves us, sooner or later, according to God's will and gets there, tell him I hope ... he will not forget me.

Bishop Ullathorne[6] put aside past differences on the Shrewsbury Will affair and wrote generously about Ambrose to Laura.

> ... He did a great work in his day, and he did it with a simple and pure heart. One must look back to his earliest days to see how religion took hold of him, and how family position and all else in the world were as nothing in his eyes when he heard in his soul the call of God.

As might be expected, the Bishop emphasised those achievements of Ambrose of which he approved:

> his childlike fervour in the work of restoring monasticism and of boldly bringing the Catholic religion into open view, at a time when others had not the courage or generosity of these things. One must remember what his example did in setting others to work to lift up the prostrate condition of the Faith in this land ...

On Ambrose's work for reunion, a single sentence was sufficient: 'One must recall the influence he exercised on the Oxford men at the time of the Tractarian movement'. On safer ground, he recalled Ambrose's 'love of the chant, that solemn song of the Church'. Bishop Ullathorne acknowledged, with insight, that 'through discouragement and failures and successes he [Ambrose] went on the same from beginning to end. I knew something of his sacrifices and something of the difficulties that came upon sacrifice, to give life the taste of trial'.

Turning to Anglican sources, Gladstone told Ambrose's biographer[7] that he had 'been an Israelite indeed, in whom was no guile . . . he only attempted to make converts of whom he had formed a high opinion'. Lord Halifax[8], President of the English Church Union, much at the same time told Purcell[9] 'Mr de Lisle was a most beautiful and interesting character and I do not think it easy to exaggerate the debt we owe him'.

Owen Chadwick in his contribution[10] to a symposium compiled in 1967, wrote of both Halifax and Ambrose (whom he referred to by the earlier name of Phillipps) and compared their achievements:

> Both the Victorians who succeeded in doing something irenic between Rome and Canterbury had a touch of the best kind of simplicity; Ambrose Phillipps from the side of Rome, Lord Halifax from the side of Canterbury. Both were country squires, both laymen, suspected and sometimes feared by their respective hierarchies, both with money to spend, and both with that simple faith which leaps over barriers too high for bishop or monsignor . . . Neither of these generous idealists ever had much chance of carrying with them the authorities of their denominations. Sometimes each of them did damage to the cause of peace, damage such as is easily done by high-minded but imprudent peacemakers. But each came astonishingly close to securing an important step forward.

Owen Chadwick feels that the palm must be awarded to Halifax, since his was the more powerful mind, more masculine character, more profound learning, harder head. 'Phillipps had more of romance in him'. But he goes on to say that Phillipps' endeavours 'were conducted in an even more difficult time for peace'; i.e. the reign of Pius IX rather than Leo XIII. An outline of Ambrose's approaches on reunion with the Oxford Men follows, and Chadwick comments:

> The proposal does not now look hopeful. It did not look hopeful in 1841. Newman thought it impossible. But I mention it, partly because it holds the place of honour as the first of several such schemes . . .

The fact that Ambrose continued with enthusiasm throughout a long life, receives notice: 'Against every discouragement he continued warm-hearted, charitable, hopeful . . . and the strange thing about Phillipps is that he never became absurd

> It was all genuine, large-hearted, true. His generous love of souls covered a multitude of impossible suggestions, and he was liked and forgiven.

This tribute gives recognition to Ambrose's very real qualities of vision, determination and resilience, even if it minimizes both the anguish that many of his schemes caused him, and the strength of his detractors, by whom it is doubtful whether he *was* much liked or easily forgiven. The time has come to examine a question formulated in chapter 1: to what extent Ambrose was prophet, ecumenist or meddler?

During the span of his adult life, almost without a break, he set himself a series of challenges and self-appointed tasks. (In his attempts to achieve them he was often an isolated figure, for he acted most frequently of his own volition; occasionally he worked with a handful of allies). One was the restoration of monasticism, where he succeeded in the foundation of Mount St Bernard as a Cistercian Abbey, the first in England since the Reformation; another, closely associated, was the re-introduction of the use of plain chant in English churches and gothic architecture for church buildings. The three chapels he caused to be built on his estate, and the Abbey itself, were examples of both these features. There is ample evidence that they became influences that were followed. The patronage given to Pugin by Lord Shrewsbury was crucial in launching him as a much sought-after church architect in the gothic style and designer of gothic ornaments, but the friendship of Ambrose was important too, as a steadying hand. Ambrose's writings were not of great consequence, for reasons that will be discussed; his book on unity was brushed aside as impudent, and much of the one on prophecy as 'untenable'. The two remaining pursuits were far the most important: evangelism in the Roman Catholic cause and the reunion of the Roman Catholic, Anglican and Orthodox Churches.

There is nothing in Ambrose's work on the subject of prophecy which would qualify him to be considered seriously as a prophet; the issues of Anti-Christ and the Millenium have become academic ones. But he can be seen in several of his attitudes and policies as a fore-runner of things to come. The main cause of opposition against him, particularly as Ultramontane views began to take hold, was on account of his daring as a layman in the Church. In a manner considered highly improper, he initiated and operated evangelistic and unity schemes of his own, because he realised that suggestions from the laity were not welcome. He was not content merely to respond to clerical direction. Eighty years after Ambrose's death, the Second Vatican Council brought profound changes. Part of the Decree on the Apostolate of the Laity[11] read as follows

> As sharers in the role of Christ . . . the laity have an active part to play in the life and activity of the Church. Their activity is so necessary within church communities that without it the apostolate of the pastors is generally unable to achieve its full effectiveness.

Moreover, Ambrose suggested certain changes which might encourage the work of evangelism. During a visit to the Rhineland, he wrote to Newman[12] from Wiesbaden; the state of religion was good and devotion intelligent:

> This I attribute partly to the fact that in the Rheinist Church there has always been a much larger use of the vernacular tongue than elsewhere.

Everything was well sung, he continued: the only churches where there was anything like it were the Anglican Ritualistic churches. He often wrote to Lee in the same vein:

> It is a fact that *we* find it difficult with our Latin liturgy to make much way among the People . . . something considerable has been done, and a certain number of people won back to the

antient Faith . . . yet we fail to be anything like what might be termed an English Church . . .[13]

These were prophetic words, for the Second Vatican Council in its Decree on the Liturgy[14] permitted the use of the Vernacular. Moreover, the Dogmatic Constitution on the Church[15] allowed for the diversity for which Ambrose had continued to plead, and for the importance of local churches[16].

As an ecumenist Ambrose had shortcomings, but undoubtedly, as Owen Chadwick has suggested, a place that was prophetic; his schemes were 'the first of several'. Among the limitations, Ambrose did not deal with more than certain 'wings' of believers in his reunion plans; not with whole Churches, and never with every part of Christendom. He did not, for instance, include Evangelicals nor Dissenters. His was a selective, and therefore, from a modern point of view, defective ecumenism. He was drawn to those with whom he had religious, social, political and cultural affinity. In the absence of post-Second Vatican Council ecclesiology concerning the implications of a common baptism, Ambrose allowed himself to be guided by other principles. He did not go so far, therefore, as the Council's Decree on Ecumenism[17], although he pleaded for the avoidance of excess and extravagances in the discussion of religious differences; he can be seen to have anticipated the paragraph on the 'hierarchy of truths'[18] in that same Decree. In short, here was a beginning in inter-Church relations which few others had the courage to initiate or follow for some decades. Ambrose's methods were by present standards amateur and personal: conversation, correspondence, pamphlets privately printed, persuasion, hospitality, were the keynotes. They were the precursors of official dialogue, committees, conferences and Final Reports. (In addition, his belief that his many children, also, would be more likely to benefit from encouragement and praise, rather than suppression and censoriousness, has a modern ring).

At the same time, a strong case can be made for Ambrose as a meddler, if it is denied that he had certain rights as a layman to act when his strong sense of personal illumination prompted him to do so; the visionary side of him was sometimes regarded with scepticism and more often with annoyance. In relation to his estates he viewed his position as giving him a certain responsibility towards the spiritual well-being of his neighbours and tenants. Bishops and clergy increasingly saw this activity as meddling; the help that was expected from him was financial. Quite apart from his lay status, there were other problems: his knowledge of theology had been acquired by a voracious and eclectic appetite for reading religious books, not by a sytematic programme of training. The curtailing of Ambrose's time at the university and his sparse formal higher education, showed itself most clearly in his writings; they were defuse and repetitive and easily construed as concerning matters on which he had no business to be giving an opinion. His determination to put as many resources as possible towards church building in England persuaded him to fight the long and expensive legal battles in relation to the Shrewsbury Will; in the opinion of his contemporaries, here was meddling indeed.

Yet posterity can afford to take a more lenient view. His belief in his causes, his courage in withstanding hostility and ridicule and his good relations with clergy and lay people of Communions other than his own[19], earn him, in the words of Newman, a special place in history.

Who should be asked to write Ambrose's biography had been discussed in his life-time. He had made it known that he favoured F. G. Lee. Bishop Ullathorne wrote a long protest to Laura on 14 December 1878[20]; Lee, to his knowledge, had been guilty of extreme exaggeration in the past in relation to the strength of enthusiasm for corporate reunion; he was an unsuitable candidate. (Lee's tendency to exaggerate was certainly no less than Ambrose's own; it was he who urged Lee in several instances[21] that it was important 'to put forward as good a case as possible' in publicising the reception of their reunion plans). The matter did not go any further.

In 1884 Bloxam considered the publication of the letters which he, Ambrose and others had exchanged in 1841–2; they were contained in a folder entitled 'Reunion'[22]. He sought Lockhart's opinion on the advisability of such a step. Lockhart replied[23]

> I should be much interested to consult with you on the subject of the publication of the letters of our dear Friend A. L. P. –

for this reason I should like to accept your offer of a bed at some future time, for the reading of letters takes time. I have a great inclination to offer to write something which you might make use of it you thought proper, as a justification of de Lisle's hopeful view of the Anglican Church and the possibilities of corporate reunion. I mean a justification before A. L. P.'s co-religionists, by whom he was never understood and whether they think corporate reunion possible or desirable, they ought to understand A. L. P.'s mind and his loyalty to the Holy See, in order to understand what he meant.

When he had read the letters, Lockhart felt that they required editing; Bloxam withdrew his intention to publish.

It was not until early in 1896, that a fresh search for a biographer resulted in an invitation to E. S. Purcell who was a journalist, and, unlike Lee, a Roman Catholic. He accepted, and had written the major part of the two-volume book, when he died without completing it; Edwin de Lisle did so. In his Preface, Edwin wrote of the controversy that had been faced by Laura's choice of Purcell.

> ... Mrs de Lisle was not unaware that she was running the risk of hostile criticism, especially from members of her own Communion.

E. S. Purcell had just completed his two-volume biography of Cardinal Manning. Manning, according to Edwin's footnote[24] in Purcell's eventual biography of his father, had 'by means of his influence' closed down the *Westminster Gazette* of which Purcell was editor, and 'effected its ruin'. The biography of Manning was not universally well received. The de Lisle family were sensitive in regard to Ambrose's posthumous reputation, and it may well be, partly because Purcell received this clear message, and partly because he was still smarting after the criticism of his biography of Manning, that his book on Ambrose became so eulogistic in tone. Still, Ambrose's children were not satisfied: Edwin added a number of glosses as footnotes, lest there be misconception of his father's orthodoxy or regard for the Holy See[25]. Margaret de Lisle likewise, took it upon herself to defend Ambrose's attitude towards the Vatican Decrees of 1870; she exchanged several letters with Gladstone[26].

To Amo was left the burden of clearing up Ambrose's debts. It would seem that they amounted to about £18,000; a large sum in 1878. Amo was unable to meet all the claims by the time of his own death in 1883 and it fell to Edwin to discharge them during the 1890s.

Reference has already been made to Tondini's letter which acquainted his superiors of Ambrose's death; he later told of the circumstances of the funeral:

> He was buried on Saturday at the Trappist monastery of which he is the founder, where at the same time a place is prepared for Madame de Lisle, who in spite of her extraordinary strength of Christian soul will not perhaps be long in rejoining him.

Tondini was wrong, for Laura lived another eighteen years as a widow. On 19 August 1896 her coffin was carried into the Abbey church at Mount St Bernard. With Home Office permission for a burial within a public building, her earthly remains were interred beside those of her husband.

Notes

ABBREVIATIONS

Hansard Parliamentary Debates	H.P.D.
Letters and Diaries of J. H. Newman, Various editors, Oxford Clarendon Press	*L. and D. of J. H. Newman*
Magdalen College Archives	M.C.A.
Propaganda Fide Archives, Scritture Riferite nei Congressi	P.F.A., S.R.n.C.
Propaganda Fide Archives, Sac. Congregazioni Particolare	P.F.A., S.C.P.
E. S. Purcell, *Life and Letters of A.P. de Lisle*, Macmillan, 2 Volumes, 1900	Purcell, *de Lisle*
Rosminian Archives, Stresa	R.A., Stresa.
Vatican Archives, Spoglie dei Cardinali	V.A., S.d.C.
Wilfred Ward, *Life and Times of Cardinal Wiseman*, Longmans, 1900	Ward, *Wiseman*

Chapter 1   Youth

1. 27 May, R. A., Stresa.
2. Remarkable monuments in Shepshed Church were also erected to him and his grandfather.
3. He assumed the additional name of Phillipps in 1771.
4. Lucy March Phillipps, *Records of the Ministry of the Revd E. T. Phillipps*, Longmans, 1862.
5. ibid, p.134.
6. *Chronological Tables of Events in Leicestershire*, 1863, C. Norman, Printers, Covent Garden.
7. L. M. Phillipps, *Ministry of the Revd E. T. Phillipps*, p.147.
8. Now the Retreat House of the diocese of Leicester.
9. 11 February 1817 Harrowby Archives C II, 3rd.
10. 1774–1860; later in parliament again from 1820–31.
11. 1781–1835; son of 4th Duke of Rutland.
12. Considerable landowners: of Sutton Bonington, Ibstock, Lubenham etc.
13. 26 June 1818.
14. 3 July 1818.
15. ibid.
16. Purcell, *de Lisle*, Vol. I, p.113. Likely to have been an exaggeration.

17. 1759–1833; Philanthropist.

18. 1805–73; Bishop of Oxford 1845; of Winchester 1869.

19. 30 November 1821; A. R. Ashwell, *Life of Samuel Wilberforce*, John Murray, 1880, Vol. I, p.16.

20. 1806–47; great-grandson of 2nd Earl of Glasgow.

21. 1807–66; Partner in Hoare's Bank, 1845.

22. 4 March; Bodleian Library Wilberforce MSS Correspondence, 1822–44. C7–11, folio 1–4.

23. 20 September 1822; ibid.

24. Of Lockington Hall. His name reappears on several occasions in Ambrose's future.

25. Edward Viscount Stuart 1807–57; 3rd Earl of Castlestewart 1854.

26. 31 October 1823; ibid, d 32, 10.

27. Purcell, *de Lisle*, Vol. I, p.20.

28. L. M. Phillipps, *Ministry of Revd E. T. Phillipps*, p.22.

29. The 'prince of Christ's enemies', often visualised as a person, rather than an evil principle at this period; see first Letter of John and 2 John 7, where Anti-Christ is identified with those who deny the Incarnation.

30. Purcell, *de Lisle*, Vol. I, p.29.

31. *Mahommetanism in Relation to Prophecy*, Charles Dolman, 1855.

32. Lancelot Andrewes, Bishop of Winchester, Christopher Sutton, Prebendary of Westminster, William Laud, Archbishop of Canterbury, Richard Montague, Thomas Jackson, William Forbes, Bishop of Edinburgh, George Herbert, John Bramhill, Archbishop of Armagh, John Cosin, Bishop of Durham, Herbert Thorndyke, Henry Hammond, Jeremy Taylor, were the most prominent.

33. First published 1650 and 1651.

34. First published 1707; republished with notes by C. E. Corrie, CUP, 1858.

35. *Or Familiar Conversations on the Principal duties of Christianity*, first published 1823; reprinted Dublin, Clarke & Son, 1853.

36. Purcell, *de Lisle*, Vol. I, p.19; a statement echoed by Pope Paul VI in 1970.

37. Elizabeth Phillipps, eldest daughter of the Revd E. T. Phillipps; 8 March 1823; to Hathern. Harrowby Archives MSS Vol. CII, No. 19.

38. ibid, No. 28.

39. Purcell, *de Lisle*, Vol. I, p.22.

40. The Revd (later Canon) Thomas Macdonnell.

41. Referred to in a letter 11 February 1839 to S. A. Proctor O. P., Dominican Archives, Newcastle.

42. Notably Edward Stuart; see Chapter 3, i, p.51.

43. Harrowby Archives.

44. The Catholic Emancipation Act did not become law until 1829.

45. Especially in the case of Leicester and Birmingham.

46. Fellow of Trinity 1820; Vice-Master 1843–4; Archdeacon of Bristol 1836–73; Rector of Kemerton, Glos. 1839–73, where Ambrose continued to visit him.

47. 1800–80; writer and illustrator.

Chapter 2   Cambridge and Rome

1. Later Member of Parliament.

2. 1776–1836.

3. A sale catalogue of Digby's books printed after his death, gave a clue as to the range of his sources; from Froissart's Chronicles and those of Holinshed, Sir William Dugdale; Monasticon Anglicanum, a 17th century Baronage of England, Mrs Jamie-

son's Legends of the Monastic Order, to several volumes of the Tales of the Brothers Grimm (Bernard Quartich 25 June 1881).

4. See p. 79.

5. To read those copies lodged in the Bodleian Library in Oxford, for example, requires recourse to a paper knife; pages remain uncut after 150 years.

6. Longmans Green, 2 Vols., 1872.

7. Longmans Green, 1874.

8. 11 November 1827, Arch. Prov. Ang. S. J.

9. 31 October, Purcell, *de Lisle*, Vol. II, p.14.

10. 1809–85; created Lord Houghton 1863; see p.168.

11. 1809–83.

12. Published at first anonymously 1859.

13. 1762–1827.

14. 9 February 1827; Purcell, *de Lisle* Vol. I, p.145.

15. B. Ward, *St Edmund's College Chapel*, C.T.S., 1903, p.22.

16. 1761–1844; a Belgian Dominican, born in Ypres.

17. Dominican Archives Newcastle.

18. Archives Dormer family.

19. Alfred McKinley Terhune, *Life of Edward Fitzgerald*, OUP, 1947, p.22.

20. In the *Lichfield Mercury* at the time of George Spencer's conversion.

21. 1 May 1828, Cambridge Record Office.

22. Who 'received the cruel intelligence' while staying at Brislington with his sick mother and left immediately in a post chaise, travelling all night.

23. B. Ward, *Dawn of Catholic Revival, 1781–1803*, Longmans Green, 1909, Vol. I, p.140–3. These issues became of considerable relevance when Gladstone

came to write his first pamphlet on the Vatican Decrees, with Ambrose beside him at Hawarden.

24. Now in the Waterloo Chamber, Windsor Castle.

25. Born Spoleto 22 August 1760; Nuncio to Switzerland 1793; to Cologne 1794; to Paris 1814. (Austria had vetoed one of the other candidates).

26. 1802–65; Rector English College 1828–40; Co-adjutor Midland District 1840; Vicar Apostolic London District 1848–50; Cardinal Archbishop of Westminster 1850–65.

27. *Recollections of Four Popes*, Hurst & Blackett, 1858.

28. J. Derek Holmes, *The Triumph of the Holy See*, Burns Oates, 1978, p.82.

29. 6 March 1829; Archives Dormer family.

30. ibid.

31. To Fr Pagani; see letter Pagani to Rosmini 17 January 1841, R. A. Stresa.

32. Ambrose's father's account of the episode is rather different; no great notice was taken of the attack, which was soon over; the rest of the party continued their sight-seeing without interruption. Diary of Charles March Phillipps; de Lisle Archives.

33. 1790–1858; 7th Lord Clifford 1831; married Mary Lucy, daughter of Thomas (later Cardinal Weld).

34. Born Liverpool 1787; d. 1843.

35. p.204.

36. Joseph Hirst, *Memoir and Letters of Lady Mary Arundell, The Ratcliffian*, Leicester, 1894, p.26. (On her husband's death in 1836, she reverted to an earlier title.)

37. 1550–68; a young Polish nobleman of exemplary life and piety

who died in the first few months of his Jesuit noviciate.

38. Everard, her husband.

39. Thomas Glover S. J., 1781–1849; sent to Rome in 1825 as agent of the English Jesuit Province.

40. *The Little Gradual or Chorister's Companion*, London, James Toovey, 1847.

41. ibid p.vii–ix.

42. 1797–1855; priest, philosopher and educationalist; founder of the Institute of Charity (Rosminians) 1828.

43. To Mgr Lushin 28 February 1829; ed. Casale, *Epistolario Completo di Antonio Rosmini-Serbati*, Giovanni Pane, 1887–94, Vol. III, 954.

44. Assistant Secretary of State.

45. The required majority.

46. 1761–1830; member of a noble family of Ancona.

47. p.234.

48. Casale, *Epistolario*, III, 971.

49. Preface to his book *The Diurnal of the Soul or Maxims of the Saints*, Thomas Rivington, 1869.

50. From Garendon 28 September 1829; in the possession of the Dormer family.

51. 28 September 1829, ibid.

52. Abbé Genet, *Vie et révélations de la Soeur de la Nativité*, Paris, 1819.

53. 7 September 1828; Arch Pro Ang S J.

54. ibid.

55. Susan March Phillipps, formerly Lisle; from Brislington Hall, 20 December 1831; Purcell, *de Lisle*, Vol. I, p.37.

Chapter 3 The English Mission
(i) Plans.

1. From Ryde 21 July 1810 to the Hon. Robert Spencer; ed. M. M. Wyndham, *Correspondence of Sarah Lady Lyttelton 1787–1870*, John Murray, 1912, p.109.

2. ibid, p.244.

3. 16 February 1830 from Hagley to the Hon Mrs Pole -Carew, ibid, p.257.

4. 4 January 1830; Purcell, *de Lisle*, Vol. I, p.44–6.

5. *Catholic Magazine*, No.XXVII, Vol. III, April 1839.

6. 1786–1859; Dean of Ripon 1847.

7. His father did the opposite; 'spoke sharply to G. Spencer'; Charles March Phillipps recorded in his diary; de Lisle Archives.

8. Letter begun 21 December 1829 and completed 10 February 1830; Arch. Prov. Ang. S. J.

9. Edward Viscount Stuart, whose father, not able to prevent his title descending to him, nevertheless deprived his eldest son of any financial inheritance; see PRO, Belfast D 1618/15/8/1.

10. 1 April 1830.

11. This was Aunt Cowper who became in her widowhood Aunt Hamilton, wife of the vicar of Shepshed. She died 17 days after the meeting.

12. 8 April 1830.

13. *List of the Patrons of the Dignities, Rectories, Vicarages etc. of the United Church of England and Ireland with the Valuation annexed of all livings not exceeding £150 p.a.*, C.J.G. and F. Rivington, 1831.

14. From figures supplied by the Northamptonshire Record Office.

15. C K Francis Brown, *History of the English Clergy*, Faith Press, 1953, p.183.

16. 18 February 1830, Urban Young, *Life of Fr Ignatius Spencer C. P.*, Burns Oates, 1933, p.48.

17. Passionist Papers, Ormskirk. The cause for the beatification of George Spencer is proceeding at present.
18. To Fr Glover, 21 December 1829–10 February 1830, op.cit.
19. To K. Digby 13 April 1830, Archives Dormer family.
20. ibid. 22 April 1830.
21. ibid. 30 March 1830. Other evidence would indicate that he was on affectionate terms with his brother and sister.
22. To Fr Glover 21 December 1829–10 February 1830, op.cit.
23. 1 November 1830, Arch. Prov. Ang. S. J.
24. 12 March 1830 to Ambrose; U. Young, *Life of Fr Ignatius Spencer C. P.*, p.51.
25. Rector of the English College in Rome 1818–28.
26. As at the Achilli trial in 1852 when Wiseman could not find important evidence in Newman's defence.
27. As he related to Fr Pagani in January 1841.
28. 13 November.
29. Dr Christopher Boylan.
30. To Rosmini 7 January 1831; Gianfranco Radice, *Annali di Antonio Rosmini-Serbati*, Marzarati Editore Milano, Vol. IV, 1829–31, 28, 1974, p.380.
31. *Epist.* III, 1333.
32. 1792–1849; first visit to England 1840; received J. H. Newman into the Roman Catholic Church 1845; beatified 1963.
33. See Chapter 7, p.200.
34. 29 November 1830; Passionist Archives, Rome.
35. Dominic Barberi sent a copy of the English translation to J. H. Newman (via J. D. Dalgairns) in December 1842.
36. April 1831, p.176.

37. 1765–1846.
38. *The Triumph of the Holy See.*
39. This establishment played an important part in Ambrose's life. It was founded by Mechitar, an Armenian (1676–1749) who reconciled part of the Armenian Church with the Holy See. Byron visited the monastery in 1886 and left a description.
40. Also a Camoldolesi monk; the Pope's vicar.
41. To Canon Macdonnell 31 August 1859; Purcell, *de Lisle*, Vol. I, p.30–1.
42. To Gentili 5 June 1831; G. Radice, *Annale di Antonio Rosmini*, op.cit. p.385.
43. From Ambrose; Claude Leetham, *Rosmini*, Longmans Green, 1957, p.158.

Chapter 3   The English Mission (ii) Achievements

1. 3 July 1831, Purcell, *de Lisle*, Vol. I, p.49
2. 13 June 1831; Passionist Archives, Ormskirk.
3. From Little Bounds; 2 May 1822; Letter 2 MS Wilberforce d. 32, Bodleian Library.
4. A. P. J. Cruikshank, *Laura de Lisle*, Art & Book co., 1897, p.35.
5. April 1831; Archives English College, Rome, 70.3, WAL.
6. 21 May 1833; ibid.
7. 10 December 1833, ibid. 32.
8. 15 August 1831, R A, Stresa.
9. 1815–58.
10. 9 December 1831; Dominican Archives, Newcastle.
11. To the Hon. Mrs Doughty, 10 January 1829, Hirst, *Lady Mary Arundell*, p.26–7.
12. To Rosmini 10 February 1832, R. A., Stresa.
13. 2 March 1832, ibid.

14. p.245–6.

15. 9 October 1832, *Epist.* 1800.

16. 17 August 1832, *Epist.* 1747.

17. To Ambrose 16 July 1831, Young, *Life and Letters of Fr Dominic*, p.58.

18. To the same 19 October 1831, ibid. p.61.

19. 29 October 1831, Passionist Archives Rome.

20. To Rosmini 15 August 1831, R. A., Stresa.

21. To the same 4 November 1832, ibid.

22. To the same 2 March 1832, ibid.

23. To the same 1 October 1833, ibid.

24. Born 1774.

25. 1728–1823.

26. 1746–1818.

27. Born 1783.

28. A relative of Laura, enobled by King Charles X of France.

29. 30 June 1833, Hirst, *Lady Mary Arundell*, p.46–7.

30. Lord Clifford's home in Devon.

31. 2 May 1834, ibid. p.55.

32. 13 April 1835, Purcell, *de Lisle*, Vol. I, p.65.

33. 27 December 1832, Archives Westminster Cathedral.

34. 1782–1854, Priest, writer, philosopher and pioneer of French liberalism.

35. 1810–1870; son of a French peer, politician and prolific writer on monasticism.

36. 1802–1861; priest, later Dominican, Member of the French Academy and outstanding preacher.

37. 12 November 1832, Passionist Archives, Ormskirk.

38. P. F. A., S. R. C. Anglia VIII.

39. Hirst, *Life and Character of Revd Andrew Egan*, 1890, p.12–20.

40. Hirst, *Lady Mary Arundell*, p.112.

41. A tendency to operate independently of the Holy See; named after a movement in the 18th cent. French Church which had this characteristic.

42. 6 October 1833; Epist. IV 2077.

43. February 1834.

44. 19 May 1835; Hirst, *Lady Mary Arundell*, p.38.

45. 27 June 1835, ibid. p.39.

46. A memorandum asking the Pope to make changes and improvements, was handed to the Pope in 1832 by Count von Lutzow, the Austrian Ambassador (uncle to Laura de Lisle).

47. 13 August 1835 to Avvocato Vincenzo Bianchi of Domodossola.

48. 8 November 1835, Epist. 2660.

49. 14 July 1835, R. A., Stresa.

50. Born 1769.

51. 25 March 1835; Robert Smith OCSO, *History of the Cistercian Order*, Thomas Richardson, 1852, p.271.

52. *Relexions de Dom Antoine*, September 1835, Archives Grande Trappe, 78.

53. May 1835; U. Young, *Life of Fr Ignatius Spencer C. P.*, p.80.

54. Archives Archdiocese of Birmingham, B.204.

55. Stapehill Archives.

56. Archives Archdiocese of Birmingham, B.245. 22 April 1836.

57. 4 April 1837; ibid. B.302.

58. This was not achieved until 1848.

59. 29 May 1830; Archives Westminister Cathedral.

60. 24 June 1831; ibid.

61. 27 December 1832; ibid.

62. 26 September 1833; ibid.

63. 18 November 1834; Archives Dormer family.

64. 11 January 1835; ibid.

65. Published 1834.

66. 22 January 1836; Archives Archdiocese of Birmingham B.234.

67. 22 September 1836; ibid. B.263.
68. See letter to Bishop Walsh, 22 April 1836, ibid. B.245.
69. Born Charmouth 1782; Valet to Thomas Weld at Lulworth; joined Community there 1808 where he learned to read and write; to Melleraie 1817, then Nantes; Prior Mt St B. 1841; Abbot 1848; died 1852.
70. 7 November 1838; Stapehill Archives.
71. The future V. C., born 28 May 1835.
72. Born 31 October 1836.
73. 1785–1844; see Philbin de Rivières, *Vie de Mgr. Forbin-Janson*, Paris 1891, in which the date of meeting is wrongly put as 1837.
74. 16 October 1836; R. A., Stresa.
75. 1806–60; formerly spiritual director of the Seminary at Novara.
76. 18 November 1839; Epist. 3891.
77. Epist. 4024.
78. Charles Januarius Acton; 1803–47; born Naples; second son of Sir John Francis Acton.
79. Undated; posted in Boulogne on his return to France.

Chapter 4 'Negotiations with the Oxford Men' (i) Prelude

1. Dialogue between a group of Anglicans and Roman Catholics at Malines at the invitation and under the leadership of Cardinal Mercier.
2. It was later printed in the *Dublin Review*, 1939, p.160–73.
3. 1797–1874; godfather to Ambrose's 7th son, Edwin in 1852.
4. 1809–98; M.P. 1832; Prime minister 1868, 1880, 1886, 1892.
5. (ed) M. R. D. Foot, *The Gladstone Diaries*, 1825–32, Oxford, 1968, p.425.
6. ibid. p.482.
7. See C. Leetham, *Rosmini*, p.94–6, et. seq.
8. 1799–1890; Bavarian Church Historian; Professor of Ecclesiastical History, University of Munich 1826. Became close to Old Catholics after 1870 promulgation of Papal Infallibility.
9. See P. Devine, *Life of the Very Revd. Father Dominic of the Mother of God*, R. Washbourne, 1898, p.42–7.
10. Letter to the Revd J. Bonomi 11 May 1858; *Ampleforth Journal*, May 1910, p.280.
11. 29 December 1838, M. R. D. Foot, *The Gladstone Diaries*, Vol II 1833–39, p.542.
12. 1808–1892; ordained in the Church of England 1833; married the same year; his wife died 1835; became Roman Catholic 1851; Archbishop of Westminster 1865.
13. 1801–90; Vicar of St Mary's Oxford; Became Roman Catholic 1845; Cardinal 1879.
14. ibid.
15. 1803–36; Fellow of Oriel College, Oxford 1826.
16. *Essays on Various Subjects*, Dolman, 1853, Vol. 11, p.94n.
17. Fano Papers; quoted B Fothergill, *Nicholas Wiseman*, Faber & Faber, 1963, p.79
18. English College Archives 83.1.
19. ibid. 56.
20. ibid. 58.
21. ibid. WAL 70.3.21.
22. V.A., S.d.C. Acton.
23. To F. C. Husenbeth 26 July 1840; see his biography of Weedall.
24. 8 June 1840, English College Archives.
25. To Mgr Acton 1 September 1840; V.A., S.d.C, 3.361.
26. 1800–47; missioner at Wolverhampton.

27. 1807–47.
28. 1 April 1841; Ward, *Wiseman*, Vol. I, p.385.
29. To Mgr Acton, 16 July 1839, V.A., S.d.C., Acton 3.325.
30. *An Apology for a Work entitled Contrasts*, Booker & Dolman, 1837, p.4.
31. Ward, *Wiseman*, Vol. 1, p.348.
32. To Canon Estcourt 2 June 1860, *L and D of J. H. Newman*, Vol. XIX, p.352.
33. Issue of July 1839.
34. 1775–1847; Irish politician and patriot who agitated for the repeal of the union of English and Irish Parliaments.
35. 1811–79.
36. From Oscott 3 February 1840; Passionist Archives, Ormskirk.
37. From Oscott, 24 January 1840; English College Archives.
38. H. F. C. Logan 1800–84; member of the staff at Oscott.
39. 1807–91; curate to J. H. Newman 1837–40.
40. 18 December 1840; Purcell, *de Lisle*, Vol. 11, p.214.
41. ibid, p.225.
42. Charles March Phillipps, father of Ambrose.
43. 1773–1842.
44. 1785–1873.
45. He had read No.4 relating to the Eucharist, written by John Keble, as early as January 1834.
46. 1812–73.
47. *Catholic Historical Journal*, April 1954, Vol. XL, p.1–2.
48. *L'Univers*, issue of 19 March 1840, No.284.
49. 25 January 1841, M.C.A. MS 459.

Chapter 4 'Negotiations with the Oxford Men' (ii) Finale

1. To Fr S. A. Proctor 1 June 1839, Purcell, *de Lisle*, Vol. 1, p.360.
2. ibid. p.191.
3. A theological quarterly to which many Tractarians contributed articles.
4. 12 January 1841; ibid, p.106.
5. 9 January 1841; Clifford Archives, Ugbrook.
6. *Newman and Bloxam*, an Oxford Friendship, OUP.
7. 1812–82; Fellow of Balliol College 1834–45.
8. 1814–63; Fellow of University College 1837–42.
9. 1818–76.
10. 1802–80; in charge of Margaret Street Chapel 1839–45.
11. 1627–1704; Bishop of Meaux.
12. A similar criticism of Newman persisted until his reputation was redeemed by the outcome of the Second Vatican Council.
13. Bishops with territorial sees, as against those with titles only.
14. J. Derek Holmes, *The Triumph of the Holy See*, p.30.
15. 9 February 1841, M.C.A., MS335, p.23.
16. Begun on 6 February, but not sent until 23 February 1841, ibid. p.53.
17. 1 February 1841, Vol. XXXIX, 6 February, 1841, p.83.
18. Inferring that their principles were new, and those of Edward Bouverie Pusey 1800–82; Regius Professor of Hebrew 1828.
19. The Revd Joseph Rathbone, 22 September 1841, *Tablet* Vol. LXXII.
20. The voluminous correspondence between Ambrose and Gladstone began in 1873.
21. M. R. D. Foot and H. C. G. Matthew, *The Gladstone Diaries*, Vol 111, 1840–47, OUP, 1974, p.84.
22. 4 February 1841, *L'Univers* 21 February 1841.

23. 18 February, ibid. 5 March 1841.

24. 22 February 1841, M.C.A. MS 459.

25. Archives Mount St Bernard.

26. 25 February 1841, M.C.A. MS 335.

27. Published 27 February 1841.

28. Undated and unsigned in Newman's handwriting; M.C.A. MS 335, p.63–7.

29. 28 February 1841, ibid. MS 459.

30. 2 March 1841, ibid. MS 335.

31. 4, 6 and 10 March 141, ibid MS 459.

32. 15 March 1841, ibid, MS 335.

33. James Henry and James Parker, Oxford and Rivingtons, p.v–vi.

34. 15 March 1841.

35. 1798–1871; Canon of Christ Church 1830; Principal of King's College, London 1844–68.

36. 28 March 1841, M.C.A. MS 335.

37. 17 March 1841, ibid. No.87.

38. 24 March 1841, ibid. No.109.

39. 1812–80; Fellow of Exeter College.

40. 25 March 1841, ibid, p.131.

41. Numero 563, 13 April 1841.

42. Ward, *Wiseman*, Vol. 1, p.382–3.

43. 1 April 1841, ibid, Vol. 1, p.383–4.

44. To Bloxam 29 March 1841, M.C.A., MS 459.

45. John Henry Parker, 1841.

46. *Some Remarks on A Letter addressed to the Revd R. W. Jelf in Explanation of Tract 90*, Charles Dolman, 1841.

47. 5 and 8 April 1841, original drafts Archives Birmingham Oratory.

48. 7 April 1841, ibid.

49. 9 April 1841, Purcell, *de Lisle*, Vol. 1, p.284–6.

50. 14 April 1841, Archives Birmingham Oratory.

51. Sabbato in Albis (12 April) 1841, Purcell, *de Lisle*, Vol. 1, p.216–8.

52. 1815–1903; Fellow of Magdalen College 1836–39; Rector of Ledenham 1839–42.

53. To Bloxam 2 May 1841, M.C.A. MS 459.

54. W Ward, *W G Ward and the Oxford Movement*, Macmillan, 1890, p.190.

55. 7 May 1841, M.C.A., MS 335.

56. Ward, *Wiseman*, Vol. 1, p.391–2.

57. Dated 5 May 1841, published as Appendix to U. Young, *Life and Letters of Fr Dominic*, Burns, Oates and Wasbourne, 1926.

58. 29 May 1841, Ward, *Wiseman*, Vol. 1. p.392.

59. 5 June 1841, M.C.A., MS 459.

60. 10 June 1841, ibid. MS 335, p.237.

61. 11 June 1841, ibid. MS 459.

62. 12 June 1841, Ward, *Wiseman*, Vol. 1, p.394–5.

63. 28 June 1841; draft Archives Birmingham Oratory.

64. 30 June 1841, ibid. 30.

65. 29 June 1841, ibid. 29.

66. 23 July 1841, published 8 August 1841, Numero 665.

67. 22 July 1841, published 1 August 1841, Numero 657, and 10 August 1841 published 21 August 1841, No.674.

68. English Rosminian.

69. 12 September 1841 (draft) Archives Birmingham Oratory.

70. 17 September 1841; M.C.A. MS 335, p.367.

71. 1792–1879; incumbent in Ryde, Isle of Wight 1830–41.

72. 12 October 1841, ibid. MS 335.

73. 1804–86; first Bishop of Plymouth 1851; Wiseman's co-adjutor 1855–62; later taught at Prior Park.

74. To Ambrose 28 October 1841, ibid. MS 335.

75. 13 October 1841; published *L'Univers* 17 October 1841 No.725.

76. 15 October 1841, M.C.A. MS 459.

77. 28 October 1841, ibid. MS 335.

78. ibid. MS 335, p.427.

79. ibid. MS 335, p.429.

80. *Dublin Review*, (ed) Louis Allen Vol. 228, No.463, p.61–2.

81. (ed) H Reeve, *A Journal of the Reign of Queen Victoria*, Longmans, 1885, Vol. 11, p.25.

82. 12 September 1841.

83. See *Final Report of the Anglican-Roman Catholic International Commission*, C.T.S./S.P.C.K., 1981.

Chapter 5   Young England (i) The Ideals

1. Note on Liberalism; 1967 edition; ed. Martin Svaglic, OUP, p.254.

2. 1804–81; Conservative statesman and writer; first entered parliament 1837; Prime Minister 1874–80.

3. William Lamb, 2nd Lord Melbourne 1779–1848; Whig Prime Minister 1834: 1835–41

4. 1800–90; Public Health Administrator; knighted 1889.

5. 2ndBaronet,1788–1850;Conservative Prime Minister 1834 and 1841.

6. 1818–1906; 2nd son of 5th Duke of Rutland; M. P. 1841–80.

7. William Ewart Gladstone 1804–98; Liberal politician; Prime minister 1868, 1880, 1886, 1892.

8. 1818–57; eldest son of 6th Lord Strangford; M.P. 1841–52.

9. 1816–90; Conservative M.P. for 40 years; created Lord Lamington 1880.

10. 1804–85; M.P. for Invernesshire 1840–68.

11. 1805–52; M.P. 1834–7; 1841–7.

12. 1811–57; M.P. 1841–57.

13. 1809–89.

14. p.332.

15. 1774–1843; Poet and historian.

16. Published December 1839 by J.G.F. and J. Rivington.

17. Henry Colburn, 1844.

18. 2 Vols. Longmans Green, 1872.

19. *Poems*, 2nd edition, Thomas Richardson, 1857, p.209.

20. Archives Belvoir Castle.

21. Published 1890 under the title *In the Days of the Dandies*, William Blackwood.

22. 1820–87; Churchman, politician and writer; M.P 1841–52; 1857–9; 1865–87.

23. 1808–62; owner of the *Deepdene*.

24. H. W. and I Law, *The Book of the Beresford Hopes*, Heath Cranton, 1925, p.112, et seq.

25. C. Whibley, *Lord John Manners and his Friends*, William Blackwood, 1925, Vol. 1, p.84–5.

26. W. F. Monypenny, *Life of Benjamin Disraeli*, John Murray, 1912, Vol. 11, p.167.

27. 20 November 1842, Passionist Archives, Ormskirk.

28. 22 December 1842, Purcell, *de Lisle*, Vol. 1, p.109.

29. 1806–89; Vicar Apostolic Western District 1846; Central District 1848; Bishop of Birmingham 1850.

30. Letter to Dr Pagani 7 July 1850; G. B. Pagani, *Life of the Revd Aloysius Gentili*, Richardson, 1851, p.324.

31. New series, Vol. 1, 1843, p.122–3.

32. Laura's cousin, the former Mary Lucy Clifford.

33. Philip Ziegler, *Life of Lady Diana Cooper*, Hamish Hamilton, 1981, p.10

34. C. Whibley, *Lord John Manners and his Friends*, Vol. 1, p.81.

35. Pseudonym Anglo-Catholicus, *A Letter to Lord Edward Howard*, W. E. Painter, 1841.

36. 6 February 1843, *Dublin Review*, (ed) Louis Allen, Vol. 228, No.464, 2nd quarter 1954, p.201–2.

37. 6 April 1843, Belvoir Archives.
38. He re-entered parliament again in 1833, but was not re-elected in 1841.
39. See p.232.
40. 16 May 1839 from University College, Oxford; Archives Belvoir Castle.
41. 21 October 1840; Archives London Oratory, Vol. 17.
42. Belvoir Archives.
43. H.P.D., Vol. LXVIII, 30 March 1843, p.203.
44. January, February and March issues, New series, Vol. 1.
45. *A Plea for National Holy Days*, Painter, 1843.
46. H.P.D., Vol. LXVII, 14 March 1843, p.872.
47. Vol. XXXIII, April quarter 1843, p.411.
48. *Catholic Magazine*, New series, Vol. 1, p.355

Chapter 5 Young England (ii) The Outcome.

1. H.P.D., Vol. LXVI, 23 February 1843, p.1221.
2. ibid. Vol. LXVIII 30 March 1843, p. 183–4.
3. ibid. p.1217.
4. 5 April 1843, No. 152, Vol IV, 8 April 1843, p.213, 25 April No.155, Vol IV, 29 April 1843, p. 260.
5. ibid. 22 April 1843, No 154, Vol. IV, p.244.
6. H.P.D., Vol. LXX, 11 July 1843, p.919.
7. ibid. 19 July, 1843, p.111–2.
8. 1818–94; M.P. 1847–65; 1868–85; inherited *The Times* from his father.
9. H P D, Vol. XLIX 1839, p. 250.
10. See p.264.
11. *Coningsby*, 1870 edition, p.129.
12. Mrs. Victor Urban, who repeated this to the writer.

13. J. T. Ward, Young England at Bingley, *Journal of Bradford Textile Society*, (1965–6), p 49–59.
14. 16 May 1845; Belvoir Archives.
15. H.P.D., 16 April 1845, Vol. LXXIX, p.825.
16. By a Layman, J. G. F. and J Rivington.
17. 2 June 1847, p.724.
18. Quoted in Norman St John Stevas, The Victorian Conscience, *Wiseman Review*, No 493, Autumn 1962, p.254.
19. C. Whibley, *Lord John Manners and his Friends*, Vol. 11, p. 153.
20. C. C. F. Greville, *A Journal of the Reign of Queen Victoria*, Vol. 11, p.195.
21. H.P.D. 1841, Vol. LXIX, p. 717.
22. A. C. Benson and Lord Esher, (eds). *Letters of Queen Victoria 1837–61*, John Murray, 1907, Vol. 11. p.19.
23. 11 November 1841, Purcell, *de Lisle*, Vol. 1, p.299–302.
24. Dolman, 1842.
25. C. C. F. Greville, *A Journal of the Reign* of Queen Victoria, Vol. II, p.391–2.
26. To J. W. Croker, 22 August 18 ?, J. T. Ward, *Sir James Graham*, Macmillan, 1967, p.326.

Chapter 6 Leicestershire Squire

1. 14 October 1834 to K. H. Digby from Barmouth, Archives Dormer family.
2. *Pèlerinage en Angleterre.*
3. 3 August 1837, Hirst, *Lady Mary Arundell*, p.114–5.
4. 31 August 1837 to Mrs. Doughty, ibid. p.92–3.
5. 2 March 1845.
6. 12 June 1845, Ugbrook Archives.
7. Hirst, *Lady Mary Arundell*, p.114–5.

8. To Laura de Lisle from Fr Nicholas Lorrain for many years chaplain at Grace Dieu, after his departure; from France. de Lisle archives.

9. 1 May 1862, *Loughborough News*, p.8.

10. 7 October 1857, Bodleian Library Eng.Lett.d.391, 13–14.

11. ibid. 10 October 1857, 11–12.

12. 1803–79; his father's name had been Purcell, but in common with frequent 19th century practice, he changed it on the death of his father-in-law.

13. 4 July 1836, To James Allen, later Archdeacon of Salop, (ed) William Aldis Wright, *Letters of Edward* Fitzgerald, Macmillan, 1894, Vol. I, p.35–6.

14. ibid, p.48–9.

15. L. M. Phillipps, *Ministry of E. T. March Phillipps*, p.311.

16. 13 August 1837 (in Italian) R. A. Stresa.

17. *My Life and What I shall do with it*, Longmans Green, 1860; also several other works with titles such as *Strong and Free* or *First Steps towards Social Science*, and *The Battle of the Two Philosophies*.

18. 8 April 1842, Bodleian Library MSS Erskine collection 18.

19. 'Feast of St Peter's Chair in Rome', 1842., ibid.

20. The same.

21. 1784–1864; educated Eton and Christ Church, Oxford.

22. W. Hextall, Ashby-de-la-Zouch, 1837.

23. 13 April 1830 to Christopher Wordsworth, son of Wordsworth's brother Christopher; (ed) Alan. G. Hill, *Letters of William and Dorothy Wordsworth*, V, the Later Years, Part.2., OUP, 1979, p.231.

24. 1806–76; Daughter of Charity of St Vincent de Paul; beatified 1933; canonized 1947.

25. *To the Inhabitants of Whitwick*, 10 February 1836.

26. *To the Inhabitants of Whitwick*, second edition, Daniel Cartwright, Loughborough, 17 February 1836.

27. *Special Pleadings in the Court of Reason and Conscience*, Leicester, 1836.

28. W. &. J. Hextall, Ashby-de-la-Zouch, 1845.

29. Achived by the Second Vatican Council in the Decree *De Accomodata renovatione* of 28 October 1965.

30. Passionist Archives, Ormskirk.

31. 3 December 1837, ibid.

32. 21 February 1835, Ugbrook Archives.

33. 15 August 1845, V.A., S.d.C. Acton 2.155.

34. This was effected in 1848.

35. 19 September 1891; Ratcliffe College Archives.

36. Charles Dolman, 1842 (no traces of these girls remain in the towns to which visitors once flocked).

37. 29 September 1844; Purcell, *de Lisle*, Vol. 1, p.137.

38. Two other local cases were Augusta, widow of the 8th Earl Ferrers of Stanton Harold, who married Captain Walsh and the widow of the 7th Lord Buron of Thrumpton, who became the wife of the Revd Paul Douglas.

39. They had changed their name from that of Shore.

40. R. P. Lecanuet, *Montalembert d'apres son journal et sa correspondance*, Paris, 1896, Vol. 11, p.92 ff.

41. September 1836, Purcell, *de Lisle*, Vol. 1, p.69.

42. 2 October 1839, ibid. p.78.

Chapter 7   Some Crises

1. Darton, Longman & Todd, 1975, p.388.
2. 29 February 1840. RA, Stresa.
3. 30 March 1840, ibid.
4. Hirst, *Lady Mary Arundell*, p.100 et. seq.
5. A French Rosminian.
6. ibid., p.102–3.
7. *A History of the Pastoral addressed to the Faithful of the Western District on the occasion of the feast of Lent 1840.*
8. *A Letter addressed to Sir Charles Wolseley, Bart. on the Lenten Pastoral of 1840.*
9. P.F.A., S.C.P., Anni 1827–42, Vol. 156, 229.
10. 15 June 1840.
11. 6 December 1841, B Ward, *Sequel to Catholic Emancipation*, Longmans, Vol. 11, p.278–9.
12. Hirst, *Lady Mary Arundell*, p,103.
13. 3 March 1840, Westminster Cathedral Archives.
14. 26 January 1840, R. A., Stresa.
15. 16 April, Purcell, *de Lisle*, Vol. 1, p.105–6.
16. 26 January 1840.
17. To Rosmini, 15 June 1840.
18. To the same, 7 September 1840.
19. A contended heresy that a man can move towards salvation by his own efforts, apart from the help of divine grace.
20. 2 July 1840.
21. A benefactress living with the Cannington nuns.
22. 14 September 1840.
23. Alphonsus Liguori, 1696–1787; founder of the Redemptorists; moral theologian.
24. 17 January 1841, R. A., Stresa.
25. 8 January 1841, ibid.
26. A Trappist who had taken on the mission.

27. To Rosmini 10 May 1841, ibid.
28. 11 June 1841, MCA, MS 31.
29. *The Tablet*, No LVII, 12 June 1841, p.385.
30. To Bloxam 25 June 1841; M.C.A., MS 32.
31. 10 August 1841.
32. 'A very serious case'.
33. Passion.
34. 9 June 1842; R. A. Stresa.
35. 8 March 1842, ibid.
36. 15 March 1842, ibid.
37. 3 and 10 March 1842, Archives Birmingham Oratory.
38. 8 March 1842, ibid.
39. To Lord Shrewsbury, 23 October 1842, Purcell, *de Lisle*, Vol. 1, p.257–60.
40. 22 July 1842, ibid, p.230–38.
41. ibid, p.112.
42. St Clement 1842, V.A., S.d.C. 3.431.
43. Vol. I, p.89. He incurred a good deal of criticism for drawing attention to his subject's so-called unhappy dealings with the Society of Jesus in his *Life of Cardinal Manning*, Macmillan, 2 Vols. 1896.
44. Arch. Prov. Ang. S. J.
45. O.M.I. General Council 24 March 1848.
46. Pagani to Rosmini 9 September 1843, R. A., Stresa.
47. *Apologia pro Vita Sua*, (ed) M. Svaglic, p.162.
48. 1 September 1843, *Correspondence with John Keble and Others*, (1839–45) p.250.
49. 22 August 1843, R. A., Stresa.
50. Sibthorpe returned to the Roman Catholic Church in 1865, but his outlook remained ambivalent; see Chapter 12.
51. To Gentili 26 July 1844.
52. 1778–1864; Maria von Lutzow, m Josef Freiherr von Weichs 1804.

53. Under the pseudonym Cordelia, she wrote novels with a strong religious flavour; several are to be found in English collections, notably the British Library.
54. Now in a chapel near Mount St Bernard.
55. 6 August 1846, *Dublin Review*, (ed. Louis Allen) No.464, 2nd quarter 1954, p.204.
56. Vol. VI, No.267, 14 June 1846.
57. Urban Young, *Dominic Barberi in England*, Burns Oates, 1935, p.128.
58. Urban Young, *Life and Letters of Father Dominic*, p.256.
59. Frederick Sellwood Bowles, 1818–1900; joined the Oratory in 1848, but left in 1860; became a secular priest on the Isle of Wight.
60. Richard Stanton 1820–1901; joined the Oratory and sent by Newman to London 1849.
61. ibid. p.259.
62. 19 October 1845, *L and D. of J. H. Newman*, Vol. XI, p.19.
63. 15 October 1845, Archives Birmingham Oratory.
64. 1812–89; became a Roman Catholic in 1845 and made several journeys between the two Churches.
65. *Verses on Various Occasions*, Burns Oates, 1868, p.270–1.
66. 1819–85; Vicar of St Mary Magdalen, Oxford 1843–5; became a Roman Catholic December 1845; joined the Oratorians 1848; Redemptorists 1850; Bishop of Southwark 1882–5.
67. 1810–80.
68. For fuller details of these family relationships, see David Newsome, *The Parting of Friends*, John Murray, 1966.
69. An event of extraordinary significance; see Chapter 8.
70. 29 January 1848, R A, Stresa.

71. 28 February 1848, ibid.

Chapter 8   Clerical Victory

1. Repeated in a letter to J. H. Newman, 28 May 1848, Archives Birmingham Oratory.
2. ibid.
3. Faber's terminology for a statue of the Blessed Virgin Mary.
4. 29 May 1848, ibid.
5. 3 June 1848, ibid and *L. and D. of J. H. Newman*, Vol. XII, p.212–3.
6. 5 June 1848, ibid.
7. See p.82
8. 15 June 1848, ibid.
9. 19 June 1848, ibid. Bishop Ullathorne wrote to Rome in 1851 (see p.258), suggesting that Newman was unsuited to be a bishop as he lacked tact and could not manage men. Newman's handing of Ambrose on this occasion earned him the latter's life-long respect and admiration.
10. 8 December 1848, Purcell, *de Lisle*, Vol. II, p.208–9.
11. Faber's manner of writing the definite article.
12. John Henry Newman.
13. 1710–73; author of *Lives of Fathers, Martyrs and other Principal Saints*, 1756–9; Mission Priest in the Midland District 1746–66; from 1766 Principal of English College, St Omer.
14. A periodical supported by 'old' Catholics.
15. Archives Archdiocese of Birmingham B. 1096.
16. B Ward, *The Sequel to Catholic Emancipation*, Vol. II, p.246–8.
17. 30 October 1848, *L and D of J. H. Newman*, Vol. XII, p.316.
18. 1 December 1848, Archives Archdiocese of Birmingham, B.1322.
19. Date unknown, Purcell, *de Lisle*, Vol. II, 218n.

20. 2 July 1850, *Dublin Review*, (ed. Louis Allen), No.465, 3rd quarter 1954, p.323.
21. As well as his manual of plain chant published in 1847, he published some sequences and proses in 1867, and 9 Gregorian Masses in 1868, which included one written by himself.
22. Purcell, *de Lisle*, Vol. II, p.186–198.
23. 8 July 1851, de Lisle Archives.
24. 1 December 1839, Purcell, *de Lisle*, Vol. II, p.222.
25. 22 November 1839, P.F.A., S.R.n.C. 1839, Anglia, Vol. IX 762. (he had been educated at St Omer).
26. 1 December 1839, Archives English College, 70.6., WAL 56.
27. 5 June 1852, *Dublin Review* (ed. Louis Allen) No.465, 4th quarter 1954, p.443–4.
28. His mental illness.
29. By Pope Gregory XVI.
30. The inside casing of the lead coffin which was then placed in a wooden one. Sophia was buried in the crypt of Grace Dieu Chapel, but re-interred in June 1880, on the death of George, in a grave next to his at the Monastery.
31. To Laura 29 May 1851, de Lisle Archives. Henry Manning was ordained into the Roman Catholic priesthood ten weeks after his reception, so highly did Wiseman regard him. He said Mass in Grace Dieu Chapel twelve days later.
32. 22 September 1847, Purcell, *de Lisle*, Vol. I, p.328.
33. 18 March 1848 To Nicholas Wiseman, newly arrived in the London Vicariate; Archives Ushaw College, 524.
34. With which Bishop Walsh eventually dissociated himself.

35. P.F.A., Scr. Orig. Cong. Generali, Vol. 956, 1839, 287–341.
36. He commented submissively on the two decrees sent to England from Rome; the one on Indulgences would 'prove to be most effective in stimulating a spirit of devotion and piety among the faithful'; the second would put an end of the spirit of jealousy which had impeded religious progress.
37. P.F.A., S.R.C., Anglia, 1839, Vol. IX, 543.
38. 3 May 1847, ibid, 1846–7, Vol. XI, 339–368 et seq. Gentili sent fourteen documents to Rome over 18 months, in all over 80,000 words.
39. 15 December 1847, Purcell, *de Lisle*, Vol. I, p.327–8.
40. 1792–1878.
41. 1773–1859; Foreign Minister of Austria from 1809.
42. 29 May 1848, Archives Birmingham Oratory.
43. 1816–86; 3rd son of Baron Talbot of Malahide. Received into the Roman Catholic Church 1843; Priest in the London Vicariate 1847; Papal Chamberlain July 1850; Consultor Propaganda Fide; retired to mental institution in France 1868.
44. Archives English College, Talbot Papers.
45. Dated 7 October 1850, published as Appendix N. to B. Ward, *The Sequel to Catholic Emancipation*, Vol. II.
46. *Address and Protest of the Archbishops and Bishops of the Church of England* (except the Bishops of Exeter and St Davids).
47. *Pio Nono*, Eyre and Spottiswoode, 1960, p.142.
48. His allocution *Quibus Quantisque* from Gaeta, dated 20 April

1849, made his future outlook plain.

49. 19 October 1850, *The Times*, No.20,624, p.4.

50. Ward, *Wiseman*, Vol. I, p.534–6.

51. *A Letter to the Earl of Shrewsbury on the Re-establishment of the Hierarchy of the English Catholic Church*, Charles Dolman, dated 28 October 1850.

52. 8 November 1850, *L and D of J. H. Newman*, Vol. XIV, p.121.

53. *An Appeal to the Reason and Good Feeling of the English People*. T Richardson & Son, 1850.

54. 13 November 1850, Archives Westminster Cathedral.

55. *A Few Words on the Letter of Lord John Russell to the Bishop of Durham*.

56. 24 December 1850, *The Times*, No.20,680, p.4.

57. 25 November 1850, from Naples, Purcell, *de Lisle*, Vol. I, p.327.

58. V.A., S.d.C. Acton, 2,389, (undated).

59. To Lord Zetland, 20 November 1850, Ward, *Wiseman*, Vol. II, p.15.

60. To Lord Beaumont, 28 November 1850, ibid.

61. He was reconciled shortly before his death.

62. To J. M. Capes, 18 February 1851, *L. and D. of J. H. Newman*, Vol. XIV, p.213.

63. 22 March 1851, Propanganda Fide Acta 213, 281.

64. 6 March 1851, P.F.A., S.R.C. Anglia Vol. XII, 949: 'Egli non governa a casa sua. Per quanto lo rispetti, non posso chiudere gli occhi all ? essere egli uomo rinchiuso e senza volunta o tatto a manegiare altri. Per questo solo motivo due dei Suoi sono gia partite.'

65. 1791–1866; A Franciscan who followed Ullathorne as Vicar Apostolic of the Western District and then was appointed first Bishop of Clifton in 1850. He was translated to Nottingham in 1851 and retired through ill health in 1853.

66. 27 October 1853, W. Ward, *Aubrey de Vere*, Longmans Green, 1904, p.226.

67. 14 November 1849, Archives Birmingham Archdiocese B. 1740.

68. William Joseph Vavasour, 1822–60, m. 1846 the Hon. Mary Constantia Clifford.

69. Relations of Lord Camoys.

70. 19th Baron Stourton 1802–76; m. 1825 the Hon. Mary Lucy Clifford.

71. William Constable-Maxwell, 1822–76; in 1858 the dormant barony of Herries was revived in his favour.

72. 1806–70; 3rd Bart.

73. Charles George Noel, 1818–81, Viscount Campden, Earl of Gainsborough 1866; became a Roman Catholic 1851.

74. A Privy Council opinion.

75. 1834–1902; 8th Bart., created 1st Lord Acton 1869; educated Oscott and Munich; Regius Professor of Modern History, Cambridge 1895.

76. Rudolph William Basil, 1823–92; 8th Earl of Denbigh 1865.

77. 1818–82; inherited large fortune from his mother; M P for Bucks 1841–5; became Roman Catholic 1844.

78. 1813–1903; Fellow of Wadham College, Oxford 1833–41; became a Roman Catholic 1850.

79. 1807–73; 4th and youngest son of William; Newman's pupil at Oriel; became a Roman Catholic 1850; a journalist.

80. 1802–57; 2nd son of William;

Archdeacon of the West Riding; became a Roman Catholic in 1854.

81. Became a Roman Catholic 1847; later a Dominican and writer; left for Unitarianism 1873.

82. 5 October 1848, Archives Rosminian English Province.

83. 1818–83; 2nd son of 13th Duke of Norfolk; M.P. 1848–68; 1st Baron Howard of Glossop 1869; m. Winifreda daughter of Ambrose de Lisle as his second wife 1863; much concerned with Catholic education.

84. Archives Westminster Cathedral.

Chapter 9   The Association for the Promotion of the Unity of Christendom.

1. 1816–70; Bishop of Southwark 1851; educated Ushaw; Rector of the English College in Rome 1844–51.

2. See Shakespere's Henry VI Part I for a romanticised version of his exploits against the army of Joan of Arc.

3. Mena had been thrown from her horse a few days earlier and had forfeited her place.

4. 11 April 1854, Archives Birmingham Archdiocese, B. 3134.

5. *Mahometanism and its Relation to Prophecy*, Charles Dolman.

6. Association for the Promotion of the Unity of Christendom.

7. Purcell, *de Lisle*, Vol. II, p. 339.

8. He was wrong.

9. 1800–73;   Sergeant-at-Law; became a Roman Catholic 1850.

10. 1804–99; Vicar of Arlington 1843–52; after becoming a Roman Catholic, he studied in Rome and later received new orders in 1857.

11. The Will stated 'for their absolute use and benefit and discharged from the trusts declared in my said Will'.

12. 12 April 1853; National Library of Ireland MSS 8318 (2).

13. 8 May 1854, Archives Birmingham Archdiocese B. 3149.

14. Le Chevalier Zeloni, *Life of Gwendoline Talbot, Princess Borghese*, Burns Oates, 1894.

15. Under the inscription: Here repose the ashes of the Mother of the Poor Princess Gwendolin Borghese.

16. 1812–73; Fellow of Merton College, Oxford, a parliamentary lawyer and friend of Newman; became a Roman Catholic in 1851.

17. In compliance with the 17th Earl's Will, he took the name of Talbot. After a distinguished parliamentary career, he was created Viscount Fitzalan of Derwent.

18. 1803–68; served in the Royal Navy and took part in several battles at sea; retired as a Rear Admiral.

19. Vol. II, p.340n.

20. 1802–79.

21. 1809–53; Spanish nobleman; writer on political philosophical and theological subjects.

22. 5 June 1852, *Dublin Review*, (ed Louis Allen) No.466, 4th quarter 1954, p.443.

23. Current term for this language.

24. 1813–83; Editor of *L'Univers* 1843–83; strong opponent of modern ideas; advocate of the temporal sovereignty of the Pope and Papal Infallibility.

25. 1806–67, Editor of *Annales Archeologiques* and author of *Christian Iconography*, (trans. E. J. Millington).

26. 1795–1858; a celebrated preacher at Notre Dame in Paris 1837–46; a spiritual director of influence.

27. 31 January 1851; Archives Clifford family.

28. p.212.

29. p.214.

30. 12 June 1855; Archives Rosminian English Province.

31. 16 March 1855.

32. 25 December 1876.

33. By that time Henry Manning.

34. *The End of the World or the Second Coming of Our Lord and Saviour Jesus Christ.*

35. c 1132–1202.

36. 1613–58; one of his works on the Book of Revelation had been reprinted in 1849.

37. 1731–1801; the book was banned by the Holy Office in 1824 and again in 1941.

38. 29 October 1848; Archives Rosminian English Province.

39. Ambrose congratulated Bishop Ullathorne on his book on the Holy Mountain of La Salette and added that great good had resulted in consequence of the apparitions; 22 August 1854, Archives Birmingham Archdiocese. B.3194).

40. Viscount Adare, *Experiences with Spiritualism with D,D, Home*, with Introductory Remarks by the Earl of Dunraven, Thomas Scott, 1869.

41. 20 April 1848, Hexham Hogarth MSS. I am indebted to the unpulished B. Litt thesis of Pauline Adams of Somerville College, Oxford, for drawing my attention to this letter.

42. 17 December 1857; de Lisle Archives.

43. See p.291.

44. 4 April 1857, ibid.

45. 1806–88, former parish priest in Chelsea; Cistercian 1847.

46. Description by Montalembert.

47. 27 June 1855, Archives Rosminian English Province.

48. 27 June 1855, ibid.

49. 5 December 1856 ibid.

50. He reported the conversation in English.

51. 26 June 1855, Archives Birmingham City Archives.

52. 1827–1919; received as a Roman Catholic at Grace Dieu 1857; became a Cistercian at Mount St Bernard 1861.

53. Also written Rudulph; the spelling of the children's names was never very consistent.

54. 1832–1903; Herbert Vaughan, 4th Archbishop of Westminster 1892; then a student in Rome.

55. There was no money.

56. 21 February was the first day without pain.

57. 7 March 1855, Archives Birmingham Archdiocese B.3304.

58. 2 June 1855; Archives Rosminian English Province.

59. 11 February 1857, de Lisle Archives.

60. Name given to those Churchmen who refused to give their allegiance to William and Mary, having already done so to James II still living, though in exile.

61. Notably H.R.T. Brandreth, *Dr Lee of Lambeth*, S.P.C.K., 1951.

62. p.vii–viii.

63. 19 February 1857, de Lisle Archives.

64. 4 March 1857, ibid.

65. 1813–91; became a Roman Catholic under Newman's influence 1846; father of the poet Francis Thompson.

66. 4 April 1857, *L & D of J. H. Newman*, Vol. XVIII, p.12n.

67. 12 April 1857, ibid.

68. 11 March 1857, Archives Westminster Cathedral.

69. *On the Future Unity of Christendom*, Charles Dolman, 1857.

70. Alexander Penrose Forbes 1817–75; Bishop of Brechin 1847.

71. 1825–90; succeeded as Earl of Glasgow 1869.

72. 18 May 1857, P.F.A., S.R.n.C., Anglia, Vol. XIV, 118v–119r.

73. 8 June 1857, Copy in de Lisle Archives.

74. To Lee, 20 June 1857, ibid.

75. 9 June 1857, Archives Southwark diocese.

76. Grace Ramsey, *Life of Thomas Grant, First Bishop of Southwark*, Smith Elder, 1874.

77. 27 June 1857, P.F.A., S.R.n.C., Anglia, Vol. XIV, 1114r–1117v.

78. 30 June 1857, ibid, 1145r–1145r, and 17 July 1857, ibid, 1146r.

79. To Lee 5 May 1857, de Lisle Archives.

80. 22 June 1857, Archives Southwark Diocese.

81. Richard Roskell 1817–83; educated English College; Bishop of Nottingham 1853, (where he was younger than the youngest priest); retired 1876.

82. Ambrose to Lee 24 June 1857; de Lisle Archives; 'he was amazed. He seemed like a man suddenly awaken from a deep sleep, he declared it was one of the most wonderful things he had ever heard of'.

83. 30 June 1857, ibid.

84. In his report to Propaganda Fide of 24 December 1857; S.P.n.C., Anglia, 1857, Vol. XIV, 1255r–1264v.

85. ibid. 1264v–1265r (wrongly dated in some printed versions).

86. 107 pages in three different sets of handwriting, ibid. 977r–1026r.

87. (undated) ibid. 975r–976v. I am indebted to Fr John McFadden C.S.Sp. and his unpublished thesis for his guidance in these matters.

88. Shane Leslie repeated this assertion in his biography *Henry Edward Manning, His Life and Labours*, Dublin, Clonmore and Reynolds, 1953, p.75.

89. 17 August 1857, Original in the Archives of Southwark Diocese.

90. To Lee, 4 September 1857, de Lisle Archives.

91. 31 August 1857; P.F.A., S.R.n.C. Anglia, Vol. XIV 1857, 1268.

92. 30 September 1857, ibid, 1027r–1030v.

93. New Series, VIII 1857, p.140–5.

94. Vol. 43, 1857, p.201.

95. 10 July 1857, Purcell, de Lisle, Vol. II, p.255.

96. *L. and D. of J. H. Newman*, Vol. XVIII, p.70–1.

97. In a letter to Lee 2 April 1857, de Lisle Archives.

98. 30 July 1857, *L and D. of J. H. Newman*, Vol. XVIII, p.105.

99. 9 July 1857, ibid, p.88.

100. 1829–88; ordained as an Anglican and after his reception as a Roman Catholic accepted only minor orders; taught at St Edmund's, Ware.

101. Cuthbert Butler, *Life and Times of Bishop Ullathorne*, Vol. I, p.345.

102. Only recently come to light; they give a vivid account of his experiences in the Mutiny; de Lisle Archives.

103. At this time not awarded posthumously, but regulations changed and the award was gazetted in 1907.

104. 29 May 1857; P.F.A., S.R.n.C., Anglia, Vol. XIV, p.1080.

Chapter 10 The 1860s

1. Titular Archbishop of Trebizond; Former Bishop of Plymouth; see p.135.

2. 23 March 1857, Richard J. Schiefen, *Nicholas Wiseman and the Transformation of English Catholicism*, Patmos Press, 1984, p.253.

3. (undated) English College Archives, 80–4. These communications became a habit. Later at the time of the debate on whether Roman Catholics should attend English universities, Vaughan reported to Talbot on a Low Week meeting and warned Talbot not only that Ullathorne was conspiring against him, but that he regarded Talbot to have been 'for twelve years *the pest* of the English bishops'. (Only date given 6 May).

4. Rambler 3rd series, 1, 1859, p.198–20.

5. 1803–93; cousin and close friend of Laura de Lisle; Bishop of Clifton 1857.

6. 15 February 1861; To J. L. Patterson (copy) Archives Westminster Cathedral W3/20.

7. 6 June 1863, Talbot to Manning, E. S. Purcell, *Life of Cardinal Manning*, Macmillan, 1895, Vol. II, p.173.

8. 1820–76, Vicar of Mitcham 1844; became Roman Catholic 1846; editor of the Rambler 1858.

9. 12 March 1860; (copy) Pusey House.

10. 25 February 1860, Purcell, *de Lisle*, Vol, 1, p.188.

11. 3 November 1860, *Dublin Review*, (ed) Louis Allen, No.299. No468, 2nd quarter 1955, p.202.

12. 9 March 1864, Purcell, *de Lisle*, Vol. II, p257.

13. 14 March 1864, ibid. Vol. II, p391–2.

14. 15 March 1864, Ward, *Wiseman*, Vol. II, p462.

15. Attached to Bishop Ullathorne's first letter to his clergy on the A.P.U.C., see p.315.

16. In his second Letter to the Clergy of his diocese, see p.320.

17. 26 April and 21 May 1864, P.F.A., S.R.d.C. Anglia, XVIII, 1864–66, 155r–159v and 197r–198v.

18. 1819–94; Edmund Salisbury ffoulkes; became a Roman Catholic 1855; returned to the Church of England 1870.

19. 10 November 1864.

20. 11 February 1865 (copy) Archives Birmingham Oratory and *L. and D. of J. H. Newman*, Vol. XXI, p.415n.

21. On the Syllabus of Errors.

22. 13 February 1865, ibid. p.415.

23. 18 September 1864, ibid. p.228.

24. 3 November 1864, wrongly dated in Purcell, *de Lisle*, Vol. 1, p.389–90.

25. 15 November 1864, ibid. p.392–3.

26. To Ambrose 18 November 1864; Ward, Wiseman, Vol. II, p.490–1.

27. Purcell, *de Lisle*, Vol, 1, p.400.

28. *A Letter on the Association for Promoting the Unity of Christendom addressed to the clergy of the diocese of Birmingham*, Thomas Richardson.

29. A reference to the papal audience granted to the Revd George Nugee, a member of the A.P.U.C., to whom Pius IX had said 'Mio interno sentimento voluntario'; an event described to Wiseman by Ambrose in a letter 11 April 1864; Archives Westminster Cathedral.

30. *A Reply to Bishop Ullathorne's Pastoral against* the A,P,U,C, G. J. Palmer, 1864.

31. To Ambrose, 19 December 1864: Purcell, *de Lisle*, Vol. I, p.400.

32. 13 June 1865, Archives Oblates of St Charles.

33. 18 July 1865, Purcell, *Life of Cardinal Manning*, Vol. II, p.281.

34. Now only to be found in printed form, such as ibid, with the disappearance of the originals in the English College.

35. 19 February 1866, (copy) Pusey House.

36. In several letters 1865–66; Archives English College.

37. 24 August 1865, Shane Leslie, *Henry Edward Manning*, p.177.

38. *A Letter to the Revd E B Pusey*, Longmans Green, 1865.

39. John Parker, 1860.

40. *The Church of England, a Portion of Christ's one Holy Catholic Church and a means of restoring visible unity.* An Eirenicon in a Letter to the Author of the Christian Year. John Henry and James Parker, 1865.

41. *The Anglican Theory of Union as maintained in the Appeal to Rome and Dr Pusey's Eirenicon*, Burns, Lambert and Oates, 1865.

42. Religious tests for university entrance had been removed in 1854.

43. E. S. ffoulkes proposed to Ambrose joining together in a committee, under the chairmanship of Lord Edward Howard, to found a Catholic College at Oxford.

44. *Apologia pro Vita Sua*, first published in the Spring of 1864.

45. Born 1834, died aged 41, Gillow's *Biographical Dictionary of English Catholics*, Burns Oates, 1885, records his 'impulsive and fiery nature which led him into various disputations and futile troubles; and curious stories are told of his eccentricities'.

46. Originals Downside Abbey.

47. Appointed lecturer in moral philosophy 1851; assistant lecturer in dogmatic theology 1852 which caused a stir on account of Ward's lay status; he resigned in 1858.

48. 1809–79.

49. 1804–83; ordained as a Roman Catholic 1845; became chaplain to Lord Shrewsbury 1846; he left England 1853 and returned to the American Church.

50. On account of these problems and in spite of Mother Connelly's efforts, papal approval of the rule of the S.H.C.J. was not obtained until 1893, after her death, by which time the Order had developed and spread in England and overseas.

51. Mary Andrew Armour, *Cornelia*, S.H.C.J., 1979, p.68.

52. 1823–91, Prime Minister of New Zealand 1864, Governor of Western Australia 1870; of Tasmania 1874; of the Straits Settlements 1880; G.C.M.G. 1880; see Alice Lady Lovat, *A Pioneer of Empire*, John Murray, 1914.

53. 8 February 1859, Dorset Record Office.

54. 1815–92; A solicitor in Salisbury; educated at Downside; Poor Law Inspector 1857; first Permanent Secretary of the Local Government Board 1871; K.C.B. 1879, P.C. 1885.

55. 1829–90; Prebendary of Salisbury 1864; Canon of St Paul's and Dean Ireland Professor of Exegesis at Oxford 1870.

56. 1822–97, became a Roman Catholic 1842; to Newman's University in Dublin 1854; Inspector of

Catholic schools in England 1864; Keeper of Antiquities British Museum 1886, Knight 1896.

57. de Lisle Archives.

58. ibid.

59. 20 June, Archives Rosminian English Province.

60. 1840–71; one of the twelve children of Sir Richard Sutton.bt., one time Master of the Quorn.

61. 7 September 1861, de Lisle Archives.

62. Archives Downside Abbey.

63. Ambrose to his father; de Lisle Archives.

64. He died deeply in debt and worn out by dissipation in 1868 aged 26. He caused great scandal in 1864 by eloping, shortly before her projected marriage, with Lady Florence Paget, daughter of the Marquess of Anglesey. Her fiancé, Henry Chaplin, was a friend of the Prince of Wales. They met, by assignment, at Marshal and Snelgrove and went straight to St George's Hanover Square, and were married. Henry Blyth, *The Pocket Venus*, Weidenfeld and Nicolson, 1966.

65. To George Ryder 19 February 1849, *L and D. of J.H. Newman*, Vol. XIII, p.58

66. She was one of five sisters, all of whom became nuns.

67. Winifreda suffered likewise in 1865, though specialists, rightly, were hopeful of a cure.

68. 1820–89; Professor of Greek and Latin at Newman's University in Dublin in 1854, in a letter of 19 December 1857 in the *Weekly Register*.

69. 5 September, from Bashika Bay; de Lisle Archives.

70. The letter to Rome of the 198 Anglicans had also made this distinction.

71. He died three months later.

72. Outstanding debts still owed to Bishop Ullathorne of several thousand pounds and nearly thirty years' standing.

73. Friend of Dr Döllinger, he later wrote on the Vatican Council in a manner unsympathetic to ultramontane opinion.

74. 1819–92; Vicar of Wymering, Sussex 1859; founded St Augustine's Priory, Walworth, 1877.

75. Copies are now hard to find; the most complete series would seem to be Gladstone's at S Deiniol's Library, Hawarden, since he was a subscriber; his annotations in the margins provide interesting reading.

76. Vol. IV, 1866, p.221.

77. Vol. III, 1864, p.236.

78. Vol. II, 1864, p.327.

79. Vol. IV, 1866, p.82–99.

80. 18 September 1864, *L and D of J.H. Newman*, Vol. XXI, p.228.

81. *A Letter to the Revd E. B. Pusey on his Recent Eirenicon*, Longmans Green and Dyer, 1866.

82. 7 February 1866, *L. and D. of J. H. Newman*, Vol. XXII, p.146–7.

83. He was 66.

84. 27 February 1866, ibid. p.165.

85. *A Pastoral Letter to the Clergy*, Longmans Green, 1866. There was a further equally umcomprising Letter from Manning in 1867, *England and Christendom*.

86. 3 March 1866, *L. and D. of J. H. Newman*, Vol. XXII, p.170–2.

87. 'I know you are full of good works', Newman wrote to Ambrose on 15 February 1867, who sent £10 a month later.

88. Edition of 6 April 1867.

89. 6 April 1867, Ward, *Life of Cardinal Newman*, Vol. II, p.143. There were 178 names in the

original document; others were added later.

90. ibid. 25 April 1867, p.146–8.

91. *Deus, Natura, Gratia*, Lyons, 1634.

92. *The Validity of the Holy Orders of the Church of the Church of England Maintained*, J. T. Hayes, 1869.

93. *Essays on Reunion of Christendom by Members of the Roman Catholic, Orthodox and Anglican Communions*, 1867.

94. *Union Review*, Vol. VI, 1868, p.539–59.

95. Laura's book of Medical Recipes gave prescriptions for such varied ills as cholera (calomel, Dover's powders and prepared chalk); for the poor when debilitated (quinine and sulphuric acid) and dropsy (calomel and squills). de Lisle Archives.

96. ibid.

Chapter 11 The First Vatican Council – Last Days

1. Cardinal de Luca would seem to have been especially interested in this aspect; see Dom Franco de Wyel's article 'Le Concile du Vatican et l'Union' in *Irenikon* Tome 3, 1929, Juin-Aout p.369–372.

2. Purcell, Manning, Vol,II, p.420.

3. 21 July 1867, *L. and D. of J. H. Newman*, Vol. XXIII, p.271–4.

4. 11 August 1867, *The Oscotian* for July 1886, p.148

5. The official statement proclaimed the Council had been called 'in order to bring necessary and salutary remedies to the many evils whereby the Church is oppressed'.

6. 4 April 1867, Archives St Edmund's Ware, B. 4529.

7. 11 April 1866, *Dublin Review*, (ed. Louis Allen) 1955, Vol. 229., No. 468, p.205–6.

8. *The Authority of Doctrinal Decisions*, Burns, Lambert and Oates, 1866.

9. 17 November 1865, *L. and D. of J. H. Newman*, Vol. XXII, p.103.

10. 1837–1907; eldest son of George Ryder; *Idealism in Theology, a Review of Dr Ward's Scheme of Dogmatic Theology*, Longmans Green and Co. 1867.

11. 11 June 1867, Purcell, *de Lisle*, Vol. II, P.36–7.

12. 3 May 1867, Archives Nottingham Diocese.

13. *A Letter to the Very Revd J H Newman, DD*, by a Catholic layman.

14. Died 638; Pope from 625.

15. 21 June 1868; *L. and D. of J. H. Newman*, Vol. XXIV, p.90.

16. 13 October 1869, Archives Pembroke College, Oxford.

17. 17 July 1867, Purcell, *de Lisle*, Vol. II, p.34.

18. 9 December 1869, Pusey House.

19. See J. Jurich, S. J., *The Ecumenical Relations of Victor De Buck S. J. with Anglo-Catholic Leaders on the Eve of Vatican I. Preludes 1854–68*, Université Catholique de Louvain, 1970.

20. 5 October 1868, Pusey House.

21. In his letter of 9 December 1869 to Bishop Forbes.

22. *L. and D. of J. H. Newman*, Vol. XXIV, p.151n.

23. ? April 1869, Pusey House.

24. August and October 1869, Purcell, *de Lisle*, Vol. II, p.259–262. Montalembert died on 13 March 1870, described by *L'Univers* as 'of all the laymen of our time, the one who has given to the Church the greatest and most devoted service'.

25. In 1872 Bishop of Salford and later later Manning's successor as Archbishop of Westminster.

26. In his letter of 9 December 1869.

27. For example *Hansard* CLXXII, 1863, p.325n.

28. *L. and D. of J. H. Newman*, Vol. XXIV, p.325n.

29. ibid. p.334.

30. Longmans Green and Co. 1869.

31. The first was a Lenten Pastoral on the value of 'old' Catholic Faith and practice; the second *A Pastoral Letter to the Faithful*.

32. *L. and D. of J. H. Newman*, Vol. XXIV p.349.

33. C Butler, *Life and Times of Bishop Ullathorne*, Vol. II, p.49–50.

34. Longmans Green, 1930.

35. (ed) Edmund Campion, *Lord Acton and the First Vatican Council*, A Journal, Catholic Theological Faculty, Sydney, 1975, p.67.

36. 6 April 1870, Archives Birmingham Oratory; in part *L. and D. of J. H. Newman*, Vol. XXV, p.81n.

37. 11 Bishops from France and 19 from Germany.

38. 7 April 1870, ibid. p.81–2.

39. 28 January 1870, ibid, p.18–20.

40. ibid. p.164.

41. Notably in the *Letter to the Duke of Norfolk*, of 1875.

42. 26 February 1872, de Lisle Archives.

43. National Library of Ireland, Dublin, MS 8318 (2).

44. Alice played the organ.

45. 17 November 1873, *L. and D. of J. H. Newman*, Vol. XXVI, p.386–7.

46. 19 April 1876, de Lisle Archives.

47. 1847–1900; became a Roman Catholic in 1868.

48. H. C. G. Matthew, *The Gladstone Diaries*, Vol. VIII, p.398.

49. Vicar of Thorpe Acre.

50. 13 October 1873, de Lisle Archives.

51. After Ambrose's death, Margaret and Gladstone exchanged letters for several years; hers are now in the British Museum; his at the Mill Hill Convent.

52. 68 letters between 1873 and 1876.

53. k506–66, Francois Louis de Blois; Flemish Benedictine who revitalised the spirit of monastic life.

54. Published 1872.

55. 1 April 1874; Purcell, *de Lisle*, Vol. II, p.78.

56. 2 April 1874, de Lisle Archives.

57. 1812–73; became a Roman Catholic 1851; friend of Newman from 1837.

58. Purcell, *de Lisle*, Vol. II, p.79–80.

59. ibid. p.80–82.

60. 20 May 1874, ibid, p.83–4.

61. 8 July 1874, ibid. p.87.

62. ibid, p.87–89.

63. de Lisle Archives.

64. 1829–1912; acted as Private Secretary to Gladstone at various periods; later Lord Stanmore.

65. Matthew, *The Gladstone Diaries*, Vol. VIII, p.539.

66. 4 November 1874, quoted ibid. p.539n5.

67. 7 August 1874, *L. and D. of J. H. Newman*, Vol. XXVII, p.104.

68. October 1874, Purcell, *de Lisle*, Vol. II, p.292n.

69. Archives Birmingham Oratory and in part *L. and D. of J. H. Newman*, Vol. XXVII, p.147n.

70. 1825–1902; 2nd son of 6th Duke of Manchester; M.P. 1859–80 in the Liberal interest.

71. 8 November 1874, Archives Birmingham Oratory.

72. Letter to Ambrose 6 November 1874, *L. and D. of J. H. Newman*, Vol. XXVII, p.152–3.

73. Just before his death in 1875, St John translated Bishop Fessler's work on Infallibility.

74. To Ambrose 15 November 1874, ibid. p.156.

75. ibid. p.156n.

76. 9 January 1875, ibid, p.185.

77. 12 January 1875, ibid. p.218.

78. 14 February 1875, ibid. p.221n.

79. Edwin Gilpin Bagshawe 1829–1915; appointed 1874; described by Ambrose as 'forced on the Nottingham diocese in spite of the Chapter by Cardinal Manning'.

80. 14 February 1875, ibid. p.221.

81. 22 February 1875, Purcell, *de Lisle*, Vol. II, p.66.

82. 19 February 1875, *L. and D. of J. H. Newman*, Vol. XXVII, p.224.

83. 8 March 1875; ibid, p.243.

84. 23 May 1875, Purcell, *de Lisle*, Vol. II, p.34–40.

85. A Church which maintains its own language, rites and canon law, yet enters into a union of obedience; i.e. Melkites and Maronites in the Near East.

86. 3 May 1875; Archives Birmingham Oratory.

87. Angela Maxwell gave birth to premature triplets, a boy and two girls, in February 1876; they were born alive, but died almost immediately, having been baptised by their father. Subsequently, she had two more daughters in January and December of 1877; even by Victorian standards, a considerable family in two years.

88. The Colonial Secretary.

89. He made a further visit to Garendon in 1882, when Laura noted in her diary that he ate little else but bread and butter. Disraeli based upon Manning the character of Cardinal Grandison in his novel *Lothiar* (published in 1870) and echoed the meagre nature of his diet.

90. 23 November 1875, Purcell, *de Lisle*, Vol. II, p.22.

91. ibid. p.23–4.

92. 17 January 1876, ibid. p.24–6.

93. 19 January 1876, *L. and D. of J. H. Newman*, Vol. XXVIII p.17–18.

94. News of the Uniat proposal reached Rome and was given space in the *Civilta Cattolica*, Vol. XI 9th series for August 1876 p.640.

95. 27 January and 21 May 1876, *L. and D. of J. H. Newman*, Vol. XXVIII, p.20 and p.66.

96. Curate of St Michael's Brighton, another energetic pamphleteer; he spent some months in the monastery established by Joseph Leycester Lyne.

97. Also to hear Irving read Macbeth.

98. Purcell, *de Lisle*, Vol. II, p.154.

99. de Lisle Archives.

100. ibid.

101. *The Bulgarian Horrors and the Question of the East*. It sold 40,000 copies in 4 days.

102. Purcell, *de Lisle*, Vol. II, p.157–8.

103. ibid, p.160.

104. War broke out between Russia and Turkey in April 1877.

105. R. T. Shannon, *Gladstone and the Bulgarian Agitation, 1876*, 1963, p.194–5.

106. He was currently in Disraeli's second Cabinet as Postmaster-General.

107. Vol. II. p.28.
108. ibid, p.29–31.
109. Documents in Pusey House.
110. To Fr Tatum, one time Chaplain at Magdalen College, who became a Roman Catholic in 1883, in a letter dated 14 January 1909, from Herald's College, E.C.
111. 20 June 1921.
112. 30 June 1921.
113. 1914–1980; ordained 1942; Assistant Secretary Church of England Council for Foreign Relations.
114. *Dr Lee of Lambeth*, SPCK, 1951.
115. To Fr Thurston, Archives Pusey House.
116. *Episcopi Vagantes and the Anglican Church*, S.P.C.K, 1947.
117. 27 November 1866, *de Lisle* Archives.
118. Born Lodi 1839; died 1907.
119. The correct name of the Congregation was Regular Clerics of St Paul.
120. Born St Petersburgh 1804.
121. By the Brief *Apositum Super Nobis* dated 30 April 1872, and extended to include prayers for return to Catholic unity by rescript of 13 May 1877.
122. He and Gladstone exchanged some letters.
123. The collection is now in the Barnabite Casa Generalizia on the Janiculum in Rome; given are free translations.
124. Of the English Roman Catholic nobility to Pius IX in May 1877; Winifreda had taken her sister Margaret.
125. 17 July 1877.
126. 24 August 1877.
127. 21 January 1878.
128. Dated 17 January 1878; Archives Nottingham Diocese.
129. Pius IX died 7 February 1878.

Chapter 12   Epilogue

1. Purcell, *de Lisle*, Vol. II, p.566.
2. 16 April 1867, *L. and D. of J. H. Newman*, Vol. XXIII, p.165.
3. To the same, 20 August 1869, ibid, Vol. XXIV, p.316–7.
4. 22 July 1878, ibid, Vol. XXVIII, p.388.
5. 18 January 1878, ibid, p.302.
6. Reprinted in the *Oscotian*, July 1886.
7. 28 January 1897, Purcell, *de Lisle*, Vol. II, p.77n.
8. 1839–1934; Charles Lindley Wood, Second Viscount Halifax; responsible for initiating, on the English side, the conversations between the Church of England and the Holy See; first in the 1890's and secondly in the 1920's (called the Malines Conversations).
9. 29 June 1896, ibid. p.371.
10. (ed) E. G. W. Bill, *Anglican Initiatives in Christian Unity*. S.P.C.K, 1967, p.77–8.
11. *Apostolicum Actuositatem* para 10, see (ed) Walter M. Abbott, S. J., *The Documents of Vatican II*, Geoffrey Chapman, 1965, p.500
12. 21 September 1868, Archives Birmingham Oratory.
13. 15 May 1858, de Lisle Archives.
14. *Sacrosanctum Concilium*, Abbot, *The Documents of Vatican II*, p.137 et. seq.
15. *Lumen Gentium*, para 32, ibid. p.58.
16. *Lumen Gentium*, para 13, ibid. p.32.
17. *Unitatis Redintegratio*, Abbott, *The Documents of Vatican II*, p.341. et seq.
18. ibid. para 11, p.354.
19. Ambrose said of his former Tutor, Archdeacon Thorp, whom he continued to visit into old age, 'A man to do honour to

any Church'. To Lee 4 April 1857, de Lisle Archives.

20. Archives Mount St Bernard.

21. de Lisle Archives.

22. Still extant in Archives Magdalen College.

23. 19 July 1884, ibid.

24. Vol. II, p.169.

25. An explanation of Ambrose's use of the term 'broken unity' was a case in point, ibid. Vol. I, p.185.

26. See p.362.

Bibliography

Addington, Raleigh. *Faber, Poet and Priest, Selected Letters 1833–1863.* Cowbridge; D. Brown, 1974.

Allchin, A. M. *The Silent Rebellion: Anglican Religious Communities 1845–1900.* SCM Press, 1958.

Allies, Mary H. *Life of Pius VII.* Burns and Oates, 1875.

Almond, Cuthbert, OSB. *History of Ampleforth Abbey.* R&T Washbourne, 1903.

Altholz, J. *The Liberal Catholic Movement in England.* Burns & Oates, 1962.

Anon. *Life of Robert Rodolph Suffield 1821–1891.* London, 1893. (In fact written by the Revd Charles Hargrove).

Anson, P. F. *The Call of the Cloister: Religious Communities and Kindred Bodies in the Anglican Communion.* SPCK, 1955.

—— *Bishops at Large.* Faber & Faber 1964.

—— *Fashions in Church furnishings, 1840–1940.* USA; Maxwell, 1966.

—— *Building up the Waste Places: the revival of monastic life.* Leighton Buzzard; Faith Press, 1973.

Armour, Mary Andrew. *Cornelia.* SHCJ, 1979.

Ashwell, A. R. *Life of Samuel Wilberforce.* (vol. I only) John Murray, 1880.

Aveling, H. *The Handle and the Axe*: the Catholic recusants in England from Reformation to Emancipation. Blond & Briggs, 1976.

Barberi, Dominic. *The Lamentation of England or the Prayer of the Prophet Jeremiah applied to the same.* Leicester; A. Cockshow, 1831.

Battiscombe, Georgina. *John Keble: a Study in Limitations.* Constable, 1963.

—— *Shaftesbury. A Biography of the 7th Earl.* Constable, 1974.

Beck, G. A. (ed.) *The English Catholics, 1850–1950.* Burns and Oates, 1950.

Benson, A. C. & Esher, Lord. (ed.) *Letters of Queen Victoria 1837–1861.* Murray, 1907.

Berkeley, Joan. *Lulworth and the Welds.* Gillingham, Dorset; the Blackmore Press 1971.

Bill, E. G. W. (ed.) *Anglican Initiatives in Christian Unity.* SPCK, 1967.

Blake, Robert (Lord Blake) *Disraeli.* Eyre & Spottiswood, 1966.

Blakiston, Noel. *The Roman Question.* Extracts from the Despatches of Odo Russell from Rome 1858–1903. Chapman and Hall, 1962.

Bloxam, J. R. *A Register of the Members of St Mary Magdalen's College, Oxford* (vols I–VII). Oxford, 1853.

Blyth, Henry. *The Pocket Venus: A Victorian Scandal.* Weidenfeld & Nicolson, 1966.

Bodenham, Countess de. *Mrs Herbert and the Villagers.* Or Familiar Conversations on the principal duties of Christianity. 1823, reprinted Dublin, Clarke & Son, 1853.

Bossy, John. *The English Catholic Community 1570–1850.* DLT, 1975.

Bowden, John Edward. *Life and Letters of F. W. Faber.* Thomas Richardson, 1869.

Brady, W. Mozière. *Annals of the Catholic Hierarchy in England and Scotland 1585–1876.* J. M. Stark, 1883.

Brandreth, H. R. T. *Ecumenical Ideals of the Oxford Movement.* S P C K, 1947.

—— *Episcopi Vagantes and the Anglican Church.* SPCK, 1947.

—— *Dr Lee of Lambeth.* SPCK, 1951.

Bricknell, W. S. (ed.) *The Judgement of the Bishops upon Tractarian Theology.* Oxford, 1845.

Brown, C. K. Francis. *History of the English Clergy.* Faith Press, 1953.

Butler, Dom Cuthbert. *The Life & Times of Bishop Ullathorne.* (2 vols.) Burns and Oates, 1926.

Butler, Dom Cuthbert. *The Vatican Council 1869–1870.* Collins and Harvill Press, 1930.

Campion, Edmund. *Lord Acton and the First Vatican Council. A Journal.* Sydney; Catholic Theological Faculty, 1975.

Chadwick, Owen. *The Mind of the Oxford Movement.* Adam and Charles Black, 1960.

—— *The Victorian Church.* Adam and Charles Black, Part I 1966, Part II 1970.

Chapman, Ronald. *Father Faber.* Burns & Oates, 1961.

Church, R. W. *The Oxford Movement 1833–1845.* Macmillan, 1891.

Cooke, Fr Robert, O. M. I. *Sketches of the Life of Mgr de Mazenod, Bishop of Marseilles.* (2 vols) Burns and Oates, 1879.

Cruikshank, Alexander. *Laura de Lisle.* London and Leamington; Art and Book Co 1897.

Cwiekowski, F. J. *English Bishops and the Vatican Council.* Louvain, 1971.

Davenport, Christopher (Franciscus a Sancta Clara). *Deus, Natura, Gratia.* Lyons, 1634.

—— *Paraphrastica Expositio Articulorum Confessionis Anglicanae.* (ed. Lee, F. G.). London; J. T. Hayes, 1865.

Davidson, Thomas Randall & Benham, W. *Life of Archibald Campbell Tait, Archbishop of Canterbury.* (2 vols) Macmillan, 1891.

de Lisle, Ambrose Phillipps. *Life of St Elizabeth of Hungary.* (trans from the French of C. Montalembert) 1839.

—— *Some Remarks on a Letter addressed to the Revd R. W. Jelf in Explanation of Tract 90.* Charles Dolman, 1841.

—— *The Little Gradual or Chorister's Companion.* London; James Toovey, 1847.

—— *A Letter to the Earl of Shrewsbury on the Re-establishment of the Hierarchy of the English Catholic Church.* Charles Dolman, 1850.

—— *A Few Words on the Letter of Lord John Russell to the Bishop of Durham.* 1850.

—— *Mahometanism in its Relation to Prophecy,* or An Inquiry into the Prophecies concerning Antichrist. Charles Dolman, 1855.

—— *On the Future Unity of Christendom.* Charles Dolman, 1857.

—— *The Diurnal of the Soul* or *Maxims and Examples of the Saints*. Thomas Richardson, 1869.

de Lisle, Edwin. *A Comparison between the History of the Church and the Prophecies of the Apocalypse*. (trans. from the German). Burns and Oates, 1874.

—— *Pastoral Politics*: A Reply to Dr Bagshawe, Catholic Bishop of Nottingham. Loughborough; H. Wills, 1885.

—— *The Majesty of London*. Edward Stamford, 1885.

de Rivières, Philbin. *Vie de Mgr Forbin-Janson*. Paris, 1891.

de Vere, Aubrey. *Recollections*. New York, 1897.

Devine, P. *Life of the Very Revd Father Dominic of the Mother of God*. R. Washbourne 1898.

Digby, Kenelm. *The Broadstone of Honour*, Rules for the Gentlemen of England. 1822.

—— *Godefridus*. 1827.

—— *Mores Catholici* or Ages of Faith. (11 volumes) Joseph Booker, 1831–1842.

Disraeli, Benjamin. *Coningsby or the New Generation*. 1844 Dent. Everyman edition reprinted 1967.

—— *Lothair*, 1870. Reprinted OUP, 1975.

Dunbabin, J. P. D. *Rural Discontent in 19th Century Britain*. Faber, 1974.

Ellis, J. T. *Cardinal Consalvi and Anglo-Papal Relations 1814–1824*. Washington; Catholic University of American Press, 1942.

Faber, F. W. *Poems* 3rd Edition Thomas Richardson, 1857.

Ferrey, B. *Recollections of A. W. N. Pugin and of his Father Augustus Pugin*. reprinted The Scholar Press, 1978.

Fessler, Joseph. *The True and the False Infallibility of the Popes*: a controversial reply to Dr Schulte (trans from 3rd edition by Ambrose St John of the Oratory) Burns and Oates, 1875.

ffoulkes, E. *Experiences of a 'vert*. reprinted from the Union Review. J. T. Hayes, 1865.

Figgis, J. N. and Laurence, R. V. (ed.) *Selections from the Correspondence of the First Lord Acton*. Longman & Green, 1917.

Fitton, R. S. and Wadsworth, A. P. *The Strutts and The Arkwrights 1758–1830*. Manchester University Press, 1958.

Fitzpatrick, W. J. *Life, Times and Correspondence of the Rt Revd Dr Doyle, Bishop of Kildare and Leighlin*. Dublin; James Duffy, 1861. (2 vols).

Forbes, A. P. Bishop of Brechin. *An Explanation of the 39 Articles*. Oxford; Parker, 1867

Fothergill, B. *Nicholas Wiseman*. Faber & Faber, 1963.

Fowler, John. *Life of R. W. Sibthorpe*. W. Skeffington & Son, 1880.

Froude, Richard Hurrell. *Remains*. (4 vols) Rivington, 1838–1839.

Gash, N. *Aristocracy and People: Britain, 1815–1865*. Edward Arnold, 1979.

Gasquet, Aidan. (ed.) *Lord Acton and his Circle*. Burns & Oates, 1906.

Genet, Abbé. *Vie et Révélations de la Soeur de la Nativité*. Paris, 1819.

Gladstone, W. E. *The Vatican Decrees in Their Bearing on Civil Obedience; a Political Expostulation*. John Murray, 1874.

—— *Vaticanism, an answer to Replies and Reproofs*. John Murray, 1875.

—— *The Bulgarian Horrors and the Question of the East*. John Murray, 1876.

Girouard, Mark. *The Victorian Country House*. Oxford; Clarendon Press, 1971.

—— *The Return to Camelot*. Yale University Press, 1981.

Greville, C. C. F. *A Journal of the Reign of Queen Victoria*. ed. H. Reeve. Longmans, 1885.

Gwynn, Denis. *The Struggle for Catholic Emancipation*. Longmans Green 1928.

—— *A Hundred Years of Catholic Emancipation*. Longmans Green, 1929.

—— *Cardinal Wiseman*. Dublin; Browne & Nolan, 1929.

—— *Second Spring*. Burns & Oates, 1942.

—— *Lord Shrewsbury, Pugin and the Catholic Revival*. Hollis & Carter, 1946.

—— *Father Dominic Barberi*. Burns & Oates, 1947.

—— *Father Luigi Gentili*. Dublin, Conmore & Reynolds, 1951.

Haile, Martin and Bonney, Edwin. *Life and Letters of John Lingard, 1771–1851*. Herbert and Daniel, 1912.

Hales, E. E. Y. *Pio Nono*. Eyre & Spottiswoode, 1960.

—— *Revolution and the Papacy, 1796–1846*. Eyre & Spottiswoode, 1965.

Harrison, J. F. C. *The Second Coming*. Routledge & Kegan Paul, 1979.

Hibbert, Christopher. *Disraeli and his World*. Thames & Hudson, 1978.

Hibbert, Marguerite. *The Very Revd Robert Cooke. OMI*. Burns & Oates, 1874.

Hill, R. L. *Toryism and the People 1832–1846*. Constable, 1929.

Hirst, The Very Rev. Joseph. *Life and Character of Revd Andrew Egan*. Market Weighton 1890.

—— *Memoir and Letters of Lady Mary Arundell*. Leicester; Ratcliffe College, 1894.

Hollis, Patricia. *Class and Conflict in 19th Century England, 1815–1850*. Routledge 1973.

Holmes, J Derek. *The Triumph of the Holy See*. Burns & Oates, 1978.

—— *More Roman than Rome*. Burns & Oates, 1978.

Horn, Pamela. *Labouring Life in the Victorian Countryside*. Macmillan of Canada, 1976.

Howard of Glossop, Winefred, Lady. *Journal of a Tour in the USA, Canada and Mexico*. London; Sampson Low, Marston & Co. Ltd, 1897.

Husenbeth F. C. *The Life of the Rt Revd Mgr. Weedall; DD*. Longmans, 1860.

Inglis, K. S. *Churches and the Working Classes in Victorian England*. Routledge & Kegan Paul, 1963.

Jones, O. W. *Isaac Williams and his Circle*. SPCK, 1971.

Jurich, J, SJ. *The Ecumenical Relations of Victor De Buck, SJ with Anglo-Catholic Leaders on the Eve of Vatican I*. Louvain, 1970.

Kenyon, J. G. *The Crisis in the East and the attitudes of Catholics*. Burns & Oates 1876.

Lacunza, Manuel de, y Ziaz. *La Venida del Mesias en gloria y majestad.* 1790.

Lamington, Lord. *In the Days of the Dandies.* William Blackwood, 1890.

Le Canuet, R. P. *Montalembert d'après son journal et sa correspondance.* Paris, 1896. (2 vols.)

Lee, F. G. *The Validity of Holy Orders of the Church of England Maintained.* J. T. Hayes, 1869.

—— (ed.) *Essays on Reunion of Christendom by Members of the Roman Catholic, Oriental and Anglican Communions.* 1st, 2nd & 3rd series.

Leetham, Claude. *Rosmini.* Longmans Green 1957.

—— *Luigi Gentili. A Sower for the Second Spring.* London; Burns & Oates, 1965.

Leslie, Shane. *Henry Edward Manning, His Life and Labours.* Burns & Oates, 1921.

Liddon, H. *Life of E. B. Pusey.* (4 vols.) Longmans Green, 1893–7.

Lingard, John. *History of England.* (up to vol X 6th edition) Dublin, James Duffy, 1878.

Lovat, Alice, Lady. *The Life of Sir Frederick Weld: A Pioneer of Empire.* John Murray, 1914.

Luddy, Ailbe. J., O. Cist. *The Story of Mount Melleray.* M. H. Gill & Son Ltd, 1946.

Lupton, J. H. *Archbishop Wake and the Prospect of Union between the Gallican and Anglican Churches.* George Bell & Sons, 1896.

McClelland, V. A. *Cardinal Manning, his Public Life and Influence. 1865–92.* OUP, 1962.

McCormack, Arthur. *Cardinal Vaughan.* Burns & Oates, 1966.

MacKay, Donald J. *Bishop Forbes, a Memoir.* Kegan Paul, 1888.

Manners, Lord John. *England's Trust* and other poems. J. G. F. and J. Rivington, 1839.

—— *A Plea for National Holydays.* Painter, 1843.

—— *A Letter to Lord Edward Howard.* (under pseudonym Anglo-Catholicus). W. E. Painter, 1841.

Manning, Henry, Cardinal. *The Working of the Holy Spirit in the Church of England; A Letter to E. B. Pusey.* Longmans Green 1864.

—— *The Reunion of Christendom; A Pastoral Letter to the Clergy.* Longmans Green, 1866.

—— *England and Christendom.* Longmans Green, 1867.

—— *The Ecumenical Council and the Infallibility of the Roman Pontiff; a Pastoral Letter to the clergy.* Longmans Green, 1869.

Manzoni, Count Alexander. *A Vindication of Catholic Morality* or a Refutation of the Charges brought against it by Sismondi in his 'History of the Italian Republics during the Middle Ages. Keating & Brown, 1836.

Marie Thérèse, Mother SHCJ. *Cornelia Connelly, A Study in Fidelity.* Burns & Oates, 1961.

Marindin, G. E. *Letters of Frederic, Lord Blachford.* (2 vols) Murray, 1896.

Masefield, Muriel. *Peacocks and Primroses.* A survey of Disraeli's novels. Geoffrey Bles, 1953.

Mathew, David. *Catholicism in England 1535–1935.* Longmans Green, 1936.

——*Acton, the Formative Years*. Eyre & Spottiswoode, 1946.

——*Lord Acton and his Times*. Eyre & Spotiswoode, 1968.

Matthew, H. C. G. and others. *The Gladstone Diaries*, Oxford; Clarendon Press

'Members of the University of Oxford'. *Tracts for the Times*. (7 vols). J. G. & F. Rivington, 1834–41.

Merewether, Francis. *Popery, a New Religion*. Ashby de la Zouche; W. Hextall, 1835.

——*To the Inhabitants of Whitwick*. Ashby de la Zouch; W. Hextall, 1836.

——*Special Pleadings in the Court of Reason and Conscience*. Leicester, 1836.

——*Letter to Dr Pusey and others*. Ashby de la Zouch; W. Hextall 1837.

——*Address to the Inhabitants of Whitwick on the Opening of a Monastery within the limits of that parish*. Ashby de la Zouch; W. & J. Hextall, 1845.

——*A Letter to Ambrose Lisle Phillipps Esq. on his Remarks on the Future Unity of Christendom*. Rivingtons, 1857.

Middleton, R. D. *Magdalen Studies*. SPCK, 1936.

——*Newman and Bloxam, an Oxford Friendship*. OUP, 1947.

——*Newman at Oxford: His Religious Development*. OUP, 1950.

Monckton-Milnes, R. *One Tract More*. By a Layman. J. & F. & J. Rivington, 1841.

Montagu, Lord Robert, M. P. *Foreign Policy, England and the Eastern Question*. (1877)

Montalembert, Charles. *Monks of the West*. John Nimmo, 1861–79 (English edition).

Monypenny, W. F. *Life of Benjamin Disraeli*. John Murray, 1912.

Moorman, John R. H. *A History of the Church in England*. Adam and Charles Black, 1953.

Newman, John Henry. *Open Letter to Dr Jelf*, 1841.

——*Letter to the Bishop of Oxford*. John Henry Parker, 1841.

——*Tract 90 on Certain Passages in the 39 Articles*. with a Historical Preface by E. B. Pusey. Oxford; Parker, 1865.

——*Verses on Various Occasions*. Burns & Oates, 1868.

——*A Letter addressed to His Grace the Duke of Norfolk on the occasion of Mr Gladstone's recent Expostulation*. Pickering, 1875.

——*Apologia Pro Vita Sua*. 1967 edition ed Martin J. Svaglic, OUP

Newsome, David H. *The Parting of Friends*: A study of the Wilberforces and Henry Manning. John Murray, 1966.

Norman, Edward. *The English Catholic Church in the 19th Century*. Oxford, Clarendon Press, 1984.

Oliphant, Mrs M. *Memoir of Count de Montalembert*, A chapter of recent French history. Edinburgh, 1872.

Ollard, S. L. *Short History of the Oxford Movement*. Mowbrays, 1915.

——*Reunion*. Robert Scott, 1919.

Ornsby, Robert. *Memoirs of James Robert Hope-Scott*. (2 vols). John Murray, 1884

Oxenham, H. N. (ed.) *Proposal for Catholic Communion by a Minister of the Church of England*. 1704. New edition with Introduction under title *An Eirenicon of the 18th Century*. Rivington, 1879.

Oxenham, H. N. *Rudolf de Lisle*. Chapman and Hall, 1886.

Pagani, Giovanni Battista. *Life of Aloysius Gentili*. London; Richardson, 1851.

——*The End of the World or the Second Coming of Our Lord and Saviour Jesus Christ*. Charles Dolman, 1855.

Pagani, G. B. (the younger). *Vita di Luigi Gentili*. Rome; Desclée, 1904.

Perry, W. A. P. *Forbes, Bishop of Brechin, the Scottish Pusey*. SPCK, 1939.

Phillipps, Lucy. *My Life and what I shall do with it*. Longmans Green, 1860.

——*Records of the Ministry of the Revd E. T. March Phillipps*. Longmans Green, 1862.

Pope-Hennesy, J. *Monckton-Milnes, The Years of Promise: 1809–1851*. Constable, 1949.

——*Monckon-Milnes, The Flight of Youth: 1851–1885*. Constable, 1951.

Presbyter Anglicanus (E. S. Grindle). *Christianity or Erastianism*. John Batty, 1875.

——*Do they well to be angry*. John Batty, 1876.

Pugin, A. W. N. *An Apology for a work entitled 'Constrasts'*: being a defence for the assertions advanced in that publication, against the various attacks lately made upon it. Birmingham; R. P. Stone, 1837.

——*Contrasts, or A parallel between the noble edifices of the Middle Ages and corresponding buildings of the Present Day*. Second Edition, Charles Dolman, 1841 Reprinted by the Victorian Library, Leicester University Press, 1969.

——*A Treatise on Chancel Screens and Rood Lofts*. Charles Dolman, 1851.

——*The True Principles of Pointed or Christian Architecture*. W. Hughes, 1851.

Purcell, E. S. *Life of Cardinal Manning*. (2 vols). Macmillan & Co, 1895.

——*Life and Letters of Ambrose Philipps de Lisle*. (2 vols) ed. and finished by Edwin de Lisle. New York; Macmillan & Co. Ltd, 1900.

Pusey, E. B. *The Working of the Holy Spirit in the Church of England*. 1864.

——*The Church of England, a Portion of Christ's one Holy Catholic Church and a means of restoring visible Unity. An Eirenicon in a Letter to the Author of the Christian Year*. John Henry & James Parker, 1865.

Quirinus (Lord Acton) part author of *Letters from Rome*. Rivington, 1870.

Ramsay, Grace. *Life of Thomas Grant, First Bishop of Southwark*. Smith Elder, 1874.

Reid, Wemyss. *The Life, Letters and Friendships of Richard Monckton-Milnes, first Lord Houghton*. (2 vols). Cassell, 1890.

Renouf, Peter Le Page, Sir. *The Condemnation of Pope Honorious*. Longmans Green 1869.

——*University Education for English Catholics, A Letter to the Very Revd J. H. Newman*.

Roe, W. G. *Lammenais and England*. OUP, 1966.

Rosmini, Antonio. *Annali di Antonio Rosmini-Serbati 1829–31* (ed Radice, Gianfranco) Milan; Marzarati Editore. 1974.

——*Epistolario Completo di Antonio Rosmini-Serbati*. (ed Monferrato Casale) (13 vols). Giovanni Pane, 1887–94.

——*Maxims of Christian Perfection*. (trans. W. Johnson), Hinckley; S. Walker, 1948.

——*Counsels to Religious Superiors*. (trans. & ed C. Leetham). Burns & Oates, 1962.

Rouse, Ruth and Neill, Stephen Charles. *A History of the Ecumenical Movement 1517–1948*. SPCK, 1954.

Rowland, Christopher. *The Open Heaven*. SPCK, 1982.

Ryder, Ignatius Dudley Fr. *Idealism in Theology, a Review of Dr Ward's Scheme of Dogmatic Theology*. Longmans Green, 1867.

Schenk, H. G. *The Mind of the European Romantics*. Constable, 1966.

Schiefen, Richard J. *Nicholas Wiseman and the Transformation of English Catholicism*. Patmos Press, 1984.

Shannon, R. T. *Gladstone and the Bulgarian Agitation*. Nelson, 1963.

Simpson, W. J. Sparrow. *Roman Catholic Opposition to Papal Infallibility*. John Murray, 1909.

Smith, B. A. *Dean Church: The Anglican Response to Newman*. OUP, 1958.

Smith, Robert, OCSO. *History of the Cistercian Order*. Thomas Richardson, 1852.

Smythe, George Augustus Frederick Percy Sydney, later Lord Strangford. *Historical Fancies*. Henry Colbury, 1844.

Stanton, Phoebe. *Pugin*. Thames & Hudson, 1971.

Strangford, Lady. *Memoir of Lord Strangford*.

Sykes, Christopher. *Two Studies in Virtue*. Collins, 1953.

Sykes, Norman. *William Wake, Archbishop of Canterbury 1657–1737*. (2 vols). OUP, 1957.

Terhune, A McK. *Life of Edward Fitzgerald*. OUP, 1947.

Thompson, F. M. L. *English Landed Gentry in the 19th Century*. Routledge & Kegan Paul 1963

Trappes-Lomax, M. *Pugin*. A mediaeval Victorian. Sheed & Ward, 1932.

Ullathorne, W. B. *A Letter on the Association for Promoting the Unity of Christendom*. Thomas Richardson, 1864.

——*The Anglican Theory of Union as maintained in the Appeal to Rome & Dr Pusey's Eirenicon*. Burns, Lambert & Oates, 1865.

——*From Cabin Boy to Archbishop*. Burns & Oates, 1941.

Vaucher, A. F. *Une Célébrité Oubliée: Le P Manual de Lacunza y Ziaz*. Collonges-sous-Salève, 1941.

Ward, Sister Benedicta, SLG. *Miracles and the Mediaeval Mind; Theory, Record and Event*. Scholar Press, 1982.

Ward, Bernard. *History of St Edmund's College*. Kegan Paul 1893.

——*St Edmund's College Chapel*. Catholic Truth Society, 1903.

——*Dawn of Catholic Revival, 1781–1803*. (2 vols). Longmans Green, 1909.

——*The Eve of Catholic Emancipation*. (3 vols). Longmans Green, 1911–12.

——*The Sequel to Catholic Emancipation*. (2 vols). Longmans Green, 1915.

Ward, Wilfred. *W. G. Ward and the Oxford Movement*. Macmillan, 1889.

——*W. G. Ward and the Catholic Revival*. Macmillan, 1893.

——*Life and Times of Cardinal Wiseman*. Longmans Green, 1897.

——*Aubrey de Vere: a Memoir.* Longmans Green, 1904.

——*The Life of John Henry, Cardinal Newman.* Longmans Green, 1912.

Ward, W. G. *The Ideal of a Christian Church.* 1844.

——*The Authority of Doctrinal Decisions.* Burns, Lambert & Oates, 1866.

Watkin, E. I. *Roman Catholicism in England from the Reformation to 1950.* OUP, 1957.

Whibley, C. *Lord John Manners and his Friends.* (2 vols). William Blackwood, 1925.

Wickham Legge, J. *English Church Life 1660–1833.* Longmans Green, 1914.

Wilberforce R. G. *Life of Samuel Wilberforce.* Vols II & III. John Murray, 1881–2.

Williams, Michael E. *The Venerable English College Rome.* A History 1579–1979. London; Associated Catholic Publications Ltd, 1979.

Wiseman, Cardinal Nicholas. *Letter respectfully addressed to the Revd J. H. Newman upon his letter to the Revd Dr Jelf.* Dolman, 1841.

——*A Letter on Catholic Unity addressed to the Rt Hon the Earl of Shrewsbury.* Dolman, 1841.

——*Three Lectures on the Catholic Hierarchy.* Richardson & Son 1850.

——Pastoral Letter '*From the Flaminian Gate*'. 1850.

——*An Appeal to the Reason and Good Feeling of the English People.* T. Richardson & Son 1850.

——*Essays on various subjects.* (2 vols). Dolman 1853.

——*Recollections of Four Last Popes.* Hurst and Blackett, 1858.

Wright, William Aldis. *Letters of Edward Fitzgerald.* (2 vols). Macmillan, 1894.

Wyndham, M. M. *Correspondence of Sarah, Lady Lyttelton, 1787–1870.* John Murray, 1912.

Young, Urban, C. P. *Life & Letters of the Venerable Father Dominic.* [Barberi], C. P., Founder of the Passionists in Belgium and England. Burns Oates & Washbourne Ltd 1926.

——(ed and translated) *Ven. Dominic Barberi in England, A New Series of Letters.* Burns Oates & Washbourne Ltd, London, 1935.

——*Life of Father Ignatius Spencer, C. P..* London; Burns, Oates & Washbourne Ltd 1935.

Zeloni, Le Chevalier. *Life of Gwendolin Talbot, Princess Borghese.* Burns & Oates 1894.

ARCHIVE COLLECTIONS

Barnabite in Rome
Belvoir Castle
Birmingham Oratory
Bodleian Library MS Collections
British Museum MS Collections
Clifford at Ugbrook
De Lisle at Quenby Hall, Leics.
De Lisle at Stockerston Hall, Leics.
Dominican in Edinburgh

Doria Pamphilj in Rome
Dormer family
Downside Abbey
English College, Rome
Grande Trappe
Harrowby, Earl of
Jesuit English Province
London Oratory
Magdalen College Oxford
Mill Hill Convent
Mount St Bernard,
National Library of Ireland
Oscott
Passionist Archives, Ormskirk
Passionist Archives in Rome
Propaganda Fide in Rome
Pusey House, Oxford
Ratcliffe College
Rosminian English Province, Wonersh
Rosminian Central Collection, Stresa
St Deiniol's Library Hawarden
St Dominic's Convent, Stone
Stapehill Convent
Ushaw College
Vatican

DIOCESAN COLLECTIONS

Birmingham Archdiocese
Clifton
Nottingham
Southwark
Westminster

SCOTTISH EPISCOPAL CHURCH DIOCESAN ARCHIVES

Brechin at Dundee

RECORD OFFICES

Belfast
Cambridge
Dorset

Leicestershire
Northamptonshire
Nottingham
Somerset

JOURNALS, NEWSPAPERS, REPORTS

Ampleforth Journal
Anglican-Roman Catholic Internation Commission; reports of
     Bedfordshire Times & Independent
British Critic
Catholic Directory
Catholic Historical Review
Catholic Magazine
Daily Telegraph
Dolman's Magazine
Downside Review
Dublin Review
Fraser's Magazine
Hansard Parliamentary Debates
Guardian
Leicestershire Journal
Lichfield Mercury
Loughborough Monitor
Loughborough News
Month
Morning Post
Oscotian
Pilot
Rambler
Recusant History
The Tablet
The Times
Union
Union Review

FOREIGN

Civiltá Cattolica
Correspondant
Irenikon
Osservatore Romano
L'Univers

DIARIES

de Lisle, Laura (née Clifford), 1840–96; de Lisle Archives, Quenby Hall.

W. E. Gladstone. *The Gladstone Diaries*. ed M. R. D. Foot 1825–32, 1833–39. with H. C. G. Matthew 1840–47; H. C. G. Matthew remainder of series.

J. H. Newman. *Letters and Diaries of J. H. Newman*. ed C. S. Dessain & others.

Charles March Phillipps, 1805–62; de Lisle Archives, Stockerston Hall.

Acknowledgements

The Author and Publishers are grateful to acknowledge the permission given by the following, to quote from their copyright material:

Geoffrey Chapman for (ed) Walter M. Abbott SJ, *The Documents of Vatican II*, 1965.
The estate of the late Brian Fothergill for *Nicholas Wiseman*, Faber and Faber 1963
Longmans Group UK for Claude Leetham, *The Life of Antonio Rosmini*, 1957
Macmillan for J. T. Ward, *Sir James Graham*, 1967
Oxford University Press for extracts from *The Letters and Diaries of J. H. Newman* and from *The Gladstone Diaries*
The Patmos Press, Shepherdstown, USA, for Richard J. Schiefen, *Nicholas Wiseman and the Transformation of English Catholicism*, 1984.
S.P.C.K. for (ed) E.G.W. Bill, *Anglican Initiatives in Christian Unity*, 1967.

And to those who hold the copyright of archive material which has been quoted, to which reference is made in the Notes:

The Archivist, Birmingham Archdiocesan Archives
The Archivist, Birmingham City Archives
The Bodleian Library, Oxford
The Birmingham Oratory
The Lord Clifford
The English Dominican Archives, Edinburgh
Michael Dormer Esq.
The Abbott and Community of Downside
The Rector of the English College in Rome
The Earl of Harrowby
The Fr Provincial of the English Province of the Institute of Charity
The London Oratory
The President and Fellows of Magdalen College, Oxford
The Librarian of the National Library of Ireland
The Bishop of Nottingham
The Fr Provincial of the English Province of Passionists
The Master and Fellows of Pembroke College, Oxford
The Principal and Chapter of Pusey House, Oxford
The Duke of Rutland
The Librarian, Ushaw College
The Cardinal Archbishop of Westminster

Index